Wissenschaftliche Untersuchungen
zum Neuen Testament · 2. Reihe

Edited by
Jörg Frey, Martin Hengel, Otfried Hofius

157

Eric Sorensen

Possession and Exorcism in the New Testament and Early Christianity

Mohr Siebeck

ERIC SORENSEN, born 1961; 1984 B.A. in English and Classics from Pacific Lutheran University; 1987 M.A. in Classics from the University of Washington; 1991 M.Div. in Scripture and Interpretation from Harvard Divinity School (Cambridge, MA); 2001 Ph.D. in Biblical Studies from the University of Chicago Divinity School.

ISBN 3-16-147851-7
ISSN 0340-9570 (Wissenschaftliche Untersuchungen zum Neuen Testament 2. Reihe)

Die Deutsche Bibliothek lists this publication in the Deutsche Nationalbibliographie; detailed bibliographic data is available in the Internet at http://dnb.ddb.de.

© 2002 by J. C. B. Mohr (Paul Siebeck), P.O. Box 2040, D-72010 Tübingen.

The book was printed by Druck Partner Rübelmann GmbH in Hemsbach on non-aging paper and bound by Buchbinderei Schaumann in Darmstadt.

Mache dich, mein Herze, rein,
  Ich will Jesum selbst begraben.
Denn er soll nunmehr in mir
  Für und für
Seine süße Ruhe haben.
  Welt, geh aus, laß Jesum ein.

—Bach, *Matthäus-Passion*

Preface

This book represents a revision of my doctoral dissertation, "The Temple of God, the House of the Unclean Spirit: Possession and Exorcism in the New Testament and Early Christianity," submitted to the Divinity of the University of Chicago in December 2001. Though based upon a dissertation, my hope is that a broad audience will find the study accessible, and that readers will recognize the sometimes extensively annotated footnotes as a resource for, rather than a distraction from, the main text. I express my thanks to Dr. Henning Ziebritsky, Theology Editor at Mohr Siebeck in Tübingen for his initial interest in my manuscript, and to Dr. Jörg Frey of the Evangelisch-Theologische Fakultät, University of Munich, who, as Managing Editor read and approved the selection of my work for the WUNT 2 series. Among Dr. Frey's helpful suggestions was to present the material on "Ancient Israel and Early Judaism" as a chapter independent of the ancient Near Eastern material. I also thank the support staff at Mohr Siebeck for their patient and always friendly assistance in bringing this manuscript to print.

I would like to acknowledge my appreciation of the University of Chicago generally, which not only provided a curriculum that engendered the research topic, but a community of interested scholars and specialists who offered their time and suggestions, and whose own teachings and writings have informed the following pages. I extend my particular thanks to my dissertation committee — Adela Yarbro Collins (advisor, now of Yale Divinity School), Hans Dieter Betz, and Elizabeth R. Gebhard — for their careful reading of my work and their substantive suggestions for delineating its boundaries. I am grateful to have had the friendship and respect that they have held for each other over the years also directed toward my own scholastic development. Informal readers have included Erica Reiner and Robert Biggs of the University of Chicago's Oriental Institute, who read through various incarnations of the section on ancient Mesopotamia and offered useful bibliographic suggestions. Bruce Lincoln of the Divinity School and John J. Collins (now of Yale Divinity School) offered critical readings and constructive comments on the sections that pertained respectively to Zoroastrianism and Ancient Israel and Early Judaism. I am also grateful to the students and faculty who participated in the Divinity School's New Testament Dissertation Seminars of 1997 and 1999 for their valuable criticism and guidance; Margaret M. Mitchell's participation in the latter year proved especially fortunate. Matthew W. Dickie, of the University of Illinois at Chicago, and Peter Brown, of Princeton University, also provided helpful bibliographic guidance for the classical world as well as a shared interest in magic in antiquity.

I received a Charlotte W. Newcombe Dissertation Fellowship in 1996, and am indebted to the encouragement that Mrs. Newcombe's gift offered at that stage. I would also like to thank Wallace A. Alston, Director of the Center of Theological Inquiry in Princeton, New Jersey, who offered me the resources of the Center for the fellowship year. Those resources extended to privileges at the Princeton Theological Seminary and Princeton University libraries, as well as at Princeton's Index of Christian Art. I would also like to express my appreciation to the CTI staff, and other residents during the 1996–1997 year, especially William Lazareth who, as acting director prior to Dr. Alston's tenure, had initially extended the invitation for residency to me.

Finally, I would like to acknowledge the good-natured interest and support that my friends and family have shown toward my endeavor over the years. In particular, I would like to thank my wife Maureen for her keen eye and helpful suggestions during the final stages of editing and formatting, as well as my brother, Philip Sorensen, and my sister, Joan Sorensen Rice, and their families. Finally, I would like to thank my parents Janice Joyce Sorensen, and † Reuben Erling Sorensen, to whom I dedicate this work.

TABLE OF CONTENTS

LIST OF TABLES

NOTE ON STYLE

The Bibliography includes all works cited in the dissertation. I have presented them in accordance with the guidelines set forth in *The SBL Handbook of Style: For Ancient Near Eastern, Biblical, and Early Christian Studies*, Patrick H. Alexander et al., eds. (Peabody, Mass.: Hendrickson Publishers, 1999). I have also followed *The SBL Handbook of Style* for the journal and serial abbreviations found in the notes, and have provided the unabbreviated titles in the Bibliography. Abbreviations of early Jewish, Christian and patristic titles follow *The SBL Handbook of Style*. Abbreviations used for titles by Greek and Roman classical authors are included in the Reference Index after their full Latin titles. When I have quoted a translation for a classical work I have cited the edition of the translation and included it in the Bibliography. Translations of ancient authors in Greek or Latin without citations are my own. For the biblical passages I have referred to *Biblia Hebraica Stuttgartensia*, edited by K. Elliger and W. Rudolph (Stuttgart: Deutsche Bibelgesellschaft, 1983); *Septuaginta*, edited by Alfred Rahlfs (Stuttgart: Deutsche Bibelgesellschaft, 1979); Nestle-Aland, *Novum Testamentum Graece* (27th ed.; Stuttgart: Deutsche Bibelgesellschaft, 1993). Unless otherwise indicated, biblical quotations in English are from the New Revised Standard Version. Translations of the Septuagint are my own.

Chapter 1

Introduction: The Christian Exorcist
in the Greco-Roman World

1.1 Definition of Terms

It is important at the outset to define some central concepts of this study.
Jonathan Z. Smith interprets the "demonic" as a label for what is marginal,
protean, and unstructured within a given society, so that when identifying the
demons one should not ask "who" they are but "what" they represent.[1] For
Smith, demons are the reifications of human anxieties over what is uncertain,
and they serve to identify the boundaries or liminalities of social structures.
Smith's deconstruction is helpful in understanding the concept of the demonic,
but the question still remains how given societies envision their liminalities.
As for the early Christians, they interpreted them as demons, which in turn
dictated how they acted towards them, and it is these demons as discrete
spiritual entities with which this present study is concerned. Within the
context of the New Testament, demonic possession may be defined as a
culturally shared belief in the potential for a maleficent spiritual being to
disrupt, often in a way observable to others, the well-being of an unwilling
host.[2] In the same context, exorcism may be defined as the forced removal of

---

[1]"The demonic is a relational or labeling term which occurs only in certain culturally
stipulated situations and is part of a complex system of boundaries and limits" (Jonathan Z.
Smith, "Towards Interpreting Demonic Powers in Hellenistic and Roman Antiquity," *ANRW*
2.16.1 [1978] 429). Compare also Jeffrey Burton Russell's assessment of evil and its
personification as a part of the human experience: "The Devil is the hypostasis, the
apotheosis, the objectification of a hostile force or hostile forces perceived as external to our
consciousness" (Jeffrey Burton Russell, *The Devil: Perceptions of Evil from Antiquity to
Primitive Christianity* [Ithaca: Cornell University Press, 1977] 34).

[2]Erika Bourguignon, who takes into account the biblical record in her cross-cultural
anthropological study of possession, has noted that the phenomenon of possession requires a
culturally shared belief: "Possession beliefs and rituals then reflect and express both social
structures and the personalities of the participants. They are not simply matters of historical
inheritance. When such inheritance loses its social significance and profound personal
psychological meaning, the beliefs will disappear and possession trance rituals will become
theatrical performances" (Erika Bourguignon, *Possession* [Chandler and Sharp Series in Cross

such a hostile spirit for the purpose of restoring the victim of demonic possession to well-being. Exorcism is accomplished by a person, the exorcist, who engages and mediates a superior spiritual power[3] against the offending demon in order to accomplish its removal from the possessed and its relocation elsewhere.[4]

1.2 Argument and Scope of the Present Study

The present study argues for the adaptation of exorcism in early Christian mission to the cultural sensibilities of the non-Christian Greeks and Romans. The subject arises when noting that exorcism was an unconventional activity in Greco-Roman society during Christianity's early centuries. Despite this, by the middle of the third century of the Common Era, as we learn from a letter of Cornelius, Bishop of Rome, to Fabius, Bishop of Antioch, the church of Rome had "fifty-two exorcists, readers and doorkeepers" on its roster of 154 clergy.[5] This letter raises the question of how a phenomenon held at the

---

Cultural Themes; San Francisco: Chandler & Sharp, 1976] 49). Following this, I interpret the presence and effectiveness of exorcism also to be socially conditioned. Given the social belief in demonic possession and exorcism in first century Palestine, and given the fact that Jesus is considered by his followers and foes alike to have engaged in exorcism, I find it likely that Jesus did perform exorcisms as part of his historical activity. In his medical anthropological approach to healing in the New Testament, John Pilch also emphasizes the role society plays in constructing models for both understanding illness and applying treatment. Exorcism would fit into this context as follows: "In other words, healing boils down to meaning and the transformation of experience. The change or transformation is created by all participants who effectively enact culturally authorized interpretations. When demons are exorcized, the anxious client believes the cause of the problem is gone. This conviction is affirmed by the healer and encouraged by the social circle. It alters the client's cognitive processes from apprehension to calm" (John J. Pilch, *Healing in the New Testament: Insights from Medical and Mediterranean Anthropology* [Minneapolis: Fortress, 2000] 35).

[3]The spiritual power sometimes lies in the background of exorcism stories as that quality of divine favor in which the authors portray their miracle workers (e.g., in the synoptic authors' portrayal of Jesus, in Josephus' of Eleazar [*Ant.* 8.45–49], and Philostratus' of Apollonius [*Vit. Apoll.*]).

[4]Smith draws attention to exorcism as a relocation of the possessing spirit, and he describes the re-locative aspect of early rituals associated with demons in this manner: "The demon is 'placed' by being named, entrapped and removed to its proper realm (e.g. exorcism) or redirected to a 'proper' goal (i.e. to somewhere or someone else, as in so-called 'hostile' magic)" (Smith, "Towards Interpreting Demonic Powers," *ANRW* 2.16.1:428–29).

[5]ἐξορκιστὰς δὲ καὶ ἀναγνώστας ἅμα πυλωροῖς δύο καὶ πεντήκοντα (Eusebius, *Hist. eccl.* 6.43.11. English translation in Eusebius, *The Ecclesiastical History*, translated by Kirsopp Lake and J. E. L. Oulton [2 vols. LCL; Cambridge: Harvard University Press, 1964–1965]). The letter, recorded by Eusebius and dated to 251, does not specify the number of exorcists among the fifty-two. It also does not say to what extent the

periphery of conventional healing activity not only survived in the early church, but apparently flourished to make the transition from superstition to institution in the Greco-Roman world.

Within the context of the Christian scriptural background the logic behind exorcism's eventual institutionalization is understandable.[6] Jesus' own exorcistic activity as presented in the synoptic gospels, and his command to his disciples to do the same, grant to exorcism a place of consequence in early Christian tradition.[7] But it also makes it a subject with which the church would eventually have to come to terms in its missionary appeal to Greek and Roman audiences. The continuation of exorcism in the westward expansion of early Christianity is noteworthy because it appears to have survived in an environment that relegated its demonology and the human powers involved with it to a magical or an occult status rather than a cultic one. In Greece the charge of magic is brought against neither medical practitioners nor the activities of the Asclepius healing cult. On the one hand, doctors rarely claim to do the extraordinary, but follow instead a naturalistic therapy of diagnoses and prognoses based upon observed precedent.[8] Even should they solicit

---

exorcists may have worked within or outside of the church community. The others on Cornelius' list include one bishop, forty-six presbyters, seven deacons, seven sub-deacons, forty-two acolytes, and over 1500 widows and others in distress.

[6]Compare the Ordinal begun in the Byzantine Church which, "from doorkeeper to bishop," justifies by an example from the life of Christ each of the grades of clergy. (Referred to in J. N. Hillgarth, ed., *Christianity and Paganism, 350–750: The Conversion of Western Europe* [Philadelphia: University of Pennsylvania Press, 1986] 179).

[7]Jesus commands his followers to perform exorcisms in his name when he commissions the Twelve Apostles (Mark 3:14–15//Matt 10:1; Mark 6:7–13//Matt 10:7–8//Luke 9:1–6), and the seventy disciples (Luke 10:17–20). After the resurrection Jesus gives a final commission to the eleven remaining apostles in the longer ending of Mark, where casting out demons is considered one of the signs that will accompany anyone who believes and is baptized (Mark 16:15–18). The idea of imitation occurs throughout a variety of New Testament works, from the gospels to the Pauline and catholic epistles, with the object of imitation ranging from the divinity ("God"—Eph 5:1; "Christ"—Matt 10:24; John 13:15–17; 1 Cor 4:16; 11:1; 1 Thess 1:6–7; 1 Pet 2:21–25), to the early apostolate ("Paul"—1 Cor 4:16; 11:1; 1 Thess 1:6–7; 2 Thess 3:9), subsequent leaders of the church ("Timothy"—1 Tim 4:12; "leaders"—Heb 6:11–12; 13:7; "presbyters"—1 Pet 5:3–4), and the congregation as a whole for other congregations ("Thessalonians"—1 Thess 1:6–7; "Churches of Judaea"—1 Thess 2:14–16). Hence, supervisors and peers become models of faith and activity within the Christian community. See R. J. S. Barrett-Lennard's summary of healing in early Christianity, and the precedent for such found in the New Testament (R. J. S. Barrett-Lennard, *Christian Healing after the New Testament: Some Approaches to Illness in the Second, Third and Fourth Centuries* [New York: University Press of America, 1994]. Note especially Chapter 5: "Irenaeus: Demon-Possession and Exorcism").

[8]One occasionally comes across statements in the medical writings that all things are curable. Consider this passage from the pre-Common Era *The Sacred Disease* included in the Hippocratic corpus of writings: "This disease styled sacred comes from the same causes as others, from the things that come to and go from the body, from cold, sun, and from the

divine powers in this process the method remains essentially unchanged.[9] On the other hand, although the Asclepius cult claims to do the miraculous, it

---

changing restlessness of winds. These things are divine. So that there is no need to put the disease in a special class and to consider it more divine than the others; they are all divine and all human. Each has a nature and power of its own; none is hopeless or incapable of treatment." (Αὕτη δὲ ἡ νοῦσος ἡ ἱερὴ καλεομένη ἀπὸ τῶν αὐτῶν προφασίων γίνεται ἀφ' ὧν καὶ αἱ λοιπαὶ ἀπὸ τῶν προσιόντων καὶ ἀπιόντων, καὶ ψύχεος καὶ ἡλίου καὶ πνευμάτων μεταβαλλομένων τε καὶ οὐδέποτε ἀτρεμιζόντων. ταῦτα δ' ἐστὶ θεῖα, ὥστε μηδὲν δεῖ ἀποκρίνοντα τὸ νόσημα θειότερον τῶν λοιπῶν νομίσαι, ἀλλὰ πάντα θεῖα καὶ πάντα ἀνθρώπινα· φύσιν δὲ ἕκαστον ἔχει καὶ δύναμιν ἐφ' ἑωυτοῦ, καὶ οὐδὲν ἄπορόν ἐστιν οὐδὲ ἀμήχανον.) (Hippocrates, *Morb. sacr.* 21. English translation in *Hippocrates*, translated by W. H. S. Jones et al. [8 vols. LCL; Cambridge: Harvard University Press, 1972–1995]). This passage likely represents the confident flourish of a rhetorician, but it nevertheless reveals a current opinion that whether or not a cure was known, it did in fact exist and merely awaited discovery. In general, however, and beginning with the historical Hippocrates, we see a concern to bring credibility to the healing art that includes an acknowledgment of its limitations. Also from the Hippocratic Corpus the author of *The Art* defines the tasks and limitations of medicine as follows: "In general terms, it is to do away with the sufferings of the sick, to lessen the violence of their diseases, and to refuse to treat those who are overmastered by their diseases, realizing that in such cases medicine is powerless. " (τὸ δὴ πάμπαν ἀπαλλάσσειν τῶν νοσεόντων τοὺς καμάτους καὶ τῶν νοσημάτων τὰς σφοδρότητας ἀμβλύνειν, καὶ τὸ μὴ ἐγχειρεῖν τοῖσι κεκρατημένοις ὑπὸ τῶν νοσημάτων, εἰδότας ὅτι ταῦτα οὐ δύναται ἰητρική.) (Hippocrates, *De arte* 3 [Jones, LCL]. See also *De arte* 8). Such a public admission of its limitations ultimately served to strengthen the medical profession by setting the patient's expectations in proper perspective. Even *The Sacred Disease* itself illustrates medicine's limitations where it mentions epilepsy's potential "overmastery" of the sufferer: "In fact, when the disease has become chronic it then proves incurable, for the brain is corroded by phlegm and melts, and the part which melts becomes water, surrounding the brain outside and flooding it, for which reason such people are attacked more frequently and readily." (οὕτω δ' ἔχει καὶ τῷ ἀνθρώπῳ· ὁπόταν γὰρ ὁ χρόνος γένηται τῇ νούσῳ, οὐκ ἔτι ἰήσιμος γίνεται· διεσθίεται γὰρ ὁ ἐγκέφαλος ὑπὸ τοῦ φλέγματος καὶ τήκεται, τὸ δὲ ἀποτηκόμενον ὕδωρ γίνεται, καὶ περιέχει τὸν ἐγκέφαλον ἐκτὸς καὶ περικλύζει· καὶ διὰ τοῦτο πυκνότερον ἐπίληπτοι γίνονται καὶ ῥᾷον.) (Hippocrates, *Morb. sacr.* 14 [Jones, LCL]).

[9]That absolutes cannot be drawn between categories of medicine as a secular craft distinct from religious healing becomes clear on several counts. The definitions blur, for example, on the role of divine power in medicine. Although it is generally true that medicine depends solely on human knowledge to discern cause and cure of a given malady, on rare occasions the practitioners also implore the gods through prayer to assist in the healing (e.g., from the Hippocratic Corpus, *On Dreams* 90 [*Regimen* Book 4]). One also finds acknowledgment of the role of gods in the restoration of health, so that the sixth chapter of *Decorum* even attributes cures in medicine to gods, with physicians merely acting as the means toward that end. In addition to such prayers, there is also the commitment to the gods sworn to by the physician in the opening lines of the *Hippocratic Oath* itself: "I swear by Apollo Physician and Asclepius and Hygieia and Panaceia and all the gods and goddesses, making them my witnesses, that I will fulfill according to my ability and judgment this oath and this covenant

operates within a healing tradition whose authority is recognized by the state. The accusation of magic, then, rests not upon extraordinary activity per se, but ultimately upon the authority from which that activity is perceived to derive. This is echoed in the Palestinian setting for the synoptic portrayals of Jesus, where critics question Jesus' authority to heal, not his ability to do so.[10]

Granted, the demarcation between magic and socially accepted religious practices in antiquity is a fluid one, and depends more upon the perspective of the one who distinguishes between the two than on any intrinsic qualities they may have held, but it is just this subjective criterion of perception that is of relevance for the present study.[11] The fact that some Greeks and Romans in positions of political power and cultural influence associated Christianity with magic and superstition was a perception that early Christian missionaries would have to have taken into account.[12]

..." (Ὀμνύω Ἀπόλλωνα ἰητρὸν καὶ Ἀσκληπιὸν καὶ Ὑγείαν καὶ Πανάκειαν καὶ θεοὺς πάντας τε καὶ πάσας ἵστορας ποιεύμενος ἐπιτελέα ποιήσειν κατὰ δύναμιν καὶ κρίσιν ἐμὴν ὅρκον τόνδε καὶ ξυγγραφὴν τήνδε) (Ludwig Edelstein, *Hippocrates The Oath: Or the Hippocratic Oath* [Baltimore: Ares Publishers, 1943] 2–3). Although Hippocratic medicine itself originated out of the Asclepius cult and doctors of this tradition were called Asclepiads, or "sons of Asclepius," one cannot assume that priests of Asclepius were necessarily Hippocratic doctors, and vice versa. The testimonia for the cult suggest no systematic interest in diagnosis and prognosis of ailments as were essential to Hippocratic medicine.

[10]In the synoptics, note especially the Beelzeboul controversy (Matt 12:22–30; Luke 11:14–23; cf. Mark 3:22–27), where the practice of exorcism is considered legitimate for other Jews.

[11]John Gager reflects this social view of magic, and says of any attempt to define it: "... the only justifiable (answerable) historical question about magic is not 'What are the characteristics of, for example, Greek magic?' but rather 'Under what conditions, by whom, and of whom does the term "magic" come to be used?'" (John Gager, *Curse Tablets and Binding Spells from the Ancient World* [New York: Oxford University Press, 1992] 25). Fritz Graf intentionally avoids giving a "rigid and artificial terminology" to the subject of "magic" in his study that spans from the sixth century B.C.E. to the end of antiquity, but seeks instead to understand how it was used by the early Greeks and Romans themselves in their "discourse on the relationship between the human and the supernatural" (Fritz Graf, *Magic in the Ancient World* [Revealing Antiquity 10; Cambridge: Harvard University Press, 1997] 18–19). Although I run the risk of undermining his subtlety by attempting to gather his findings into a cohesive summary, I interpret Graf to consider magic a form of religion, whose practitioners use persuasive analogies in their communications with the divine.

[12]A charge that early anti-Christian polemic makes against Jesus was that he performed his miracles by means of magic learned in Egypt. Celsus first makes the connection: "... Jesus ... having hired himself out as a servant in Egypt on account of his poverty, and having there acquired some miraculous powers, on which the Egyptians greatly pride themselves, returned to his own country, highly elated on account of them, and by means of these proclaimed himself a God." (τὸν Ἰησοῦν . . . διὰ πενίαν εἰς Αἴγυπτον μισθαρνήσας, κἀκεῖ δυνάμεών τινων πειραθείς, ἐφ' αἷς Αἰγύπτιοι

The foreignness of the Jewish and Christian practices of exorcism to the Greco-Roman world becomes readily apparent in the context of healing. The synoptic gospels and Acts portray exorcism either explicitly as a healing activity (Matthew, Luke and Acts), or as a closely related event (Mark). In contrast, the practice of exorcism and demonic possession as an illness are noticeably absent from conventional Greek healing traditions until the turn of the era, and as a consequence exorcism does not play a role in medicine or the healing cults. The Hippocratic Corpus and the writings of noted medical practitioners as late as Galen (ca. 129–199) are unconcerned with the phenomena of demonic possession and exorcism or, where discussed, treat them polemically.[13] Prior to the turn of the era, even the religious healings attributed to the god Asclepius appear to deal neither with possession as a malady from which their patients suffer nor for which they seek a cure.[14]

With the locus of Greek medicine in the Asclepieia, both medical and religious healing offered culturally sanctioned alternatives to magical practices, and they likewise would have benefited from magic's discreditation. On the one hand, this explains the absence of such references in earlier Greek literature, though the presence of exorcism in early magical contexts, too, is by and large wanting. On the other hand, the apparent irrelevance of possession and exorcism to culturally sanctioned healing, and the lack of evidence for it even in magic, raises the question of how exorcism was to prove effective as a missionary activity if no apparent demand for exorcism existed in Greek society prior to the Common Era.

σεμνύνονται, ἐπανῆλθεν ἐν ταῖς δυνάμεσι μέγα φρονῶν, καὶ δι᾽ αὐτὰς θεὸν αὐτὸν ἀνηγόρευσε.) (Celsus, *True Doctrine* = Origen, *Cels.* 1.28 [*ANF* 4.408; PG 11.713]). See, Robert L. Wilken, *The Christians as the Romans Saw Them* (New Haven: Yale University Press, 1984) 98–101, 109. See also Morton Smith, *Jesus the Magician* (San Francisco: Harper & Row, 1978).

[13]*The Sacred Disease* first states a current superstitious interpretation of epilepsy as possession by a deity, then refutes it in favor of a physiological explanation. Klaus Thraede finds exorcistic reference in Galen, *fac. simpl. med.* 6.68 (Klaus Thraede, "Exorzismus," *RAC* 7:51).

[14]This conclusion is based upon a survey of the evidence published in Emma J. and Ludwig Edelstein, *Asclepius: A Collection and Interpretation of the Testimonies* (2 vols.; Baltimore: Johns Hopkins, 1975). Robert Garland notes that at least 320 Asklepieia existed around the Mediterranean by the second century Common Era (Robert Garland, *Introducing New Gods: The Politics of Athenian Religion* [Ithaca, N.Y.: Cornell University Press, 1992] 122, note 2), which, depending upon the degree of their discovery and excavation, suggests that a great amount of material evidence remains to be examined. Later literary sources do attribute exorcisms to Asclepius. In the *Acts of Pilate* (ca. late third century) Pilate credits Jesus' power to exorcize to the authority granted him by Asclepius (*Acts Pil.* ch. 1). Likewise, Philostratus (ca. 170–ca. 245) says that Asclepius heals wounds caused by demons, not by carelessness (*Ep.* 18).

In literary contexts as well exorcism remains a field untrodden, and is undocumented in Roman society until late in the first century Common Era.[15] Then, Josephus (37–ca. 100), writing in Greek to a Roman audience, mentions Eleazar having exorcized a demon before Vespasian.[16] In his account Josephus mentions both the technique and proof of that exorcism, as well as the pedigree of the practice in general, which he claims to stem from Solomon. It would appear to be something of a novelty to his readers. From the second century onward exorcists become occasional subjects of Greco-Roman literature in genres as diverse from Josephus' historiography as the jurisprudence of Ulpian (fl. 212–217), who distinguishes exorcism from proper medicine;[17] the philosophy of Marcus Aurelius (121–180), who treats the exorcist with disdain;[18] the satire of Lucian (ca. 120–ca. 180), who treats

---

[15]Although Pliny the Elder (23/24–79 C.E.) mentions magic and popular healing techniques in chapters 20–32 of his *Natural History*, he does not record any incidents of exorcism.

[16]Josephus, *Ant.* 8.45–49.

[17]Domitius Ulpianus, *De omnibus tribunalibus*, Book 8: *De extraordinariis cognitionibus*. The passage was incorporated into Justinian's digest of Roman law (Ulpian, *Dig.* 50.13.1.1–3). Ulpian states that the work of obstetricians and medical specialists are justly paid positions because of their concern with health (*salutis hominum ... curam agant*), but in contrast: "... one must not include people who make incantations or imprecations or, to use the common expression of imposters, exorcisms. For these are not branches of medicine, even though people exist who forcibly assert that such people have helped them." (*non tamen si incantauit, si inprecatus est, si, ut uulgari uerbo impostorum utar, si exorcizauit: non sunt ista medicinae genera, tametsi sint, qui hos sibi profuisse cum praedicatione adfirment.*) (Theodore Mommsen and Paul Krueger, eds., *The Digest of Justinian*, trans. Alan Watson [4 vols.; Philadelphia: University of Pennsylvania Press, 1985] 4:929). Tony Honoré argues that Ulpian wrote during a period of heightened cultural syncretism. This was evident even in traditional Roman law, which recognized the Punic, Gallic and Assyrian (i.e., Aramaic) languages in addition to Greek and Latin, as valid for drafting certain legal documents. The metropolitan climate was most affected by the *constitutio Antoniniana* (212 C.E.), an imperial edict that granted citizenship to virtually every free inhabitant of the Roman Empire. Ulpian's prolific summation of Roman law during the reign of M. Aurelius Antoninus (Caracalla) (211–17) amounted to the systematic publication of that law for the new citizenry. This move toward political inclusion, however, did not extend to toleration of marginal social activities. As Honoré says: "Superstition, for example Judaism, or imposture, for instance that practised by exorcists, is condemned" (Tony Honoré, *Ulpian* [Oxford: Clarendon Press, 1982] 31).

[18]Marcus Aurelius (121–80) says that he understood from the example of one Diognetus: "... not to be taken up with trifles; and [not] to give credence to the statements of miracle-mongers and wizards about incantations and the exorcizing of demons and such like things." (τὸ ἀκενόσπουδον· καὶ τὸ ἀπιστητικὸν τοῖς ὑπὸ τῶν τερατευομένων καὶ γοήτων περὶ ἐπῳδῶν καὶ περὶ δαιμόνων ἀποπομπῆς καὶ τῶν τοιούτων λεγομένοις.) (Marcus Aurelius, *Ad se ipsum* 1.6. English translation in Marcus Aurelius Antoninus, *The Communings with Himself*, translated by C. R. Haines [LCL; Cambridge: Harvard University Press, 1961]).

exorcists as fraudulent entrepreneurs in a superstitious world;[19] and the hagiography of Philostratus (ca. 170–ca. 245), who shows the first century wise man Apollonius of Tyana to perform his miracles under a cloud of suspicion and misunderstanding by the Roman authorities.[20]

Exorcism, not without reason, leaves an exotic impression upon these literati, an "easternness" which they tend to interpret as "foreignness." Thus, Vespasian encounters a Jew adept in a craft excelled in by Jews.[21] For Lucian, a connection with the east is a near prerequisite for exorcistic conjuration. He notes Egypt for its familiarity with magic in general,[22] and in particular he mentions a contemporary Syrian exorcist famous for his work in Palestine,[23] a "Chaldean" from Babylonia who successfully casts spells and incantations,[24] and an Arab who possesses a ring used to control demons.[25] Philostratus mentions that Apollonius received an education in eastern wisdom,[26] which in part translated into his ability to discern and control spirits.

These critical assessments of the exorcist and his craft nevertheless record their underlying popular fascination and appeal. The story of Lucian's Arab itself attests to this interest in conjuration and its conveyance to Greece from the east. Accordingly, the Arab gives the ring to Eucrates, a Greek, and teaches

---

[19]Lucian, *Philops.* 16–17. Brenk notes: "Lucian's ridicule of all these [exorcistic] practices is surely typical of the attitude of many Greek intellectuals of the time" (Frederick E. Brenk, "In the Light of the Moon: Demonology in the Early Imperial Period," in *ANRW* 2.16.3, W. Haase, ed. [New York: Walter de Gruyter, 1986] 2.16.3:2112). In another work, Lucian also corroborates Ulpian's higher expectations for medicine when he says that the physician Paetus acted in a manner unfitting of his profession by believing in the deceits of Alexander of Abonoteichus, the "false" prophet of Asclepius (Lucian, *Alex.* 60).

[20]Philostratus, *Vit. Apoll.* 1.2. Philostratus was commissioned to write the *Life of Apollonius* by the Syrian princess Julia Domna, Septimius Severus' second wife, whose intellectual circle also included Ulpian (Honoré, *Ulpian*, 31). This attests to a range of views with regard to exorcism within the intellectual and social elite at this time. Wizardry is a constant charge against Apollonius, and one which Philostratus assiduously refutes (see below, Chapter 6). Lucian also views Apollonius of Tyana and a student of his, whom he identifies only as a γόης, unfavorably as the teachers of Alexander (Lucian, *Alex.* 5).

[21]Josephus, *Ant.* 8.45–49.

[22]Lucian, *Philops.* 31. See also Origen, *Cels.* 1.28. Klaus Thraede considers exorcism a magical practice picked up by the Jews from the priestly magical traditions of Babylon and Egypt during the Hellenistic period, but that Egypt was the dominant source of inspiration for exorcism as it continued to spread throughout the Mediterranean during the Hellenistic period (Thraede, "Exorzismus," *RAC* 7:57).

[23]Lucian, *Philops.* 16–17.

[24]Lucian, *Philops.* 9–11.

[25]Lucian, *Philops.* 17; cf. 24.

[26]Philostratus, *Vit. Apoll.* 1.2. As a Pythagorean, Apollonius also inherited the reputation for eastern wisdom once attributed to Pythagoras himself (cf. Pliny, *Hist. nat.* 24.156; 25.13; 30.8–9). The Indian sage Iarchas also performs an exorcism (Philostratus, *Vit. Apoll.* 3.38).

him along with it "the spell of many names";[27] it is precisely the type of practice ridiculed by the critics. The Arab's ring and spell converge with the magical papyri, amulets, and curse tablets that have survived from the early Common Era as a growing corpus of firsthand evidence of conjuration's popularity at this time.[28] These sources, however, essentially confirm exorcism's place in the eddies of the cultural mainstream.

Even while pagan authors offer their criticisms of the exorcist, Justin Martyr (ca. 100–165) and Tertullian (ca. 160–240) appeal to exorcism in their defenses of Christianity. The references to exorcism made by the apologists differ from the contemporary magical evidence in that they are directed publicly toward the civil authorities, some of whom have maligned the practice in their own writings.[29] Throughout their apologies both Justin and

---

[27]ἡ ἐπῳδὴ ἡ πολυώνυμος (Lucian, *Philops.* 17. English translation in *Lucian*, translated by A. M. Harmon et al. [8 vols. LCL; Cambridge: Harvard University Press, 1959–1967]).

[28]We can add to this evidence the collection of books found at Nag Hammadi, and the New Testament Apocrypha and Pseudepigrapha. See also, Marvin Meyer and Richard Smith, eds., *Ancient Christian Magic: Coptic Texts of Ritual Power* (San Francisco: HarperSanFrancisco, 1994) for texts from the first to the eleventh/twelfth centuries. Numerous curse tablets and binding spells attest to the prevalence of phenomena similar to exorcism among non-Christians, that is, the conjuring of spiritual powers to further one's intentions (see, e.g., John G. Gager, *Curse Tablets and Binding Spells*). Some of the Greek Magical Papyri from the fourth century C.E. onward show the interest among exorcists themselves of passing on the formulae they have inherited and developed. See especially the exorcistic passages in *PGM* 4.86–87; 1227–64; 3007–86; 5.96–172; 7.429–58; 579–90; 12.270–350; 13.1–343 (242–44); 94.17–21; 114.1–14.

[29]Justin addresses his apologies to Marcus Aurelius (called here Verissimus the Philosopher), as well as the Emperor Antoninus Pius, Lucius, the holy Senate (ἱερᾷ συγκλήτῳ), and all the Romans (δήμῳ παντὶ ʻΡωμαίων) (Justin, *1 Apol.* 1.1). In his *Second Apology*, Justin says that Jesus became incarnate: "... for the sake of believing men, and for the destruction of the demons. And now you can learn this from what is under your own observation. For numberless demoniacs throughout the whole world, and in your city, many of our [Christian] men exorcising them in the name of Jesus Christ, who was crucified under Pontius Pilate, have healed and do heal, rendering helpless and driving the possessing devils out of the men, though they could not be cured by all the other exorcists, and those who used incantations and drugs." (ὑπερ ... τῶν πιστευόντων ἀνθρώπων καὶ <ἐπὶ> καταλύσει τῶν δαιμόνων, <ὡς> καὶ νῦν ἐκ τῶν ὑπ᾿ ὄψιν γινομένων μαθεῖν δύνασθε. Δαιμονιολήπτους γὰρ πολλοὺς κατὰ πάντα τὸν κόσμον καὶ ἐν τῇ ὑμετέρᾳ πόλει πολλοὶ τῶν ἡμετέρων ἀνθρώπων [τῶν Χριστιανῶν] ἐπορκίζοντες κατὰ τοῦ ὀνόματος Ιησοῦ Χριστοῦ, τοῦ σταυρωθέντος ἐπὶ Ποντίου Πιλάτου, ὑπὸ τῶν ἄλλων πάντων ἐπορκιστῶν καὶ ἐπαστῶν καὶ φαρμακευτῶν μὴ ἰαθέντας, ἰάσαντο καὶ ἔτι νῦν ἰῶνται, καταργοῦντες καὶ ἐκδιώκοντες τοὺς κατέχοντας τοὺς ἀνθρώπους δαίμονας.) (Justin *2 Apol.* 6.5–6. Greek text from Miroslav Marcovich, ed., *Iustini Martyris Apologiae pro Christianis* [PTS 38; Berlin: Walter de Gruyter, 1994] 146). Tertullian addresses his apology to the Roman religious authorities (*Romani imperii antistites*) (Tertullian, *Apol.* 1.1), and at several places mentions the success of Christian

Tertullian join with their audiences in condemning magic. In order simultaneously to uphold the legitimacy of exorcism the apologists redefine Christianity for their Roman audience as an authentic religion. Having once established the legitimacy of their faith the apologists can then rehabilitate exorcism's reputation insofar as it is practiced within that faith. With Christian exorcism thus liberated from the realm of magical deception, the apologists can appeal to it as a practice that exposes the falsity of other religions while at the same time substantiates its own: by drawing their authority to perform exorcisms from the Christian godhead, Christian exorcists are able to control the so-called gods of pagan belief.[30]

It is in the area of Christian mission, where Christian values confront non-Christian sensibilities, that one would expect the practice of exorcism to undergo the greatest adaptation. Yet, at face value the exorcisms referred to by the apologists appear consistent with the exorcisms of the synoptic tradition. The most marked departure from the synoptic precedent occurs not in the exteriority of mission, but within the confines of the church itself. The differences in form and meaning of exorcism within Christianity are highlighted when we look several centuries after the evangelists to an early example of a Christian liturgical exorcism.[31] In the *Apostolic Tradition*, attributed to

---

exorcists in subduing the supposed pagan gods by the power of the one true God. References to exorcism by Christians occur at 21.17; 23.6–7, 16; 27.5–6; 32.2–3; 37.9 (cf. 43.2); and 46.5.

[30]In the 23rd chapter of his *Apology*, Tertullian shows how exorcism validates Christianity: "Produce someone before your tribunals, who is admittedly demon-possessed. Let any Christian you please bid him speak, and the spirit in the man will own himself a demon—and truly—just as he will elsewhere call himself a god, falsely. Similarly bring forward some one or other of those persons who are supposed to be god-possessed ... if they do not confess they are demons, not daring to lie to a Christian, then shed that impudent Christian's blood on the spot! What could be plainer than such a deed? What proof more reliable?" (*Edatur hic aliqui ibidem sub tribunalibus vestris quem daemone agi constet. Iussus a quolibet Christiano loqui spiritus ille tam se daemonem confitebitur de vero quam alibi dominum de falso. Aeque producatur aliquis ex his qui de deo pati existimantur ... nisi se daemones confessi fuerint Christiano mentiri non audentes, ibidem illius Christiani procacissimi sanguinem fundite! Quid isto opere manifestius? Quid hac probatione fidelius?*) (Tertullian, *Apol.* 23.4–7. English translation in Tertullian, *Apology*, translated by T. R. Glover [LCL; Cambridge: Harvard University Press, 1966]). In the fourth century, Athanasias reiterates the claim that any Christian worth his salt can cast out demons, which he supports by referring to Matthew 10:8 (Barrett-Lennard, *Christian Healing after the New Testament*, 213).

[31]The earliest reference to renunciation of the devil as part of the Christian baptismal ceremony is found in the gnostic writings of Theodotus of Rome (fl. early II C.E.), as preserved in the writings of Clement of Alexandria. The relevant passage reads as follows: "For this reason baptism is called death and the end of the old life, since we renounce the evil principalities; it is called life according to Christ, since he is the master of this life." (Ταύτη θάνατος καὶ τέλος λέγεται τοῦ παλαιοῦ βίου τὸ βάπτισμα, ἀποτασσομένων ἡμῶν ταῖς πονηραῖς Ἀρχαῖς, ζωὴ δὲ κατὰ Χριστόν, ἧς

Hippolytus (ca. 170–ca. 236), but perhaps a composite work that in its extant form dates to the early fourth century,[32] the author describes exorcism's place

---

μόνος αὐτὸς κυριεύει.) (Francois Sagnard, ed., *Extraits de Théodote* [2d ed., SC 23; Paris: Cerf, 1970] Excerpt 77; citation and translation in Barrett-Lennard, *Christian Healing after the New Testament*, 156, n. 87). Further along Theodotus also notes the tenacity of demons and the need to safeguard against them even into the very baptismal waters: "It is proper to come to baptism rejoicing, but since often unclean spirits also descend [into the water] with someone, accompanying and receiving the seal with him, and becoming incorrigible thereafter, fear mixes with joy, so that each one descends alone, pure. For this reason fasts, entreaties, prayers, [laying on] of hands, and genuflexions are done to save a soul from the world and from the maw of lions ..." ('Επὶ τὸ βάπτισμα χαίροντας ἔρχεσθαι προσῆκεν ἀλλ' ἐπεὶ πολλάκις συγκαταβαίνει τισὶ καὶ ἀκάθαρτα Πνεύματα, <ἅ>, παρακολουθοῦντα καὶ τυχόντα μετὰ τοῦ ἀνθρώπου τῆς σφραγῖδος, ἀνίατα τοῦ λοιποῦ γίνεται, [ἃ] τῇ χαρᾷ συμπλέκεται φόβος, ἵνα τις μόνος καθαρός αὐτὸς κατέλθη. Διὰ τοῦτο νηστεῖαι, δεήσεις, εὐχαί, <θέσεις> χειρῶν, γονυκλισίαι, ὅτι ψυχὴ «ἐκ κόσμου» καὶ «ἐκ στόματος λεόντων» ἀνασώζεται·) (*Extraits de Théodote*, 83–84).

[32]The *Apostolic Tradition*, formerly known as the *Egyptian Church Order*, has generally been attributed to Hippolytus, also called the Antipope, placed in Rome, and dated to ca. 215 (Gregory Dix, *The Treatise on the Apostolic Tradition of St. Hippolytus of Rome, Bishop and Martyr* [2d rev. ed. reissued with additional corrections by Henry Chadwick; London: Alban Press, 1992] xxxv–xxxvii). Barrett-Lennard notes that the author himself considers his descriptions of church offices and procedures to represent models rather than fixed practices (cf. Hippolytus, *Trad. ap.* Prologue). Even so, he supports the early date based upon the charismatic gift of healing as an authentic yet unordained office received through revelation by God in *Apostolic Tradition* 14, in contrast to Chapter 8 of the mid-fourth century Egyptian work, the *Canons of Hippolytus*, which expects those with healing abilities to be ordained (Barrett-Lennard, *Christian Healing after the New Testament*, 250). He says: "Certainly the *Apostolic Tradition* reflects a considerably more primitive situation where it was seen to be appropriate that a lay, charismatic ministry of healing existed alongside the ministry to the sick by the leadership of the Church" (Barrett-Lennard, *Christian Healing after the New Testament*, 253). Paul Bradshaw recognizes the scholarly consensus over the attribution and date of the *Apostolic Tradition*, but warns that "one ought not automatically to assume that it provides reliable information about the life and liturgical activity of the church in Rome in the early third century" (Paul Bradshaw, *The Search for Origins of Christian Worship: Sources and Methods for the Study of Early Liturgy* [London: SPCK, 1992] 92). Bradshaw notes that the earliest manuscript evidence dates to a late fifth century copy of the Latin translation (L) of the lost Greek original (Paul Bradshaw, *Ordination Rites of the Ancient Churches of East and West* [New York: Pueblo Publishing, 1990] 3). In a preliminary analysis, Bradshaw advances Marcel Metzger's doubts with respect to the date of the *Apostolic Tradition* (Paul F. Bradshaw, "Redating the *Apostolic Tradition*: Some Preliminary Steps," in *Rule of Prayer, Rule of Faith: Essays in Honor of Aidan Kavanagh, O.S.B.*, Nathan Mitchell and John F. Baldwin, eds. [Collegeville, Minn.: Liturgical Press, 1996] 3). Bradshaw interprets the extant document to be a composite work that shows evidence of continuous revision, and he dates the work as a whole to the first quarter of the fourth century based upon its use by other documents that can be dated to later in that century (e.g. *CH* [ca. 336–340]; *AC* [ca. 375–380]). Bradshaw acknowledges, however, that the *Apostolic Tradition*'s own source material would likely be of varying dates, and he describes

in connection with Christian initiation.[33] In the *Apostolic Tradition* "exorcist" does not refer to a clerical rank, as it does in Cornelius' Rome.[34] It is, however, a clerical activity, performed during the baptismal ceremony by a bishop and presbyter with the assistance of a deacon.[35] In this context those catechumens who are set apart for baptism undergo repeated exorcisms throughout their period of instruction, and receive a final exorcism in the baptismal ceremony itself.

The method of exorcism in the *Apostolic Tradition* differs markedly from the portrayals of exorcism in the New Testament. Contrary to the predominantly verbal method of exorcising demons in the New Testament, such as by rebuke and command,[36] the baptismal ceremony of the *Apostolic*

---

the initiation ceremony in particular as "a conflation of different traditions from different periods, and very probably different places" (Bradshaw, "Redating the *Apostolic Tradition*," 15). A further clue to the date of the *Apostolic Tradition* may be found in other types of Christian literature. The liturgical prescription of catechetical and baptismal exorcism in The *Apostolic Tradition* finds a literary complement in the third century pseudo-Clementine *Recognitions*. In the *Recognitions*, an initial confrontation between Peter and Simon Magus offers an opportunity for the author to expound upon "orthodox" teaching to correct the deceptive mission of Simon Magus. This instruction involves not just the retelling of Scripture, but also the critique of the beliefs and philosophies out of which the catechumens have come. These impromptu lectures essentially serve as catechetical instruction for the uninitiated, Clement included. In the romance Peter often ends his days of teaching by summoning the sick and demon-possessed for healing and exorcism (Pseudo-Clement, *Recogn.* 2.70; 3.30; 4.7; 5.36; 10.52), and occasionally this is followed by baptism (Pseudo-Clement, *Recogn.* 6.15; 10.68–71; also Pseudo-Clement, *Hom.* 7.5). This pedagogical process also occurs in the seventh of the *Clementine Homilies*, where Peter offers the Two Ways instruction, heals (exorcism included), and advises baptism (Pseudo-Clement, *Hom.* 7.7–8).

[33]Hippolytus, *Trad. ap.* 21–22. Compare *On the Soldier's Crown* (written 201), where Tertullian says of renunciation at baptism: "Finally that I may comment upon baptism, those of us then about to approach the water, but prior to entry into the church, profess under the hand of the bishop that we renounce the devil and his ostentation and his angels." (*Denique, ut a baptismate ingrediar, aquam adituri ibidem, sed et aliquanto prius in ecclesia, sub antistitis manu, contestamur nos renuntiare diabolo et pompae et angelis eius.*) (Tertullian, *Cor.* 3.2; Latin from Q. Septimi Florentis Tertulliani, *De Corona* [Érasme; Paris: Presses Universitaires de France, 1966]).

[34]Barrett-Lennard notes in a chapter on Irenaeus: "There is nothing here [in the literary sources] that would suggest that, in the late second century, different spiritual gifts were being associated with particular offices in the church" (Barrett-Lennard, *Christian Healing after the New Testament*, 118). He finds evidence for an emerging "order of exorcists" in the third and fourth centuries, and refers to Hippolytus' *Apostolic Tradition* and Cyprian's 23rd *Epistle* as the primary evidence for this transition (Barrett-Lennard, *Christian Healing after the New Testament*, 202).

[35]Hippolytus, *Trad. ap.* 21. Hippolytus does not say who perform(s) the exorcisms during the period of catechesis.

[36]The exclusively verbal method of exorcism is true for Mark and Matthew. Luke offers an exception with his unparalleled presentation of the woman bent double. In this story Luke

Tradition uses an "oil of exorcism" (*oleum exorcismi*), and the placement of the cleric's hand upon the head of the catechumen (*manum imponens super eum*). When words are used they form a command for the catechumen to renounce Satan. This renunciation also shows how the character of the person possessed differs from the New Testament example: the tangible rituals of oil and touch are applied to one who makes a conscious decision to be relieved of demonic forces compared to the New Testament's passive victims of demonic aggression.

The context for exorcism in the *Apostolic Tradition*, now part of a private initiation ceremony, also differs from the New Testament. By its repetition during the period of catechesis, exorcism in the *Apostolic Tradition* is more similar to purification rituals than to the exorcisms performed in the New Testament for the sake of healing and the display of the exorcist's power and authority. The focus of the ceremony is not upon the priesthood, but upon the catechumen who is to receive baptism. Thus, the "possessed" rather than the exorcist takes center stage. The fact that exorcism occurs in catechetical instruction and within the baptismal ceremony itself shows that it is now no longer reserved for the unusual and extraordinary otherness of the demonically possessed as one finds them in the gospels and Acts. Instead, demonic possession and the subsequent need for the exorcists' services are applicable to the catechumen and, hence, to virtually all Christians upon their entry into the church. Consequently, exorcism is not a relic of the New Testament tradition mimicked and preserved in the early church for tradition's sake, but is a ritual that had a function of immediate relevance to every member of the Christian community, at least with regard to their initiation into that community through baptism.

The placement of exorcism in the *Apostolic Tradition*'s baptismal ceremony alters the purpose of exorcism relative to its practice in the New Testament. In the *Apostolic Tradition*, demonic possession becomes correlated to the idea of divine possession, so that exorcism now serves as a prerequisite cleansing of the body in preparation for its habitation by the Holy Spirit.[37] The two

---

thoroughly blends exorcism and healing with regard to both the interpretation of an ailment and its method of cure. He describes the woman's physical condition in terms of possession by a "crippling spirit" (πνεῦμα ἔχουσα ἀσθενείας), which Jesus "heals" (ἐθεράπευσεν) by both word and touch: "When Jesus saw her, he called her over and said, 'Woman, you are set free from your ailment' (γύναι, ἀπολέλυσαι τῆς ἀσθενείας σου). When he laid his hands on her, immediately she stood up straight and began praising God" (Luke 13:12–13). On another occasion, Luke figuratively describes Jesus to perform exorcisms "by the finger of God" (ἐν δακτύλῳ θεοῦ) (Luke 11:20).

[37]The Latin version is less explicit in the summoning of the Holy Spirit into the baptizand: "O Lord God, who has made them worthy to deserve the remission of sins through the washing of regeneration of the Holy Spirit, send into them your grace, that they may serve you according to your will ..." (*D[omi]ne D[eu]s, qui dignos fecisti eos remissionem mereri peccatorum per lauacrum regenerationis sp[irit]u[s] s[an]c[t]i, inmitte*

types of possessing entities, demonic and divine, are not brought together in this way in the gospel texts.[38] Rather, the gospels leave us with the prospect of a demoniac swept clean of his demon only to have it return again with others more evil still.[39] Consequently, this early Roman baptismal rite illustrates one means by which the activity of exorcism established itself in the church as a theologically founded activity which employed exorcism of the demonic as a preliminary step toward invocation of the divine.[40]

Franz Joseph Dölger has done much to explain the changes in early Christianity's practice of exorcism, including its incorporation into the

---

in eos tuam gratiam, ut tibi seruiant secundum uoluntatem tuam ...) (Hippolytus, *Trad. ap.* 21. Latin from Hippolyte de Rome, *La Tradition Apostolique* [SC, 2d ed.; Paris: Cerf, 1984]). In the Bohairic Coptic, as well as the Arabic and Ethiopic versions, the language more explicitly states the subsequent possession by the divinity: "... make them worthy that they may be filled with the Holy Spirit and send over them your grace that they may serve you according to your will ..." (... *fac eos dignos ut repleantur spiritu sancto et mitte super eos gratiam tuam ut* [ἵνα] *tibi serviant secundum voluntatem tuam* ...) (Hippolytus, *Trad. ap.* 21).

[38]There are a few passages in the New Testament that have some relevance for a correlation between demonic and divine possession. The most evocative but least helpful of these is the baptism and temptation sequence of Jesus. The passage is evocative for the close proximity in which it places the devil's wiles to the reception of the Holy Spirit at baptism, though in reverse sequence. It appears that Bultmann is correct in questioning "whether the linking up of Baptism and Temptation can be traced to the cultic connection of Baptism with Exorcism" at the time of Jesus. In the Marcan context Bultmann places the baptism of Jesus under the theme of messianic kingship, for which he finds no inner connection with the Temptation (Rudolf Bultmann, *The History of the Synoptic Tradition* [rev. ed. from the 2d German ed. of 1931; New York: Harper & Row, 1968] 253–57). Elsewhere in the synoptics Mark 3:29 directly correlates demonic and divine possession as mutually exclusive states of existence: to say that Jesus has a demon is to blaspheme the Holy Spirit within him. Matthew's and Mark's conclusions to the Beelzeboul controversy echo this sentiment. A more illustrative correlation comes in Acts 5:3–9, where Peter catches Ananias withholding a promised gift from the community and charges him with being filled at heart with Satan (τί ἐπλήρωσεν ὁ σατανᾶς τὴν καρδίαν σου), and of falsifying the Holy Spirit (ψεύσασθαί σε τὸ πνεῦμα τὸ ἅγιον). As a result of Ananias' own action, then, the Holy Spirit no longer abides in him (οὐχὶ μένον σοὶ ἔμενεν καὶ πραθὲν ἐν τῇ σῇ ἐξουσίᾳ ὑπῆρχεν). This illustrates the replacement of one type of possession with another.

[39]Matt 12:43–45//Luke 11:24–26; cf., the wandering spirits in 4 Ezra (2 Esdras) 7:78–99.

[40]Compare also from the *Apostolic Constitutions*: "Let us earnestly entreat God on behalf of the catechumens ... that he may cleanse them from all pollution of flesh and spirit, and dwell in them ..." (Ὑπὲρ τῶν κατηχουμένων πάντες ἐκτενῶς τὸν θεὸν παρακαλέσωμεν ... καθαρίσῃ δὲ αὐτοὺς ἀπὸ παντὸς μολυσμοῦ σαρκὸς καὶ πνεύματος, ἐνοικήσῃ τε ἐν αὐτοῖς ...) (*Const. ap.* 8.6.5-6. Greek text and English translation in David A. Fiensy, *Prayers Alleged to Be Jewish: An Examination of the Constitutiones Apostolorum* [BJS 65; Chico, Calif.: Scholars Press, 1985]).

baptismal ceremony, and some of his conclusions are worth stating here.[41] Dölger considered exorcism and baptism to have become entwined by the second century after having originally operated independently of each other in the earlier Christian communities.[42] He determined the merger to have resulted from two principal beliefs. First was Christianity's demonization of foreign pantheons and cultures, a factor aided by the otherwise morally neutral term *"daimon"* which assumed an exclusively negative sense among Jewish and Christian writers. By associating what was pagan and heretical with demons and the devil, Dölger derived a cause for exorcizing those catechumens who were coming to Christianity out of these traditions.[43]

The second impetus for the merger, related to the first, was the association made between sin and Satan. This association led Dölger to distinguish between corporal and ethical possession (*leibliche Besessenheit*; *ethische Besessenheit*).[44] To some extent, the association of moral weakness with bodily illness contributed toward the changes of method within Christian exorcism, so that, for example, the use of oil in exorcism, unattested earlier in the New Testament writings, "healed" the soul of its sins in analogy with oil's healing effects upon the body.[45] But the eventual association of exorcism with

---

[41]Franz Joseph Dölger, *Der Exorzismus im altchristlichen Taufritual: Eine religionsgeschichtliche Studie* (Studien zur Geschichte und Kultur des Altertums 3.1–2; Paderborn: Ferdinand Schöningh, 1909).

[42]Dölger says: "Consequently, not just the thought of rebirth [παλιγγενεσία], sealing [σφραγίς], and enlightenment [φώτισμα] were joined to baptism; there was also attached to it the significance of an exorcism, due to the influence of contemporary teachings about demons." (*Es wurde, sonach mit der Taufe nicht bloss der Gedanke der Wiedergeburt, Besiegelung und Erleuchtung verbunden, es wurde ihr auch unter dem Einfluss der damaligen Dämonenlehre die Bedeutung eines Exorzismus beigemessen.*) (Dölger, *Exorzismus im altchristlichen Taufritual*, 4–5).

[43]"The Devil is joined with the heathen and heretic; he lives in him." (*Mit dem Heiden und Ketzer ist der Teufel verbunden, er wohnt in ihm.*) (Dölger, *Exorzismus im altchristlichen Taufritual*, 24).

[44]Dölger, *Exorzismus im altchristlichen Taufritual*, 33–37. Dölger insists that both forms of possession constituted real beliefs in real demonic spirits that reside within the possessed; ethical possession is not merely a metaphor of human sinfulness: "By ethical possession one understood not perhaps a powerful influence of the devil upon the soul, but a real inhabitation by the demonic powers." (*Unter ethischer Besessenheit verstand man aber nicht etwa eine dynamische Einwirkung des Teufels auf die Seele, sondern ein wirkliches Einwohnen der dämonischen Mächte.*) (Dölger, *Exorzismus im altchristlichen Taufritual*, 153). Thraede also makes use of the distinction between corporal and ethical possession (also called by Dölger "spiritual possession" [*geistliche Besessenheit*]) in his study (e.g., Thraede, "Exorzismus," *RAC* 7:79).

[45]Dölger, *Exorzismus im altchristlichen Taufritual*, 77–78, 146–47. Compare the combination of oil and prayer for healing in James 5:14–16. Gabriele Winkler offers an alternative view to Dölger's. She sees the use of oil in the prebaptismal ceremony as an addition by the Syrian and Armenian theologians who, rather than as an apotropeion, applied this to baptism as a messianic rite in analogy with the anointing of kings in the Hebrew

ethical possession also had a more profound effect. Dölger considered both corporal possession and its exorcism to have been a belief and practice of Jesus and his contemporaries that became increasingly outdated among subsequent generations of Christians.[46] By demonizing humanity's sinful nature, and by applying exorcism to ethical possession in the baptismal ceremony, Dölger saw the church to have maintained a theological basis for the dominical command to exorcize.[47]

Dölger's work on the development of exorcism within Christianity has been affirmed and refined by more recent research.[48] The focus for Dölger and

---

Bible. (See Gabriele Winkler, "The Original Meaning and Implications of the Prebaptismal Anointing," *Worship* 52 [1978] 24–45). In support of Winkler's view compare the *Gospel of Philip* from the Nag Hammadi codices, where the chrism ceremony, distinct from the baptismal ceremony, serves to make one a "Christ" (*Gos. Phil.* 67d, 95). We see command and touch to play a role in exorcism also in Tertullian's *Apology*: "Thus at a touch, a breath from us, they are seized by the thought, by the foretaste of that fire, and they leave the bodies of men at our command, all against their will, in pain, blushing to have you witness it." (*Ita de contactu deque afflatu nostro, contemplatione et repraesentatione ignis illius correpti etiam de corporibus nostro imperio excedunt inviti et dolentes et vobis praesentibus erubescentes.*) (Tertullian, *Apol.* 23.16 [Glover, LCL]. Cf., 21.17; 27.5–6; 46.5).

[46]Dölger, *Exorzismus im altchristlichen Taufritual*, 127. In support of Dölger we can refer to the work of Barrett-Lennard, who has collected and commented upon written sources from the second half of the second century to the fourth century as evidence of the popularity of exorcism within Christian circles. These sources include papyrus letters of the laity, literary writings by educated leaders and pastors, and liturgical sources, which provide a wider spectrum of church thought for a given region. What is interesting is a lack of reference to exorcism in the ephemeral writings prior to the fourth century. Barrett-Lennard says of this: "… I am not aware of any pre-fourth century Christian papyrus letter which makes reference to either an act of exorcism or to a demon-possessed person. This contrasts sharply with the situation in relation to our literary and liturgical sources" (Barrett-Lennard, *Christian Healing after the New Testament*, 137).

[47]The Council of Carthage (256) offers the first evidence of exorcism and baptism unified into a single ceremony, for which it finds biblical basis in the dominical mandates to baptize and exorcize found respectively in Matthew 28:19 and Mark 16:17 (Dölger, *Exorzismus im altchristlichen Taufritual*, 12–13).

[48]For example, Thraede, "Exorzismus" *RAC* 7. Note also Elizabeth Ann Leeper's outline of the gradual institutionalization of exorcism in the church from its charismatic origins in early Christianity. Leeper concludes that exorcism as an institution aided the church's stability and growth by bringing "healing, control, and initiation" to the three liminal areas of health, orthodoxy, and ecclesial organization. She notes that exorcism's importance: "… goes back to the need of Christianity to create a new symbolic universe, to bring converts into a new order of being, and to instill in them a new identity if the movement was to survive. The church, whether aware of it or not, was involved in ordering and maintaining reality" (Elizabeth Ann Leeper, *Exorcism in Early Christianity* [Ph.D. diss., Duke University, 1991] 341). Leeper defines exorcism's role as "reality ordering" in relation to both of Dölger's forms of demonic possession: physical exorcism is a means of restoring health, and ethical exorcism is an "inner" or "social reordering" as a means of initiating the catechumen into the cosmological view of Christianity. Leeper also sets forth a third category

later researchers, however, has been upon exorcism as an "intra-mural" activity, that is, as it takes place within the church and among the converted. What I hope to do in the following chapters is to explore how exorcism also played a role in the process of conversion, as Christianity formally introduced itself to the host cultures of Greece and Rome. In order to argue the relevance of exorcism to Christian mission, one must make a case for either a change in Greek thought that led to its accommodation of the exorcist (Near Eastern influences on Greco-Roman thought and practice), or a change in the practice of exorcism that may have brought it more into synchronicity with the Greek world-view, or a synthesis of both. The issues of cultural adaptation will be discussed under five chapter headings. Chapters 2 and 3 discuss analogous practices from the ancient Near East that, although initially rejected in the biblical texts, gained a credibility during the intertestamental period that would add legitimacy to the portrayals of exorcism in subsequent Judaism and early Christianity. Chapter 4 discusses the Greek cultural background that under-mined this legitimacy. Chapter 5 discusses the various uses of exorcism in the New Testament that would have facilitated its adaptation in the early centuries of Christian expansion. Chapter 6 discusses the actual reception of the Christian exorcist as it can be gathered from the literary sources, to determine where changes may have taken place either in the Christian practice of exorcism to accommodate the sensibilities of the audience to be converted, or in the world-view of the audience that the exorcist hoped to convert. The present study's time frame for early Christianity extends from the first to the early fourth centuries of the Common Era. The closing terminus reflects Constantine's favorable recognition of Christianity, and assumes that the acceptance or tolerance of Christianity that followed thereafter would have affected the contemporary perceptions of its traditions, exorcism included.

---

not distinguished by Dölger, that of "reality maintaining," as a means of controlling the deviant and maintaining orthodoxy within the church (Leeper, *Exorcism and Early Christianity*, 342–45). Another way to think of exorcism, still compatible with Leeper's three categories, is to emphasize exorcism's role in reconciliation: reconciling the sick to creation, the schismatic to the one church, the uninitiated to the true God.

Chapter 2

Possession and Exorcism in the Ancient Near East

2.1 Introduction

This chapter presents Near Eastern evidence for possession and exorcism as it appears in ancient Mesopotamia societies and Zoroastrianism. In contrast with the official, if not popular, Hellenistic and Roman antipathy toward the exorcist, the ancient Near East had a long and respected tradition of treating demonic afflictions, the documentation of which extends back to as early as the third millennium B.C.E. Although this chapter will argue for Zoroastrianism as the primary instigator for the belief in possession and the need for exorcism by reason of its dualistic and apocalyptic beliefs and doctrines, it will also note that the practices and beliefs of the earlier Mesopotamian societies set a precedent of respect for those practitioners who mediated between humanity and the spiritual powers. For this reason the Near Eastern environment serves as the likely context in which the Christian practice of exorcism arose. It is because of this environment that the New Testament can record its stories of demonic possession and exorcism without defensiveness or self-consciousness.

2.2 Affliction and Conjuration in Ancient Mesopotamia

The Sumerians, Akkadians, Assyrians and Babylonians shared polytheism and syncretism as common features of their religious beliefs,[1] features which have hindered the systematization of those beliefs in the present day. A. Leo Oppenheim describes the nature of the ancient Near Eastern polytheistic religions as:

---

[1] A. Kirk Grayson, "Mesopotamia, History of (Assyria)," *ABD* 4:753–54; and "Mesopotamia, History of (Babylonia)," *ABD* 4:773–76. H. W. F. Saggs notes that the Sumerian scribes were able to compile a list of 3600 known names of deities (H. W. F. Saggs, *Civilization before Greece and Rome* [New Haven: Yale University Press, 1989] 277).

multifaceted structures ... characterized by the absence of centrality and by a deep-seated tolerance to shifting stresses, making possible the adaptability that such religions need to achieve their millennial lifespan.[2]

The religious heritage of the ancient Mesopotamian region represents a conglomeration of inheritances from the earlier empires joined to the provincial traditions of the newer. Thus, the traditions and beliefs of the Sumerians (early III millennium) were adapted by the Akkadians (late III millennium), and in turn by the Assyrians and Babylonians (II millennium), and Chaldeans (Neo-Babylonians, I millennium). Although the pantheons that resulted had gods of superior and inferior statuses, the gods themselves were subject to promotion and demotion within the hierarchy coincident with the region's political fluctuations. Thus, as individual city-states rose and fell in importance so, too, did their local deities. The rise in prominence of Babylon's Marduk, who eventually replaced the ancient Sumerian sky-god Enlil as the chief deity, serves as one such example.

The first part of Chapter 2 concerns possession and exorcism as they occur in the ancient Near Eastern Mesopotamian societies. Three texts are presented to illustrate the variety of interpretations for the cause of spiritual affliction: *Šurpu* highlights the cause of human transgression; *Udug-hul* highlights the occasion of unprovoked demonic aggression; *Maqlû* illustrates the occasion of spiritual affliction due not to one's personal transgression, but to the machinations and slander brought against that person by means of witchcraft. A section on divination is included here for comparative purposes. Otherwise, the diviner (*bārû*) of the ancient Near East appears to be more a learned technician than the inspired prophet familiar in Jewish (and Greek) society. A final section addresses the argument that the Mesopotamian societies did not believe in "possession" by a foreign spirit per se. The second part of Chapter 2 concerns the evidence for possession and exorcism in Zoroastrianism.

2.2.1 The Conjurer before the Common Era

Among a host of specialized professions such as the *asû* (medical practitioner), the *bārû* ("divination priest"), and non-professionals such as the *kaššāpu* and *kaššāptu* ("sorcerer," and "female sorcerer" or "witch" respectively), the *āšipu* of the ancient Mesopotamian cultures most resembles the later exorcist. The *āšipu* was a respected member of professional society, whose venues of service included the royal courts in Mesopotamia and elsewhere in the ancient Near East.[3] In contrast to the malicious conjurations

---

[2]A. Leo Oppenheim, *Ancient Mesopotamia: Portrait of a Dead Civilization*, rev. ed. by Erica Reiner (Chicago: University of Chicago Press, 1977) 182.

[3]Note, for example, the letters by conjurers from the Babylonian capital of Nineveh that date to the reigns of Esarhaddon (680–669) and Assurbanipal (669–626). Forty per cent of the letters are exorcistic or medical in content, which the editor suggests to be an indication of

of the *kaššāpu* and *kaššāptu*, which he was often called upon to remedy, the *āšipu* practiced culturally sanctioned magic that operated within the cultic framework of established religious beliefs.

What we know of the *āšipu* comes primarily from writings by his own hand, by way of correspondence and handbooks, many of which have been both published and translated from their original cuneiform script.[4] There are three principal contexts for physical and psychic disturbances in *āšipūtu* (the practice of the *āšipu*). These are instances in which gods or demons afflict the patient by reason of some transgression committed by the patient, or by reason of their own maliciousness, or by having been persuaded by witchcraft to forsake or to afflict the victim. Each of these contexts requires a similar method of diagnosis of cause and prognosis that dictated a course of treatment. In each of these categories the *āšipu* also acts as the mediator between the patient and the spirit-world in his efforts to release the victims from their sufferings. The handbooks *Šurpu*, *Udug-hul*, and *Maqlû* attend to each of these categories respectively, and serve as important reference materials for defining the activities and persons involved with ancient Near Eastern conjuration.

2.2.1.1 Šurpu *and Human Transgression*

Preserved on nine tablets that likely date to the Kassite Period (1500–1200), *Šurpu* serves as a useful introduction to the *āšipu*'s craft.[5] In *Šurpu* we find examples of the diagnosis and prognosis involved with the practice, and the metaphorical quality of the healing methods that accompany them. Erica Reiner describes the Akkadian title and something of the ritual itself, in this

---

Asarhaddon's failing health (Simo Parpola, ed., *Letters from Assyrian and Babylonian Scholars* [*State Archives of Assyria* 10; Helsinki: Helsinki University Press, 1993]). As to the international reputation of its healing practitioners, which included the *āšipu*, Babylonia shared its expertise by exporting its sages and medical writings to such kingdoms as Hatti (G. Beckman, "Medizin. B. Bei den Hethitern," *RlA* 7:631). Common approaches to treating illness throughout the ancient Near East is also supported by the occasions of common terminology used for certain healing practitioners (P. E. Dion, "Medical Personnel in the Ancient Near East. *asû* and *āšipu* in Aramaic Garb," *ARAM* 1 [1989] 206).

[4]A. Leo Oppenheim has estimated that ca. two-thirds of the 1500 tablets of the extant Babylonian literature is scholarly and technical, such as the magical and medical corpora. The remaining one-third is more strictly literary in genre (Erica Reiner, "First-Millennium Babylonian Literature," CAH 3.2:295). For some of the epistolary evidence, see Parpola's *Letters from Assyrian and Babylonian Scholars*, in which he divides the letters according to author's occupation—astrologers, haruspices, exorcists, physicians, lamentation priests, miscellaneous—and his earlier interpretive work: *Letters from Assyrian Scholars to the Kings Esarhaddon and Assurbanipal, Part 2: Commentary and Appendices* [AOAT 5.2; Neukirchen-Vluyn: Butzon & Bercker, 1983]).

[5]On the dating of *Šurpu*, see Erica Reiner, *Šurpu: A Collection of Sumerian and Akkadian Incantations* (Archiv für Orientforschung 11; Graz: Ernst Weidner, 1958) 2.

way: "The title, «Burning», refers to the magic operation that was to be carried out while the reciting of the incantations and prayers took place."[6] Reiner says of the occasion for *Šurpu*: "*Šurpu* is performed when the patient does not know by what act or omission he has offended the gods and the existing world order."[7] In *āšipūtu* the diagnosis of a patient's symptoms typically refers back to a cause found in the spirit-world.[8]

A hallmark of the Mesopotamian cultures was divination through observation of the natural world.[9] Oppenheim considers that the major impulses at work in Mesopotamian thought were finding patterns and consistencies, recording these through such means as name lists (onomastica), and then taking note of the inconsistencies and divergencies that could likewise be categorized and understood as omens for divination:

> The main motivation for Mesopotamian man's interest in keeping the manifestations of animal and plant life, the movements of the heavenly bodies, and other phenomena under close and constant surveillance was his hope to obtain from them timely warning of impending misfortune or disaster. In a way that is never explicitly stated or even hinted at, Mesopotamian man assumed the existence of an unknown, unnamed, and unapproachable power or will that intentionally provided him with signs.[10]

---

[6]Reiner, *Šurpu*, 1.

[7]Reiner, *Šurpu*, 3

[8]Edith K. Ritter, "Magical-Expert (= *āšipu*) and Physician (= *asû*)," in *Studies in Honor of Benno Landsberger on His Seventy-Fifth Birthday April 21, 1965*, Hans G. Güterbock and Thorkild Jacobsen, eds. (AS 16; Chicago: University of Chicago Press, 1965) 305. Physiological disturbances can also trace back to bewitchment (see, Pablo Herrero, *La Therapeutique mesopotamienne* [Memoire 48; Paris: Editions Recherche sur les Civilisations, 1984] 23–24).

[9]Grayson, "Mesopotamia, History of (Babylonia)," 775. Omen collections date from the Old Babylonian (post 1750 B.C.E.) to the Seleucid periods. The collections were originally recorded in Akkadian, but translated for use in the courts of Elam, Nuzi, Hatti, Syria and Palestine (Oppenheim, *Ancient Mesopotamia*, 206).

[10]A. Leo Oppenheim, "Man and Nature in Mesopotamian Civilization" (*Dictionary of Scientific Biography* 15 Supp. 1; New York: Scribners, 1978) 641. Reiner describes one manual of the *bārû* as giving "the rationale for the interconnexions between observable phenomena (on the earth and in the sky) and the interpretations to be derived from them" (Reiner, "First-Millennium Babylonian Literature," CAH 3.2:320). She considers the collection of omens itself to be "rigorously scientific" for reasons that: "first, they are based on observation of facts, ... and more important, because they rigorously exhaust, in the best casuistic manner, all possibilities and variations according to the position and the characteristic ... of the phenomenon observed" (Reiner, "First-Millennium Babylonian Literature," CAH 3.2:316).

Divination plays a role in the diagnosis accomplished by *ašipūtu*.[11] Oppenheim considers the practitioner of *ašipūtu* to be a "divination-oriented" physician:

> who scrutinized his patient to establish the disease affecting him and to predict its outcome … These observations … like all other [in Mesopotamian literature], are made by the *ašipu* for the purpose of identifying 'signs' that portend whether or not the patient will recover and when this will happen.[12]

In both the areas of diagnosis and prognosis the *ašipu* manifests his role as diviner.[13] Even uncommon occurrences observed along the way to a patient's

---

[11]In regard to divination and healing, Stol says: "Two experts were able to predict the patient's future: the conjurer and the diviner (haruspex)" (Marten Stol, "Diagnosis and Therapy in Babylonian Medicine," *JEOL* 32 (1991–92) 55).

[12]Oppenheim, "Man and Nature," 643.

[13]It is noteworthy that in the art of divination a persistent association exists between magic and medicine, primarily in the areas of diagnosis and prognosis. It is an association also found in Greek medicine and thought. From the Hippocratic corpus we read of the physician who sees the importance of accurate prognosis as a means of obtaining the patient's faith in his abilities: "I hold that it is an excellent thing for a physician to practice forecasting. For if he discover and declare unaided by the side of his patient the past and the future, and fill in the gaps in the account given by the sick, he will be the more believed to understand the cases, so that men will confidently entrust themselves to him for treatment. Furthermore, he will carry out the treatment best if he know beforehand from the present symptoms what will take place later." (Τὸν ἰητρὸν δοκεῖ μοι ἄριστον εἶναι πρόνοιαν ἐπιτηδεύειν· προγινώσκων γὰρ καὶ προλέγων παρὰ τοῖσι νοσέουσι τά τε παρεόντα καὶ τὰ προγεγονότα καὶ τὰ μέλλοντα ἔσεσθαι, ὁκόσα τε παραλείπουσιν οἱ ἀσθενέοντες ἐκδιηγεύμενος πιστεύοιτο ἂν μᾶλλον γινώσκειν τὰ τῶν νοσεύντων πρήγματα, ὥστε τολμᾶν ἐπιτρέπειν τοὺς ἀνθρώπους σπᾶς αὐτοὺς τῷ ἰητρῷ. τὴν δὲ θεραπείην ἄριστα ἂν ποιέοιτο προειδὼς τὰ ἐσόμενα ἐκ τῶν παρεόντων παθημάτων.) (Hippocrates, *Progn.* 1 [Jones, LCL]). A passage from Philostratus' *Life of Apollonius* speculates about the discovery of the healthful and harmful qualities of plants: "… the wise sons of Asclepius would have never attained to this branch of science, if Asclepius had not been the son of Apollo; and as such had not in accordance with the latter's responses and oracles concocted and adapted different drugs to different diseases … For I do not think that men without the forecasts of prophetic wisdom would ever have ventured to mingle with medicines that save life these most deadly of poisons." (τοὺς σοφοὺς Ἀσκληπιάδας ἐς ἐπιστήμην τούτου παρελθεῖν, εἰ μὴ παῖς Ἀπόλλωνος Ἀσκληπιὸς γενόμενος, καὶ κατὰ τὰς ἐκείνου φήμας τε καὶ μαντείας ξυνθεὶς τὰ πρόσφορα ταῖς νόσοις φάρμακα . . . οὐ γάρ μοι δοκοῦσιν ἄνευ τῆς προγιγνωσκούσης σοφίας θαρσῆσαί ποτε ἄνθρωποι τὰ πάντων ὀλεθριώτατα φαρμάκων ἐγκαταμῖξαι τοῖς σώζουσιν.) (Philostratus, *Vit. Apoll.* 3.44. English translation in Philostratus, *The Life of Apollonius of Tyana*, translated by F. C. Conybeare [2 vols. LCL; Cambridge: Harvard University Press, 1960]). Nevertheless, the similarity of method (namely, observation of condition), and similarity of objective (namely, diagnosis and prognosis) have a difference of theory behind them, so that whereas the *ašipu*'s craft is truly "divinatory" in its appeal to a supernatural referent for explanation of cause and result, the

house play a role in the *āšipu*'s diagnosis, and his prognosis comes in part by the proper reading of "signs" (or "symptoms") once at the patient's home.[14]

An example of this diagnosis appears in *Šurpu* Tablet 2, which describes the patient as one who is "sick, in danger (of death), distraught, troubled ..." The nature of the illness described here is not specified, even as to whether it is physical or mental.[15] Neither is the cause of the illness known, nor, consequently, the agent who can release the patient from his affliction. In fact, of this tablet's 193 lines, lines 5–128 list possible causes of the illness, which by and large concern an affront to the social order or to a deity,[16] while lines 129–192 consist of petitions to the offended deities to release the patient from his troubles. Wrongdoing, then, was perceived as one cause of illness in ancient Mesopotamia, and part of the healing process included a "confession" of one's infractions.[17]

After the determination of a diagnosis the *āšipu* then delivers a prognosis of the patient's likelihood of recovery. A typical prognosis provided by *Šurpu* at this moment reads: "he will release him" (favorable), or "he will not be released" (unfavorable).[18] If the prognosis is favorable the *āšipu* proceeds with treatment; if unfavorable, he withdraws from the case. Insofar as these cases involve some culpability on the victim's part, the *āšipu* serves more to appease the divine wrath than to exorcize it. The process of appeasement serves not only to restore the patient to good health, but to mend his relationship with the offended deity.

Contrary to the *asû*, or medical practitioner, who worked with medications by reason of their naturopathic powers, the *āšipu* used his pharmaceuticals for their metaphorical connotations. Two examples of treatment found in *Šurpu* illustrate the metaphorical quality of the *āšipu*'s craft. *Šurpu* Tablets 5–6 describe an affliction as follows:

---

medical practitioner tends to use the same observations of a person's condition and to reason from them causes and results based on physiological principles.

[14]Ritter, "Magical-Expert," 301.

[15]In her commentary, Reiner says that *naqdu* means "'dangerously ill' and occurs frequently in diagnostic texts and hemerologies ..." (Reiner, *Šurpu*, 54). That *Šurpu* is performed with regard for physical ailments becomes more explicit elsewhere in the text, for example: "the sickness that is in my body, my flesh, my veins" (*Šurpu* 5–6.89; trans. Reiner). Of relevance to this citation in particular, Markham Geller says: "The use of the first person verbal forms represents the incantation priest reciting formulae or making declarations, as if the patient himself were speaking" (Markham J. Geller, *Forerunners to Udug-hul: Sumerian Exorcistic Incantations* [Freiburger Altorientalische Studien 12; Stuttgart: Franz Steiner, 1985] 104).

[16]For example, Tablet 2 line 68 reads: "set his hand to sorcery and witchcraft;" and line 34 reads: "his sins are against his god, his crimes are against his goddess" (trans. Reiner).

[17]Georges Roux, *Ancient Iraq* (3d ed.; London: Penguin Books, 1992) 366.

[18]Ritter, "Magical-Expert," 315.

An evil curse like a *gallû*-demon has come upon (this) man,
dumbness (and) daze have come upon him,
an unwholesome dumbness has come upon him,
evil curse, oath, headache.
An evil curse has slaughtered this man like a sheep,
his god has left his body,
his goddess (Sumerian adds: his mother), usually full of concern for him, has stepped aside.
Dumbness (and) daze have covered him like a cloak and overwhelm him incessantly.[19]

The incantation-priest then envisions a healing action by which Marduk will take the patient "to the pure house of ablutions,"[20] where he will "undo his oath, release his oath" from him,[21] which has been caused by a curse unknown to the patient, and which may be due to a familial fault rather than a personal one.[22] The metaphorical quality of *āšipūtu* manifests itself in the treatment once the diagnosis and prognosis have been determined. At this point, objects mentioned earlier in the tablet (an onion, a bunch of dates, a piece of matting, a flock of wool, goat's hair, and red wool) are unpeeled, undone, etc., by the sufferer, and cast into the fire. This undoing of the articles and their consumption by the fire symbolizes the dissolution of the oath that has bound the victim, and the consumption, and thus the cessation, of the harmful symptoms it has caused.

The metaphorical quality of the *āšipu*'s craft is also seen in *Šurpu* Tablet 7. Here, the afflictions are the *dimītu*-disease, which attacks from heaven, and the Aḫḫazu demon, who comes up from the ground. The symptoms are manifold: paralysis of hands and feet, affliction of one's skin with scabs, fear, cough and phlegm, filling the mouth with spittle and foam, and afflicting with dumbness and daze.[23] The patient is described as one "whom an 'oath' had seized."[24] The last lines of the tablet prescribe the magician's remedy. The magician must wipe the patient with coarse flour, remove it, spit on it, cast a spell on it, place it under a thorn-bush on the plain, and thereby:

entrust his "oath" [to] the Lady of the plain and the fields,
may Ninkilim, lord of the animals, transfer his grave illness to the vermin of the earth ...[25]

The patient is eventually relieved from his sufferings through the combined efforts of Damu ("the great conjurer"),[26] Gula (the "Mother whose hands are

---

[19]*Šurpu* 5–6.1–16; trans. Reiner.
[20]*Šurpu* 5–6.36–37; trans. Reiner.
[21]*Šurpu* 5–6.38–39; trans. Reiner.
[22]*Šurpu* 5–6.42–44.
[23]*Šurpu* 7.15–34.
[24]*Šurpu* 7.58–59; trans. Reiner.
[25]*Šurpu* 7.67–70; trans. Reiner.
[26]*Šurpu* 7.71–72; trans. Reiner.

cool"), who relieves his fever,[27] and Marduk, who loosens his remaining "bonds".[28] One can see how this transference ritual helps to restore the natural order. At the beginning of the tablet the illness' outbreak was described as the Aḫḫazu(-demon) "breaking through the ground like weed."[29] Presumably, the vermin of the fields would eat the discarded flour, and by way of their burrows convey its contamination groundward.

Šurpu is also important for showing the importance of divine authority in the *āšipu*'s craft. Marduk is "the patron-god" of the *āšipu*,[30] and it is primarily from him that the *āšipu* derives his own power to heal.[31] Hence, Tablet 2 says: "[r]elease it, exorcist among the gods, merciful lord, Marduk ...;"[32] and Tablet 4 begins: "Incantation. It rests with you Marduk, to keep safe and sound ..."[33] But Marduk also appears as the archetype of the *āšipu* in his own dependence upon the god Ea for instruction and permission to heal. This bestowal of duties upon and deference of the junior god to the senior god (represented here by the Akkaddian names Marduk and Ea) is reiterated in the pairing of Asalluḫi (= Marduk) and Enki (= Ea) in Sumerian literature as seen, for example, in *Udug-hul.*[34]

2.2.1.2 Udug-hul *and the Demonic Antagonist*

Udug-hul ("Evil Demons") is a serialized composition of apotropaic rituals against demons and the sorcerers who manipulate them. Preserved on sixteen tablets, the collection contains rituals that span from the Old Akkadian (2300–2200) to the Seleucid periods (300–200).[35] It is in the context of *Udug-hul* that the *āšipu* most foreshadows the New Testament exorcist in his

---

[27]*Šurpu* 7.73–75; trans. Reiner.

[28]*Šurpu* 7.76–79; trans. Reiner.

[29]*Šurpu* 7.5–6; trans. Reiner.

[30]Reiner, *Šurpu*, 3. Marduk, however, was not the only deity to whom the *āšipu* appealed for assistance. From *Šurpu* compare also the following references: "[Incantation. Be it released], great gods, [god and] goddesses, lords of absolution ..." (*Šurpu* 2.1–2; trans. Reiner); "... may stand by Enlil, lord of Nippur, may he pronounce healing for him with his unchangeable word ..." (*Šurpu* 4.90; trans. Reiner); "... may stand by Nergal, lord of the verdict, from whose presence the devils and plague creep into hiding ..." (*Šurpu* 4.100; trans. Reiner); "... may stand by Zababa, lord of the high throne, may he expel plague ..." (*Šurpu* 4.102; trans. Reiner); "... may stand by Ninkarrak (Gula), the great doctoress [*a-zu-gal-la-tu*], may she remove the weariness of his body ..." (*Šurpu* 4.107; trans. Reiner).

[31]Marduk's beneficent activities include to release from sin (*Šurpu* 4.14, 37, 41, 93), to "heal the sick" (*Šurpu* 4.16, 39, 73; trans. Reiner), and to drive away diseases, headache, and bad health from the body (*Šurpu* 4.83–86).

[32]*Šurpu* 2.134; trans. Reiner.

[33]*Šurpu* 4.1; trans. Reiner.

[34]Oppenheim, *Ancient Mesopotamia*, 195.

[35]Reiner, "First-Millennium Babylonian Literature," CAH 3.2:315; Geller, *Forerunners to Udug-hul*, 3. Geller's work focuses on the Sumerian forerunners to those incantations found in *Šurpu* Tablets 3–8, which stem from the Old Babylonian period (1700–1600).

attribution of affliction to the demons, in his dependence upon divine powers to treat those afflictions, and in his own role as the mediator between that divine assistance and the human victim which includes a confrontation with the demonic antagonist.

As in *Šurpu*, the incantations of *Udug-hul* help to restore the proper cosmic order. In this case, however, the order has been disrupted by wrongful actions done within the spirit-world rather than by one's personal transgressions. Tablet 4 of *Udug-hul* concerns the identification of demons who have come up from the netherworld and their return by Enki to their proper place.[36] Tablet 5 illustrates this in its description of the activity of seven demons called the "watchmen":

The watchmen (demons) pursue anything
created in the Netherworld, the seed of An.[37]

The watchmen constitute a sort of netherworld police force, but have left their proper domain and are misusing their authority in the upper world. In a case where the literary presentation may actually document the course of a disease, one by one the demons assault the patient in worsening stages:

the fifth one lays him there on his bed.
As the sixth one approached the distraught man, he lifts his head from his belly
As the seventh one approaches the distraught man, (the patient) had already set his mind on
    the Netherworld.[38]

Udug-hul also sets a paradigm for the conjurer's activity in the Enki – Asalluḫi dialogues, which correspond to those between Ea – Marduk of the Babylonian pantheon seen in *Šurpu*.[39] In these dialogues the junior god asks the senior for help in exorcism:

---

[36]Similarly, Marten Stol tells how the spirits ascend at night from the Netherworld together with the stars (Marten Stol, *Epilepsy in Babylonia* [Cuneiform Monographs 2; Groningen: Styx, 1993] 13).

[37]*Udug-hul* 5.377–378; trans. Geller.

[38]*Udug-hul* 5.430–432; trans. Geller. Geller notes that this incantation "is one of the few examples of an U[dug] H[ul] incantation duplicated in a medical text" (Geller, *Forerunners to Udug-hul*, 108).

[39]Ea and Marduk (Sumerian) and Enki and Asalluḫi (Akkadian) are virtually equivalent pairings of gods. The discrepancy lies in whether the names are Sumerian and/or written with Sumerograms or Akkadian. Geller, however, argues against the assertion that Enki and Asalluḫi are identical to Ea and Marduk: "The problem with this focus on the identification of Asalluḫi and Marduk is that it obscures some of Asalluḫi's individual characteristics, partially because of Marduk's rise to prominence in the Old Babylonian period. The forerunners to *Udug-hul* offer some insights into Asalluḫi, independent of his Marduk connections" (Geller, *Forerunners to Udug-hul*, 12).

"I do not know what I should do about it (i.e., the patient's affliction by evil demons). By
    what will he [recover from it?"]
Enki [answered] his son Asalluḫi,
"My son, what do you not know? What can I add to it?
Asalluḫi, what do you not know? What can I add to it?
What I know, you also know.
Go my son Asalluḫi."[40]

Another example of the incantation priest's authority appears further down in
Udug-hul:

[I] am the chief incantation priest of [the pure] *Eridu* [rite],
and I am the messenger, herald of Enki.
I am Asalluḫi, the wise *mašmaš*-priest, chief son of [Enki]; I am the messenger.
I am the incantation [priest] of Eridu, and I am his [clever incantation].[41]

Udug-Hul includes several passages which illustrate well the confrontation
between the *āšipu* and the demonic presences he seeks to drive out. These
passages refer to the *āšipu*'s making known his source of authority,[42] and
threats made against the demons not to harm him.[43] From Tablet 6 of the
collection we read:

---

[40]*Udug-hul* 3.192–197; trans. Geller. Geller sees in Enki's polite rejoinder—"what do I
know that you do not already know"—a means both of establishing the authority for the
incantations that Asalluḫi (and the incantation-priest) will then use, and of securing the
patient's confidence in the *āšipu*'s abilities (Geller, *Forerunners to Udug-hul*, 15). Geller
adds: "The Enki-Asalluḫi dialogue in its original form was not a discussion between
colleagues about diagnosis, but instructions from the divine exorcist to his servant/son. Thus
Asalluḫi's role in these incantations cannot be equated with that of Enki's. The evidence, in
fact, from UHF [*Udug-hul* Forerunners] suggests that Asalluḫi originally acted as a
functionary, able to apply Eridu incantations [Eridu being the earliest Sumerian settlement],
but he lacked independent authority as an exorcist" (Geller, *Forerunners to Udug-hul*, 15).
Instead of disqualifying Asalluḫi as an exorcist, this dependence upon authority qualifies him
as such. It is typical of later exorcists to draw upon a higher authority, and so to mediate its
power toward the exorcism of the possessing spirits.
[41]*Udug-hul* 8.867–870; trans. Geller.
[42]For example, in *Udug-hul* Tablet 3 the *āšipu* treats a patient who suffers from "the
grievous *asag*-disease in his body" (3.20; trans. Geller). The incantation priest says that he
himself has been sent to the patient's house by the "great lord Enki" (3.6; trans. Geller) to
approach the sick man.
[43]For example, the incantation priest assures his own continued health by adjuring the
numerous demons who may otherwise convey their illness to him:
    the evil Udug, evil Ala demon, evil ghost,
    evil Galla, evil bailiff, Dimme,
    Dimme-lagab, Lil,
    (female Lil), and maiden Lil demons,
    the evil Namtar, the bitter *asag*-disease — his serious illness being virulent —
    may they not approach me. (*Udug-hul* 3.220–225; trans. Geller).

I am the incantation priest, the *sangamah* of Enki.
The Lord (Enki) sent me to him (the victim), he sent to him me, the vizier of the Abzu.
You shall not shriek behind me,
nor shall you shout after me.
O evil man, may you not lift your hand (against me).
O evil demon, may you not lift your hand (against me).[44]

Udug-hul also makes known the *āšipu*'s uncompromising stance against the demons' requests. From Tablet 8 the priest adjures the demon to depart:

Do [not say, "let me] stand [at the side]."
[Go] out, [evil Udug-demon,] to [a distant place],
[go] away, [evil Ala-demon], to [the desert].[45]

These passages show the *āšipu*'s dependence upon and confidence in divine support for his craft, and an aggressive attitude toward the demons that one also finds in connection with the New Testament exorcists.

2.2.1.3 Maqlû *and the Defense against Witchcraft*

The hostile activities of sorcerers and witches was another means by which people were thought to acquire demonic afflictions in the ancient Mesopotamian societies. The text known as *Maqlû* (that is, "Burning") consists of nearly 100 incantation rituals recorded upon nine tablets (eight tablets of incantations, and the ninth the Ritual Tablet). The composition in its present form likely dates back to the first millennium.[46] Contrary to *Šurpu* and *Udug-hul*, *Maqlû* concerns a known cause. Namely, it deals with the afflictions brought against someone by the human agency of a witch or sorcerer through the medium of maliciously hostile magic.[47] In this text we see that the "magic" practiced by the *āšipu* operated under a culturally sanctioned aegis not bestown upon those magical arts practiced outside of official cultic contexts.[48]

---

[44] *Udug-hul* 6.567–572a; trans. Geller.

[45] *Udug-hul* 8.873–875; trans. Geller.

[46] Tzvi Abusch, "*Maqlû*," *RlA* 7:347.

[47] Tzvi Abusch considers *Maqlû* to be "the single most important source for the study of Mesopotamian witchcraft" (Tzvi Abusch, *Babylonian Witchcraft Literature: Case Studies* [Atlanta: Scholars Press, 1987] 2).

[48] In the course of his study of the Babylonian witchcraft material, Tzvi Abusch has discerned a tension that developed between the *kaššaptu* as a kind of "folk magician," who practiced illicit witchcraft, and the *āšipu* as the "learned exorcist" with ties to the established temple cults and the upper echelons of society. He considers the *āšipu* to have "reshaped the image of the witch," and to have set her up as the polar opposite of himself: "First, a malevolent woman, a folk magician, and opponent in court; then, a wind or demon that is part of the divine world and sends harmful dreams, finally, merging into a cosmic force that makes its rounds and must be expelled" (Tzvi Abusch, "The Demonic Image of the Witch in

The primary participants in the *Maqlû* ritual are the exorcist and his patient.[49] As to the theory behind the rituals, Tzvi Abusch considers the ceremony to represent three judicial audiences. The first consists of the heavenly night court of Anu and the netherworld court of Ereskigal. The second comprises the heavenly court of Enlil and the chthonic court of Ekur. Over the third presides the sun god Šamaš with his retinue of the morning sky, and the subterranean abyss of Ea and Asalluḫi.[50] The theory behind these hearings is that a witch or sorcerer has slandered the victim before the gods, and so caused them to forsake or to afflict him. The legal setting of *Maqlû* gives an importance to words and speech as the instruments of accusation and refutation in the confrontation between the *āšipu* and the witch or sorcerer. The *āšipu* herein acts as the patient's advocate and pleads his case before the juries. In the process, the *āšipu* also reveals the treachery of the bewitcher, who is present in effigy. If justified, the patient is released from bewitchment.

One can see from *Šurpu*, *Udug-hul*, and *Maqlû* that the *āšipu* relates his healing craft to the spirit-world: maladies are the result of spiritual activity, whereby gods or demons afflict the patient either out of their own maliciousness, or by reason of some transgression committed by the patient, or because they have been persuaded by witchcraft to forsake or to afflict him. Consequently, the *āšipu* acts as the mediator between the patient and the spirit-world in his efforts to release the patient from his sufferings, and in some cases he represents the divine powers in his confrontations with malicious demons.

2.2.2 The Bārû *and Prophecy*

As the "diviner," the *bārû* is worth mentioning because in Israel as well as in Greece prophecy is one area that can involve spiritual possession.[51] Unlike the prophets and seers of ancient Israel and early Greece, however, the *bārû* does not actually serve as the receptacle of the god.[52] *Bārûtu* ("the act of

---

Standard Babylonian Literature: The Reworking of Popular Conceptions by Learned Exorcists," in Jacob Neusner, ed., *Religion, Science, and Magic: In Concert and Conflict* [New York: Oxford, 1989] 50). Abusch refers to the *āšipu* as "temple-affiliated exorcists" (Abusch, "Demonic Image," 28), a connection substantiated by a document which cites three family members as "exorcists of the Temple of Assur" (Abusch, "Demonic Image," 52, n. 7).

[49]Abusch, "*Maqlû*," *RlA* 7:347. A contemporary letter mentions the king as a patient in the *Maqlû* ritual (Parpola, *Letters from Assyrian and Babylonian Scholars*, 215, No. 274).

[50]Abusch, "*Maqlû*," 349.

[51]The University of Chicago's *Assyrian Dictionary* offers as one definition of the verb *bārû* "to inspect exta [extispicy], to observe omens, to check, to establish by observation" ("*Bārû*," *The Assyrian Dictionary* 2:115). Parpola describes the substantive as "experts in the art of consulting the divine will and prognosticating the future by extispicy and lecanomancy" (Parpola, *Letters from Assyrian and Babylonian Scholars*, XXXIV).

[52]Oppenheim says that amidst the vast range of means for divination the human being, whether through the interpretation of dreams or ominous births, or through prophetic ecstacy,

divination"),[53] manifested itself in the ancient Near East primarily through hauruspicy (divination by liver inspection, which the *bārû* performed primarily on sheep or lambs), lecanomancy (divination based on observing the reaction of oil thrown on water), or libanomancy (divination derived from observation of the motion of smoke from a censer).[54]

The *bārû* had connections with the military,[55] and he served both in the royal court, and in the king's provincial administrations. Apparently he applied his craft toward any issue for which the future outcome was of concern. As a consequence, in addition to military inquiries the *bārû* entertained questions as diverse as concerns over livestock[56] and issues of health. With respect to health, the diviner's role seems to have dealt mostly with diagnoses which would then lead to prognoses. The *bārû* cooperated with other healing professionals, though how he did so remains unclear. Perhaps the *bārû* through a preliminary diagnosis or prognosis then provided a recommendation to obtain the services of the *āsipu* or the *asû*. In the following medical correspondence, for example, an *asû* recommends that the king also seek the aid of a *bārû* in a difficult case:

> The king, my lord, keeps on saying to me: "Why do you not diagnose the nature of this illness of mine and bring about its cure?" — formerly I spoke to the king at the audience and

---

is of minor importance as the vehicle for such (Oppenheim, *Ancient Mesopotamia*, 221). Where ecstasis does occur it tends to be on the western outskirts in the late Assyrian period, which shows Aramaic influence. This reflects a common practice in Syria and Palestine. Those who practiced prophetic ecstacy held socially marginal positions, and were often associated with witchcraft. Oppenheim mentions the priestesses and priests of Ishtar as the sole exception to this, "who pronounced the will of the deity either as an edict, in the third person, or in the first person, identifying themselves with the deity who spoke through them" (Oppenheim, *Ancient Mesopotamia*, 221).

[53]"*Bārûtu*," *The Assyrian Dictionary* 2:131.

[54]"*Bārû*," *CAD* 2:121–22. Note, however, the editor's remark: "After the O[ld] B[abylonian] period, there is no evidence for the *bārû*'s performing libanomancy or lecanomancy, although the latter activity is still mentioned in the 'handbook' for the *bārû* ..." ("*Bārû*," *CAD* 2:125). To these methods of divination compare the varieties disclosed in the text from Sultantepe discussed by Reiner in "Fortune Telling in Mesopotamia," *JNES* 19 (1960) 23–35. One method divines by observing the manner in which a recumbent ox reacts to having water poured on its forehead (Reiner, "Fortune Telling," *JNES* 19 (1960) 28–29). This, and other unusual techniques were likely performed by the *mašmašu*, "who could assume the functions of a diviner in such divination techniques as were not reserved for the *bārû*" (Reiner, "Fortune Telling," *JNES* 19 [1960] 30).

[55]So, for example, we read: "I captured the diviner PN, who marches in front of their (the Babylonian's) army, together with them (the soldiers);" and again: "the diviner will participate in the battle and defeat the enemy" ("*Bārû*," *CAD* 2:124).

[56]So, for example, we read: "take a lamb from the flock to the diviner and find out the (divinatory) pronouncement about my herds and flocks" ("*Bārû*," *CAD* 2:121).

could not clarify his symptoms. ... If it suits the king, my lord, let the haruspices [logogram LU.HAL.MES = *bārû*] perform an extispicy on account of this.[57]

Here we have evidence of cooperation between the offices, and evidence for the *bārû* as one who helps the *asû* to arrive at a diagnosis. Based upon this and other examples the *bārû*'s role is evidently advisorial and, though it could in that sense be considered prescriptive, it is distinct from medical practice and *āsipūtu* in that it nowhere appears to be therapeutic.[58]

2.2.3 Indwelling Possession in the Ancient Near East

A point of comparison between the New Testament exorcism stories and its Near Eastern antecedents lies in the notion of a demon that occupies the victim's body. Marten Stol objects to the use of the term "exorcism" for the analogous activities in ancient Near Eastern texts because he considers actual demon possession to have had no correspondent in Assyrian and Babylonian traditions: one is not properly "possessed" by a demon, but externally affected by it. Stol says of possession:

> Normally, a spirit "reaches" or "seizes" a human being and he is closest when he is "tied" to his victim. There is no evidence that he enters and settles in his body. Demons and diseases "overthrow" the patient, or "cover" him like a garment. So far as I am aware there is no Babylonian evidence for possession at all ... The term "exorcism" presupposes possession ... If possession was not known to the Babylonians, the word "exorcist" is less apt as the translation of Akkadian *āsipu*; we prefer "conjurer."[59]

Thus, Stol considers exorcism to be a phenomenon later than his period of study (ca. 1800 – 450 B.C.E.), and the origin of which "cannot be sought in Babylonian-Assyrian beliefs."[60]

---

[57]Parpola, *Letters from Assyrian and Babylonian Scholars*, 254–55, #315.

[58]Compare also these references from *Ludlul Bēl Nēmeqi* ("The Prayer of the Righteous Sufferer") to the *bārû*'s role in diagnosis: "The omen of the diviner [*bārî*] and dream priest [*sa'-i-li*] does not explain my condition" (*Ludlul Bēl Nēmeqi* 1.52; trans. W. G. Lambert, "The Poem of the Righteous Sufferer: *Ludlul Bēl Nēmeqi*," in *Babylonian Wisdom Literature* [Oxford: Clarendon, 1960]). "The diviner [*bārû*] with his inspection has not got to the root of the matter,/ Nor has the dream priest [*sa'ilu*] with his libation elucidated my case" (*Ludlul Bēl Nēmeqi* 2.6–7; trans. Lambert).

[59]Marten Stol, *Epilepsy in Babylonia*, 52. Stol refers to an analogous argument presented in Wesley D. Smith's article, "So-called Possession in Pre-Christian Greece," *TAPA* 96 (1965) 403–26. Therein, Smith argues that possession was virtually unknown to Greeks of the Classical and Hellenistic eras. Smith's conclusion for the Greeks, however, is refuted by early evidence found, for example, in Greek tragedy and in the Hippocratic tract *The Sacred Disease*. For fuller discussion see below, Chapter 4: "Possession and the Treatment of the Possessed in Early Greece."

[60]Stol, *Epilepsy in Babylonia*, 53.

Stol's claim for the Assyrian and Babylonian periods, however, is not without exception. Among the rituals in *Udug-hul*, Enki on one occasion says to his son Asalluḫi:

"Go, my son, Asalluḫi,
pour water in an *anzam*-cup,
and put in it tamarisk and the *innuš*-plant."
(He recited the Eridu [incantation]). Calm the patient, and bring out the censer and torch for
him,
so that the Namtar demon existing in a man's body, may depart from it.[61]

The last line of the cure describes the affliction in terms of demonic possession. This example from *Udug-hul*, however, is an exception to the rule. Exterior tormentors otherwise clearly dominate the portrayals of demonic antagonists in these ancient Near Eastern texts.

2.3 Pollution and Purification in Zoroastrianism

The Sumerian, Akkadian, Assyrian, and Babylonian societies of the ancient Near East had well established beliefs and practices with respect to the conjuration of the spirit-world. They lacked, however, description of indwelling possession as a consequential aspect of the spirit-world's relationship with humanity. Only very seldom do these spirits enter into the human body. In the belief of the day it was sufficient to see them as exterior agents. From the first half of the first millennium B.C.E., however, the association of one's identity with a foreign spirit became an integral part of another belief system on the geographic periphery of these Mesopotamian societies: Zoroastrianism of eastern Iran.

The majority of contemporary scholars would date Zarathushtra, the reformer of old Iranian religious beliefs and the prophet of Ahura Mazda ("Lord Wisdom"), to the first half of the first millennium B.C.E.[62] He is thought to have lived in the northeastern region of Iran and, according to the hymns (Gāthās) attributed to him, his beliefs gained a foothold there through

---

[61] *Udug-hul* 7.669–674; trans. Geller.

[62] On the early side of this time frame Mary Boyce would date Zarathushtra to the end of the second millennium B.C.E. (Mary Boyce, *Zoroastrianism: Its Antiquity and Constant Vigour* [Columbia Lectures on Iranian Studies 7; Costa Mesa, Calif.: Mazda Publishers, 1992] xi). William Malandra dates Zarathushtra to the VI B.C.E. (William W. Malandra, *An Introduction to Ancient Iranian Religion: Readings from the Avesta and Achaemenid Inscriptions* [Minneapolis: University of Minnesota Press, 1983] 17). The tradition of a sixth century B.C.E. date for Zarathushtra goes back to Heraclides of Pontus (IV B.C.E.), who sought to make him a contemporary and fellow student with Pythagoras at Babylon. P. Kingsley has argued that this late date is unwarranted (P. Kingsley, "The Greek Origin of the Sixth-Century Dating of Zoroaster," *BSOAS* 53 [1990] 245–65).

the patronage of a local ruler, Kavi Vishtaspa.[63] Although several prominent scholars hesitate to accredit Zoroastrianism with an expansion beyond this region before the fourth century B.C.E., prior to that era some form of Ahura Mazdeism appears to have taken hold in western Iran where it found support among the Median priests. These magi would in turn come to hold positions of influence in the religious and governmental activities of Persia's Achaemenian rulers (ca. 550–330 B.C.E.) and Ahura Mazdeism is consequently evident in their religious beliefs.[64] The Parthians (ca. 247 B.C.E. –224 C.E.) and Sassanians (ca. 224–651 C.E.), who ruled the region after the Achaemenians and Seleucids, were adherents of Zoroastrianism.

2.3.1 Zoroastrian Sources

Zoroastrianism began as oral tradition and did not start to assume written form until the Parthian era.[65] It was not until the Sassanian period, during the fifth and sixth centuries of the Common Era, that the writings were assembled into the 21 *nasks* ("bundles," "books") of the *Great Avesta* to form a written canon.[66] It is in the later Pahlavi texts, written after the fall of the Sassanid Empire, that systematized Zoroastrian beliefs first appear.[67] The reliance

---

[63]Mary Boyce, *A History of Zoroastrianism* (3 vols.; Leiden: Brill, 1975–91) 1:187. In the early *Gathas* Vishtaspa's name appears in *Yasnas* 28.7; 46.14; 51.16; 53.2. Vishtaspa is rendered Hystaspes in Greek. Thus, compare the attribution of the late-hellenistic work *Oracles of Hystaspes* (Emil Schürer, *The History of the Jewish People in the Age of Jesus Christ [175 B.C.–A.D. 135]* rev. and ed. by Geza Vermes et al. [3 vols.; Edinburgh: T&T Clark, 1986] 3.1:654–56).

[64]On the one hand, Mary Boyce is a chief proponent of an early infusion of Zoroastrianism upon western Iran. Boyce considers that Zoroastrian missionaries first gained a foothold in Media then Persia, so that the religion was already in place by the time of Cyrus' conquest of that region (Mary Boyce, *History of Zoroastrianism*, 2.49). Arthur Christensen, on the other hand, following E. Beneviste and H. S. Nyberg, has argued that the religion of neither the Medes nor the Persians was Zoroastrian at the time of Herodotus (V B.C.E.): "*la religion de Xerxès n'était pas le zoroastrisme*" (Arthur Christensen, *Essai sur la démonologie iranienne* [Historisk-filologiske Meddelelser 27.1; Copenhagen: Ejnar Munksgaard, 1941] 42). Christensen argues that the magi who held positions of influence in the Persian government practiced a form of Ahuramazdeanism (*le culte d'Ahuramazdāh*) that differed from that of the Zoroastrianism of eastern Iran. It was this western version adapted to Median preferences that was the cultic practice of the Persian kings (Christensen, *Essai sur la démonologie iranienne*, 45–46).

[65]Geo Widengren, "Leitende Ideen und Quellen der iranischen Apokalyptik," in *Apocalypticism in the Mediterranean World and the Near East*, David Hellholm, ed. (2d ed.; Tübingen: Mohr, 1989) 87.

[66]Boyce, *History of Zoroastrianism*, 1.20; Anders Hultgård, "Persian Apocalypticism," in John J. Collins, ed., *The Encyclopedia of Apocalypticism, Vol. 1: The Origins of Apocalypticism in Judaism and Christianity* (New York: Continuum, 1998) 65.

[67]The *Indian* rather than the *Greater Bundahishn* of the Pahlavi literature likely offers an earlier account of creation that appears to follow along traditional Mazdean lines. R. C. Zaehner notes as one indication of the better reliability of the *Indian* over the *Greater*

upon an oral tradition over such an extended period has made it difficult for modern scholars to determine what ideas were original to Zarathushtra and what were later additions to Zoroastrianism. My interest here, however, is not necessarily with issues of Zoroastrian orthodoxy (e.g., the Zervanite heresy), or with issues of what teachings are authentically traceable to Zarathushtra. What is of interest are those views which held status within Zoroastrianism before the Common Era, and so were in a position to influence early Jewish and Christian beliefs. Although one must turn to such late compilations as the *Bundahishn* (IX C.E.) for a coherent Zoroastrian narrative myth, the principles of dualism with its discrete good and evil spirits, the choice that has to be made between the two, and an eschatology that includes final judgment followed by reward and punishment, are already present in the earliest literature.[68]

Zoroastrianism's earliest sacred writings are contained in the *Avesta* (the "Injunction" [of Zarathushtra]), which includes the 17 *Gathas* ("Hymns") attributed to Zarathushtra himself, *Yashts* (hymns to divine beings), and the *Vendidad* ("Against the Daevas"), an antidemonic purity code that likely originated among the magi in Media.[69] The *Yashts* and *Vendidad* are preserved in the Young Avestan language, and date to before the Common Era.[70] The *Gathas*, preserved in Old Avestan and linguistically dated to before 500 B.C.E.,

---

Bundahishn its fewer traces of overt Zervanite doctrine: "In the accounts of the creation that have come down to us it is not always easy or possible to draw a clear distinction between what may be called Mazdean and what may be called Zervanite. The *Indian Bundahishn*, however, pays little attention to Time (Zurvan) and, with a few modifications, may therefore be taken as our basic text for the Mazdean cosmology" (R. C. Zaehner, *Zurvan: A Zoroastrian Dilemma* [Oxford: Clarendon Press, 1955] 91).

[68]Concerning choice and the spirits of good and evil, see *Yasna* 30.3. Concerning judgment and its consequences, see *Yasna* 30.2; 31.20; 33.1; 43.5; 46.10–11; 48.4; 49.3; 51.9, 13–15.

[69]Mary Boyce, *Textual Sources for the Study of Zoroastrianism* (Textual Sources for the Study of Religion; Totowa, N.J.: Barnes & Noble Books, 1984) 1–2. Demonology was a fundamental trait of Median religiosity, and Christensen (following Nyberg) underscores the considerable contrast between the mentality of the *Yashts* and that of the *Vendidad*: "the new spirit of the Median priests, imbued with an infinitely pedantic formalism and by a somber and adamant fanaticism, [is] very different from the heroic mentality of the Yashts." (*l'esprit nouveau, bien différent de la mentalité héroïque des Yašts, esprit des prêtres mèdes, imbu d'un formalisme infiniment pédantesque et d'un fanatisme sombre et dur*). (Christensen, *Essai sur la démonologie iranienne*, 29). The distinction applies equally well between the *Vendidad* and *Gathas*.

[70]Boyce dates the *Vendidad* to the first half of the first millennium B.C.E. (Boyce, *History of Zoroastrianism*, 2:222). Christensen assigns it to the end of the Achaemenian era, or to the transition between that era and the subsequent rule by the Arsacids (Christensen, *Essai sur la démonologie iranienne*, 28, 46).

constitute the sole source for Zarathushtra's original teachings.[71] Although they present a challenge for translators, the *Gathas* likely reveal in the reformer's own words the salient features of his religious views.[72]

2.3.2 Zoroastrian Dualism and the Doctrine of Choice

Dualism is a principal feature of Zoroastrian doctrine, a feature that necessitates choice.[73] Zarathushtra established a religion involving two spirits who make choices. Spenta Mainyu ("Virtuous Spirit"), the holy spirit of Ahura Mazda, chose good, while Angra Mainyu ("Deceitful Spirit") chose evil.[74] The decisive moment of choice is described in a passage from an early Gathic hymn:

---

[71]Jean Kellens and Eric Pirart note that a definitive attribution of the *Gathas* to Zarathushtra is impossible to make. They do concede that "If the *Gathas* are not the work of Zarathushtra, the posthumous celebration of Zarathustra is the work of the *Gathas*." (*Si les Gāθā ne sont pas l'oeuvre de Zaraθuštra, la célébrité posthume de Zaraθuštra est l'oeuvre des Gāθā.*) (Jean Kellens and Eric Pirart, *Les Textes Vieil-Avestiques* [3 vols.; Weisbaden: Ludwig Reichert Verlag, 1988] 1:22). Emile Benveniste assigns a pre-500 B.C.E. date to the *Gathas* (Emile Benveniste, *The Persian Religion according to the Chief Greek Texts* [Ratanbai Lecture Series 1; Paris: Librairie Orientaliste Paul Geuthner, 1929] 41). Malandra notes that the archaic quality of words used in the Avesta could simply reflect the conservative retention of archaisms typical in religious traditions (Malandra, *Introduction to Ancient Iranian Religion*, 17). Yet, the retention of archaic language is different from the composition in such. It seems unlikely that the *Gathas* were composed at a late date deliberately in a obscure, archaizing language, since doing so would create the risk that they would be unintelligible to their intended audience.

[72]Even by the Sassanian period the *Gathas* were apparently nearly incomprehensible, as Zaehner reports: "It must, however, be borne in mind that in the Sassanian period the *Gathas* were scarcely understood at all and that commentators could and did make them mean more or less what they liked" (Zaehner, *Zurvan*, 149). Stanley Insler says of the translation difficulties: "... overshadowing all the difficulties inherent in properly understanding the Gāthās is the problem of disentangling the intricacies of their syntax. Because, as long as little certainty exists in the establishment of definite rules for interpreting the various possibilities of syntactic coordination within the special eloquence of Zarathustra's poetry, there can be no assurance that the translation of a given passage approaches the intentions originally formulated by the prophet. When this lack of certitude exists for the greater number of verses within the limited corpus of the Gāthās, then we are faced with the realization that much of our knowledge of these poems is highly doubtful" (Stanley Insler, *The Gāthās of Zarathustra* [Acta Iranica 8; Leiden: Brill, 1975] 2).

[73]Zaehner considers dualism of spirit an original Iranian contribution to the history of religions (Zaehner, *Zurvan*, 4), and choice as "the original doctrine of Zoroaster" (Zaehner, *Zurvan*, 120). Arthur Christensen notes that monotheism and dualism are paradoxical tendencies of the *Gathas*, neither of which is fully developed there. ("*La religion des Gathas présente une tendance double, vers le monothéisme et vers le dualisme. Ni l'un ni l'autre ne sont pleinement réalisés.*") (Christensen, *Essai sur la démonologie iranienne*, 5).

[74]Over the centuries Ahura Mazda's name was transformed into Ahuramazda, Ohrmazd, and Ormazd. Angra Mainyu is "Ahriman" in Middle Persian (Boyce, *Zoroastrianism*, xii).

2. Listen with your ears to the best things. Reflect with a clear mind — man by man for himself — upon the two choices of decision, being aware to declare yourselves to him before the great retribution.

3. Yes, there are two fundamental spirits, twins which are renowned to be in conflict. In thought and in word, in action, they are two: the good and the bad. And between these two, the beneficent have correctly chosen, not the maleficent.

4. Furthermore, when these two spirits first came together, they created life and death, and how, at the end, the worst existence shall be for the deceitful but the best thinking for the truthful person.

5. Of these two spirits, the deceitful one chose to bring to realization the worst things. (But) the very virtuous spirit, who is clothed in the hardest stones, chose the truth, and (so shall those) who shall satisfy the Wise Lord continuously with true actions.

6. The gods did not at all choose correctly between these two, since the deceptive one approached them as they were deliberating. Since they chose the worst thought, they then rushed into fury, with which they have afflicted the world and mankind.[75]

The choices made by these two spirits lead them into an irreconcilable hostility. Their decisions serve as paradigms for humanity: matters of salvation and damnation are subject to human effort, and the decision for good or evil that each individual makes puts him or her forever on the side of one of these who were first to choose.

With choice as its premise, Zarathushtra's teaching guides one in the right decision to join with Ahura Mazda. From the "creed" *Fravarane* ("I Profess"), the worshipper says:

I forswear the company of the wicked Daevas ... and the followers of Daevas, of demons and the followers of demons, of those who do harm to any being by thoughts, words, acts or outward signs. Truly I forswear the company of all this as belonging to *the Lie* [Drug], as defiant (of the good); even as Ahura Mazda taught Zarathushtra in each instance, at all deliberations, at all encounterings at which Mazda and Zarathushtra spoke together.[76]

To these examples of the righteous chooser, compare the person who chooses evil:

By reason of this, the conception of the deceitful person misses the true (conception) of the honest man. His soul shall vex him at the Bridge of the Judge surely, in that he has disappeared from the path of truth by reason of his own actions and (the words) of his tongue.[77]

---

[75] *Yasna* 30.2–6; trans. Insler, *Gāthās of Zarathustra*, 33. See also *Yasna* 45.2 concerning this initial choice.

[76] *Yasna* 12.4–5; trans. Boyce, *Textual Sources*, 57.

[77] *Yasna* 51.13; trans. Insler, *Gāthās of Zarathustra*, 107. The "Bridge of the Judge" is the place where the soul is judged after death. If judged evil it is cast into the abyss spanned by the bridge. If good, it continues on to the house of Good Intention and Righteousness.

In the choice between good and evil, Zoroastrianism offers guidance in the decision between right and wrong behavior, and so offers an ethic by which the faithful may live their lives.[78]

2.3.3 Pollution and Zoroastrian Cosmogony

What the Zoroastrian struggle between good and evil adds to the world view of the other ancient Near Eastern societies is an overarching plan to creation: there is a singular end to the world as it presently exists and creation helps to accomplish it.[79] The early *Gathas* identify Ahura Mazda with his virtuous spirit (Spenta Mainyu) as the creator of all that is good,[80] and they attribute the worst things to the deceitful Angra Mainyu.[81] Not only did Ahura Mazda fashion the good creation, but he did so with a purpose, namely, that it assist him in his anticipated conquest of evil.[82] It is because of Angra Mainyu's confrontation with the good creation that evil enters into human experience.[83] Thus, under the tutelage of their patrons evil and good seek the other's destruction. There are no passive beings in creation. Each must make a choice to serve good or evil, and each thereby joins in the cosmic struggle between the two.

The ethical dualism that dominates Zoroastrian doctrine manifests itself in one's permeation by the good or the evil that one chooses.[84] The metaphor of

---

[78]Malandra notes: "It is essential to understand from the outset that Iranian religion, especially Zoroastrianism, was founded on the idea of an all-inclusive ethical dualism" (Malandra, *Introduction to Ancient Iranian Religion*, 13).

[79]Widengren calls Zarathushtra the first apocalypticist of Iranian religion for converting the conception of time from cyclical to linear, whereby history comes to a definitive conclusion (Widengren, "Leitende Ideen und Quellen," 85).

[80]E.g., *Yasna* 44.3–7; 51.7.

[81]E.g., *Yasna* 30.2–5; 51.10.

[82]This notion is articulated well, but late, in a passage from the *Greater Bundahishn*: "First, [Ahura Mazda] created Sky as a defense; second, He created Water, to defeat the demon of thirst, ... sixth, He created the Just Man, to smite the Evil Spirit together with the devs and to make them powerless" (*Greater Bundahishn* 1.1–4; trans. Boyce, *Textual Sources*, 48).

[83]E.g., *Yasna* 29.1; 30.2–5; 45.1–2.

[84]The spirit of Ahura Mazda is said to be with the one who chooses good (*Yasna* 33.14), and one can assume the same of the evil spirit for those who choose evil. Mary Boyce underscores the importance of possession in Zoroastrian doctrine, though its scriptures tend to describe it only in a subtle manner: "The concepts of divinity and of humanly possessed power seem frequently to blend, through the thought of that power proceeding from the divinity, who has himself actually entered into the person. This adds a further dimension to the doctrine of the immanence of the Heptad [i.e., the seven prototypes of creation: sky, water, earth, plant, cow, man, fire] in the world; but the belief is very difficult to convey in translation, and some modern translators of the Gathas, concentrating on the power or quality alone, fail to give a sense also of the indwelling divinity" (Boyce, *Textual Sources*, 13–14; cf. Boyce, *History of Zoroastrianism*, 1:85–88).

the body as a receptacle of the foreign spirit that characterizes later Jewish
and Christian thought does not appear to apply to the earlier Zoroastrian way
of thinking. After one has chosen between good and evil, a kind of alliance, or
a mutually supportive symbiosis, takes place between the individual and the
spirit of choice. An early *Yasna* expresses this fusion well: after Ahura Mazda
has first given to his adherent the powers of good thinking and truth, he
himself gains strength from the worship, good words and deeds thereafter
generated by the adherent.[85] Thus, along with the adherent's appeal to Ahura
Mazda for assistance against evil, Zoroastrianism also recognized the
advantage humanity's good thoughts and deeds bring to the god.[86]

Choice in Zoroastrian belief thus leads to identity: by the alliance one
makes with good or evil, one becomes identified with that spiritual presence.
Thus, the *ashawan* is one who "possesses" or is "associated" with *Asha*
("Truth"). The *dregvant* is one who "possesses" or is "associated" with *Drug*
("Deceit"), and it is used both of the Deceitful Spirit, as well as of an evil
person. We see something of this allegiance-identity in passages from the early
Gathas. From *Yasna* 43:

7. And I have already realized Thee to be virtuous, Wise Lord, when he attended me with
good thinking and asked me : *"Who art thou? To which side dost thou belong? How, this
day, wouldst thou begin to explain these revelations among thy creatures and thine own?"*
8. Then I said to him first: *"(I am) Zarathustra. If I were able, I would be a true enemy to
the deceitful one but a strong support to the Truthful One."* That, while I continue to praise
and eulogize Thee, Wise One, I would begin (to explain) the endeavors of Him who rules at
His wish.
9. Yes, I have already realized Thee to be virtuous, Wise Lord, when he attended me with
good thinking. To his question, *"Whom dost thou wish to serve?"* I then replied: *"Thy fire.
As long as I shall be able, I shall respect that truth is to have a gift of reverence."*[87]

And from *Yasna* 49:

4. Those who, with ill will, have increased fury and cruelty with their own tongues among
the cattle-breeders, these non-cattle-breeders whose evil effects one has not yet defeated with
good effects, they have served the [old] gods, which is the conception of a deceitful person.

---

[85]*Yasna* 33.12.

[86]Stanley Insler sees this in *Yasna* 31.6–7, of which he says: "Man also must intercede
to preserve the existence of god, for the power of god derives its strength from the enactment
of his essence and principles in the world of man. ... To bring happiness and the good to
mankind, the Wise Lord was moved by his benevolent spirit to create truth and good
thinking. Yet for the lord to grow in his rightful power, mankind must also be moved by the
same spirit founded upon truth and good thinking. The destiny of the world of man and the
destiny of the world of god are thus linked in this cooperative function" (Insler, *Gāthās of
Zarathustra*, 179).

[87]*Yasna* 43.7–9; trans. Insler, *Gāthās of Zarathustra*, 63.

5. But that man, Wise One, is both milk and butter (for Thee), namely, the one who has allied his conception with good thinking. Any such person of piety is of the (same) good lineage with truth and all those (other forces) existing under Thy rule, Lord.[88]

In the identification of persons with their good or evil patrons we see a convergence with the rhetoric later used by Jewish sectarians and early Christians to sanctify their fellow adherents or to demonize their opponents.[89] The ethical dualism found in the earliest Zoroastrian writings also provides precedent for the ethical dualism one encounters in turn-of-the-era Jewish and Christian writings.[90]

In Zoroastrian belief the effects of evil also extend beyond moral contaminations to affect the physical body. Some of the laws of the *Vendidad* provide purifications from physical contaminations by demons such as are present in death, sickness, and women *in menses*, to name but a few.[91] Thus, Angra Mainyu is the author of 99,999 diseases that plague humanity,[92] and the deformations of physical bodies are called the "brands wherewith Angra Mainyu stamps the bodies of mortals."[93] Pollution as a physical taint appears in death, where the corpse becomes a lodging place for demons and a source of demonic contamination for any who touch it:

If a man alone by himself carry a corpse, the Nasu rushes upon him, to defile him, from the nose of the dead, from the eye, from the tongue, from the jaws, from the sexual organs,

---

[88]*Yasna* 49.4–5 (cf., *Yasna* 32.2–5); trans. Insler, *Gāthās of Zarathustra*, 95. The gods referred to in stanza 4 are the *daevas*, the old gods rejected under Zoroastrian reform.

[89]For this usage among Jewish and Christian groups, see Elaine H. Pagels, *The Origin of Satan* (New York: Random House, 1995). A difference, however, appears to be that, whereas Jewish sectarians and Christians tended to demonize opponents within their own faiths, the Zoroastrians tended to demonize non-Zoroastrians.

[90]It is tempting to see in the earliest Zoroastrian hymns the origins for the Two Ways metaphor of ethical instruction that one finds fully articulated in early Christian writings (cf. also Prodicus' "Heracles at the Crossroads," quoted by Xenophon in *Memorabilia* 2). The early *Gathas*, however, never use "path" to describe the course of one who has chosen evil. For the "path" of goodness in Zoroastrianism, see e.g. *Yasna* 33.5; 43.3; 51.13; cf. 50.6–7.

[91]It is with the *Vendidad* that physical purity appears to have entered into a Zoroastrian tradition that had otherwise been concerned with ethical purity as seen in the *Gathas*. For the sake of its authority in Zoroastrianism before the Common Era I include a discussion of it here. Of the *Vendidad*'s purpose Darmesteter says: "Purity and impurity have not in the Vendîdâd the exclusively spiritual meaning which they have in our languages: they do not refer to an inward state of the soul, but chiefly to a physical state of the body. Impurity or uncleanness may be described as the state of a person or a thing that is possessed of a demon; and the object of purification is to expel the demon. The principal means by which uncleanness enters man is death, as death is the triumph of the demon" (James Darmesteter, trans., *The Zend-Avesta: Part 1. The Vendîdâd* [Sacred Books of the East. 3d American ed.; New York: Christian Literature Company, 1898] 1:lxxii).

[92]*Vendidad* 22.2.

[93]*Vendidad* 2.29; trans. Darmesteter, *Zend-Avesta*, 1.17.

from the hinder parts. This Drug Nasu falls upon him, [stains him] even to the end of the nails, and he is unclean, thenceforth, forever.[94]

Whether demonic possession was physical as in the case of touching a corpse, or moral as an aspect of ethical dualism, Zoroastrianism provided prescriptive means for preventing contamination and cleansing it when it did occur.

2.3.4 Purification and Zoroastrian Eschatology

If pollution is an aspect of Zoroastrian cosmogony, purification finds its *raison d'être* in Zoroastrian eschatology. Whereas purification becomes necessary in so far as evil continues to contaminate the good creation, it becomes a possibility in the assumption of good's dominion over evil. As the idea of an embattled cosmos explains the current experience of humanity embroiled in the conflict between good and evil, so the domination and overthrow of a demonic presence through divine agency shows the power of good over evil in that conflict, and foreshadows the destined triumph of Ahura Mazda and his holy spirit over Angra Mainyu.[95]

The closest analogy to exorcism in the early Zoroastrian literature is a reference to the followers of the Wise Lord (Ahura Mazda) as "the expellers of fury."[96] The "fury" of this passage refers to Aeshma, which some have identified as the only demon mentioned by name in the *Gathas*.[97] The texts themselves, however, do not require the term to be anything more than an abstract quality, and even as a demon the reference to Aeshma would appear to be as much to its adherents as to the demon itself. Unlike early Christian accounts of demonic possession in which a demon invades the human body and can be cast out to restore the body to its natural state of health, the early Zoroastrian hymns envision the physical and spiritual worlds as allied in causes for good or evil. In the Zoroastrianism of the *Gathas* evil and good are holistic aspects: the person who sides with evil is not a victim of maliciousness from whom the evil influence may be driven away; rather, by choice one has implicated oneself with evil. As a consequence, where "expulsion" occurs it is much less a matter of driving off evil demons than of

---

[94] *Vendidad* 3.14; trans. Darmesteter, *Zend-Avesta*, 1.26–27. Darmesteter says of "Nasu": "The word Nasu has two meanings: it means either the corpse (nasâi), or the corpse-demon (the Drug Nasu, that is to say the demon who takes possession of the dead body and makes his presence felt by the decomposition of the body and infection)" (Darmesteter, *Zend-Avesta*, 1.27, n. 1).

[95] Cf., *Yasna* 48.2–4.

[96] *Yasna* 48.12. Kellens and Pirart translate the phrase *"adversaires de la Rage"* (Kellens and Pirart, *Textes avieil-avestiques*, 1:171).

[97] *Yasna* 29.2; 30.6; 48.12 (Boyce, *History of Zoroastrianism*, 1:87; Manfred Hutter, "Asmodeus," *DDD*[2] 106).

driving off and destroying those who ally themselves with evil, and suppressing the quality of evil as such.[98]

Of the writings in the *Avesta*, the *Vendidad* is most concerned with rituals for physical purification against demons, and the power of words comprises much of its arsenal toward this objective.[99] This illustrates an important feature of Zoroastrianism, as of any belief system that attributes a demonic cause to human affliction: when a malady is personified it is expected to understand and to react to human language. A lengthy section of the *Vendidad* illustrates the importance of language in combating the intentional hostility Angra Mainyu brings against humanity. In *Vendidad* Chapter 10 Angra Mainyu sends a demon against Zarathushtra to kill him, but Zarathushtra wards him off with a hymn:

> From the region of the north, from the regions of the north, forth rushed Angra Mainyu, the deadly, the Daêvas. And thus spake the evil-doer Angra Mainyu, the deadly: "Drug, rush down and kill him," O holy Zarathustra! The Drug came rushing along, the demon Bûiti, who is deceiving, unseen death.
>
> Zarathustra chanted aloud the Ahuna-Vairya: "The will of the Lord is the law of righteousness. The gifts of Vohu-manô to the deeds done in this world for Mazda. He who relieves the poor makes Ahura king."
>
> He offered the sacrifice to the good waters of the good Dâitya! He recited the profession of the worshippers of Mazda!

---

[98] *Yasna* 48.12; cf., *Yasna* 32.16; 43.14; 44.14; 49.3; 53.9.

[99] For the importance of words used to purify, compare the example of *Vendidad* Chapter 10, which in its entirety offers hymns to be recited by priests in order to drive off the "Drug who from the dead rushes upon the living" (Darmesteter, *Zend-Avesta*, 1:136–42). Further, the beginning of the *barashnom-i no shaba* ceremony ("Washing of the Nine Nights") says the following: "... thou, O Zarathustra ... shalt recite *Nemaskâ yâ ârmaitis îzâkâ*; and the man defiled shall repeat, *Nemaskâ yâ ârmaitis îzâkâ*. The Drug becomes weaker and weaker at every one of those words which are a weapon to smite the fiend Angra Mainyu, to smite Aêshma of the murderous spear, to smite the Mâzainyu fiends, to smite all the fiends" (*Vendidad* 9.12–13; trans. Darmesteter, *Zend-Avesta*, 1:126). Compare also chapter 11, which adjures evil demons to depart with incantations made up of lines from the *Gathas* followed by "victorious, most healing words" (trans. Darmesteter, *Zend-Avesta*, 1:142–48). The physical maladies attended to in the *Vendidad* were also addressed through means other than words, as seen in the following illustrative passage: "If several healers offer themselves together, O Spitama Zarathustra! namely, one who heals with the knife, one who heals with herbs, and one who heals with the Holy Word, let one apply to the healing by the Holy Word: for this one is the best-healing of all healers who heals with the Holy Word; he will best drive away sickness from the body of the faithful" (*Vendidad* 7.44; trans. Darmesteter, *Zend-Avesta*, 1:87). Thus, though the religious nature of the *Vendidad* recommends the priestly course in this instance, the alternatives of surgery and pharmacology suggest that the Zoroastrians, like the peoples of Mesopotamia before them, entertained a pragmatic approach to healing with different methods of therapy.

The Drug dismayed, rushed away, the demon Bûiti, who is deceiving, unseen death.[100]

The passage continues as Angra Mainyu negotiates with Zarathushtra to preserve his evil creation, but his efforts prove futile, and the section closes with Zarathushtra learning from Ahura Mazda what invocations destroy the evil *Drug*.[101]

The *Vendidad* resonates with Mesopotamian conjuration and the exorcisms of Christianity in the human conjurer's petition for divine support. In one passage from the *Vendidad* the petitioner first calls upon the support of Ahura Mazda and his holy spirit and then, with words as bold as if they were spoken by the divinity himself, adjures evil to depart:

> Keep us from our hater, O Mazda and Ârmaiti Spenta! Perish, O fiendish *Lie* [Drug]! Perish, O brood of the fiend! Perish, O creation of the fiend! Perish, O world of the fiend! Perish away, O *Lie*! Rush away, O *Lie*! Perish away, O *Lie*! away to the regions of the north, never more to give unto death the living world of Righteousness![102]

We find the petition for divine support also in the homages paid to the Heptad (the sevenfold pantheon of Zoroastrianism) and lesser deities praised in the *Yashts*. In a passage from the *Yasht* to Ashi (goddess of "reward," "recompense") Zarathushtra says:

> Grant me boon, good tall Ashi, that I may be victorious over all the *daēwas* from Mazandarn, so that, frightened, I may not out of terror flee before the *daēwas*, (rather) may all the *daēwas*, unwilling, frightened, flee before me; frightened may they run into darkness.[103]

---

[100] *Vendidad* 10.1–3; trans. Darmesteter, *Zend-Avesta*, 1:209–10.

[101] From *Vendidad* 10.4–16: "Again to him said the Maker of the evil world, Angra Mainyu: 'Do not destroy my creatures, O holy Zarathuṣtra! Thou art the son of Pouruṣaspa; by thy mother I was invoked. Renounce the good Religion of the worshippers of Mazda, and thou shalt gain such a boon as Vadhaghna gained, the ruler of nations.' Spitama Zarathuṣtra said in answer: 'No! never will I renounce the good Religion of the worshippers of Mazda, either for body or life, though they should tear away the breath!' ... Zarathuṣtra asked Ahura Mazda: 'O Ahura Mazda ... How shall I free the word from that Drug, from that evil-doer, Angra Mainyu? How shall I drive away direct defilement? How indirect defilement? How shall I drive the Nasu from the house of the worshippers of Mazda? How shall I cleanse the faithful man? How shall I cleanse the faithful woman?' Ahura Mazda answered: 'Invoke, O Zarathuṣtra! the good Religion of Mazda. Invoke, O Zarathuṣtra! though thou see them not, the Amesha-Speṇtas who rule over the seven Karshvares of the earth. ...'" (trans. Darmesteter, *Zend-Avesta*, 1:210–14). The importance of words as a defense against demons also appears in the *Yasht* to the *Frawashi* ("ancestor spirits"), among whom Zarathushtra is himself counted. Here, Zarathushtra is called the one "who first of the material world proclaimed *daēwa*-repudiating words which follow ahuric doctrine" (*Yasht* 13.90; trans. Malandra, *Introduction to Ancient Iranian Religion*, 114.

[102] *Vendidad* 8.21; trans. Darmesteter, *Zend-Avesta*, 1:101.

[103] *Yasht* 17.25; trans. Malandra, *Introduction to Ancient Iranian Religion*, 134.

A later *Yasht* also garners divine support, where Zarathushtra receives Ahura Mazda's holy names as weapons against evil. Zarathushtra asks the god what name is most protective against the powers of Angra Mainyu in order to

... overcome all *daēwas* and (evil) men, so that I may overcome all sorcerers and witches, so that no one may overcome me, neither a *daēwa* nor yet an (evil) man, neither a sorcerer nor yet a witch.[104]

Ahura Mazda replies that it is the god's own twenty names that he seeks, and he assures Zarathushtra that these will protect the righteous against any evil foe:

And these twenty names stand ready as (his) support and fortification against the invisible Lie [*Drug*], the concupiscent, deceiving (Lie) and against the destructive conjurer, against the all-destructive Deceiver (Angra Mainyu), as if a thousand men would watch over one man.[105]

Another passage from the *Yashts* converges with later exorcism in its recitation of a formula, in this case a prayer, to drive off the demons:

Before his time the *daēwas* would move about visibly, visibly (their) orgies would take place, visibly they would drag women away from (their) men. The *daēwas* would violate them crying and lamenting.
Then, alone, the Ahuna wairya, which righteous Zarathushtra recited four times with (the proper) pauses and then in a loud recitation, drove down all the *daēwas* (so that they became) concealed in the earth, unworthy of worship, unworthy of praise.[106]

These passages from the *Vendidad* and *Yashts* illustrate not only the immediate victories of good over evil, but allude also to the ultimate triumph of Ahura Mazda over Angra Mainyu.

2.3.5 The Influence of Zoroastrianism in the Eastern Mediterranean

The influence of Zoroastrianism upon Hellenism and Judaism has so far been difficult to prove. The evidence currently available suggests a mutual exchange of Zoroastrian and Hellenistic ideas. The first evidence cited for a Greek awareness of Zoroastrian ideas has been seen in the cosmologies of the pre-Socratic Ionian philosophers Thales, Anaximander, and Anaximenes of

---

[104]*Yasht* 1.6; trans. Malandra, *Introduction to Ancient Iranian Religion*, 52. This list of opponents is repeated in several of the other *Yashts*, where it also includes "tyrants, kawis [i.e., chieftains, or princely rulers], and karapans [i.e., priests of the old religion who were hostile to Zarathushtra]" (*Yasht* 5.13, 22, 26; *Yasht* 10.34; *Yasht* 14.62; *Yasht* 19.76).

[105]*Yasht* 1.19; trans. Malandra, *Introduction to Ancient Iranian Religion*, 53.

[106]*Yasht* 19.80–81; trans. Malandra, *Introduction to Ancient Iranian Religion*, 95. In the passages from *Yashts* 17.25 and 1.6 quoted above, the *daēwas* may simply refer to hostile human beings, albeit persons allied with evil. In this passage they appear more clearly as evil spirits.

Miletus, and especially the philosophy of Heraclitus of Ephesus, who were active during the late Archaic and early Classical periods (ca. 550–480 B.C.E.).[107] Further traces have also been detected in Attica during the Classical period,[108] but it is not until the early Common Era that beliefs specifically attributed to Zoroaster, namely, the cosmic battle between Oromazes (Ahura Mazda) and Areimanius (Angra Mainyu), are clearly stated.[109] For its part, Zoroastrianism appears to have been subject to western influences from as early as the conquest of Persia by Alexander, and of which the Zervanite heresy may offer one example.[110]

---

[107]Walter Burkert, however, notes the indeterminate quality of the evidence for Iranian influence upon the pre-Socratics: "For a long time the possibilities concerning an Iranian influence on Anaximander and Heraclitus have been discussed back and forth. The situation with the sources is that the witnesses do not overlap, so a definitive proof is not possible. Thus there is, regrettably, room for the exercise of the individual preferences of friends or foes of the East." (*Man hat über die Möglichkeiten eines iranischen Einflusses auf Anaximandros und Heraklit seit langem hin und her diskutiert. Die Quellenlage is derart, dass die Zeugnisse nicht unmittelbar ineinandergreifen, ein zwingender Beweis also nicht möglich ist; so bleibt ein bedauerlicher Spielraum für individuelle Vorlieben der Freunde oder Feinde des Orients.*) (Walter Burkert, "Apokalyptik im frühen Griechentum: Impulse und Transformationen," in David Hellholm, ed., *Apocalypticism in the Mediterranean World and the Near East* [2d ed.; Tübingen: Mohr, 1989] 242).

[108]Zoroastrian elements have been detected in some of Plato's writings and those of the Academy, for example, the dualistic metaphysics of the bad and good world souls (*Laws* 10) (Boyce, *History of Zoroastrianism*, 2:259). Aristotle held a high regard for the eastern magi, to whom he granted a greater antiquity of learning than the Egyptian magi, which included a dualism that pitted Zeus/Oromasdes against Hades/Areimanias (Aristotle, *Phil.* frag. 6 as preserved in a single quotation by Diogenes Laertius 1.8. Cited in Boyce, *History of Zoroastrianism*, 2:280–81). Boyce also cites Herodotus, himself born a Persian subject in Halicarnassus in ca. 484 B.C.E., as one who had some knowledge of Persian religion that coincides with Zarathushtra's doctrines (Boyce, *History of Zoroastrianism*, 2:165–71, 179–83). Emile Benveniste has argued against Herodotus' knowledge of Zoroastrianism per se, however, and suggests instead that he was familiar with Persian religion as it incorporated the "polytheism ... and deified forces of nature" of Iranian beliefs that existed prior to Zarathushtra's reforms (Benveniste, *Persian Religion*, 29–30). It is during the reign of Artaxerxes II (404–359 B.C.E.) in the late Classical period of Greece that Greek writers such as Theopompus (b. ca. 378 B.C.E.) and Eudemus of Rhodes (2/2 IV B.C.E.) appear to reveal a general familiarity with Iranian – Persian ideas (as preserved through Plutarch, e.g., *Is. et Os.* 369D–F). Hultgård finds Iranian apocalyptic influence in the "Oracles of Hystaspes," which he considers "undeniably an important testimony to the impact of Persian apocalyptic ideas on the western Greco-Roman world" (Hultgård, "Persian Apocalypticism," 76).

[109]For example, Plutarch, *Isis and Osiris* 369A–370C, in which Plutarch cites Theopompus (IV B.C.E.) as a source. Benveniste has argued, however, that Plutarch's discussion represents not the teachings of Zarathushtra, but Zervanite beliefs, with their tenets of equi-lateral dualism and Time as the Supreme Being (Benveniste, *Persian Religion*, 114–16).

[110]In its move westward Zoroastrianism encountered Time as a separate deity (e.g., Chronos of the Greeks), whom the Zoroastrian priests accommodated into their pantheon as

Striking affinities between Zoroastrianism and Judaism have been noted by others. The angelologies, demonologies, and the subjugation of evil evident in late canonical and intertestamental writings such as Tobit, Daniel, and Qumran's *Community Rule* offer tantalizing suggestions of Zoroastrianism's influence upon Jewish thought.[111] Much of Judaism's affinity with Zoroastrianism appears in its apocalyptic texts, and it has been suggested that Iranian ideas "propelled" Jewish apocalyptic thought by showing the way to a personified evil, to a doctrine of good and evil spirits and the ethical dualism they represent, and to the opposition between them that culminates in an eschatological battle.[112]

Zurvan (*zurvan* = "time" in Avestan), the father of the twins Ahura Mazda and Angra Mainyu (Boyce, *History of Zoroastrianism*, 2:231–32). The heresy lies in the primacy given to Zurvan over Ahura Mazda. Darmesteter found it convenient to divide Zoroastrianism into pre- and post-Alexandrian periods, the latter of which he considered to be influenced by Greek thought (Neo-Platonism), Judaism, and Buddhism (Darmesteter, *Zend-Avesta*, 1:lxviii–lxix). Zaehner also considers Zoroastrianism to have lost some of its doctrinal rigor and purity beginning with the Hellenistic era: "There can, however, be little doubt that during the Seleucid and Parthian epochs Hellenistic influences made themselves felt which may even then have penetrated into the Zoroastrian religion itself" (Zaehner, *Zurvan*, 7).

[111]Boyce argues that Zoroastrian influence was possible and likely upon Judaism during the Hellenistic period. Of the affinity between Zoroastrianism and Judaism, Boyce says: "... each upheld an ancient and ethically noble prophetic religion that was essentially monotheistic, and each sustained it by a regular and (at its strictest) exacting devotional life, with complex purity laws" (Boyce, *History of Zoroastrianism*, 3:392). For Zoroastrian influence upon Judaism, see Boyce, *History of Zoroastrianism*, 3.401–36. John Collins finds Persian overlap in the Qumran *War Scroll*, in which he sees "a combination both of Jewish traditions and of Persian myth" (John J. Collins, "The Mythology of Holy War in Daniel and the Qumran War Scroll: A Point of Transition in Jewish Apocalyptic," *VT* 25 [1975] 608). The most explicit evidence of Zoroastrian views on early Judaism is the demon Asmodeus in Tobit (II B.C.E.). The name Asmodeus derives from the Avestan words *aēšma daēuua* ("Demon of Wrath"); it is a name that appears in the later *Yashts* (*Yasht* 10.8, 97; 11.15; 57.10.25). *Aēšma* also appears without *daēuua* in the Old-Avestan Gathic writings (*Yasna* 29.2; 30.6; 48.12), which would suggest it more as an abstract quality in these texts than a personified demon (cf. Hutter, "Asmodeus," *DDD*² 106–8).

[112]Hultgård, "Persian Apocalypticism," 79–81. Samuel K. Eddy argues for the simultaneous development of eschatological and apocalyptic thought in Egypt, Persis and Judah during the period of Seleucid rule as "the necessary response of a people who could not overcome the Greek by force alone ..." (Samuel K. Eddy, *The King Is Dead: Studies in the Near Eastern Resistance to Hellenism 334–31 B.C.* [Lincoln: University of Nebraska Press, 1961] 253–54). Sven Hartman agrees that apocalyptic thinking came out of Iranian rather than Greek cultural influence. He sees a specific example of this in the figure of the devil, whom he considers the Jews to have modelled after Ahriman (Angra Mainyu) after their exposure to the Achaemenian and Parthian periods of dominance in the Near East (Sven S. Hartman, "Datierung der jungavestischen Apokalyptik," in David Hellholm, ed., *Apocalypticism in the Mediterranean World and the Near East* [2d ed.; Tübingen: Mohr, 1989] 61–75). In contrast to the Iranian beliefs, Walter Burkert observes that the Greeks had a concept of natural law (φύσις) by which the world operated. Although apocalyptic forerunners are present in early

2.4 Conclusion

This overview of beliefs and practices with regard to possession and exorcism in the ancient Near East highlights several themes that carry into the New Testament and early Christianity. The Mesopotamian societies accorded respect to the conjurer. The conjurer's craft also included the features of discovery, verbal confrontation with the possessing spirits, and support sought from the divine spiritual world. Zoroastrianism in particular converges with later Judaism and Christianity, and its own apocalypticism suggests this type of thought as a nurturing ground for the ideas of possession and exorcism generally. Zoroastrianism also offers an analogy to Jewish and Christian concepts of possession to the extent that it teaches an intimate contact between the spirit world and its human host. Further, by its use of words to ward off spirits and by its enlistment of divine support to aid in their expulsion, Zoroastrianism also converges with Judaism's and Christianity's interest in exorcism.

Greek literature, apocalypticism as a breaking-through of this natural law is essentially contrary to Greek thought (Burkert, "Apokalyptik im frühen Griechentum," 235).

Chapter 3

Possession and Exorcism in Ancient Israel and Early Judaism

3.1 Introduction

The Hebrew Bible and intertestamental Jewish literature offer a scenario different from the cultural pluralism evident among the Mesopotamian societies. Instead of a policy of religious conglomeration, the Hebrew Bible advocated the exclusive theism of its national God. The cultic practices that catered to polytheistic beliefs found themselves out of place and out of favor in the presence of this official Jewish monotheism. Yet, a transition took place in Jewish society that allowed some practices such as exorcism to shift from their earlier prohibition as occult activities to their gradual absorption into the cult of Yahweh. Such a transition appears at first to have met with resistance in ancient Israel, but gradually gained credibility there, so that early figures such as Moses and Solomon would be rewritten as great magi of yore who validated the professions of Jewish exorcists and wonder workers at the turn of the era.

Chapter 3 discusses three collections of early Jewish literature: the canonical books of the Hebrew Bible and Septuagint, the non-canonical pseudepigraphic writings that expanded upon the canonical traditions, and the sectarian texts from Qumran. With the Israelite and early Jewish writings we come across not only a verifiably direct influence upon Christianity, but also the mediation of Near Eastern thought to the western Greek speaking world. The Septuagint offers the translation of Near Eastern ideas into Greek, and many of the apocryphal and pseudepigraphic materials were either composed in Greek, or translated into that language early on.

3.2 Possession and Exorcism in the Hebrew Bible and Septuagint

The Hebrew Bible presents an apparently anomalous situation for the Israelites and Jews relative to their neighbors. Here we find little reference to demonic possession, as well as an uncompromising stance against magic.[1]

---

[1]E.g., see the prohibitions of magical activity in Exod 22:18 (17) ("sorceress" [מכשפה]); Lev 19:26b ("divine" by omens [נחש], "practice soothsaying" [ענן]), 31 ("necromancer" [אוב],

Where the *aŝipu*-type figure does occur in the Hebrew Bible, he is accurately counted among the wise men of foreign courts, but shown by the authors to be inferior in power to Yahweh and his emissaries.[2] Such is the case in the encounters of Joseph,[3] and Moses and Aaron[4] with the wise men in Egypt, and Daniel's with those in Babylon.[5]

This, however, reaffirms the social issues that ultimately define magic as an activity practiced outside the established cult. Within the Hebrew Bible there are many instances of "magical" acts similar to what one finds in the surrounding cultures, but which receive approval because they are performed within the cult of Yahweh. The cases of Joseph, Moses, Aaron, and Daniel, illustrate this well. We see that Joseph and Daniel have reputations for the correct interpretation of dreams and for the divination of signs, respectively. These are the same skills practiced by the wise courtiers first looked to by the Egyptian and Babylonian kings. When the training of the wise men fails the rulers turn to Joseph and Daniel, who address the same issues, and use the same techniques,[6] but derive satisfactory interpretations from within their cult of Yahweh. Because of their surpassing abilities they usurp the wise men in the royal courts and, in the case of Daniel and his companions, assume the

---

communication with a "familiar spirit" [ידעני]) (likewise 20:6, 27); Deut 18:10–11 (those who: "practice divination" [קסם], "divine" by signs [מעונן, מנחש], "practice sorcery" [מכשף], "bind" by a spell [חבר], "seek oracles" [שאל אוב], "necromance" [דרש אל־המתים, ידעני]); 1 Sam 15:23a ("divination" [קסם]); 28:8–9 (אוב and ידעני); 2 Kgs 17:17 (קסם, נהש); 21:6 (עֹנן, נהש, ידעני אוב); 23:24 (אוב and ידעני); 2 Chr 33:6 (עֹנן, נהש, כשף, אוב, ידעני).

[2]*Aŝipu* occurs several times as a Babylonian loan word in both the Hebrew and Aramaic portions of Daniel (Hebrew אשף: Dan 1:20; Aramaic אשף: Dan 2:10, 27; 4:7; 5:7, 11, 15). Theodotian, who wrote his Greek translation of the Hebrew Bible in the second century C.E., consistently translates this as μαγοί; the Old Greek LXX also uses φαρμακοί (Dan 2:27).

[3]Gen 41:1–45. The terms used are: HB — חרטמים ("magicians"; literally "engravers" or "writers", this word shows the close association between magic and the occult knowledge associated with literacy in a foreign language) and חכמים ("wise men"); LXX — ἐξηγηταί ("interpreters") and σοφοί ("wise men").

[4]Exod 7:8–19. The terms used are: HB — חרטמים, מכשפים ("sorcerers," from Assyrian *kaŝŝâpu*), חכמים; LXX — σοφισταί ("experts," cf. this Greek term with the Hebrew חרטמים which it translates for their associations with literacy), φαρμακοί ("magicians" who work with drugs [φάρμακα]), ἐπαοιδοί ("magicians" who use verbal charms, i.e., "enchanters").

[5]Dan 1:17–21; 2:1–49; 4:4–9, 24–28; 5:7–17. The terms used are: HB — אשפים, חרטמים ("conjurer;" probably a Babylonian loan word from the Assyrian *aŝipu*), כשדים, מכשפים ("Chaldeans;" from Babylonian *Kasdu*, via Assyrian *Kaldu, Kaldû*); LXX — σοφισταί, φιλόσοφοι ("philosophers") (Dan 1:17–21); ἐπαοιδοί, μάγοι (e.g., "dream interpreters," "wizards"; from *Magian*, i.e., one from Media), φαρμακοί, σοφοί, Χαλδαῖοι ("Chaldeans"). "Chaldeans" and "wise men" also serve here as collective designations for these professionals (Dan 2:1–49; 4:7). Theodotian consistently uses γαζαρηνοι as a transliteration of the Aramaic technical term גזרין ("determiners" of fate); thus, at Dan 2:27; 4:4; and 5:7, 11.

[6]Daniel and his three companions spend three years in the Babylonian court for just such training (Dan 1:1–21).

same responsibilities as those whom they have replaced. Likewise, Moses and Aaron, and the Egyptian wise men achieve similar results in their initial tests of miraculous power, and do so by the same device of miracle-conjuring rods.[7] Both parties, however, draw upon different sources of authority for their wondrous acts — the wise men from their learning, Moses and Aaron from Yahweh — the latters' of which eventually proves superior.

The importance of cultic authority is a central point in each of these stories. The miracle workers and wise men, among whom the exorcist would eventually be included, represent given traditions. They engage in contests that accredit and validate of their traditions, and their individual success or failure in these contests impacts the audience's bias for or against those traditions. These contests also occasion cultural interaction, as seen with the Israelites and Jews in the courts of foreign rulers. This scenario will also prove analogous to Judaism and Christianity in the Common Era, where these beliefs would engage the views of the broader culture. The case of Eleazar before Vespasian is one such example within the Jewish tradition. But the same can be said of the Christian exorcists to whom Justin and Tertullian refer in their apologies addressed to the Roman authorities.

One reason for the more subdued character of possession and exorcism in the Hebrew Bible is that demons rarely appear as viable entities that either act beyond divine supervision or are subject to conjuration. This holds true also for the apocryphal literature, which builds upon the angelology of the Hebrew Bible without articulating a parallel demonic world.[8] Thus, although divine warriors frequent 2 Maccabees, and God is there called "Defender of the

---

[7]Compare also the tradition of the brothers Jannes and Jambres as the magicians, who (raised up by Belial in the Damascus Document) compete against Moses and Aaron in Egypt (CD 5.17–20; 2 Tim 3:8–9; *The Book of Jannes and Jambres* [*OTP* 2.427–42]). A recent presentation of the early manuscript evidence for the apocryphal book can be found in Albert Pietersma, ed., *The Apocryphon of Jannes and Jambres the Magicians: P. Chester Beatty XVI (with New Additions of Papyrus* vindobonensis *Greek inv. 29456 + 29828* verso *and British Library Cotton Tiberius B. v f. 87)* (Religions in the Graeco-Roman World 119; Leiden: Brill, 1994).

[8]Personal names for certain demons first appear in the apocryphal and intertestamental literature. Asmodeus occurs in Greek in Tobit 3:8, 17 (for the Persian origins of "Asmodeus," see above Chapter 2, note 111). Though mentioned in the Hebrew Bible, it is only later that Azazel became demonized: "The process of the demonization of Azazel was intensively pursued in early Judaism under the influence of dualistic tendencies ..." (Bernd Janowski, "Azazel עזאזל," *DDD*[2] 130). Later revisions of the Septuagint sometimes recognize the individuality of demons glossed over by the Old Greek. Thus, לילית "Lilith" from Akkadian *lilitu*, from Sumerian *lil* (Isa 34:14; Old Greek = ὀνοκένταυροι "demon"; Aquilla = λιλίθ; Theodotian = λαμία "devourer of men's flesh"), עזאזל "Azazel" (Lev 16:8(2x), 10(2x), 26; Matt 12:43; cf. Αζαήλ in *1 En.* 8.1; 9.6; 10.4–8; 13.1), and עלוקה "Aluqqah" (a "pan-Semitic" word found in Syriac, Arabic, Ethiopic, and Akkadian meaning "leech", or "vampire" in a demonic context [Prov 30:15]). See, Manfred Hutter, "Lilith לילית," *DDD*[2] 520–21. See, Ronald S. Hendel, "Vampire עלוקה," *DDD*[2] 887.

nation," the enemies they rally against are the forces marshaled by Hellenistic kings rather than their demonic counterparts in apocalyptic writings.[9] Likewise, in 2 Maccabees we find illness under divine surveillance and the result of divine displeasure. There, God brings fatal illness to Antiochus and seriously debilitates Heliodorus until the high priest Onias makes sacrifices of atonement on his behalf.[10] To restore health one must appease God. We also see that the apocryphal wisdom literature adds Wisdom herself to the divine retinue as a personified being without juxtaposing a "spirit of stupefaction," or the like.[11] Only Tobit offers a demonology that acts independently of the divine order. Here we find Asmodeus as the representative of this independence, whose mischief is brought to an end by a pharmaceutical prescribed by the angel Raphael.[12]

3.2.1 Possession in the Hebrew Bible and Septuagint

The Hebrew Bible and the apocryphal Jewish texts of the Septuagint make few references to demonic possession. The most explicit instances of such in the Hebrew Bible appear in the "spirit of jealousy,"[13] the "lying spirits" that enter the mouths of Ahab's prophets,[14] the suggestive spirit that God puts into Sennacherib that causes him to return to Assyria with his army,[15] the indwelling "spirit of whoredom" that leads astray,[16] and perhaps the alteration of Nebuchadnezzar's state-of-mind.[17] To this we can add the concept of the *engastrimythos*, or "belly talker," a term that occurs several times in the Hebrew Bible within the lists of banned practices, and is applied also to the medium of Endor visited by Saul.[18] Aside from the lying spirits of

---

[9]Divine warriors appear in 2 Maccabees 3:22–40; 5:1–4; 10:29–31; 11:6–13; 15:22–24. Cf., 2 Kings 19:35 for an example of this kind of angelic help also in the Hebrew Bible. God as "Defender of the nation" appears at 2 Maccabees 14:34.

[10]Antiochus: 2 Macc 9:5–29; Heliodorus: 2 Macc 3:22–40. Both of these cases have symptoms similar to the "sacred disease" of Greek medicine. In the Hebrew Bible, God inflicts illness in e.g. Genesis (20:18) Exodus (15:26), Numbers (8:19; 11:33; 12:1–16, et al.), and Deuteronomy (7:15; 28:21–22, 27–28, 35, 59–61; 32:23–24).

[11]Wis 1:4–6; 6:12–20; Sir 1:9–20; 24:1–22. Cf. the "spirit of sleep" (רוח תרדמה) brought upon Israel by God in Isaiah 29:10 (LXX "spirit of stupor" [πνεῦμα κατανύξεως]) and Romans 11:8 that dulls its ability to discern the divine will.

[12]Tob 3:7–17; 6:1–17; 8:1–3. Internal evidence suggests that Tobit was written sometime while Zerubbabel's temple was standing, and probably before the Maccabean era, ca. late III – early II B.C.E. (Schürer, *History of the Jewish People*, 3.1:222–32).

[13]Num 5:14–15, 30.

[14]1 Kgs 22:19–24; 2 Chr 18:18–23.

[15]2 Kgs 19:7; Isa 37:7.

[16]Hos 5:4; cf. 3:12.

[17]Dan 4:16. Compare also God's "hardening the heart" of one (את־לבם לחזק; κατισχῦσαι τὴν καρδίαν) (Josh 11:20; cf. Deut 2:30; Dan 5:20).

[18]1 Sam 28:1–25 (Old Greek version of the LXX). The term is discussed at greater length in Chapter 4: "Possession and the Treatment of the Possessed in Early Greece."

Ahab's prophets and the *engastrimythoi*, the other examples could simply refer to changes in character rather than foreign spiritual presences. Otherwise, demons appear as non-possessing figures in the service of God;[19] attributes that are also applicable to Satan during this period.[20]

The apocryphal texts 4 Ezra (2 Esdras) and 4 Maccabees offer explanations for evil as presences that exist within each person.[21] 4 Ezra also illustrates the exchange of influences upon the individual: once the evil root was established in the human heart "what was good departed, and the evil remained."[22] Neither 4 Ezra nor 4 Maccabees, however, personify the inner evil inclinations as demonic presences. Although the evil spirit that plagues Saul in 1 Samuel does not actually appear to enter into his body, this account is important in that it shows a similar transferal of spirits: the departure of the "spirit of the Lord" (רוח יהוה; πνεῦμα κυρίου) from Saul allows an "evil spirit" (רעה רוח; πνεῦμα πονηρόν) to approach the king and trouble him.[23] In this it appears similar to the phenomenon of a protective spirit that abandons one and leaves one open to misfortune as found in Mesopotamian writings.

Influence of the divine spirit upon humanity appears throughout the biblical texts. The spirit of God as an indwelling presence is occasionally used in the anthropological sense of the life-giving presence that animates and invigorates creation.[24] We see this divine spiritual influence used to promote artistic skill,[25] to produce spectacular deeds,[26] and to generate profound

---

[19]Judg 9:23; Job 4:12–16. Compare God's striking panic, madness, and blindness upon Israel's neighboring nations (Zech 12:4; cf. 14:13).

[20]1 Chr 21:1; Job 1:6–19.

[21]4 Ezra 3:20–27. 4 Macc 2:21-3:5. The composition of 4 Ezra dates to the late first century C.E. (B. M. Metzger, "The Fourth Book of Ezra," *OTP* 2:520).

[22]"Thus the disease became permanent; the law was in the hearts of the people along with the evil root; but what was good departed, and the evil remained." (*Et facta est permanens infirmitas et lex cum corde populi cum malignitate radicis; et discessit quod bonum est et mansit malignum.*) (2 Esdras [=4 Ezra] 3:22).

[23]1 Sam 16:14–23; 18:10–12; 19:9–10. Judges 16:19–20 also shows the spirit of God to abandon Samson, and thus to expose him to misfortune.

[24]In Genesis, God says that his spirit will not "abide in" mortals forever (ב ידון; καταμείνῃ ... ἐν — Gen 6:3). Compare also Job 27:3; 34:14–15; Ps 104:30; Ezek 37:5–6, 14; 4 Ezra 16:61–62.

[25]God "fills" (אמלא; ἐνέπλησα) the designers of the tabernacle with his spirit to heighten their skills of craftsmanship (Exod 31:1–6; 35:30–36:2). This is the closest the Hebrew Bible comes to the Greek poetic practice of invoking the Muses. There is nothing comparable, for example, in the Psalms to suggest that the hymn writers received their inspiration from God.

[26]The spirit of God is manifest among the deeds of the judges: the spirit of God "was upon" Othniel (עליו ותהי; ἐγένετο ἐπί — Judg 3:10) and Jephthah (Judg 11:29); Gideon "puts on" the spirit of God (לבשה; ἐνέδυσεν — Judg 6:34); the spirit of God typically "rushes upon" Samson (עליו ותצלח; κατηύθυνεν ἐπ᾽ αὐτόν — Judg 14:6, 19; 15:14).

judgment,[27] qualities of leadership,[28] and prophetic powers.[29] Though the language used is most often in terms of an external influence, such as the spirit of God "being upon," or "clothing" someone, there are a few exceptions. Thus, the spirit of God enters into Ezekiel and Daniel to stimulate their prophecy or skills at divination.[30] Other passages from Ezekiel and one from Psalms also show how the spirit of God within a person indicates one's

---

[27]In the Apocrypha the spirit of wisdom enters into the body. Thus, from Wisdom of Solomon: "wisdom will not enter a deceitful soul, or dwell in a body (κατοικήσει ἐν σώματι) enslaved to sin. For a holy and disciplined spirit will flee from deceit ..." (Wis 1:4–5). These verses also show a belief in the repulsion that exists between what is holy and what is sinful: the two do not occupy the same space, but one drives out the other (see also Wis 7:7 and Sir 1:9–10). Compare also 1 Kings 3:28, where the wisdom of God within Solomon permits him to execute justice.

[28]God identifies Joshua as one "who has the spirit in him," prior to his commissioning by Moses (אֲשֶׁר־רוּחַ בּוֹ; ὅς ἔχει πνεῦμα ἐν ἑαυτῷ — Num 27:18–23; Deut 34:9). God also "rushes upon" Saul (עַל ... תִּצְלַח; ἐφήλατο ... ἐπί — 1 Sam 11:6–7), and David (עַל ... תִּצְלַח; ἐφήλατο ... ἐπί — 1 Sam 16:13). The spirit of God "clothes" Amasai (לָבְשָׁה; ἐνέδυσε — 1 Chr 12:19), and an excellent spirit is "in" Daniel (ἐν αὐτῷ — Dan 6:4). The presence of God in qualities of judgment and leadership are also found in Isaiah, where the spirit of God "rests upon" (נָחָה עַל; ἀναπαύσεται ἐπί — Isa 11:2–4), is "poured out upon" (יְעָרֶה עָלֵינוּ; cf. ἐπέλθη ἐπί — 32:15; עַל ... אֶצֹּק; cf. ἐπιθήσω ... ἐπί — 44:3), and is "bestown upon" one (עַל ... נָתַתִּי; ἔδωκα ... ἐπί — 42:1). Compare also the words of Elihu to Job, who says that "it is the spirit in a mortal (בֶאֱנוֹשׁ; ἔστιν ἐν βροτοῖς), the breath of the Almighty, that makes for understanding" (Job 32:8).

[29]God takes a portion of the spirit that is upon Moses and "places" it "upon" the seventy elders (שַׂמְתִּי עַל; ἐπιθήσω ἐπί — Num 11:17, 24–30), and the spirit is "established" or "rests upon" them so that they prophesy (כְּנוּחַ עַל; ἐπανεπαύσατο ... ἐπί). Balaam's prophecy comes when the spirit of God "was upon" or "in" him (תְּהִי עַל; ἐγένετο ... ἐν — Num 24:2–3). Saul prophesies in ecstasis with a band of prophets once the spirit of the Lord "rushes upon" him (צָלְחָה עַל; ἐφαλεῖται ἐπί — 1 Sam 10:5–6, 9–13), and the spirit of the Lord "was upon" Saul's messengers to cause them also to enter into prophetic frenzy (תְּהִי עַל; ἐγενήθη ... ἐπί — 1 Sam 19:20–24). The spirit of God "clothes" Zechariah so that he prophesies (לָבְשָׁה; ἐνέδυσεν — 2 Chr 24:20). At the outset of his proclamation of God's good news to his people, Isaiah writes: "The spirit of the Lord God is upon me" (יְהוָה עָלָי; רוּחַ אֲדֹנָי; πνεῦμα κυρίου ἐπ᾽ ἐμέ — Isa 61:1; cf. 59:21). Ezekiel most explicitly describes the spirit of God to enter into the prophet's body rather than just upon it. In the Hebrew he speaks of a spirit that "enters into" (תָּבֹא בִי) him and causes him to prophesy (Ezek 2:2–5; 3:22–27). The Greek uses the more external expression "it came upon me" — ἦλθεν ἐπ᾽ ἐμέ). Daniel also has "the holy spirit of God in him" that enables his divination (בַהּ רוּחַ־אֱלָהִין קַדִּישִׁין; ὃς πνεῦμα θεοῦ ἅγιον ἐν ἑαυτῷ — Dan 4:8–9, 18; 5:11–12, 14). Joel says that God will "pour out" his spirit "upon all flesh" (עַל־כָּל־בָּשָׂר ... אֶשְׁפּוֹךְ; ἐκχεῶ ... ἐπὶ πᾶσαν σάρκα) to cause them to prophesy, dream, and see visions (Joel 2:28–29 [3:1–2]). Micah, "filled with the spirit of the Lord" (מָלֵאתִי כֹּחַ אֶת־רוּחַ יהוה; ἐμπλήσω ἰσχὺν ἐν πνεύματι κυρίου), makes his prophetic proclamation to Israel (Mic 3:8).

[30]Ezek 2:2–5; 3:22–27; Dan 4:8–9, 18; 5:11–12, 14.

relationship to God, or establishes one as God's representative.[31] One metaphor, popularized in the New Testament but virtually lacking in the Hebrew Scriptures, is that of the body of the individual, or the corporate body of a community, as the temple in which the divinity dwells.[32] The source for this New Testament usage has been traced out of Greco-Roman culture, where the body could be understood as a temple in which the god dwelt as a cult shrine.[33]

3.2.2 Exorcism in the Hebrew Bible and Septuagint

In the Hebrew Bible, exorcism finds its closest analogies in two passages: David's soothing of Saul in 1 Samuel,[34] and God's rebuke of Satan in the book of Zechariah.[35] In the first instance, although the evil spirit is not actually said to possess Saul's body, David's lyre playing serves an exorcistic function by causing the evil spirit to depart, and thus restores Saul to a state of well being, however temporary. From this story we can see how exorcistic psalms were attributed to David among the scrolls from Qumran.[36] David's own reputation for soothing the soul, combined with his successor's vast wisdom, led to Solomon's reputation as the exorcist *par excellence*. A passage from the Septuagint's Wisdom of Solomon attests to this reputation, where Solomon gives thanks to God for having given him "unerring knowledge of what exists, to know ... the powers of spirits" ($\pi\nu\epsilon\upsilon\mu\acute{\alpha}\tau\omega\nu$ $\beta\acute{\iota}\alpha\varsigma$).[37] Solomon is also apparent as a great exorcist in the later pseudepigraphic *Testament of*

---

[31]Psalm 51:10 includes the phrase "put a new and right spirit within me," which both the Hebrew and Greek more explicitly phrase with reference to the inwardness of the body, as 'in my inmost parts' (רוח נכון חדש בקרבי; $\pi\nu\epsilon\tilde{\upsilon}\mu\alpha$ $\epsilon\dot{\upsilon}\theta\dot{\epsilon}\varsigma$ $\dot{\epsilon}\gamma\kappa\alpha\acute{\iota}\nu\iota\sigma\upsilon$ $\dot{\epsilon}\nu$ $\tau\tilde{o}\iota\varsigma$ $\dot{\epsilon}\gamma\kappa\acute{\alpha}\tau\upsilon\iota\varsigma$ $\mu\upsilon\upsilon$ — Psalm 51:10–12 [50:10–14]; see also Ezek 11:19–20; 36:25–27). Compare also where God's spirit accompanies Isaiah in his role as God's messenger (Isa 48:16), and God's consecration of Jeremiah (Jer 1:5–10).

[32]Compare the Hebrew Bible's concept of God dwelling within the corporate community (e.g., Ezek 11:19–20; 36:26–27; 39:29), manifested in part by the images of the ark and tabernacle as visible signs of God among the Israelites (Exod 25:1–9; 1 Sam 4:3–9). For the metaphor of the temple in the New Testament, see 1 Cor 3:16–17; 2 Cor 6:16–18; John 2:21; Eph 2:19–22. Among the apostolic and apocryphal writings, see, *Barn.* 16.6–10 and *T. Isaac* 4.15 (ca. II C.E.); cf., *Herm.* Vision 3.2–7.

[33]J. Haussleiter, "Deus internus," *RAC* 3:826.

[34]1 Sam 16:14–23. Compare *Pseudo-Philo* 60.1–3.

[35]Zech 3:1–2. Compare God's rebuke of the locust that would desolate the land (Mal 3:11).

[36]*11QPsalms^a* (11Q5 27.9).

[37]Wis 7:15–22. Compare also Wis 17:7–8, where Solomon decries the practitioners of magic ($\mu\alpha\gamma\iota\kappa\tilde{\eta}\varsigma$) "who promised to drive off the fears and disorders of a sick soul," while they were themselves the victims of what they promised to cure; it is a description of practices not far removed from those of the *āšipu*. David Winston considers the reign of Gaius "Caligula" (37–41 C.E.) as the most probable date for the Wisdom of Solomon's composition (David Winston, "Solomon, Wisdom of," *ABD* 6:122–23).

Solomon, in the magical papyri, and in the artifacts of magical rings and charms from the early centuries of the Common Era.

In the second passage, God's rebuke of Satan offers a confrontational context and language similar to what one later finds in the New Testament exorcisms. Zechariah 3:1–2 occurs within a court proceeding where the high priest Joshua stands before the angel of the Lord with Satan as his prosecutor. The second verse reads:

> And the Lord said to Satan, "The Lord rebuke you, O Satan! The Lord who has chosen Jerusalem rebuke you (יגער יהוה בך השטן; Ἐπιτιμήσαι κύριος ἐν σοί, διάβολε)! Is not this man a brand plucked from the fire?"

This passage has a parallel in the New Testament epistle of Jude, where the archangel Michael contests with the devil (διάβολος) over the body of Moses, and says to him "The Lord rebuke you!" (ἐπιτιμήσαι σοι κύριος).[38] Both Zechariah and Jude use the same term for "rebuke" that one finds in several exorcistic passages in the New Testament.[39] The passages from Zechariah and Jude also converge with the New Testament exorcisms in their appeal to the Lord's higher authority in controlling the offending presence.

Of the apocryphal books in the Septuagint only Tobit contributes toward the idea of exorcism.[40] Tobit is set during the Assyrian period of domination in the Near East. The action takes place in the Assyrian capital of Nineveh, where Tobit and his family dwell, and in Ecbatana the capital of Media, the region east of Assyria, where Sarah, the daughter of Tobit's kinsman and the future bride of Tobit's son, Tobias, lives. On seven previous occasions the demon Asmodeus has plagued Sarah's bridal chamber by killing her newlywed husbands. God sends Raphael, the angel of healing, "to bind the evil demon Asmodeus."[41] Asmodeus is driven off by an apotropaic ritual that Tobias has learned from Raphael, and Raphael binds Asmodeus in the furthest reaches of Egypt. The contribution this story makes to the later portrayals of exorcism is

---

[38]Jude 9.

[39]For New Testament references, see "The Terminology of Exorcism" in Chapter 5, below. Compare Zechariah 2:13's command to all flesh to be silent out of respect for the presence of the Lord, which occurs just before the confrontation between the angel of the Lord and Satan. Silencing is also a factor in Jesus' rebuke of the demoniac in the synagogue (φιμώθητι — Mark 1:25; Luke 4:35), and his silencing the demons while staying at the home of Simon's mother-in-law (ἐπιτιμῶν οὐκ εἴα αὐτὰ λαλεῖν — Luke 4:41); cf. the stilling of the storm (σιώπα, πεφίμωσο — Mark 4:39). The usage in Zechariah differs from these New Testament passages, however, in that Zechariah's rebuke and command to silence are directed at two different parties.

[40]Tob 4:17; 6:13–17; 8:1–3.

[41]δῆσαι Ασμοδαυν τὸ πονηρὸν δαιμόνιον (Tob 3:17; cf. 8:3).

in Asmodeus' apparent autonomy: Asmodeus appears to plague Sarah by his own volition rather than at God's behest.[42]

Although the Hebrew Bible does not offer explicit evidence of exorcism, the Hellenistic period does introduce the semantic groundwork for the demonology that would become standard to the later presentations of exorcism in the New Testament.[43] During this time the Hebrew Bible was translated into Greek, and most of the apocryphal documents were composed in Greek. Though Near Eastern demonic personalities do not enter into the early Greek translation of the Hebrew Bible (Old Greek version), δαίμων and its derivatives are used to translate various Hebrew terms for spiritual entities.[44] These will come to refer often and exclusively to evil spirits in the New Testament.

The biblical texts serve as a kind of linguistic brokerage house during the Hellenistic period, in which Near Eastern concepts were rendered from the Semitic Hebrew and Aramaic languages into Greek. The eastern magical professions serve as relevant examples of this linguistic exchange for the early Greek equivalents they received in the Septuagint. By their variety, the following tables hint at the highly specialized nature of these professions as they had evolved in the east, which occasionally find close convergences with technical terms already existing in the Greek. Though none of these professionals perform exorcisms in the biblical passages, they do operate within the realm of occult knowledge that would come to include exorcists in the first centuries of the Common Era. The first column gives the relevant terms as they occur in the Biblical Hebrew or Aramaic. The second column presents their etymologies outside of the scriptural languages. The third column shows how they appear in the Old Greek (OG) version of the Septuagint as derived from the manuscripts of *Codices Vaticanus* (B),

---

[42]Asmodeus does, however, conveniently protect Sarah's virginity for Tobias, the man for whom she was destined "from eternity" (Tob 6:17).

[43]On semantics, see J. P. Louw, *Semantics of New Testament Greek* (Philadelphia: Fortress, 1982). See also, Emanuel Tov, "Greek Words and Hebrew Meanings," in Takamitsu Muraoka, ed., *Melbourne Symposium on Septuagint Lexicography* (SBLSCS 28; Atlanta: Scholars Press, 1990) 83–126. In this article, Tov discusses the difficulties in translating Greek words used for Hebrew terms in that they either bring specialized meanings to the Greek terms (from the translator's view), or they alter the meaning of the Greek words for Greek readers. Ralph Marcus concludes of Jewish and Greek influences in the Septuagint: "the Greek elements of the LXX are merely superficial and decorative while the Jewish elements are deep-lying, central and dominant" (Ralph Marcus, "Jewish and Greek Elements in the Septuagint," in *Louis Ginzberg Jubilee Volume on the Occasion of His Seventieth Birthday* [New York: American Academy for Jewish Research, 1945] 227–45).

[44]Thus, δαιμόνιον translates the following Hebrew terms: שֵׁד "demon," from Assyrian *sedu* (Deut 32:17; Ps 105[106]:37), שָׂעִיר "satyr," "demon" (Isa 13:21; 34:14), קֶטֶב "pestilence" (Ps 91:6), אֱלִילִים "worthless (gods)" (Ps 96:5), גַּן Phoenician "god of fortune" (Isa 65:3, 11) (see, Werner Foerster, "δαίμων et al." *TDNT* 2:10–16).

Sinaiticus (א), and *Alexandrinus* (A).[45] The remaining three columns provide, when known, the Greek terms used by the later translators of the Scriptures as collated by Origen: Aquilla (A), Symmachus (Σ), and Theodotian (Θ).[46] These last three were made during the first centuries Common Era, and have bearing upon the social status of magical practitioners at that time.

Table 1: Genesis 41:1–45 (Joseph in Pharaoh's Court)

Biblical Term	Origin	OG (mid III BCE)	A (128 CE)	Σ (end II – early III CE)	Θ (mid I BCE– end II CE)
חרטמים ("magi"; literally "engravers," "writers") 41:8, 24		ἐξηγηταί ("interpreters") 41:8, 24	κρυφιασταί ("dream interpreters") 41:8, 24	μάγοι ("magicians" fr. Magian, i.e., one from Media) 41:8, 24	σοφισταί ("experts") 8:24
חכמים ("wise men") 41:8	Late Hebrew fr. Assyrian ḫakāmu "to know"	σοφοί ("wise men") 41:8			

Table 2: Exodus 6:28–12:36 (Moses and Aaron in Egypt)

Biblical Term	Origin	OG	A	Σ	Θ
חכמים 7:11		σοφισταί 7:11			
מכשפים ("sorcerers") 7:11	Assyrian kassâpu ("sorcerer," as one involved with illegal witchcraft)	φαρμακοί ("magi" who work with drugs [φάρμακα]) 7:11			
חרטמים 7:11, 22; 8:3, 14, 15; 9:11(2x)		ἐπαοιδοί ("magi" who use verbal charms, i.e., "enchanters") 7:11, 22; 8:3, 14,15 φαρμακοί 9:11(2x)	κρυφιασταί 7:11	ἐπαοιδοί 7:11	ἐπαοιδοί 7:11

---

[45]The Hebrew Bible was first translated into Greek from the mid-third century to the late second century B.C.E. (Leonard J. Greenspoon, "Versions, Ancient [Greek]," *ABD* 6:793). The Pentateuch received the earliest attention, the translation of which the *Letter of Aristeas* places during the reign of Ptolemy II Philadelphus (285–247 B.C.E.). Textual and lexical evidence combine to corroborate a third century date for the Pentateuch's first translation into Greek (see, J. A. L. Lee, *A Lexical Study of the Septuagint Version of the Pentateuch* [SBLSCS 14; Chico, Calif.: Scholars Press, 1983] 129–44). Daniel was translated into Greek toward the end of the second century B.C.E. shortly after its original composition in Hebrew and Aramaic, the visions of which date to the beginning of the Maccabean period (early II B.C.E.) (John J. Collins, *Daniel: A Commentary on the Book of Daniel* [Hermeneia; Minneapolis: Fortress, 1993] 8–9).

[46]Origen, *Origenis Hexaplorum quae supersunt sive Veterum interpretum graecorum in totum Vetus Testamentum fragmenta*, Friedrich Field, ed. (2 vols.; Oxford: Clarendon Press, 1875). For dates of the early Greek revisions of the Septuagint, see Emanuel Tov, *Textual Criticism of the Hebrew Bible* (Minneapolis: Fortress, 1992) 144–48.

"Chaldeans" and "wise men" also serve in Daniel as collective designations for these professionals.[47] The connection between literacy and occult knowledge in eastern wisdom is found in the grammatical connotations of חרטמים, which the Old Greek captures by ἐξηγηταί, and Theodotian by σοφισταί in the passage from Genesis. From the stories of Joseph, Moses, and Daniel, four of the six terms used of magical practitioners (חכמים, מכשפים, כשׂדים, אשׁפים) have their origins in the Mesopotamian cultures of Assyria and Babylonia. Linguistically, then, the Mesopotamian cultic and occult practices influenced how Hellenistic Judaism interpreted magic and illicit conjurations even when those practices take place in Egypt. The "foreignness" of these professionals derives from their easterness relative to those who contest them.

Table 3: Daniel 1:1–5:31 (Daniel in the Babylonian Court)

Biblical Term	Origin	OG (late II BCE)	A	Σ	Θ
חרטמים Hebrew: 1:20; 2:2 Aramaic: 2:10, 27; 4:4, 6; 5:11		σοφισταί 1:20, 4:18 ἐπαοιδοί 2:2, 27 σοφοί 2:10			ἐπαοιδοί 1:20; 2:2, 10, 27; 4:7, 9, 5:11 σοφοί 4:18
אשׁפים ("conjurer") Hebrew: 1:20; Aramaic: 2:2, 10, 27; 4:4; 5:7, 11, 15	Probable Babylonian loan word from the Assyrian āšipu	φιλόσοφοι ("philosophers") 1:20 μαγοί, 2:10 φαρμακοί, 2:27 (ἐπαοιδοὶ καὶ φαρμακοί 5:7)			μαγοί 1:20; 2:2, 10, 27; 4:7; 5:7, 11, 15
מכשפים Aramaic: 2:2		φαρμακοί 2:2			φαρμακοί 2:2
כשׂדים ("Chaldeans") Hebrew: 2:2, 4 Aramaic: 2:5, 10(2x); 4:4; 5:7, 11	Babylonian Kasdu, via Assyrian Kaldu, Kaldû	Χαλδαῖοι ("Chaldeans") 2:2, 4, 5, 10(2x); 5:7			Χαλδαῖοι 2:2, 4, 5, 10(2x); 4:7; 5:7, 11
חכמים Aramaic: 2:12, 13, 14, 18, 24(2x), 27, 48; 4:3, 15; 5:7, 8, 15		σοφοί 2:12, 27 (5:11) σοφισταί 2:14, 18, 24(2x), 4:8 (ἐπαοιδοί, φάρμακοι, γαζαρηνοί 5:8)		σοφοί 2:48	σοφοί 2:12, 13, 14, 18, 24(2x), 27, 48; 4:6, 18; 5:7, 8, 15
גזרין ("determiners" of fate) Aramaic 2:27; 4:4; 5:7, 11		γαζαρηνοί (transliteration of the Aramaic) 2:27; 5:7		θύται ("haruspex") 2:27 (see Jerome's note in Field 2.910.24)	γαζαρηνοί 2:27; 4:7; 5:7, 11 (15)

To these passages we can add the prohibitions against magic cited in footnote 1 above:

---

[47]Dan 2:1–49; 4:7.

Table 4: Magical Practices Prohibited in the Hebrew Bible

Biblical Term	Origin	OG	A	Σ	Θ
נחש ("divine" by omens) Lev 19:26; Deut 18:10; 2 Kgs 17:17; 21:6; 2 Chr 33:6		οἰωνίζεσθαι ("take omens from birds") Lev 19:26; Deut 18:10; 2 Kgs 17:17; 21:6; 2 Chr 33:6	κληδονίζεσθαι ("to divine") Lev 19:26		
ענן ("practice soothsaying") Lev 19:26, Deut 18:10; 2 Kgs 21:6; 2 Chr 33:6		ὀρνιθοσκοπήσεσθαι ("take omens from birds") Lev 19:26 κληδονίζεσθαι Deut 18:10; 2 Kgs 21:6; 2 Chr 33:6			
אוב (communication with "spirit of the dead," thus "necromancer") Lev 19:31; 20:6, 27; Deut 18:11; 1 Sam 28:9; 2 Kgs 21:6; 23:24; 2 Chr 33:6 שאל אוב ("seek oracles") Deut 18:11	cf. Assyrian massaku sa sa'ili ("skin- vessel of the oracle-seeker")	θελητής "wizard," lit. "one who wills" 2 Kgs 21:6; 23:24 ἐγγαστρίμυθοι ("one who delivers oracles through ventriloquism") Lev 19:31; 20:6, 27; Deut 18:11; 1 Sam 28:9; 2 Chr 33:6			
ידעני (communication with "familiar spirit") Lev 19:31; 20:6, 27; Deut 18:11; 1 Sam 28:9; 2 Kgs 21:6; 23:24; 2 Chr 33:6		τερατοσκόπος ("diviner through signs") Deut 18:11 γνώστης, ("diviner," lit. "one who knows"), 2 Kgs 21:6 γνωρισταί, ("diviners") 2 Kgs 23:24 ἐπαοιδοί, Lev 19:31; 20:6, 27; 1 Sam 28:9; 2 Chr 33:6			
קסם ("practice divination") Deut 18:10; 1 Sam 15:23; 2 Kgs 17:17		μαντεύεσθαι ("to divine") Deut 18:10; 2 Kgs 17:17 οἰώνισμα ("omen from birds") 1 Sam 15:23			
כשף ("practice sorcery") Deut 18:10; 2 Chr 33:6 מכשפה "sorceress" Exod 22:18 (17)	fr. Assyrian kaššāpu	φαρμακός Exod 22:17; Deut 18:10 φαρμακεύειν 2 Chr 33:6			
חבר ("bind" by a spell) Deut 18:11	cf. Assyrian ubburu	ἐπαείδειν Deut 18:11			
דרש אל־המתים ("necromance," lit. "inquire of the dead") Deut 18:11		ἐπερωτῶν τοὺς νεκρούς Deut 18:11			

Compared to the stock characters used in the above stories, as legal and practical guides these prohibitions give more detail to the proscribed activities.

This chart shows that the illicit practices all have comparable translation values in the Old Greek without recourse to transliterations or borrowed words.

These passages reveal the terms that expressed a negative view of magical practices in Jewish (and then Christian) circles during the Hellenistic and Roman periods. What we see in the above tables is a variety of often interchangeable translation values for the Hebrew and Aramaic terms. We should note, though, that the Hebrew and Aramaic are themselves importing these professions into polemical contexts. Even though Joseph and Daniel eventually replace the indigenous wise men in the royal courts by reason of their greater aptitude at the same skills, the Bible still views negatively the professions at which they excel. This is seen in the promiscuous use of terms to identify the Babylonian wise men as *aššaphim* (אשפים) and *məkaššəphîm* (מכשפים) in Daniel. These terms derive from the names for two different practitioners in ancient Mesopotamia: the one the legitimate *āšipu*, the other the outlawed sorcerer (*kaššāpu*) whose conjurations the *āšipu* sought to thwart. The origins and specifics of the terms may have been lost on the writer of Daniel, but the very variety of terms used would indicate an effort on the author's part universally to discredit Babylonia's learned elite.

3.3 Possession and Exorcism in the Jewish Pseudepigrapha

Demonology and the practice of exorcism become more pronounced in content as well as semantics in other Jewish intertestamental literature. Some of the documents among the Old Testament Pseudepigrapha and the scrolls from the Judean desert, especially in their testaments and apocalypses, provide closer-to-contemporary and contemporary views of possession and exorcism as they occur in the New Testament, and serve as indicators that Near Eastern beliefs and practices had moved into the same Palestinian environment from which the synoptic sources and other New Testament writings were to emerge.[48] The closing two sections of this chapter will deal first with earlier texts included among the Jewish Pseudepigrapha, followed by documents peculiar to Qumran.

---

[48]E.g., from the Old Testament Pseudepigrapha: *1 Enoch, Sibylline Oracles* (especially with regard to divine possession), *Apocalypse of Abraham, Apocalypse of Elijah, Testament of Abraham, Jubilees, Ascension of Isaiah, Life of Adam and Eve, Pseudo-Philo.* E.g., from Qumran: *1QRule of the Community* (1QS), *Damascus Document* (CD), *1QGenesis Apocryphon* (1Q20 20.22, 29), *4QPrayer of Nabonidus* (4Q242), *4QSongs of the Sage* (4Q510–511), *4QAgainst Demons* (4Q560), *11QPsalms^a* (11Q5), *11QApocryphal Psalms^a* (11Q11), *11QMelchizedek* (11Q13).

3.3.1 Possession in Early Jewish Pseudepigrapha

The Old Testament Pseudepigrapha identifies a modern collection of ancient texts that refer back to the figures of the Hebrew biblical tradition.[49] Their dates of original composition range from the third century B.C.E. to the fifth century C.E., with Christian redaction at work from the first through fifth centuries.[50] It is often impossible to determine for some of the texts whether they were originally composed within Jewish or Christian communities. However, for those texts that are decidedly early we gain an insight into Jewish beliefs during the intertestamental period that are not always exhibited in the canonical books, including beliefs about possession and exorcism. This section draws upon texts that are generally believed to have been composed before the Common Era, or within the first century thereof. Texts attributed to a later period (for example, the *Testament of Solomon* and *The Testaments of the Twelve Patriarchs*, which likely are preserved in Christian redaction) will be discussed in the final chapter.

The demonology that developed within Judaism in the late Second Temple period finds clearer expression in the Jewish (early Old Testament) Pseudepigrapha. Here, we find significant portions of texts devoted to explaining the origins and following the activities of demonic and angelic beings alike. Possession of the spirit can simply be a matter of anthropology, the equivalent of the "life giving soul" that animates the human being,[51] but there are also several instances where human thoughts or actions are attributed to foreign spiritual presences. Although only a few passages resonate with demonic possession, some of these suggest it as a bodily affliction similar to its portrayal in the New Testament. Thus, in *1 Enoch* the fallen angel Kasadya (Beqa) is responsible for "flagellations of all evil — of the souls and the demons, the smashing of the embryo in the womb so that it may be crushed,

---

[49]The collection I have referred to for my research is that of James H. Charlesworth, ed., *The Old Testament Pseudepigrapha* (2 vols.; New York: Doubleday, 1985).

[50]James H. Charlesworth, "Pseudepigrapha, OT," *ABD* 5:537–40.

[51]For example, in the Coptic *Apocalypse of Adam* the Lord says to Adam: "Do you not know that I am God who created you, and that I breathed into you a spirit [or "breath"] of life for a living soul?" (*Apoc. Adam* 2.5; trans. G. MacRae, "Apocalypse of Adam," *OTP* 1). The text dates from I to IV C.E. (G. Macrae, "Apocalypse of Adam," *OTP* 1:708). After Death kills Abraham's servants, God "sends upon" (ἀπέστειλεν ... ἐπί) them the spirit of life (*T. Ab.* 18.1–11). The text dates from I to II C.E. (E. P. Sanders, "Testament of Abraham," *OTP* 1:874–75). In *Jubilees* God creates an "upright spirit" for humanity (*Jub.* 1.20, 23). The text dates to II B.C.E. (O. S. Wintermute, "Jubilees," *OTP* 2:43–44). *Pseudo-Phocylides* talks about the spirit (and soul) as being on loan to the body from God (*Ps-Phoc.* 104–115). The text dates from I B.C.E. to I C.E. (P. W. van der Horst, "Pseudo-Phocylides," *OTP* 2:567–68). Compare the soul's place in the body (*Apoc. Sedr.* 9.1–10.4). From the biblical Apocrypha, cf. also how the "spirit" or "soul" is given to the body by God, and departs the body after death (4 Ezra 7:75–101).

the flagellation of the soul, snake bites, sunstrokes, ..."[52] In *3 Baruch* the angel Michael includes among the plagues to bring against humanity the punishment of besetting "their children with demons" (τὰ τέκνα αὐτῶν ἐν δαιμονίοις).[53] Animals also become demonically possessed in the Jewish Pseudepigrapha, as when the devil uses the serpent as a "vessel" (σκεῦος) for deceiving Eve.[54] This shows manipulation of one's body by the possessing spirit for purposes of deceit.[55]

In addition to demonic possession, beneficent possession by the divinity also appears in the Jewish Pseudepigrapha. Some of the language describes divine "possession" as an external influence upon the person, as when the spirit of truth "descends upon" Rebecca and gives her the words to bless Jacob;[56] a spirit of prophecy "comes down upon" the mouth of Levi;[57] the spirit of the Lord is "with" Joseph,[58] or "upon" (בו; ἐπί) him;[59] the Spirit of God "came upon" (*incidit in*) Miriam to cause her to see a prophetic dream;[60] Kenaz "was clothed" (*indutus est*) with a spirit of power that enables him to defeat his enemies.[61] Beneficent spiritual attention also recurs as the inspiration for prophecy. Thus, a beneficent spirit that is "poured over"

---

[52] *1 En.* 69.12. The composite text of *1 Enoch* dates from III B.C.E. to I C.E. This section falls within the "Similitudes," which date from ca. the second half I B.C.E. to ca. 75 C.E. (George W. E. Nickelsburg, "Enoch, First Book of," *ABD* 2:512–13).

[53] *3 Bar.* 16.3 (Greek) (Greek in *PVTG* 2). The Slavonic version translates "bring them ... demons to strangle their children" [*3 Bar.* 16.2]). H. E. Gaylord dates *3 Baruch* from the first to third centuries C.E. (H. E. Gaylord, "3 [Greek Apocalypse of] Baruch," *OTP* 1:655–66). Compare the afflictions against children by demons in *T. Sol.* 1.1–13; 9.1–7; 18.25.

[54] The *Life of Adam and Eve* has the words, "Do not fear; only become my vessel, and I will speak a word through your mouth by which you will be able to deceive him" (*LAE* 16.5; 17.4). The devil also speaks through Eve to deceive Adam (21.3). Later in the text Seth drives off the serpent with words of rebuke similar to those found in exorcism (*LAE* 39.1–3). M. D. Johnson dates this text to I C.E. (M. D. Johnson, "Life of Adam and Eve,"*OTP* 2:252). Compare where Samael or the devil "took the serpent as a garment" (*3 Bar.* 9.7).

[55] In the late Old Testament Pseudepigrapha this is used in an allegorical fashion, where the Antichrist is said to enter a small fish. By this means the Antichrist then infiltrates the Christian community: caught by the twelve fisherman, Judas receives the fish and sells it for thirty pieces of silver to a young maiden, who becomes impregnated by it, and gives birth to the Antichrist (*Apoc. Dan.* 9.2–13). The *Apocalypse of Daniel* dates to ca. IX C.E. (G. T. Zervos, "Apocalypse of Daniel," *OTP* 1:756–57).

[56] *Jub.* 25.14. The text of *Jubilees* is preserved in Ethiopic, for which I have referred to the translation by O. S. Wintermute, "Jubilees," *OTP* 2:35–142.

[57] *Jub.* 31.12.

[58] *Jub.* 40.5.

[59] *Jos. Asen.* 4.7. The text dates from I B.C.E. to II C.E. (C. Burchard, "Joseph and Aseneth," *OTP* 2:187–88).

[60] *Ps-Philo* 9.10. The text dates to the first century C.E. (D. J. Harrington, "Pseudo-Philo," *OTP* 2:299).

[61] *Ps-Philo* 27.10. In this same passage divine assistance also takes the form of helping angels.

Enoch enables him to foresee the future for Methuselah;[62] divine possession describes the prophetic ecstasy of the prophetess in the *Sibylline Oracles*;[63] a holy spirit "dwells in" (*habitans in*) Kenaz,[64] and another "abides in" (*mansit ... in*) Saul to cause each to prophesy.[65]

Other passages grant more interiority to divine possession. We see this in the generous endowments of what is commendable in humanity, such as the spirits of wisdom, thoughtfulness, knowledge and strength bestowed upon the Elect One of the Lord of the Spirits.[66] In an early *Sibylline Oracle* the Sibyl says that God will "dwell in" (ἐν σοί ... οἰκήσει) the maiden.[67] This increasing emphasis on indwelling possession relates possession language to a context not so much concerned with physical afflictions, but with ethical decision making. From the second century B.C.E., *Jubilees* uses the language of the evil "inclination" (יצר [*yetzer*]) to convey an idea of deceitfulness.[68] Within this internal context demonic and divine possession become to some extent correlated either as competing forces that exist simultaneously within the human body, or as presences whose polarities force the other to depart. In

---

[62]*1 En.* 91.1. This verse falls within the "Testamentary Narrative" of Ethiopic *1 Enoch*, which dates to II B.C.E. (Nickelsburg, "Enoch," *ABD* 2:511–12). I have refered to the translation by E. Isaac, "1 (Ethiopic Apocalypse of) Enoch," *OTP* 1:5–89.

[63]See especially the onsets of prophecy experienced by the Sibyl, and her wearied pleas for rest at their conclusions (*Sib. Or.* 2.4–5; 3.1–7; 3.489–91; 4.18–23). *Sibylline Oracles 1* and *2* date to the turn of the Common Era, with Christian redaction likely between 70 to 150 C.E. (J. J. Collins, "The Sibylline Oracles, Books 1 and 2," *OTP* 1:331–32). The fourth oracle dates to the early Hellenistic period, with Christian redaction at ca. 80 C.E. (J. J. Collins, "The Sibylline Oracles, Book 4," *OTP* 1:381–82). Compare where the Sibyl suspects some will interpret her negatively as "a messenger with frenzied spirit" (*Sib. Or.* 11.315–18). The eleventh oracle dates to ca. the turn of the Common Era (J. J. Collins, "The Sibylline Oracles, Book 11," *OTP* 1:430–32).

[64]*Ps.-Philo* 28.6.

[65]*Ps-Philo* 62.2.

[66]*1 En.* 49.1–4 ("Similitudes," ca. second half I B.C.E. to ca. 75 C.E.). Compare also 4 Ezra 5:22–23.

[67]*Sib. Or.* 3.787. The oracle dates to mid II B.C.E. (J. J. Collins, "The Sibylline Oracles, Book 3," *OTP* 1:354–55). Compare how the Virgin receives God into her bosom by inspiring the words spoken by the archangel Gabriel (*Sib. Or.* 8.460–69). The oracle dates toward the end of the second century C.E. (J. J. Collins, "The Sibylline Oracles, Book 8," *OTP* 1:416–17). The later *Apocalypse of Sedrach* says that divine love "dwelt in the heart of Abel ... it made David the dwelling place of the Holy Spirit" (ἠκόνησεν ἐν τῇ καρδίᾳ τοῦ Ἀβέλ ... αὐτὴ τὸν Δαυὶδ οἰκητήριον τοῦ ἁγίου πνεύματος ἐποίησεν) (*Apoc. Sedr.* 1.18; trans. S. Agourides, "Apocalypse of Sedrach," *OTP* 1.609). In the same text the divine spirit causes one to seek baptism (*Apoc. Sedr.* 14.5).

[68]*Jub.* 35.9. For the dating of *Jubilees* to II B.C.E., see James C. VanderKam, "Jubilees, Book of," *ADB* 3.1030–31. Of related interest is the reference in the apocryphal 4 Ezra to the "evil heart" (*cor malignum*), also called the "evil of the root" (*malignitas radicis*), implanted first in Adam, and made a "permanent disease" (*permanens infirmitas*) of his descendants (4 Ezra 3:20–27). This evil heart causes God's people to trangress the laws.

this latter context the good or evil inclination of the individual helps to determine which corresponding force shall reside within.

3.3.2 Exorcism in Early Jewish Pseudepigrapha

Evidence of exorcism in the early Jewish Pseudepigrapha is elusive. Although references to exorcism do occur in some of the later documents (often with apparent allusion to Jesus),[69] only hints of such practice appear in the earlier texts. *1 Enoch* is one such source. There, on the one hand, "magical medicine, incantations, the cutting of roots, and knowledge of plants" are taught by the rebellious angels to women, which suggests the more illicit forms of conjuration.[70] On the other hand, Enoch himself learns from the Holy and Great One "the word of understanding so that I may reprimand the Watchers, the children of heaven."[71] Later in the book, Enoch hears in his vision the angel Phanuel "expelling the demons and forbidding them from coming to the Lord of the Spirits in order to accuse those who dwell upon the earth."[72] Exorcism also appears to lie behind Michael's acquisition of the secret name of Beqa, a fallen angel responsible for various physical afflictions; a name that causes all the distresses he arouses to tremble when used in an oath.[73] It is a knowledge that Michael then passes on to humanity.

---

[69]E.g., *T. Adam* 3.1. The text dates from II to V C.E. (S. E. Robinson, "Testament of Adam," *OTP* 1.990). In the *Apocalypse of Elijah* (I to IV C.E.), Elijah says of the benefits of the fasting done by one who is pure: "It releases sin./ It heals diseases./ It casts out demons./ It is effective up to the throne of God for an ointment and for a release from sin by means of a pure prayer" (*Apoc. El.* 1.21–22; trans. O. S. Wintermute, "Apocalypse of Elijah," *OTP* 1). Though extant in its entirety only in Coptic, the apocalypse is considered to have been composed in Greek (Wintermute, "Apocalypse of Elijah," *OTP* 1:729). Compare the *Testament of Jacob*'s " ... do not slacken from prayer and fasting ever at any time, and by the life of the religion you will drive away the demons" (*T. Jac.* 7.17). W. F. Stinespring dates the work, extant in Arabic, Coptic and Ethiopic, to ca. II–III C.E. (W. F. Stinespring, "Testament of Jacob," *OTP* 1:913). This apocalypse mentions exorcism again as one of the signs performed by the antichrist, "the son of lawlessness" (*Apoc. El.* 3.10). Compare the Beelzeboul controversy, and the house divided against itself in the New Testament (Matt 12:22–30; 9:32–34; Mark 3:22–27; Luke 11:14–15, 17–23).

[70]φαρμακείας καὶ ἐπαοιδὰς καὶ ῥίζοτομίας καὶ τὰς βοτάνας (*1 En.* 7.1–8.4; cf. 4Q201, 4Q202). This section falls within the "Book of the Watchers," dated to the second half of the third century B.C.E. (Nickelsburg, "Enoch," 509).

[71]ἔδωκεν ἐλέγξασθαι ἐγρηγόρους τοὺς υἱοὺς τοῦ οὐρανοῦ (*1 En.* 14.3 ["Book of Watchers," second half III B.C.E.]; trans. E. Isaac, "1 [Ethiopic Apocalypse of] Enoch," *OTP* 1.20). Isaac notes that the text may be corrupt. Manuscripts B and C offer the reading: "As he has created man and given him the word of understanding, and likewise he has created me and given me the (authority of) reprimanding" (Isaac, "1 [Ethiopic Apocalypse of] Enoch," *OTP* 1.20, note 14.b).

[72]*1 En.* 40.7 ("Similitudes," second half I B.C.E. to ca. 75 C.E.; trans. Isaac, *OTP* 1).

[73]*1 En.* 69.12–15 ("Similitudes," second half I B.C.E. to ca. 75 C.E.).

The instruction that Michael gives in *1 Enoch* evokes comparison with the instruction involved in conjuration seen earlier in the Ea-Marduk, Enki-Asalluḫi dialogues of *Šurpu*. A similar instruction is seen in a passage from the *Apocalypse of Abraham* (I–II C.E.), where Abraham recalls from his vision how the angel Iaoel advised him to deal with the evil angel Azazel:

> Say to him, "May you be the firebrand of the furnace of the earth! Go, Azazel, into the untrodden parts of the earth. For your heritage is over those who are with you, with the stars and with the men born by the clouds, whose portion you are, indeed they exist through your being. Enmity is for you a pious act. Therefore through your own destruction be gone from me!" And I said the words as the angel had taught me.[74]

This passage contains the elements of knowing the demon's name, identifying its offences, and commanding it to depart. The preceding section also contains the element of discovery, where Abraham, perplexed at the presence of an unclean bird that speaks to him, learns that its name is Azazel. These are all features found in the diagnosis and treatment of spiritual afflictions in earlier Near Eastern *āšiputu*, and which will re-emerge in the exorcisms of the first centuries Common Era.[75]

3.4 Possession and Exorcism in the Dead Sea Scrolls

Most of the texts from Qumran represent books from the Hebrew Bible, Septuagint, and Jewish Pseudepigrapha. Since the manuscripts found there range in date from III B.C.E. to I C.E., their discovery testifies to the early origins of some of the pseudepigrapha. Since the language of demonic possession also occurs in some of Qumran's sectarian writings, their discussion in the closing sections of this chapter will add further insight into

---

[74]*Apoc. Ab.* 14.5–8; trans. R. Rubinkiewicz, "Apocalypse of Abraham," *OTP* 1.695–696. The apocalypse is preserved only in Old Slavonic. Compare also Noah's prayer to God to relieve his children from the sufferings caused by the evil spirits led by Mastema. God commanded nine-tenths of the spirits to be bound, and the rest were allowed to roam the earth under Satan's power. To counter the hardships they bring to humanity the angels taught Noah the pharmacopoeia necessary to deal with them. Noah wrote the teachings in a book, which he then handed down to his son Shem (*Jub.* 10.1–14).

[75]In the New Testament, the story of the Gerasene demoniac involves first a command to the unclean spirit to depart, then a discovery of its name "Legion" (Mark 5:6–13). In the case of the possessed boy, the discovery consists of Jesus learning the demon's activities from the boy's father, and then in his rebuke of the demon that identifies its destructive activities: "You spirit that keeps this boy from speaking and hearing ..." (Mark 9:14–29).

the beliefs in possession and exorcism that circulated in Judaism during the intertestamental period.[76]

3.4.1 Possession in the Dead Sea Scrolls

The sectarian texts from Qumran make occasional references to spiritual afflictions that affect the physical body.[77] But, as with the contemporary pseudepigrapha, the language of demonic possession tends to be associated with ethical behavior. From the *Community Rule* we read, "I will not keep Belial within my heart" (בליעל לוא אשמור בלבבי).[78] From the *Hymns* a spirit of degeneracy "rules over" (משל) one,[79] and "Belial is manifest in their (evil) inclination" (בליעל עם הופע יצר).[80] The concern for inner purity is evident in this passage from the *Psalms*:

Lord, cleanse me from the evil plague, and let it not return to me. Dry up its roots within me, and permit not its leaves to flourish in me.[81]

This passage also resembles the returning demon in the parable told by Jesus (Matt 12:43–45; Luke 11:24–26), and it is in this context of ethical possession that one can explain the eventual application of exorcism to Christian initiation. We find a good illustration of both physical and ethical influence upon the human being by demonic forces in another passage from the *Psalms* from Qumran:

Let not Satan rule over me, nor an evil spirit; let neither pain nor evil purpose take possession of my bones.[82]

---

[76]Unless otherwise noted, Dead Sea Scroll enumerations are from Florentino García Martínez, *The Dead Sea Scrolls Translated. The Qumran Texts in English*, trans. by Wilfred G. E. Watson (2d ed. Leiden: Brill, 1996).

[77]Thus, the phrase "if the spirit enters the head or the beard" (בזקן או {ו} בראש הרוח באה) is important in the regulations concerning ringworm (4Q267 Frag. 9 I. Compare the hymn against demons in the *Apocryphal Psalms*, which says: "those possessed [...] the volunteers of your tr[uth, when Ra]phael heals them." ([הפועו]ים [אשר] /([... שלמ]ם פאל ר[א] נרבי) (11Q11 4.2–3; trans. in García Martínez, *The Dead Sea Scrolls Translated*, 377. Hebrew in DJD 23:198).

[78]1QS 10.21; trans. Geza Vermes, *The Complete Dead Sea Scrolls in English* (New York: Allen Lane/Penguin, 1997) 114.

[79]1QH[a] 5.21.

[80]1QH[a] 15.3; trans. Vermes, *Complete Dead Sea Scrolls*, 275.

[81] סהרני יהוה מנגע רע   ואל יוסף לשוב אלי
יבש שורשיו ממני   ואל ינצו על[ל]ץ בי

(11Q5 24 [Psalm 155] 12–13; trans. Vermes, *Complete Dead Sea Scrolls*, 304. Hebrew in DJD 4:71).

In this psalm, demonic spiritual presences describe both the "physical" and "intentional" aberrations as they occur within the individual. A related concept that recurs in the sectarian texts is that of the good or evil "inclination" (*yetzer*) that draws one towards God or Belial respectively.[83]

If we see "Belial's hand" as possession, then it is in the sense of a possession that affects moral discernment rather than the body, and as that which causes one to stray from the path of righteousness.[84] The same can be said for some of the hymns against demons found at Qumran. In the *Songs of the Sage*, the author writes:

> And I, the Master, proclaim the majesty of his beauty to frighten and ter[rify] all the spirits of the destroying angels and the spirits of the bastards, the demons, Lilith, the howlers (?) and [the yelpers ...] they who strike suddenly to lead astray the spirit of understanding and to appal their heart ...[85]

This is not an exorcism, but it conveys the use of the deity against the demonic hosts. The passage also shows that what the demons affect in this case is not the body, but the mind and its capacity to make sound judgments.

The examples of possession from the Dead Sea Scrolls often juxtapose references to demonic and divine possession in a way that shows how one's life is corrupted or blessed according to how one associates with the two, respectively. The examples of possession we find in these texts include the warring between the spirits of truth and deceit that takes place within the human being.[86] The *Community Rule* offers a clear picture of the spiritual influences upon humanity:

> He has created man to govern the world, and has appointed for him two spirits in which to walk until the time of His visitation: the spirits of truth and injustice. Those born of truth

---

[82]בעויה אל תשלט בי שטן ורוח טמאה מכאוב ויצר רע אל ירשו בעצמי כי אתה (*11QPsalms[a]*) [11Q5 19.15–16]; Hebrew and English in García Martínez, *Dead Sea Scrolls Study Edition*, 2.1174-75).

[83]For the inclinations generally, see 4Q381 Frags. 76–77.2. For the evil *yetzer* see, for example, 4Q370 1.3; 1QH[a] 19.20; 4Q417 Frag. 2 2.12; 6Q18; cf. the "guilty inclination" (יצר אשמחכה) incited by Melki-rasha ("Evil King") 4Q280. For the good inclination see, for example, 4Q417. 4Q416 Frag. 1 refers to the "inclination of the flesh" (יצר בשר).

[84]The "hand of Belial" (יד בליעל) appears in the Dead Sea Scrolls, for example, in *11QMelchizedek* (11Q13) 2.13, 25.

[85]

4 ... ואני משכיל משמיע הוד תפארתו לפחד ולב[ן]הל[

5 כול רוחי מלאכי חבל ורוחות ממזרים שד אים לילית אחים ו[ציים]

6 והפוגעים פתע פתאום לתעות רוח בינה ולהשם לבבם ונ[פשו]הם בקץ ממשל[ת]

7 רשעה ותעודות תעניות בני או[ר] באשמת קצי <נגוע[י]>עוונות ולוא לכלת עולם

8] כי א[ם לקץ תעניות פשע] ...[

(*4QSongs of the Sage[a]* [4Q510] 4–8; trans. Vermes, *Complete Dead Sea Scrolls*, 420. Hebrew in DJD 7.216).

[86]*Community Rule* (1QS 3.6–4.26).

spring from a fountain of light, but those born of injustice spring from a source of darkness. All the children of righteousness are ruled by the Prince of Light and walk in the ways of light, but all the children of injustice are ruled by the Angel of Darkness and walk in the ways of darkness.[87]

This passage is followed in the *Community Rule* by a description of initiation and promotion within the community:

And they shall examine their spirit and deeds yearly, so that each man may be advanced in accordance with his understanding and perfection of way, or moved down in accordance with his distortions.[88]

This sets up the metaphor of the Two Ways doctrine that becomes important in such early Christian texts as the *Didache* and the *Epistle of Barnabas*. Like the *Didache*, the *Community Rule* also puts the conflict in the context of a lustration ritual:

And when his flesh is sprinkled with purifying water and sanctified by cleansing water, it shall be made clean by the humble submission of his soul to all the precepts of God.[89]

God will then purify every deed of man with His truth; He will refine for Himself the human frame by rooting out all spirit of injustice from the bounds of his flesh. He will cleanse him of all wicked deeds with the spirit of holiness; like purifying waters He will shed upon him the spirit of truth (to cleanse him) of all abomination and injustice.[90]

These passages highlight the recurrent association between the spirits in the sectarian texts, in which the two types of possession, demonic and divine, are constantly seen in relation to each other. One's personal vigilance affects which of the two spiritual presences, evil or good, shall prevail within.

---

[87]   17 ... והואה ברא אנוש לממשלת

18 חבל וישם לו שתי רוחות להתהלך בם עד מועד פקודתו הנה רוחות

19 האמת והעול במעון אור תולדות האמת וממקור חושך תולדות העול

20 וביד שר אורים ממשלת כול בני צדק בדרכי אור יתהלכו וביד מלאך

21 חושך כול ממשלת בני עול ובדרכי חושך יתהלכו ...

(1QS 3.17–21; trans. Vermes, *Complete Dead Sea Scrolls*, 101. Hebrew in Florentino García Martínez and Eibert J. C. Tigchelaar, eds., *The Dead Sea Scrolls Study Edition* [2 vols.; Leiden: Brill, 1997] 1.74).

[88] פוקדם את רוחם ומעשיהם שנה בשנה להעלות איש לפי שכלו ותום דרכו ולאחרו כנעוותו (1QS 5.24; trans. Vermes, *Complete Dead Sea Scrolls*, 105. Hebrew in *DSSSE* 1.82).

[89] בשרו להזות במי נדה ולהתקדש במי דוכי ויהכין פעמיו להלכת תמים בכול דרכי אל (1QS 3.9–10; trans. Vermes, *Complete Dead Sea Scrolls*, 101. Hebrew in *DSSSE* 1.74).

[90]   ואז יברר אל באמתו כול מעשי גבר יזקק לו מבני איש להתם כול רוח עולה מחכמי

בשרו ולטהרו ברוח קודש מכול עלילות רשעה ויז עליו רוח אמת כמי נדה מכול תועבות שקר והתגולל

(1QS 4.20–21; trans. Vermes, *Complete Dead Sea Scrolls*, 103. Hebrew in *DSSSE* 1.78).

3.4.2 Exorcism in the Dead Sea Scrolls

There is an interest in conjuration generally at Qumran, which appears to have some relevance to exorcism.[91] The most explicit evidence for the practice of exorcism includes the following passages. In the *Genesis Apocryphon* God sends a "chastizing spirit" (רוח מכדש) to afflict Pharaoh and his household after Pharaoh has taken Sarai from Abraham. Pharaoh asks Abraham to remove the affliction from him:

> "And now pray for me and my house that this evil spirit may be expelled from it." So I prayed [for him] ... and I laid my hands on his [head]; and the scourge departed from him and the evil [spirit] was expelled [from him], and he lived.[92]

From the psalms found at Qumran we learn that David, through the "wise and enlightened spirit" (רוח נבונה ואורה), the "spirit of prophecy" (בנבואה) given by God, created four "songs to be sung over the possessed" (לנגן על הפגועים ושיר).[93] The names of David and Solomon appear in one of these apocryphal exorcistic psalms:

> [Of David. Concerning the words of the spell] in the name of [YHWH ...] [...] of Solomon, and he will invoke [the name of YHWH] [to set him free from every affliction of the sp]irits, of the devils, [Liliths,] [owls and jackals.] These are the devils, and the pri[nce of enm]ity [is Belial,] who [rules] over the abyss [of dark]ness.[94]

---

[91]In the *Damascus Document* the Inspector of the community has among his responsibilities to "undo all the chains which bind [the members of the camp], so that there will be neither harassed nor oppressed in his congregation" (לבלתי היות עשוק ורצוץ בעדתו יתר כל חרצובות קשריהם) (CD-A 13.10; *DSSSE* 1.572–73). Compare also the apotropaic imagery in one of the Hymns that asks God to engrave his commandments within one "so that he can hold himself up against [fiendish] spirits" (חזק מ]... [ר על רוחות) (1QH*a* 4.23; *DSSSE* 1.148–49). Another of the *Hymns* speaks of the spells cast by those allied to Beliar, and "against which there is no incantation" (לאין חבר) (1QH*a* 13.28; *DSSSE* 1.172–73). Further down, the scroll reads "No spirit /host/ can reply to your reproach, no one can stand against your anger" (ואין להשיב על תוכחתכה) (1QH*a* 15.28–29; trans. García Martínez, *Dead Sea Scrolls Translated*. Hebrew in *DSSSE* 1.178).

[92]   וכען צלי עלי ועל ביתי ותתגער מננה רוחא דא באישתא וצליח על [ד]י [ית] רפא
הו וסמכת ידי על [ראי]שה ואתפלי מנה מכתשא ואתגערת [מנה רוחא] באישתא
(1Q20 20.28–29; trans. Vermes, *Complete Dead Sea Scrolls*, 455. Hebrew in *DSSSE* 1.42). Abraham's laying on of hands differs from the New Testament's strictly verbal method of performing exorcisms. The text is discussed in André Dupont-Sommer, "Exorcismes et guérisons dans les écrits de Qoumrân," in J. A. Emerton, ed., *Oxford Congress Volume* (VTSup 7; Leiden: Brill, 1960) 246–53.

[93]*11QPsalms*a* (11Q5 27.9–10); trans. García Martínez, *Dead Sea Scrolls Translated*, 309. Compare 1 Sam 16:14–23.

[94]

[ש]ם[	1]
[ה שלומה] [ויקר]א	2]
הרו[ח]ות] [והשדים]	3]

In *11QMelchizedek* the author interprets Psalm 82:2 ("How long will you judge unjustly and show partiality to the wicked?") as a reference to Belial and his evil spirits.[95] Melchizedek will free those who are oppressed by them.

Another important fragment is the *Hymn against Demons*, which includes references both to indwelling possession and its relief through exorcism.[96] The fragment in its entirety reads:

Col.i
1. ... Beel]zebub, you/to you [...
2. ...the midwife, the punishment of childbearers, an evil visitant, a de[mon ...
3. ... I adjure you all who en]ter into the body, the male Wasting-demon the female Wasting-demon
4. ...I adjure you by the name of YHWH, "He who re]moves iniquity and transgression," O Fever and Chills and Chest Pain
5. ...and forbidden to disturb by night in dreams or by da]y in sleep, the male Shrine-spirit and the female Shrine-spirit, breacher-demons (?) of
6. ... w]icked ... [ ] ... [ ] [ ]
7. ...] ... [ ]
8. ...

Col.ii
1. ...
2. before h[im ...
3. and ...
4. before him and ... [
5. And I, O spirit, adjure [you that you ...
6. I adjure you, O spirit, [that you ...
7. On the earth, in clouds [...
8. ...[97]

---

4 [ ]   [אלה] הש[ ]רים וש[ ]ר המשט[ ]מה
5 [ ]   א[שר] [ל תהו[ם]ך
6 [ ]   [לש] [ ]הגר[ו]ל [ ]והי

(*11QApocryphal Psalms^a* [11Q11] 1.1–6);] trans. García Martínez, *Dead Sea Scrolls Translated*, 376. Hebrew in DJD 23:189).

[95] *11QMelchizedek* (11Q13 2.11–13; *DSSSE* 2.1206-7).

[96] *4Q Against Demons* (4Q560).

[97] Translation by Douglas L. Penny and Michael O. Wise, who record the Aramaic as follows:

Col. I
1 [בעל] דכב לכי [c. 25]
2 [ ] מילרתה מרדות ילרן פקד באיש ש [יד c. 8]
3 [אנה מומה לכ כל] עלל בכשרא לחלחליא דכרא וחלחליתא נקבתא
4 [אנה מומה לכן בשם יהוה הן]שא עוֹאן ופשע אשא ועריה ואשת לבכ
5 [ואסיר לבהלה בליליא בחלמין או ביממ]ה כשנא פרכיא דכרא ופרכיתא נקבתא מחתורי
6 [ ] ר[שיעין ... [c. 6] .. [c. 9] ל [c. 2]...
7 [ ] ... [c. 26]
8 [Note: Col. *ii* 8 implies the existence of col. *i* 8.]

This fragment is significant both for the evidence it brings to the idea of a demon that infiltrates the victim's body (Column I, line 3), and for the role of an adjurer in controlling that demonic presence (Column II). Douglas Penny and Michael Wise see this turn-of-the-era formula from Qumran to stand in continuity with the magical formulae of ancient Mesopotamia, and to fill the "long gap" between those earlier traditions and the magical texts of medieval Judaism.[98]

Finally, the *Prayer of Nabonidus* found at Qumran is an early Midrashic example of a personal, albeit pseudepigraphic, testimony that involves divine healing through human agency.[99] Its five fragments, dated by paleography to 75–50 B.C.E., record the prayer the Babylonian king offered to end the seven-year affliction of a "malignant inflammation" (בשחנא באישא) brought upon him by God. The king credits a Jewish "diviner" (גזר) for having relieved him of his inflammation.[100] The reconstructed text reads:

Fragments 1, 2a, 2b, 3:

1. The words of the p[ra]yer which Nabonidus, king of [Baby]lon, [the great] king, prayed [when he was smitten]
2. with a bad disease by the decree of G[o]d in Teima. [I, Nabonidus, with a bad disease]
3. was smitten for seven years and sin[ce] G[od] set [his face on me, he healed me]

Col.II

] 1

2 קורדמו[הי

] ١ 3

4 קורדמוהי וממ]

5 ואנה רוח מומה]ן לד די

6 אומיתך רוחא] די

7 על ארעא בעננין]

8 [c. 5] ל *vacat* .

(Douglas L. Penny and Michael O. Wise, "By the Power of Beelzebub: An Aramaic Incantation Formula from Qumran [4Q*560*]," *JBL* 113 [1994] 627–50).

[98]Penny and Wise, "By the Power of Beelzebub," 629–31, 649. In this regard, compare also Hans Dieter Betz' treatment of a Jewish maternity spell found among the medieval manuscripts in the Cairo Geniza (Hans Dieter Betz, "Jewish Magic in the Greek Magical Papyri (*PGM* VII.260–71)," in Peter Schäfer and Hans G. Kippenberg, eds., *Envisioning Magic: A Princeton Seminar and Symposium* [Leiden: Brill, 1997] 45–63). Betz finds this spell to have counterparts in the *Greek Magical Papyri,* and to show continuity with ancient Mesopotamian and Egyptian healing magic.

[99]*4QPrayer of Nabonidus ar* (4Q242). The Aramaic of the prayer with translation, textual notes, and commentary is found in John Collins, "Prayer of Nabonidus: 4Q242. 4Q Prayer of Nabonidus ar," in George Brooke et al., *Qumran Cave 4, 17* (DJD 22; Oxford: Clarendon Press, 1996) 83–93.

[100]Nabonidus was Babylonia's last king, who ruled from 556–539 B.C.E. The *Prayer of Nabonidus* contains some elements considered earlier than the parallel legend in Daniel 4, such as the king's name (Daniel's Nebuchadnezzar) and his residence in Teima (Collins, "Prayer of Nabonidus," 85–87).

4. and as for my sin, he remitted it. A diviner (he was a Jew fr[om among the exiles) came to me and said:]
5. 'Pro[cla]im and write to give honour and exal[tatio]n to the name of G[od Most High,' and I wrote as follows:]
6. 'I was smitten by a b[ad] disease in Teima [by the decree of the Most High God.]
7. For seven years [I] was praying [to] the gods of silver and gold, [bronze, iron,]
8. wood, stone, clay, since [I thoug]ht that th[ey were] gods
9.]their[

Fragment 4:
1.]apart from them. I was made strong again
2.]from it he caused to pass. The peace of [my] repo[se returned to me]
3.] my friends. I was not able [
4.]how you are like [
5.] [¹⁰¹

Like the *Hymn against Demons* mentioned above, the *Prayer of Nabonidus* serves as an important reference for the relevance of sinfulness and forgiveness of sins to healing in early Judaism. A point of debate in the reconstruction and reading of the prayer, however, is whether the healer forgives sins as part of his practice, contrary to the biblical and later Jewish records generally that attribute forgiveness of sins to God alone.¹⁰² However, since the prayer can

---

¹⁰¹Fragments 1, 2a, 2b, 3:

1. מלי צ[ל]ל[ח]א די צלי נבני מלך [בב]ל מלכ[א רבא כדי כתיש הוא[
2. בשחנא באישא בפתגם א[לה]א בתימן[אנה נבני בשחנא באישא[
3. כתיש הוית שנין שבע ומן [די] שוי א[להא עלי אנפוהי ואסא לי[
4. וחטאי שבק לה גזר והוא יהודי מ[ן בני גלותא על לי ואמר[
5. החוי וכתב למעבד יקר ור[בו] לשם א[להא עליא וכן כתבת אנה[
6. כתיש הוית בשחנא כ[אישא[בתימן [בפתגם אלהא עליא[
7. שנין שבע מצלא הוי[ת קדם] אלהי כספא ודהבא [נחשא פרזלא[
8. אעא אבנא חספא מן די [הוית סב]ר די אלהין ה[מון
interlinear letters   או   [ד של [
9. ח[ ]מ[יהון[

Fragment 4:

1. [לבר המון אחלמת
2. [מנה אח[ן]ל[ף שלם של[וחי יתוב עלי[
3. [ ][]נו רחמי לא יכלח]
4. [ ]כמה רמא אנתה ל]
5. [ ] [

(Collins, "Prayer of Nabonidus," 88–93).

¹⁰²Dupont-Sommer considers the *Prayer of Nabonidus* to contradict this tradition, for which he refers to *Damascus Document* 13.10 as a parallel witness (Dupont-Sommer, "Exorcismes et guérisons dans les écrits de Qoumrân," 260). In opposition, Émile Puech calls such a reading "a new theological conception, unknown to the Bible and ancient Judaism" (*une conception theologique nouvelle, inconnue de la Bible et du judaïsme ancien*) (Émile Puech, "La prière de Nabonide [4Q242]," in R. J. Cathcart and M. Maher, eds.,

plausibly be read in a way that allows forgiveness to come from God rather than the Jewish diviner, so that it remains consistent with its contemporary texts, this is the reading followed here.[103] In the *Prayer of Nabonidus*, as in the Mesopotamian *Šurpu* ritual, appeasement and healing are results facilitated by the healer's divination, but ultimately granted by the divinity.

Together with the *Genesis Apocryphon*, André Dupont-Sommer cites the *Prayer of Nabonidus* as evidence for exorcism in the sectarian texts found at Qumran.[104] Based in part upon later usage of the verb *g^ezar* in the Talmud and various Armenian and Mandean magical texts where it has the sense of "to pronounce a conjuration," Dupont-Sommer interprets the Aramaic term (גזר — frag. 1, line 4) as "conjurer" or "exorcist," and he finds analogy for the *gāzzar* in the *āšipu* or *mašmašu*.[105] Although Dupont-Sommer's argument has found some acceptance in the scholarly community,[106] scant corroborating attestation of the noun in Aramaic, aggravated by the fragmentary state of the prayer itself, discourages such a precise translation. Nor did early translators of the term into Greek, several of whom did their work at a time when exorcism had otherwise begun to establish itself as a subject of contemporary Greek literature, suggest exorcism in their interpretations of *gāzzar*. The very transliteration of the term in the Old Greek and Theodotianic versions of the Septuagint would suggest either an assumption of currency for the Aramaic term that would have rendered translation unnecessary for contemporary readers, or an obscurity of its meaning to the minds of the translators. The rarity of the term lends support to the latter.[107]

Targumic and Cognate Studies: Essays in Honour of Martin McNamara [Sheffield: Sheffield University Press, 1996] 216).

[103]Collins, whose translation of this line follows the interpretations of Pierre Grelot, Frank Moore Cross, and Puech, notes that "if God is restored as the subject of שרי in line 3, he is also the most likely subject in line 4" (Collins, "Prayer of Nabonidus," 90).

[104]Dupont-Sommer, "Exorcismes et guérisons dans les écrits de Qoumrân," 246–61.

[105]Dupont-Sommer, "Exorcismes et guérisons," 257–58 (following Guiseppe Furlani on *g^ezar*).

[106]Dupont-Sommer's interpretation of "exorcist" has been followed recently, e.g., by Florentino García Martínez and Eibert J. C. Tigchelaar, who reconstruct and translate line 4 of the first set of fragments: "and an exorcist forgave my sin. He was a Je[w] fr[om the exiles who said to me ...]" (וחטאי שבק לה גזר והוא] גבר [יהודי מן בני גלותא והוא אמר לי]) (García Martínez and Tigchelaar, *The Dead Sea Scrolls Study Edition*, 1:486–87).

[107]The Aramaic term גזר appears in the LXX at Daniel 2:27; 4:4; 5:7, 11 (OG 2:27; 5:7; Θ 2:27; 4:7; 5:7, 11). The Brown, Driver, Briggs' *Hebrew and English Lexicon of the Old Testament* (Oxford: Clarendon Press, 1951) lists the usages of the verb as "to cut (divide), determine," and defines the plural absolute derived therefrom as "determiners" (of fate). The noun first appears in Greek as a transliteration in the OG and Θ versions of the LXX (γαζαρηνοί, see LXX chart above). The subsequent appearances, all among patristic writers, refer to Babylonian wise men, mostly in the context of Daniel. The verb's two senses of "to cut" and "to determine" appear to combine in those who performed sacrifices for the sake of divination. Symmachus (ca. II–III C.E.) appears to think so, at least, when he translates the

Unlike the *Genesis Apocryphon*, a demonic agent also is not explicitly evident in the *Prayer of Nabonidus*, and its relevance to exorcism must come from importing to the fragmented text the demonically inspired character of the illness that is here otherwise attributed to God.[108] The context of the prayer does, however, reveal the *gāzzar*'s role in attributing the origin of the king's healing to the God Most High and his prescription of praise to that God. Though the practice of diagnosis and prescription place the *gāzzar* in the company of the eastern magi, elsewhere in Jewish literature the distinctive healing and divination arts of the Mesopotamian cultures tend to serve merely as similes for the collective wisdom of the Babylonian sages. The extent to which we can expect the author of the prayer to have had an other than generic profession in mind for the *gāzzar* remains uncertain. In the initial publication of the text, J. T. Milik translated the Aramaic *gāzzar* into French as "*devin*" ("diviner"),[109] an interpretation reflected in John Collins' translation given above. The generality that "diviner" brings to the passage is also preferred in this study since it remains true to the extant context while it does not preclude the possibility for greater specificity that "exorcist" requires. What the author's use of *gāzzar* does provide, however, is a favorable view of magian practice in Jewish circles. The fragments also show how the diviner acts as a missionary to other cultures, in this case from Jewish to Babylonian, and through his success validates and publicizes his own beliefs. These are factors also apparent in the work of Christian exorcists active in the western half of the Roman Empire during the first centuries of the Common Era.

---

term as θύται for his Greek speaking audience (see LXX chart above). On the basis of the range of usages for the Aramaic verb, θύται appears to be an apt rendering, as it, too, captures a similar duality of divination and sacrifice in Greek; cf. a passage from Appian (II C.E.): "When [Cornelius Scipio] arrived he expelled all traders and harlots; also the soothsayers and diviners (θύτας), whom the soldiers were continually consulting because they were demoralized by defeat. For the future he forbade the bringing in of anything not necessary, even a victim for purposes of divination." ('Ελθὼν δὲ ἐμπόρους τε πάντας ἐξήλαυνε καὶ ἑταίρας καὶ μάντεις καὶ θύτας, οἷς διὰ τὰς δυσπραξίας οἱ στρατιῶται περιδεεῖς γεγονότες ἐχρῶντο συνεχῶς· ἔς τε τὸ μέλλον ἀπεῖπε μηδὲν ἐσφέρεσθαι τῶν περισσῶν, μηδὲ ἱερεῖον ἐς μαντείαν πεποιημένον.) (Appian, *Hisp.* 85. English translation in Appian, *Roman History*, translated by Horace White [4 vols. LCL; New York: MacMillan, 1912–1913]). Although the fragmentary *Prayer of Nabonidus* does not detail the Jewish healer's method, his use of divination to determine the cause and cure of maladies is consistent with ancient Near Eastern healing practices generally, as seen in Chapter 1.

[108]*4QPrayer of Nabonidus ar* (4Q242), fragments 1–3, lines 2 and 6.

[109]J. T. Milik, "'Prière de Nabonide' et autres écrits d'un cycle de Daniel," *RB* 63 (1956) 407–11.

3.5 Conclusion

The Hebrew Bible and intertestamental writings offer evidence of changing cultural values within Judaism. The intertestamental literature begins to articulate a dualistic framework of opposing hierarchical spiritual powers. This change in perception of the spirit-world allows for the development of human mediaries who could solicit divine assistance to deal with the burgeoning host of demons. With the attribution of such acts as exorcism to revered figures in Israel's past, the magical arts that the Hebrew Bible initially condemned were in time accepted and claimed as part of the Jewish heritage. Literature from the intertestamental period also develops the association of spiritual possession with ethical concerns, which the Qumran texts illustrate by means of the "Two Ways" metaphor. It is an association and metaphor that would recur significantly in early Christian literature.

Possession and the Treatment of the Possessed in Early Greece

4.1 Introduction

Chapters 2 and 3 provided an overview of possession and exorcism in the ancient Near East, including the milieu of hellenistic Palestine. Chapter 4 presents evidence for spiritual possession and exorcism in Greek society prior to the Common Era. The exorcisms and cases of possession that appear in the New Testament have helped to structure the emphases in this chapter: as prophecy, physical illness, and madness pertain to demonic possession and exorcism in the New Testament, their pertinance is also studied relative to spiritual possession in Greek society. Chapter 4 begins with a discussion of possession as it occurs in the early Greek sources. After first identifying the possessing entities, the manifestations of possession are then discussed with attention paid both to beneficent possession, with particular interest in prophetic inspiration, and to maleficent possession, with particular interest in madness as its most salient form. The chapter concludes with a discussion of the treatment for cases of maleficent possession. Specifically, it discusses bondage of the afflicted, medical and cultic healing, and purificatory treatments for the possessed.

4.2 Possession in Early Greece

In anticipation of the reception the Christian exorcist would have received in Greek areas of mission it is important to understand how the Greeks perceived demons to interact with human beings before the Common Era. Granted, the Greeks believed in *daimones*, that is, in intermediary beings between mortals and the fully divine gods, that provide a common ground between the Christian missionaries and those whom they wished to convert. But the belief in the indwelling possession of mortals by "foreign" spirits, that is, spirits other than one's own life force, is less well documented. Wesley D. Smith went so far as to claim that the New Testament's portrayals of demonic possession have no precise correspondent in earlier Greek literary sources.[1] In so doing, he challenged the evidence brought forth early-on by Julius Tambornino,[2] and reaffirmed by H. J. Rose,[3] which assumed a continuous belief in demonic possession in early Greek antiquity. Smith argued that, although the Greek accounts show individuals to be affected by spiritual beings, that affectation is virtually always caused by exterior agents; the accounts lack the vivid imagery of spiritual beings that enter into and possess the human body.

Smith was correct in so far as little clear evidence exists in early Greece for the type of demonic possession found in the New Testament. Malevolent *daimones* enter the literary sources as early as the Classical period, but the clearest evidence for the idea that such entities actually possess a human body doesn't begin to accumulate until a much later time, and the examples most often cited for exorcism outside of the New Testament date almost exclusively from the Common Era.[4] A paucity of evidence in the literary sources, however, could be misleading with respect to a society's belief in demonic possession. In his study of demonology in Greek literature, Frederick E. Brenk takes into account demon-belief from Homer to the third century Common Era.[5] Brenk considers that the sophisticated literary traditions "controlled" this belief, and he assumes that a substantial distance existed

---

[1]Wesley D. Smith, "So-Called Possession in Pre-Christian Greece," *TAPA* 96 (1965) 403-26. Earlier, E. R. Dodds, himself following the judgement of Levy-Bruhl, considered *daimonic* interaction with humans as "participation" rather than "possession," whereby humans become instruments of daimonic activity (E. R. Dodds, *The Greeks and the Irrational* [Berkeley: University of California Press, 1964] 40). More recently, Frederick E. Brenk says "… the idea of demons entering a person seems entirely foreign to the Greek intellectual tradition except for Philo who is obviously bending toward accommodation with Jews" (Brenk, "In the Light of the Moon," *ANRW* 2.16.3:2108).

[2]Julius Tambornino, *De antiquorum daemonismo* (RGVV 7.3; Giessen: Alfred Töpelmann, 1909).

[3]H. J. Rose, "Possession," *OCD*[2] 869; Rose's article is a reprint of the *Oxford Classical Dictionary*'s first edition. H. S. Versnel's article in the third edition notes that belief in pathological possession, such as demonic possession, increases in the post-Classical period (H. S. Versnel, "possession, religious," *OCD*[3] 1233).

[4]Thus, Rudolf Bultmann lists as non-Christian exorcisms that parallel those in the New Testament Josephus, *Jewish Antiquities* 8.2.5 (I C.E.), Lucian, *Lover of Lies* 31 (II C.E.), Philostratus, *Life of Apollonius of Tyana* 3.38 and 4.20 (III C.E.), *Pesachim* 112b/113a (Babylonian Talmud, III–IV C.E.) (Rudolf Bultmann, *The History of the Synoptic Tradition* [2nd rev. ed.; New York: Harper & Row, 1968] 231). Smith considers the first example of a pagan exorcism to appear in Lucian's *Lover of Lies* 16 (Smith, "So-Called Possession," *TAPA* 96 (1965) 409).

[5]Brenk, "In the Light of the Moon," *ANRW* 2.16.3:2068–145.

between the demonology described there and the largely undocumented folk belief.[6]

Brenk's view is helpful in explaining the lack of evidence for exorcism in early Greece, and any evidence of folk belief would be of great relevance to the social reception of Christianity. The lack of such evidence, however, reduces the value of any conclusions based upon it. Suffice it to say that, should one find examples of spiritual possession in the literary sources, rather than recording the idiosyncratic thoughts of a given author such references could draw from a well of popular belief. The sources to which I have looked for evidence of possession are tragedy and history for their portrayals of possession in mythical and social contexts respectively, oratory for its rhetorical use of possession language, and philosophy for its theories about *daimones*. The sources are diverse and abundant, but each type of literature has relevance to the cultural environment into which the Christian exorcist would tread.

4.2.1 Possessing Entities

The distinction between possession by an interior agent versus oppression by an exterior one is important in Christian thought. Whereas one's integrity of self remains intact in cases of oppression, in possession one's autonomy becomes compromised. The one possessed assumes the identity of the foreign spiritual presence, so as to become the agent of the foreign spirit's will, or his or her own will is joined into allegiance with the possessing entity. Further, what one believes about demons dictates what one does with them.[7] Exorcism in the New Testament sense of casting out a maleficent indwelling spirit becomes an option when one believes that spirits are not only capable of possessing the body, but are also hostile and thus worthy of being driven out.

Compelling examples of physical possession do appear in the literary sources, but the agents of possession are not "demonic" in the sense of the

---

[6]Brenk says on the matter: "What we have from the early Imperial period is a combination of philosophical literature, generally with reference to Plato and other earlier sources, or bits and pieces of popular belief. How accurate it is to judge from what remains is difficult to say. However, it does seem possible to deduce that philosophical authors treated the matter of demonology with some hesitancy and as an area where there was great latitude of both belief and scepticism" (Brenk, "In the Light of the Moon," *ANRW* 2.16.3:2140).

[7]For example, see Hans Dieter Betz, "Jewish Magic in the Greek Magical Papyri (*PGM* 7.260–71)," in which Betz compares Jewish, pagan Greek, and Christian iatromagical spells for the treatment of the uterus, and shows how the treatment employed by each follows their respective theological and mythological frameworks. The same extends to Greek Hippocratic medicine, which overtly treats ailments according to a philosophy of natural disorder resolved by natural therapy contrary to the apotropeic and exorcistic methods of the ancient Near Eastern, Egyptian, Jewish and Christian interpretations (Betz, "Jewish Magic," 59–60).

malicious spirits one finds in the exorcism stories of the New Testament.[8] Instead, the cases of possession that present themselves in Greek literature before the Common Era are cases of divine possession, or possession by a lesser spirit in the service of some divinity. The following section introduces some of the categories of possessing entities, and looks first at the gods, then at the intermediary spirits identified most generally by the term *daimon*, and the more specific category of avenging spirits such as the *alastor*. A closing section discusses the contribution of the Erinyes to the iconography of demons if not to possession per se.

4.2.1.1 The Gods

The Greek tragedians make several explicit references to deities as possessing agents who occupy a mortal's body. The extant plays and fragments of Sophocles make known Eros,[9] Dionysus,[10] and perhaps Ares[11] as possessing

---

[8]Even the Erinyes (literally "the Curses," or "Angry Ones"), who as avenging deities would appear to be hostile, also have the potential for blessing. In Aeschylus' *Eumenides* ("Kindly Ones") the Erinyes vow not to dishonor Athens if they should receive a shrine. In addition, they pray for good harvests, abundant flocks, civil accord for the state, and long lives for its inhabitants (Aeschylus, *Eum.* 916–87). Cf. Ἀραί ("Curses") at Aeschylus *Eum.* 415–17 with Σεμναί ("Venerable Ones") at line 1041 (cf. Pausanias 1.28.6; 2.11.4). The Erinyes were also called *Ablabiai* ("Harmless"), all of which could be construed as euphemisms since the descriptions of their actions virtually always describe their vengeful side (H. J. Rose and B. C. Dietrich, "Erinyes," *OCD*[3] 406–7). The flexibility of the spirits and deities from vengeful to appeased, and likewise of the wrongdoer's own status from impure to pure, is seen in the Selinous *lex sacra* where prior to purification the guilty party offers sacrifices to the "impure Tritopatores" (τοῖς μιαροῦς Τριτοπάτορες), and after performing the requisite cathartic rituals concludes the ceremony with a sacrifice to the now pure Tritopatores (τοῖς καθαροῖς Τριτοπάτορες) (Column A) (Michael H. Jameson et al., *A Lex Sacra from Selinous* [GRBM 11; Durham, N.C.: Duke University, 1993]).

[9]Of Eros the chorus in *Antigone* says: "the one who has [you] is mad" (ὁ δ᾽ ἔχων μέμηνεν — Sophocles, *Ant.* 790). A fragment from the *Phaedra* also records Eros' all pervading influence: "For Love comes not only upon (ἐπέρχεται) men and women, but troubles the minds even of the gods in the sky, and comes upon the sea. And not even the all-powerful Zeus can keep him off, but he too yields and willingly gives way."

> (Ἔρως γὰρ ἄνδρας οὐ μόνους ἐπέρχεται
> οὐδ᾽ αὖ γυναῖκας, ἀλλὰ καὶ θεῶν ἄνω
> ψυχὰς ταράσσει κἀπὶ πόντον ἔρχεται·
> καὶ τόνδ᾽ ἀπείργειν οὐδ᾽ ὁ παγκρατὴς σθένει
> Ζεύς, ἀλλ᾽ ὑπείκει καὶ θέλων ἐγκλίνεται).

(Sophocles, *Phaedra* frag. 684. English translation in *Sophocles*, translated by Hugh Lloyd-Jones [3 vols. LCL; Cambridge: Harvard University Press, 1994–1996]).

[10]In *Antigone* the chorus reminds the audience that Dionysus brought madness (μανία) upon Lycurgus as retribution for his having tried to subdue the bacchic-fevered Maenads (Sophocles, *Ant.* 955–65).

[11]In *Oedipus at Colonus* Oedipus says that Ares has sown (ἐμβεβληκότα) a mutual hatred into the minds of his sons Polynices and Eteocles (Sophocles, *Oed. Col.* 1389–92).

deities. In a Sophoclean fragment, Aphrodite is also said to possess. Her pervasiveness enters into the bodies of human beings and animals alike, and even of the gods:

> For she sinks into the vitals of all that have life ... She enters into the swimming race of fishes, she is within the four-legged brood upon dry land, and her wing ranges among birds ... among beasts, among mortals, among the race of gods above ... she rules over the heart of Zeus without spear, without iron.[12]

In Sophocles' *Antigone* Dionysus is said to have "enthused" (ἐνθέους) the maenads to their revels;[13] thus, to use a term that Walter Burkert describes as "an ancient name and interpretation" which means literally "within is a god."[14] Euripides also has Dionysus enter into the body to bring on forms of bacchic frenzy.[15] Pan, Hecate or some corybant is assumed to "enthuse" (ἔνθεος) Phaedra and thereby to have brought upon her ill health and lack of appetite.[16] Lyssa, madness personified, rushes into the breast of Heracles.[17]

Yet, these examples and the important term "enthusiasm" betray a distinction between the indwelling physical possession of early Greece and

---

12 (ἐντήκεται γάρ †πλευμόνωνt ὅσοις ἔνι
ψυχή· ...
εἰσέρχεται μὲν ἰχθύων πλωτῷ γένει,
χέρσου δ' ἔνεστιν ἐν τετρασκελεῖ γονῇ,
νωμᾷ δ' ἐν οἰωνοῖσι τοὐκείνης πτερόν.
...
ἐν θηρσίν, ἐν βροτοῖσιν, ἐν θεοῖς ἄνω.
τίν' οὐ παλαίουσ' ἐς τρὶς ἐκβάλλει θεῶν
εἴ μοι θέμις — θέμις δὲ — τἀληθῆ λέγειν,
Διὸς τυραννεῖ πλευμόνων ἄνευ δορός,
ἄνευ σιδήρου·)
(Sophocles, frag. 941, from an unidentified play [Lloyd–Jones, LCL]). On the pervasiveness of love, compare also Eros in Sophocles, *Phaedra* frag. 684.

13Sophocles, *Ant.* 955–65.

14Walter Burkert, *Greek Religion* (Cambridge: Harvard University Press, 1985) 109, 391 note 1. Burkert's observation comes in direct response to Smith's position. To the Greek *entheos* compare *deus in pectore* in Latin authors (Ovid, *Met.* 2.641; Vergil, *Aen.* 6.46–48; Statius, *Theb.* 4.542; referred to in Robert McQueen Grant, *Gods and the One God* [LEC 1; Philadelphia: Westminster Press, 1986] 148). Given a broad vocabulary for indicating divine and demonic possession in the New Testament it is surprising that ἔνθεος and ἐνθουσιάζω (- άω) do not occur there.

15Cf. "the god came fully into the body" (ὁ θεὸς εἰς τὸ σῶμ᾽ ἔλθῃ πολύς — Euripides, *Ba.* 300–1; εἰσέρχομαι is used of demonic possession in Mark 5:1–20; Luke 8:26–39; 22:3–6; John 13:26–31); "she was controlled by Bacchus" (ἐκ Βακχίου κατείχετ᾽ — Euripides, *Ba.* 1122–24).

16Euripides, *Hipp.* 141–50.

17"I stormed the breast of Heracles" (δραμοῦμαι στέρνον εἰς Ἡρακλέους — Euripides, *Herc. fur.* 863).

the later bifurcation of possession into the two radically different phenomena of demonic and divine possessions seen in the New Testament. Bacchic frenzy, for example, reflects the positive and negative potential within a divine visitation. Basically a beneficent form of the worship of Dionysus, bacchic frenzy becomes a form of punishment when one resists the sacred rites such as happens to Pentheus,[18] Lycurgus,[19] and the daughters of Proetus.[20] Aeschylus' description of Cassandra's divine oracular possession by Apollo, in the emotional and physical pain it causes her, also illustrates how the later distinction between divine and demonic possession as beneficent and maleficent phenomena respectively lacks similar clear definition in earlier Greek antiquity.[21] Thus, the possibility arises for seeing demonic and divine possession as essentially one in the same for earlier Greek society, whereas for purposes of Jewish and Christian theologies they become independent and contrasting phenomena.

4.2.1.2 The Greek Daimon

In the New Testament, the term "*daimon*" refers without further qualification to evil spirits, as does "demon" in Modern English.[22] In this regard, the New Testament perpetuates the belief in demons found in the later books of the Hebrew Bible and Judaism generally, and like them portrays these beings in ways distinctly at odds with the Greek view. In contrast, in the context of early Greek culture, "*daimon*" conveys a neutral sense that says nothing of the entity's good or evil intentions or qualities. In Homer it even served as a synonym for *theos*, or to indicate a generic Divine power.[23] Hesiod brought

---

[18]For example, in Euripides, *Ba.*

[19]Apollodorus, *Bibliotheca* 3.5.1; Hyginus, *Fab.* 132. Cf. Aeschylus, *Edoni* frag. 28.

[20]Hesiod, *Fr.* 131. Others attribute their possession to Hera (e.g., Acusilaus, *FGrH* 2F28). Note also the case of possession vividly described by Herodotus, in which Dionysus is called a δαίμων, and those whom he possesses are said to become mad (μαίνεσθαι) and to bacchize (Βακχεύομεν καὶ ἡμέας ὁ θεὸς λαμβάνει) (Herodotus 4.79).

[21]Aeschylus, *Ag.* 1072–1330.

[22]Δαίμων appears in the New Testament only once (Matt 8:31), compared to fifty-five appearances of the diminuative δαιμόνιον.

[23]Tambornino, *De antiquorum daemonismo*, 69. As a synonymn of *theos*, see Homer, *Il.* 1.222, 3.420, etc. As signifying divine power, see Homer, *Od.* 3.27 (citations from LSJ). Walter Burkert says of Homeric usage: "*Daimon* does not designate a specific class of divine beings, but a peculiar mode of activity" (Burkert, *Greek Religion*, 180). Brenk says of the *daimon* in Homeric literature: "... the *daimon* has no visible shape or form, no history, no parentage. It was never in a human body. This mindless being carries out no orders for higher gods or serves upon them, nor is it embarassed by an exorcist. It is limited to a number of psychic functions ... It is vaguely responsible for misfortune ... It has only the faintest association with disease ... Yet within this Homeric nucleus one can see the capability for evolution into the more distinct usages of later periods: fate, chance, fortune, character, thoughts, good or evil spirits, the divinity" (Brenk, "In the Light of the Moon," *ANRW* 2.16.3:2081).

greater clarity to the *daimones* when he defined them as the departed heroes of the Golden Age, whose spirits oversaw the welfare of the generations that followed.[24]

Hesiod's categorization lent itself to the systematic thinking of the philosophers, who developed their demonologies also with regard to the rank and origin of the *daimones* relative to other animate beings.[25] In the hands of the philosophers, the *daimones* were to retain their status between the gods and mortals as Hesiod had categorized them. In the Common Era some would extend their origins beyond the souls of heroes to include the souls of any who had died.[26] Others would maintain their independence from spirits of the dead entirely, and rank them superior in status to the departed heroes, though still lower in status to the gods.[27] Among the important early figures in the philosophical development of Greek demonology were Pythagoras (VI B.C.E.), who considered *daimones* to be "souls" (ψυχαί) that occupied the air, could be audibly and visually perceived, and were the source of divination;[28] Empedocles (ca. 493–ca. 433 B.C.E.), who considered the *daimones* capable of certain wrongdoings that would send them on journeys of purificatory transmigration through water, earth and fire eventually to restore

---

[24]Hesiod writes: "But after the earth had covered this generation — they are called pure spirits dwelling on the earth, and are kindly, delivering from harm, and guardians of mortal men ... then they who dwell on Olympus made a second generation which was silver and less noble by far."

(Αὐτὰρ ἐπεὶ δὴ τοῦτο γένος κατὰ γαῖ᾽ ἐκάλυψε,
τοὶ μὲν δαίμονες ἁγνοὶ ἐπιχθόνιοι καλέονται
ἐσθλοί, ἀλεξίκακοι, φύλακες θνητῶν ἀνθρώπων

...

δεύτερον αὖτε γένος πολὺ χειρότερον μετόπισθεν
ἀργύρεον ποίησαν 'Ολύμπια δώματ᾽ ἔχοντες
...)

(Hesiod, *Op.* 121–28. English translation in *Hesiod, The Homeric Hymns and Homerica*, translated by Hugh G. Evelyn-White [LCL; Cambridge: Harvard University Press, 1959]).

[25]Burkert, *Greek Religion*, 179–81, 329–32.

[26]Lucian, *Luct.* 24.

[27]Plutarch, *Def. orac.* 414F–415I. For a similar view, compare Diogenes Laertius who says the Stoics believe *daimones* watch over human beings in sympathy (συμπάθεια), and believe also that the souls of heroes live beyond the life of the body (Diogenes Laertius 7.151). This appears to represent Plutarch's own view rather than Hesiod's. It is consistent with the five divisions of living beings Plutarch sets forth in "The E at Delphi," in sympathy with the epsilon as the fifth letter of the alphabet (Plutarch, *E Delph.* 390E). Plutarch arranges the beings from greatest to least as θεοί, δαίμονες, ἥρωες, ἄνθρωποι, and θηριῶδες.

[28]Aristotle, *Pyth.* frag. 3 (193); Apuleius; *De deo Socr.* 20; Clement, *Strom.* 6.6.53; Diogenes Laertius 7.32 (Burkert, *Greek Religion*, 180).

them to their rightful place in air;[29] Plato (ca. 429–347 B.C.E.) for his illustration of the human soul (ψυχή) as a *daimon*;[30] and Xenocrates (fl. 339–314 B.C.E.), who included evil spirits among the *daimones*.[31] Plato aside, much of what we know of the others' demonologies comes to us second-hand through later authors, who cited the earlier philosophers as authorities in support of their own views.

"*Daimon*" is a neutral term during the Classical period that requires context to reveal the good or evil nature of a given spirit. The oldest evidence for the "good *daimon*" (ἀγαθὸς δαίμων) comes from Aristophanes, who uses it of a household god.[32] "Hostile spirits" (δυσμενέες δαίμονες) first enter the literary sources in the fifth century Hippocratic work *On the Ailments of Young Women*,[33] which critiques a popular belief that *daimones* are the cause of the sacred disease, apoplexies, and other terrors. Plato's interpretation of the human soul as a *daimon* is part of the distinction among types of *daimones* that begins to be drawn in the Classical period. In a role articulated as early as the *Symposium*, Greek cosmology views the *daimones* as intermediaries between perfect divinity and human frailty.[34] They are intermediaries both in the sense of their cosmological placement between gods and mortals, and in their role as the communicators who make the lowlier humans aware of the loftier divine essence. In this sense, they correspond properly to the heavenly "messengers" (ἄγγελοι) of biblical literature rather than to the demons of those same texts.

Plato expresses his views on cosmology, theology, and anthropology in the *Timaeus*, a work that would prove influential for the rest of antiquity.[35] In the dialogue, Timaeus, a Locrian astronomer and mathematician, illustrates his theology by means of cosmology. In the *Timaeus*, the universe represents a single hierarchical structure with the Cause (αἴτιος) and Creator (δημιουργός) of all things at the supreme head. Around this Cause rotate the

---

[29]Plutarch, *Is. et Os.* 361C; Hermann Diels, *Die Fragmente der Vorsokratiker: Griechisch und Deutsch* (3 vols.; Zurich: Weidmann, 1974–1975) 1:356–58, frag. 115.

[30]Plato, *Tim.* 90A.

[31]Plutarch, *Def. orac.* 419A (Burkert, *Greek Religion*, 332).

[32]Aristophanes, *Eq.* 107; *Vesp.* 525 (Martin P. Nilsson, *Geschichte der Griechischen Religion*; 2: *Die Hellenistische und Römische Zeit* [Munich: C. H. Beck'sche, 1961] 213–14).

[33]Hippocrates, *Virg.*; Littré, *Ouevres complétes d'Hippocrate*, 8.466. Plutarch considers "evil *daimones*" (φαύλους δαίμονας) a legacy left by Heracleon, Plato, Xenocrates, Chrysippus and Democritus (Plutarch, *Def. orac.* 419A). Brenk notes that even in Homer the *daimon*'s association with evil can be sensed: "... the *daimon* acts very much like a god, except that it tends to be unidentifiable and evil" (Brenk, "In the Light of the Moon," *ANRW* 2.16.3:2074).

[34]Plato, *Symp.* 202D–203A (see Brenk, "In the Light of the Moon," *ANRW* 2.16.3:2086–87).

[35]Burkert, *Greek Religion*, 329.

celestial bodies of stars and planets, which represent visible gods. Only as an allowance of tradition does Plato accept the gods of mythology, whom he calls *daimones*,[36] into the realm of the heavenly bodies. "The body of the cosmos" (τὸ τοῦ κόσμου σῶμα) is made of the four elements: fire, air, earth, and water,[37] and is permeated by the immortal "soul" (ψυχή).[38] Since the Creator has generated these divine beings, they take part in His immortality. The Creator also fashioned souls of lesser purity, each corresponding to a given star,[39] which He informs of the nature of the cosmos, and then scatters throughout the earth, moon, and stars.[40] The rest of creation was fashioned from the remainder of the existing elements, but fashioned by the divinities so as to ensure its imperfection and mortality.[41] This mortal creation dwells beneath the divine creation, and inhabits the realms of air, water, and earth.[42]

The *Timaeus* also offers an anthropology that parallels the hierarchical structure of the cosmos.[43] Accordingly, humanity has been fashioned from a combination of body (σῶμα) and soul (ψυχή). The assignment of the soul within the human body reflects the hierarchical structure of the cosmos. The Creator has placed the soul's highest aspects of reason and intelligence in the head. Plato compares this portion of the soul to a *daimon*.[44] By drawing upon its own instruction from the Creator, this *daimon* acts as an intermediary to assist each person to recognize his or her own place in the cosmos and connection with the divine realm. One who is able to concentrate on divine things rather than the passions and appetites is thus called "blessed" (εὐδαίμων).[45] A second portion of the soul is assigned to the chest (θώραξ), where passions reign, but upon which higher reason has some influence. Below the chest, the belly (κοιλία), as the seat of appetites, with the liver (ἧπαρ), as the receptacle of divination, holds the third and lowliest portion of the soul. Here, the soul has no share in reason and intelligence but, to use

---

[36]Plato, *Tim.* 40B-E.

[37]Plato, *Tim.* 31B–32C.

[38]Plato, *Tim.* 34B.

[39]Plato, *Tim.* 41D–42D.

[40]Plato, *Tim.* 41D–42D.

[41]Plato, *Tim.* 41B–D.

[42]Plato, *Tim.* 39E–40A.

[43]Plato, *Tim.* 69B–71D.

[44]Plato, *Tim.* 90A.

[45]"... and inasmuch as he is for ever tending his divine part and duly magnifying that daemon who dwells along with him, he must be supremely blessed." (... ἅτε δὲ ἀεὶ θεραπεύοντα τὸ θεῖον ἔχοντά τε αὐτὸν εὖ κεκοσμημένον τὸν δαίμονα ξύνοικον ἐν αὐτῷ διαφερόντως εὐδαίμονα εἶναι.) (Plato, *Tim.* 90C. English translation in *Plato*, translated by R. G. Bury et al. [12 vols. LCL; Cambridge: Harvard University Press, 1917–1929]).

Plato's imagery, as livestock at the manger it brutishly attends to the appetites.[46]

The astrological interest that led Plato to identify gods with stars and planets led others to identify the *daimones* with the moon as that celestial body which orbited closest to the earth.[47] It is a connection that helps to explain the appearance and relevance of the term σεληνιάζειν ("to be moonstruck") to demonic possession in later antiquity.[48] For the philosophers, however, the correlation had less to do with a moral judgment against the *daimones* than to distinctions between perfection and imperfection based upon material composition.[49] Xenocrates, Plato's second successor at the Academy, would illustrate the relationship between gods, *daimones*, and mortals by assigning representative triangles to each: to the perfection of the gods belonged the equilateral triangle; to the *daimones* (δαίμονες), who partake in the perfection of the gods while sharing also in the imperfection of mortals, belonged the isosceles triangle with two sides of equal length; to the imperfection of mortals (θνητοί) belonged the scalene triangle with all sides unequal.[50] The moral division between gods and *daimones* is a later development among the Greeks, which resulted from the influence of Near Eastern beliefs that juxtaposed good and evil spiritual worlds.[51]

---

[46]Plato, *Tim.* 70D–72B.

[47]The Pythagoreans believed that *daimons* resided around the moon (Brenk, "In the Light of the Moon," 2094–98), and the belief was perpetuated by Plutarch (I–II C.E.), Sextus Empiricus (fl. ca. 200 C.E.), Apuleius (II C.E.), Iamblichus (ca. 250–325 C.E.), and Proclus (ca. 410–485 C.E.) (Brenk, "In the Light of the Moon," *ANRW* 2.16.3:2088–89 and note 38).

[48]Aside from a probably late scholion on Aristophanes supplied by Johannes Tzetzes (Koster, *Scholia in Aristophanem* 4:834 [*Ra.* 507A.9]), the term first appears in the New Testament: once in a list of those who were healed by Jesus (Matt 4:24), and again with reference to the demon-possessed boy (Matt 17:14). Outside of its usage here, and by the early patristic writers in their commentaries on this passage, the term, or a close variant thereof, appears in non-Christian astrological writings. It is not used in medical texts. In his Latin translation of the Bible, Jerome (V C.E.) translated the Greek verb with the adjective *lunaticus* (*-a, -um*), itself a late arrival into Latin. In his etymology of *lunaticus*, Isidorus, Bishop of Seville (VI–VII C.E.) cites its connection with the popular belief in epilepsy: "The multitude calls these people '*lunatics*' because a possessing daemon comes to them during the course of the moon." (*Hos etiam vulgus lunaticos vocant, quod per lunae cursum comitetur eos insidia daemonum* — Isidorus, *Orig.* 4.7.6).

[49]Xenocrates associated the material composition of the *daimones* with the atmosphere around the moon, and so identified this space as their residence (Brenk, "In the Light of the Moon," *ANRW* 2.16.3:2087–90).

[50]Plutarch, *Def. orac.* 416D.

[51]Compare Plutarch (ca. 50–ca. 120), who, although his own views on demonology are greatly influenced by the earlier Greek philosophers to whom he often refers, also finds value in the demonologies of Zoroaster, the Thracian Orpheus, and the sages of Egypt, Phrygia, and Chaldea (e.g., Plutarch, *Is. et Os.* 370C; *Def. orac.* 414F).

4.2.1.3 Avenging Spirits

In Greek tragedy, Olympian gods are the leading agents of possession and affliction. But lesser deities closer in stature to the demons of the New Testament also have a place. As long as it stays within the framework of philosophical dialogue the *daimon* remains a rather abstract figure among the Greeks. It takes on a greater three-dimensionality in the poetry of the tragedians and in the speeches of the rhetoricians. One manifestation of the spiritual intermediaries between gods and mortals are the numerous avenging spirits that frequent Greek literature. The avenging spirits typically react to an initial transgression and in this way differ from the demons of the New Testament. Two passages, however, suggest that they were also understood to act maliciously of their own volition. In Euripides' *Iphigeneia at Aulis*, Clytemnaestra asks which of the avenging spirits drives Agamemnon to sacrifice his own daughter.[52] In *Electra* Orestes questions the divine origin of an oracle that would have him murder his own mother and so invoke her Erinyes against him. He thinks it to be not from Apollo, but from an *alastor* who impersonates the gods.[53]

The *alastor* is an avenging spirit that makes frequent appearances, in singular or plural, in Greek tragedy.[54] An *alastor* possesses Clytemnaestra in Aeschylus' *Agamemnon*,[55] and in the *Persians* it acts as a destructive force

---

[52]"Which of the avenging spirits subjects him" (τίς αὐτὸν οὐπάγων ἀλαστόρων — Euripides, *Iph. Aul.* 878).

[53]"Then has an avenging spirit itself spoken after taking taken the likeness of a god?" (ἆρ' αὖτ' ἀλάστωρ εἶπ' ἀπεικασθεὶς θεῷ; — Euripides, *El.* 979; cf. *Or.* 1666–70).

[54]Burkert calls the *alastor* "the personified power of vengeance for spilled blood" (Burkert, *Greek Religion*, 181).

[55]Clytemnaestra says: "Taking the semblance of the wife of this corpse, the ancient bitter *alastor* of Atreus, that grim banqueter, has offered him in payment, sacrificing a full-grown victim in vengeance for those slain youths."

(φανταζόμενος δὲ γυναικὶ νεκροῦ
τοῦδ' ὁ παλαιὸς δριμὺς ἀλάστωρ
'Ατρέως χαλεποῦ θοινατῆρος
τόνδ' ἀπέτεισεν,
τέλεον νεαροῖς ἐπιθύσας.)

(Aeschylus, *Ag.* 1500–1504. English translation [modified] in *Aeschylus*, translated by Herbert Weir Smyth [2 vols. LCL; Cambridge: Harvard University Press, 1938–1946]). The statement is not exculpatory. Elsewhere, Clytemnaestra confesses that she herself killed Agamemnon (*Ag.* 1552–53). Instead, the passage is illustrative of one becoming an *alastor* by doing what an *alastor* does. Namely, Clytemnaestra murders her husband and so avenges the sacrifice of their daughter Iphigeneia, just as an *alastor* murders Agamemnon to avenge the curse against the House of Atreus. The "possession" is the result of an internal motivation: Clytemnaestra feels that she has been wronged by her husband, and is compelled to avenge the injustice. Eduard Fraenkel notes that "In *Ag.* 1501 and 1509 the ἀλάστωρ shows the unmitigated features of a daimon" (Aeschylus, *Agamemnon*, Eduard Fraenkel, ed.

against the foreign invaders at Salamis.[56] It also makes appearances in Sophocles' plays, though not with the same infiltration of the body as envisioned by Aeschylus.[57] The *alastor* frequently turns up in the plays of Euripides, where its actions converge with those of the Erinyes.[58] In fact, the Erinyes are said to "alastorize" Orestes[59] and the house of Creon and Jason.[60] As an "avenger," the *alastor* properly responds to someone's wrongdoing,[61] and so represents one means by which the gods communicated their desires to human beings through spiritual intermediaries.

Tragedy deals with mythological stories in which the gods and spirits play active, tangible roles in human affairs. This active presence facilitates an occasional name-calling in tragedy that paints human opponents as spiritual adversaries. Thus, the chorus of Corinthian women calls Medea one of the Erinyes,[62] as does a delusional Orestes call Electra.[63] In *The Trojan Women* the chorus calls Paris an *alastor*,[64] and elsewhere Teiresias identifies Oedipus' sons as *daimones* because of their internecine strife.[65] These latter passages from tragedy draw near to the language of possession that appears in

---

[3 vols; Oxford: Clarendon Press, 1950] 3:711). The activity of a maleficent demon in the House of Atreus begins in Aeschylus' play with the chorus' accusation that Cassandra's fantastic prophecy about the death of Agamemnon was demon-inspired: "Surely some malign spirit, falling upon you with heavy swoop, moves you to chant your piteous woes fraught with death."

> (καί τίς σε κακοφρονῶν τίθη–
> σι δαίμων ὑπερβαρὴς ἐμπίτνων
> μελίζειν πάθη γοερὰ θανατοφόρα.)

(Aeschylus, *Ag.* 1174–76 [Smyth, LCL, modified]).

[56] Aeschylus, *Pers.* 353–432.

[57] In *The Women of Trachis* the *alastor* appears in plural, and would cause one to make a noxious choice (Sophocles, *Trach.* 1235). Here, Hyllus shows disgust at his father Heracles' suggestion that he marry the girl Iole, who has brought about the death of his mother and the suffering and impending death of his father. In *Oedipus at Colonnus* the *alastor* appears to be Oedipus' own spirit which Oedipus threatens will return to haunt Creon (Sophocles, *Oed. Col.* 788).

[58] Burkert calls the Erinyes "the embodied curse" (Burkert, *Greek Religion*, 181).

[59] ἠλάστρουν θεαί (Euripides, *Iph. Taur.* 934, 971).

[60] Euripides, *Med.* 1258.

[61] Such is the case, for example, with Jason who wrongly gave the fratricide Medea refuge on the Argo (Euripides, *Med.* 1330).

[62] The chorus also calls her a lioness and Skylla (Euripides, *Med.* 1258–60; cf. Aeschylus, *Ag.* 749 and Euripides, *Tro.* 457).

[63] Euripides, *Or.* 264–65. Cassandra uses the same term of herself, not in self-derision, but to emphasize her power to wreak vengeance upon Agamemnon (Euripides, *Tro.* 453–54).

[64] Euripides, *Tro.* 940–42.

[65] Euripides, *Phoen.* 886–88. The herdsmen in Taurica use the same term, though this time more in complimentary awe of Orestes and Polydes, whose physical bearing leads them to think they might be Palaimon, the Dioscuri, or sons of Nereus (Euripides, *Iph. Taur.* 267–339).

polemical contexts in the New Testament,[66] but differ from them in the potentially positive role the Greek spiritual entities play as avengers of transgression.

Elaine Pagels has located the practice of demonizing one's opponents among sectarian Jewish groups and Christians for whom Satan constituted the "intimate enemy."[67] Pagels assumes such Jewish and Christian demonizations to lack precedent in Greek society, and cites in comparison the harsh, yet non-demonic attacks engaged in by the philosophical schools.[68] Pagel's assumption also holds true for historical texts. Thus, Herodotus treats the Persians as mortals with the strengths and weaknesses of any other human, and the criteria of blood, language, religion, and habits that unite the Greeks could be used to categorize any other people as well.[69] Thucydides' *History of the Peloponnesian War* provides a forum for exposing hatreds among the Hellenic peoples themselves. The political tensions between the Spartans and Athenians, though most prominent in the history, are some of the most reserved compared to the long standing local feuds between, for example, the Plataeans and Thebans,[70] or the Athenians and Aeginetans.[71] Thucydides' numerous speeches afford the best opportunity for negatively portraying the opposition, yet even here none of the portrayals are demonic.[72]

Public oratory does, however, provide contexts where the spirits are used less as symbols of vengeance than of plague and destruction. In the intimate context of Athenian courts of law, the language used by citizens against

---

[66]For examples in the New Testament, see "Sanctification and Divine Possession" in Chapter 5.

[67]Pagels writes: "Satan is not the distant enemy but the intimate enemy — one's trusted colleague, close associate, brother. ... Whichever version of his origin one chooses ... and there are many, all depict Satan as an *intimate* enemy — the attribute that qualifies him so well to express conflict among Jewish groups" (Pagels, *The Origin of Satan*, 49).

[68]Pagels writes: "But philosophers did not engage ... in *demonic* vilification of their opponents. Within the ancient world, so far as I know, it is only the Essenes and Christians who actually escalate conflict with their opponents to the level of cosmic war" (Pagels, *The Origin of Satan*, 84).

[69]For the criteria of blood, language and religion, see Herodotus 9.7. The Greek love of freedom and equality versus a barbarian willingness to be subjugated is also a recurrent theme in the *History*, thus, 5.49, 78, 91; 6.11–12, 43; 7.135. Granted, Herodotus also draws stereotypes for different nations, for example the Egyptians are the wisest in the world (Herodotus 2.160), while cleverness is a particularly satisfying, albeit suspect, Greek trait (e.g. Herodotus 1.60; especially of Themistocles 8.80, 110, 124; cf. also the description of Antiphon in Thucydides 8.68).

[70]Thucydides 3.59.

[71]For example, Thucydides 4.57.

[72]One of the harshest examples of name-calling is the Plataeans' describing the Thebans as their "most hated" enemies (ἐχθίστοις — Thucydides 3.59). Thucydides has not recorded these speeches verbatim, but composed them himself (1.22), and so this may reflect more his own style than the rhetoric actually delivered.

citizens to discredit and deride also included demonization of the opponent. As well as addressing local and ephemeral intrigues and concerns, these orators spoke in times of great political and social changes in Athens: fluctuations between democratic and oligarchic forms of government; the decline of the Athenian empire precipitated by the Peloponnesian War and further eroded with the revolt of Athens' subjugated allies in the Social War; the threat of a growing Macedonian empire. Each new upheaval brought with it accusations by citizens against their fellows of treason and other crimes against the welfare of the state that led to confiscations of property, banishments and death sentences.

In keeping with the desperate stakes involved, the language used in court often became abusive.[73] The prominent rhetoricians of the day addressed these public and private intrigues with often vitriolic denunciations of their opponents. Demosthenes' reference to Philip II of Macedon as an "enemy" and a "barbarian" is the height of civility compared to how the orators refer to their own compatriots or resident aliens.[74] Thus, in their bitter rivalry

---

[73]Demades asks the jurors for support in response to his opponent's vitriole: "Since I have myself become exposed to the full hatred of the orators, I am asking not only for divine assistance but for your help also." (ἐμπεσὼν δ' αὐτὸς εἰς μέσην τὴν τῶν ῥητόρων δυσμένειαν, ὥσπερ τῆς παρὰ θεῶν, οὕτω τῆς παρ' ὑμῶν δέομαι τυχεῖν βοηθείας.) (Demades, *On the Twelve Years* 2. English translation in *Minor Attic Orators*, translated by K. J. Maidment and J. O. Burtt [2 vols. LCL; Cambridge: Harvard University Press, 1953–1954]).

[74]οὐκ ἐχθρός; ... οὐ βάρβαρος; (Demosthenes, *Olynthiaca* 3.16). Compare the following examples drawn from Attic oratory: "nefarious slanderers" (πονηροῖς συκοφάνταις — Lysias, *Areopagiticus* 1); "the most evil man in all Greece" (πονηροτάτου τῶν Ἑλλήνων — Aeschines, *De falsa legatione* 143; said of Demosthenes); "the common misfortune of the Greeks" (κοινὴν τῶν Ἑλλήνων συμφοράν — Aeschines, *In Ctesiphontem* 253); "slanderer" (ὁ βάσκανος οὗτος — Demosthenes, *De corona* 132; said of Antiphon); (ὦ κατάρατε — Demosthenes, *De corona* 290; said of Aeschines); "loathsome outcast," "pestilence" (ὁ φαρμακός, ὁ λοιμός — Demosthenes, *In Aristogitonem* 1.80; cf. Lysias, *In Andocidem* 53); "polluted and profane man" (ὁ μιαρὸς καὶ ἀνόσιος ἄνθωπος — Aeschines, *In Ctesiphontem* 101; said of Demosthenes); "most loathsome of all living men" (ὦ μιαρώτατε πάντων τῶν ὄντων ἀνθρώπων — Demosthenes, *In Aristogitonem* 1.28); "filthy magician" (τοῦ μιαροῦ γόητος τούτου — Dinarchos, *In Demosthenem* 92, cf. 95); "polluted man" (μιαρὸς ἄνθρωπος — Dinarchos, *In Demosthenem* 95). A common appelative is "beast" (θηρίον — e.g., Dinarchos, *In Philoclem* 19; Aeschines, *De falsa legatione* 20, 34; *In Ctesiphontem* 182 [said of Demosthenes]; Demosthenes, *Contra Macartatum* 3). Aristogeiton, nicknamed "the dog" in daily life, seems to have been especially so abused in the courts (Dinarchos, *In Aristogitonem* 10; Demosthenes, *In Aristogitonem* 1.8). Demosthenes also calls him a snake (ἔχις), and portrays him as a scorpion (σκορπίος) that moves about the agora with his stinger poised for his next victim (Demosthenes, *In Aristogitonem* 1.52). Hyperides, with Demades in mind, says of orators in general: "That orators are like snakes, in that all snakes are hateful, though some of them, the adders, are harmful to men, while others, the brown snakes, eat the adders." (Εἶναι δὲ τοὺς ῥήτορας

Aeschines calls Demosthenes "the offender against Greece," who is pursued by a demon and a fortune against which the citizens should protect themselves.[75] In response, Demosthenes implicates Aeschines in the expansion of Philip's empire, and calls him a *"daimonic* offender" for the destruction of men, land, and cities that has resulted.[76] Later on in the same speech he calls Aeschines and his friends "rogues and parasites and *alastors.*"[77] Dinarchos calls Demosthenes an "evil demonic presence" among the Athenians,[78] and the malignant "spirit" who has brought misfortune to Aristarchus.[79] Isocrates exhorts his contemporary Athenians to shun the impious example set by the Thirty oligarchs, whom he calls "madmen possessed by evil demons."[80] In a speech attributed to Lysias, the author calls Andocides an "offscouring" and a *"daimonic* offender" of which the city will do well to purify itself.[81]

ὁμοίους τοῖς ὄφεσι· τούς τε γὰρ ὄφεις μισητοὺς μὲν εἶναι πάντας, τῶν δὲ ὄφεων αὐτῶν τοὺς μὲν ἔχεις τοὺς ἀνθρώπους ἀδικεῖν, τοὺς δὲ παρείας αὐτοὺς τοὺς ἔχεις κατεσθίειν. — Hyperides, *Against Demades for Illegal Proposals* frag. 19.5 [Burtt, LCL]).

[75]τὸν τῆς Ἑλλάδος ἀλειτήριον ... ἀλλὰ καὶ τὸν δαίμονα καὶ τὴν τύχην τὴν συμπαρακολουθοῦσαν τῷ ἀνθρώπῳ φυλάξασθαι (Aeschines, *In Ctesiphontem* 157).

[76]From Demosthenes we read: "... if I am to tell the whole truth without concealment, I will not flinch from declaring him the evil genius of all the men, all the districts, and all the cities that have perished." (... εἰ μηδὲν εὐλαβηθέντα τἀληθὲς εἰπεῖν δέοι, οὐκ ἂν ὀκνήσαιμ' ἔγωγε κοινὸν ἀλειτήριον τῶν μετὰ ταῦτ' ἀπολωλότων ἁπάντων εἰπεῖν, ἀνθρώπων, τόπων, πόλεων ...) (Demosthenes, *De corona* 159. English translation in *Demosthenes*, translated by C. A. Vince et al. [7 vols. LCL; Cambridge: Harvard University Press, 1964–1989]).

[77]... ἄνθρωποι μιαροὶ καὶ κόλακες καὶ ἀλάστορες ... (Demosthenes, *De corona* 296).

[78]"If then the city must go on enjoying the fruits of Demosthenes' wickedness and ill-fortune, that we may still be plagued by an evil genius — I can find no other word for it — we should acquiesce in the present state of affairs." (εἰ μὲν οὖν ἔτι δεῖ τὴν πόλιν τῆς Δημοσθένους πονηρίας καὶ ἀτυχίας ἀπολαύειν, ἵνα πλείω κακοδαιμονῶμεν — οὐ γὰρ ἔχω τί ἄλλο εἴπω — στερκτέον <ἂν> εἴη τοῖς συμβαίνουσιν ...) (Dinarchos, *In Demosthenem* 91 [Burtt, LCL]).

[79]"And did not Aristarchus find in Demosthenes such a friend as to make him think that this was some evil spirit which had visited him and the originator of all his misfortunes?" (καὶ τοιούτῳ φίλῳ Δημοσθένει ἐχρήσατο, ὥστε δαίμονα αὐτῷ τοῦτον καὶ τῶν γεγενημένων συμφορῶν ἡγεμόνα νομίσαι προσελθεῖν;) (Dinarchos, *In Demosthenem* 30 [Burtt, LCL]).

[80]κακοδαιμονησάντων καὶ μανέντων ἀνθρώπων (Isocrates, *Areopagiticus* 73).

[81]"You should, therefore, consider that to-day, in punishing Andocides and in ridding yourselves of him, you are cleaning the city, you are solemnly purifying it from pollution, you are dispatching a foul scapegoat, you are getting rid of a reprobate; for this man is one of these." (νῦν οὖν χρὴ νομίζειν τιμωρουμένους καὶ ἀπαλλαττομένους

In the context of the Athenian courts of law, the orators mythologize or demonize their opponents to emphasize the gravity of their present circumstances; it is an illustrative technique contrary to the objectives of the historians.[82] Whether in public oratory, or in the polemical contexts of the New Testament, the intention of *daimonic* vilification is to exclude one from the community. As a consequence, although the language of possession is invoked, such charges of "demonic" possession are left at the level of accusation without recourse to exorcism.

4.2.1.4 The Erinyes

Whether as avenging spirits in tragedy or plaguing spirits in oratory, the *alastor* and its kind reflect how the ancient Greeks thought of *daimones*. Its features, however, remain unsketched and offer little legacy to the iconography of demons in later antiquity. For description of hostile spirits it is the Erinyes who most stimulated the imaginations of the poets. Euripides especially attests to the Erinyes as howling, with blood-dripping eyes, serpentine hair, dog- or gorgon-eyes or faces, black skin, wearing fiery clothing, and winged to illustrate the swiftness of their vengeance.[83] Such features become standard images of terror in Greek literature and iconography, and are used also of gleaming-eyed Lyssa.[84] Although the Erinyes hound their victims rather than possess them in Greek literature, the descriptions they

---

Ἀνδοκίδου τὴν πόλιν καθαίρειν καὶ ἀποδιοπομπεῖσθαι καὶ φαρμακὸν ἀποπέμπειν καὶ ἀλιτηρίου ἀπαλλάττεσθαι, ὡς ἐν τούτων οὗτός ἐστι.) (Lysias, *In Andocidem* 53. English translation in *Lysias*, translated by W. R. M. Lamb [LCL; Cambridge: Harvard University Press, 1960]).

[82]Thus, compare Thucydides' emphasis on the factual (Thucydides 1.21; cf. Herodotus 1.95). Compare also a passage from Aeschines that presents a contrary view, and that places the source of human wrongdoing upon the individual: "For you must not imagine, fellow citizens, that the impulse to wrong doing is from the gods; nay, rather, it is from the wickedness of men; nor that ungodly men are, as in tragedy, driven and chastised by the Furies with blazing torches in their hands. No, the impetuous lusts of the body and insatiate desire ... these are, for each man, his Fury, urging him to slay his fellow citizens, to serve the tyrant, to help put down the democracy." (μὴ γὰρ οἴεσθε, ὦ ἄνδρες Ἀθηναῖοι, τὰς τῶν ἀδικημάτων ἀρχὰς ἀπὸ θεῶν, ἀλλ᾽ οὐκ ἀπ᾽ ἀνθρώπων ἀσελγείας γίγνεσθαι, μηδὲ τοὺς ἠσεβηκότας, καθάπερ ἐν ταῖς τραγῳδίαις, Ποινὰς ἐλαύνειν καὶ κολάζειν δᾳσὶν ἡμμέναις ἀλλ᾽ αἱ προπετεῖς τοῦ σώματος ἡδοναὶ καὶ τὸ μηδὲν ἱκανὸν ἡγεῖσθαι, ... ταῦτά ἐστιν ἑκάστῳ Ποινή, ταῦτα παρακελεύεται σφάττειν τοὺς πολίτας, ὑπηρετεῖν τοῖς τυράννοις, συγκαταλύειν τὸν δῆμον.) (Aeschines, *In Timarchum* 190–91. English translation in *The Speeches of Aeschines*, translated by Charles Darwin Adams [LCL; Cambridge: Harvard University Press, 1958]).

[83]Euripides, *Or.* 253–61, 315–27; *Iph. Taur.* 285–94. Jameson et al., note that the Erinyes are called Maniai at Ake in Arkadia (Jameson, Lex Sacra *from Selinous*, 53).

[84]Euripides, *Herc. fur.* 880–86.

evoked make them a source for how demons came to be envisioned in the Common Era.[85]

4.2.2 Manifestations of Possession

Having identified some of the possessing entities, it is worthwhile to set forth some of the many ways in which their possessions manifested themselves to the early Greeks. Plato refers to three principal forms of manic possession that originate from the gods and serve a beneficial purpose both for the afflicted and for humanity in general. These are prophetic inspiration, maniai resulting from prior wrongdoing (παλαιῶν ἐκ μηνιμάτων), and the artistic inspiration of the Muses.[86] As a way of narrowing the field I have focused on those instances that correspond best with the contexts of prophecy, sickness, and derangement that coincide with demonic possession in the New Testament.

4.2.2.1 Possession and Prophetic Inspiration

The conveyance of divine messages took on a variety of forms in early Greece, which can be grouped into the two overarching categories of non-human and human vehicles of mediation.[87] In the former case, as a refined craft, prophecy involved the discernment of such omens as the flight of birds (ornithoscopy), or the appearance of the organs of sacrificed animals (extispicy). Such methods of extrapolation from observation were historically used as a prelude to Greek warfare, and in this context may have played a role not only in perceiving the outcome of battle, but of influencing it.[88] In the latter case, a

---

[85]In the pagan world, cf. Plutarch, *Dion* 55, where the demon has the face of an Erinys, and Lucian, *Philopseudes* 16, where the demon is black; see also *Philopseudes* 22 for a Fury-like being (Brenk, "In the Light of the Moon," *ANRW* 2.16.3:2113–14). Some of these translate into the features of the demons envisioned by Christians, such as the black and winged figures that emerge from the mouths of the possessed in later iconography. In literature, compare Tertullian's reference to demons as swift and winged spirits (Tertullian, *Apol.* 27), and Lactantius' reference to anger, desire, and lust as "Furies" (Lactantius, *Inst.* 6.19).

[86]Plato, *Phdr.* 244A–245A.

[87]The former concerns prophecy as a refined craft; the latter as an inspired experience. Plato differentiates between diviners (μάντεις), and prophets (προφῆται) in the *Timaeus* (Plato, *Tim.* 71D–72B). The former receive the messages in their belly, the latter use their heads to decipher the messages through reason and intelligence. Plutarch also distinguished between the prophecy made by those who hear the voice of god directly, and those who learn to decipher it through signs. It is the latter that he considers "divination" (μαντική) (Plutarch, *Gen. Socra.* 593C–D).

[88]The seers who accompanied the Greek (and Persian) armies, and caused an eight-day delay at the battle of Plataea as both Greeks and Persians hesitated to start a battle before sacrifices proved favorable, suggest the use of prophecy to influence an outcome (Herodotus 9.33–42). Herodotus says of Sparta's famous seer Tisamenus: "... by his prophesying helped

human being becomes the medium for prophetic inspiration. Divine messages sent through human agents appear in two principal social contexts: oracular cults and itinerant gifted seers.

In oracular prophecy inspiration comes with the delivery of the oracle, but the meaning of the often ambiguous message is left to the human intellect to decipher. Thus, when mediation of divine knowledge comes through human language the words themselves become the object of scrutiny. The early Greek sources record oracular responses as having been delivered to the petitioners in a language intelligible to the general population. A correct interpretation of the oracle, however, was incumbent upon the wisdom, cleverness, and ingenuity of the interpreters within the petitioning community. Although the Greeks had a technical term for those who interpreted oracles (χρησμολόγοι), the final say was not always reserved to their judgments. If others grasped the oracle's true meaning their views, too, at times influenced the consensus, thereby lending a "democratic" quality to the process of interpretation.[89]

Tragedy reveals the role of divine inspiration in prophecy in the case of Amphilytos who is inspired to prophesy,[90] and when Aeschylus calls prophecy a "divinely inspired craft."[91] Euripides also tells how Dionysus enters into the bacchants and prophesies through them.[92] Seers in Greek tragedy tend to reinforce a belief in the inevitability of fate rather than in the manipulation of outcomes. The plot thickens when those who hear their inspired words refuse to believe them, or take offense at unfavorable forecasts. The honors fluctuated for those who practiced prophecy. On the one hand,

---

them win five great contests," including Plataea (οὗτος δὲ ὕστατος κατεργάσθη τῶν πέντε ἀγώνων — Herodotus 9.35. English translation in Herodotus, *The History*, translated by David Grene [Chicago: University of Chicago Press, 1987]). Of Hegesistratus, the Greek seer for the Persian army, Herodotus says: "As for the sacrifices of Hegesistratus, he was for dismissing them and not trying to force some favorable answer; let them follow the customs of Persia and give battle." (τά τε σφάγια τὰ ῾Ηγησιστράτου ἐᾶν χαίρειν μηδὲ βιάζεσθαι, ἀλλὰ νόμῳ τῷ Περσέων χρεωμένους συμβάλλειν — Herodotus 9.41; trans. Grene).

[89]One of the more famous examples of this is Themistocles' ingenious interpretation of the Delphic oracle's "wooden wall" to protect Athens from the invading Persians (Herodotus 7.143). Themistocles interpreted the wooden wall as reliance in the strength of Athens' navy. His view won out over against a minority group, who literally interpreted the Pythian response to their own peril. Having favored building a wooden wall around the acropolis, they did so, and were slaughtered once the Persians broke through.

[90]ἐνθεάζων (Herodotus 1.63).

[91]τέχναισιν ἐνθέοις (Aeschylus, *Ag.* 1209).

[92]Euripides, *Ba.* 298–301. Compare how Cassandra distinguishes her own enthusiastic prophecy for its clarity of reason distinct from senseless bacchic frenzy. She acknowledges the spasms of her body, yet affirms that her flesh remains pure, and that her prophecy comes from a sound mind (Euripides, *Tro.* 453–54). Hecuba strikes a compromise between Cassandra and the outside observers of her behavior when she addresses her daughter as a "co-bacchant with the gods" (ὦ σύμβακχε Κασάνδρα θεοῖς — Euripides, *Tro.* 500).

the prophecy used as a prelude to Greek warfare brought great fame to some seers. On the other hand, Greek tragedy presents the spokespersons of the gods as much maligned, even though their prophecies are invariably truthful. Teiresius is one such prophet accustomed to cyclical fortunes. Of the seer's plight he says:

... Who uses the diviner's art
Is foolish. If he announces ill things,
He is loathed by those to whom he prophesies.
If, pitying them that seek to him, he lie,
He wrongs the Gods. Sole prophet unto men
Ought Phoebus to have been, who fears no one.[93]

Despite the hostile reception the prophets sometimes received, their rejection or persecution is in essence a slight to the gods whose messages they conveyed.

Inspiration and divination combine in early Greece in the phenomenon of the *engastrimythos* (ἐγγαστρίμυθος; cf. ἐγγαστρίμαντις). The term translates literally as "speech within the belly," and is commonly translated "belly talker," or, less precisely, "ventriloquist." This term refers to a type of prophet whose oracles were generated by a voice within their body. Eurycles is one such prophet known by name.[94] Originally from Lesbos, Eurycles lived in Athens during the fifth century B.C.E., and both Aristophanes[95] and Plato[96] mention him. Later scholiasts on Aristophanes and Plato both refer to Eurycles' inner voice as having come from a "*daimon*," with the scholiast on

---

[93]   ... ὅστις δ' ἐμπύρῳ χρῆται τέχνῃ,
μάταιος· ἢν μὲν ἐχθρὰ σημήνας τύχῃ,
πικρὸς καθέστηχ' οἷς ἂν οἰωνοσκοπῇ·
ψευδῆ δ' ὑπ' οἴκτου τοῖσι χρωμένοις λέγων
ἀδικεῖ τὰ τῶν θεῶν. Φοῖβον ἀνθρώποις μόνον
χρῆν θεσπιῳδεῖν, ὃς δέδοικεν οὐδένα.
(Euripides, *Phoen.* 954–59. English translation [modified] in *Euripides*, translated by Arthur S. Way [4 vols. LCL; New York: MacMillan, 1912]). Dishonored by the house of Oedipus, Teiresias returns to Thebes with a victor's wreath upon his head for the success in battle he brought to the Athenians (Euripides, *Phoen.* 852–57), only to be dishonored again by Creon.

[94] See a summary of the sources about Eurycles in A. C. Pearson, *The Fragments of Sophocles* (3 vols.; Cambridge: Cambridge University Press, 1917) 1:37, frag. 59. Fragment 59 is attributed to Sophocles' lost play *Aichmalotides*. Pearson concludes "There is nothing in these passages which is not satisfied by the simple inference that Eurycles alleged his oracles to be the voice of a demon lodged in his own breast" (Pearson, *Fragments of Sophocles*, 1:37). Wesley Smith dismisses the case of Eurycles as an aberration in classical Athens (Smith, "So-called Possession," *TAPA* 96 [1965] 425–26).

[95] Aristophanes, *Vesp.* 1019–20.

[96] Plato, *Soph.* 252C.

Aristophanes specifying that the spirit was "good".[97] Plutarch would later remark that others continued to practice this type of prophecy under Eurycles' name.[98] Although this suggests that Eurycles gave Athens' its first exposure to the *engastrimythos*, it is possible that the practice did not originate with him, but that he himself learned the craft on Lesbos or its environs.

The term *engastrimythos* is probably a derogatory one, as the references to Eurycles and other such practitioners are generally hostile. Both Aristophanes and Plato ridicule Eurycles because of his unusual talent.[99] Plato elsewhere reveals a suspicion of "diviners" (μάντεις) generally. In the *Timaeus* he identifies the belly — the unreasoning seat of appetites — as the receptacle of divination.[100] In the *Laws*, he places the bulk of diviners with that class of atheists who maliciously prey upon others' beliefs for personal gain.[101] In Hellenistic literature the Septuagint also serves as a hostile witness in its use of the term, where it places the *engastrimythos* within lists of abhorrent and forbidden pagan practices, particularly as found in Egypt.[102] In these verses it typically corresponds to the Hebrew אוב, which refers to the "skin" used to hold water or wine, and presumably describes the belly of this type of prophet.[103]

Although nothing more is known of Eurycles himself, the term *engastrimythos* appears elsewhere in Classical Greek literature in a work

---

[97]W. J. W. Koster, ed., *Scholia in Aristophanem* (Groningen: Bouma's Boekhuis, 1978) 2.1:162, line 1019b. The scholiasts considered Eurycles' prophecies to be "true" (ἀληθῆ μαντευόμενος) and from a "good daimon" (ἀγαθὸν δαίμονα).

[98]"... the *engastrimythoi*, who long ago were called 'Eurycleis,' but now 'Pythones'..." (... τοὺς ἐγγαστριμύθους, Εὐρυκλέας πάλαι νυνὶ δὲ Πύθωνας προσαγορευομένους ...) (Plutarch, *Def. orac.* 414E).

[99]In the *Wasps*, Aristophanes compares his own borrowing of ideas for his plays as similar to Eurycles' receiving messages from his inner voice (Aristophanes, *Vesp.* 1019b [in Koster, *Scholia in Aristophanem*, 2.1:162, line 1019b]). The stranger from Elis in Plato's *Sophist* calls Eurycles "out of place" (ἄτοπος), and uses him to illustrate those sophists whose arguments need no refutation by others because everything they say they themselves refute. The others in the dialogue welcome the comparison (Plato, *Soph.* 252D).

[100]Plato, *Tim.* 70D–72B.

[101]Also included are several tyrants, demagogues, generals, sophists, those who indulge in personal mysteries, and those who claim to charm mortal souls and bewitch the gods (Plato, *Lg.* 10.907D–909D).

[102]Lev 19:31; 20:6, 27; Deut 18:11; cf. 2 Chr 33:6; 35:19a (LXX); Isa 8:19; 19:3; 44:25. Philo also lists it among the nefarious and deceitful crafts practiced by the Egyptians (Philo, *Somn.* 1.220.8).

[103]It is also used of the witch of Endor (1 Sam 28:3–9; cf. 1 Chr 10:13). This coincides with the usage cited for Philochorus in the *Suda*, which says that in the third book of *On Divination* he uses *engastrimythos* of women prophets who call forth souls of the dead (Karl Müller, ed., *Fragmenta historicorum graecorum* [5 vols.; Paris: Didot, 1851–1885] 1.416, frag. 192).

attributed to Hippocrates (V B.C.E.). In the fifth book of *Epidemics*, Hippocrates uses it in his description of the congested sounds made by a woman who mortally suffers from sore throat, tracheal swelling, and high fever:

> Around the fifth day, pain at the knee, swelling of the left bodes ill: and it seems that something congests her in the heart, and she breathes as they who have been half-drowned, and she makes a light noise from the chest, as do those called *engastrimythoi*.[104]

Hippocrates does not appear to use the term in a derogatory sense, and his anatomical description significantly associates the source of such prophecy with the upper part of the torso rather than the belly. To this one can compare the more favorable Sophoclean term στερνόμαντις, or "one who prophesies from the chest."[105]

The *engastrimythos* serves as a potential example of *daimonic* possession in early Greece, but as a good *daimon* as some viewed it, its prophecies represent a useful resource to the community, and therefore is not subject to exorcism. The same can be said of prophecy in general during this period. Although the honors fluctuated for those who practiced divination and prophecy, I have found no occasion where an attempt was made to divest a prophet of his art. In contrast, the New Testament account of Paul's having dismissed the spirit of divination from the slave girl at Philippi stands apart as extraordinary, and the angry reaction of her owners would likely have met with the sympathy of other Greeks.[106]

4.2.2.2 Possession and Illness

Very seldom in early Greek literature does disease (νόσος) possess the individual in ways that resemble later demonic possession. Although Sophocles personifies Philoctetes' agonizing foot infection, and describes its chronic nature as one who returns after weary bouts of wandering, this

---

[104]Περὶ πέμπτην, γούνατος ἄλγημα, οἴδημα τοῦ ἀριστεροῦ· καὶ κατὰ τὴν καρδίην ἐδόκεέ τι ξυλλέγεσθαι αὐτῇ, καὶ ἀνέπνεεν ὡς ἐκ τοῦ βεβαπτίσθαι ἀναπνέουσι, καὶ ἐκ τοῦ στήθεος ὑπεψόφεεν, ὥσπερ αἱ ἐγγαστρίμυθοι λεγόμεναι· (Hippocrates, *Epid.* 5.63. Greek in Hippocrates, *Ouevres complétes*, Ê. Littré, ed. [10 vols.; Paris: J.-B. Bailliére, 1839–1861] 5.242).

[105]Sophocles, frag. 59. Although the context in which Sophocles used the term is lost, it was assumed synonymous with *engastrimythos* even as early as Philochorus of Athens (ca. 340–260 B.C.E.). After Philochorus, the connection was consistently made in antiquity by the lexicographers (Hesychius, "*E*," entries 123 line 2; 1774 line 1; 3307 line 1; *Suda* "ἐγγαστρίμυθος"), the scholiast on Plato, and the fourth to fifth century Christian theologian Theodoretus (*Comm. Isa.* 6.236).

[106]Acts 16:16–24.

personification does not involve possession.[107] A closer convergence comes with Sophocles' depiction of Heracles as mortally afflicted by the cloak dyed with Nessus' blood.[108] Heracles calls his affliction a *daimon*, and describes it as a possessing entity, which first affected him superficially, but now eats away from within:

It has clung to my sides and eaten away my inmost flesh, and lives with me to devour the channels of my lungs. Already it has drunk my fresh blood, and my whole body is ruined, now that I am mastered by this unspeakable bondage. ... Again a spasm of torture has burned me, it has darted through my sides, and the ruthless devouring malady seems never to leave me without torment. ... For again it is feasting on me, it has blossomed, it is launched.[109]

In the cases of both Philoctetes and Heracles, their maladies derive from a divinity or through divine agency.[110]

Epilepsy is another illness relevant to hostile possession in early Greece. Also called the "sacred disease" (ἱερῆ νούσος) in antiquity, epilepsy was popularly attributed to possession by a deity. *The Sacred Disease*, a medical tractate that likely dates to the late fifth century B.C.E.,[111] juxtaposes its own

---

[107]"It has come in person after a time, perhaps because it is weary of wandering, the sickness" (ἥκει γὰρ αὐτὴ διὰ χρόνου, πλάνης ἴσως ὡς ἐξεπλήσθη, νόσος — Sophocles, *Phil.* 758–59 [Lloyd-Jones, LCL]).

[108]Sophocles, *Trach.* 1024–30.

[109] πλευραῖσι γὰρ προσμαχθὲν ἐκ μὲν ἐσχάτας
βέβρωκε σάρκας, πλεύμονός τ' ἀρτηρίας
ῥοφεῖ ξυνοικοῦν· ἐκ δὲ χλωρὸν αἷμά μου
πέπωκεν ἤδη, καὶ διέφθαρμαι δέμας
τὸ πᾶν, ἀφράστῳ τῇδε χειρωθεὶς πέδῃ.
...
ἔθαλψέ μ' ἄτης σπασμὸς ἀρτίως ὅδ' αὖ,
διῆξε πλευρῶν, οὐδ' ἀγύμναστόν μ' ἐᾶν
ἔοικεν ἡ τάλαινα διάβορος νόσος.
...
... δαίνυται γὰρ αὖ πάλιν,
ἤνθηκεν, ἐξώρμηκεν.
(Sophocles, *Trach.* 1053–1089 [Lloyd-Jones, LCL]).

[110]For Heracles, the cloak is poisoned by Nessus' deceit, comparable to a magical potion (Sophocles, *Trach.* 568–87; 672–722; cf. 1138–42). Heracles at one point calls the poisoned cloak, the "woven garment of the Erinyes" ('Ερινύων ὑφαντὸν ἀμφίβληστρον — Sophocles, *Trach.* 1051–52). Philoctetes received his wound from the bite of a serpent (*Il.* 2.718–25). In post-Homeric accounts this takes place at the altar of Apollo, where Chryses serves as priest, and the infection comes from the god's response to Chryses' curse (cf. Sophocles, *Phil.* 191–200).

[111]Owsei Temkin dates the treatise to ca. 400 B.C.E. (Owsei Temkin, *The Falling Sickness: A History of Epilepsy from the Greeks to the Beginning of Modern Neurology* [2d rev. ed.; Baltimore: Johns Hopkins University Press, 1994] 4); Fritz Graf also favors a late fifth century date (Graf, *Magic in the Ancient World*, 30). *The Sacred Disease* 21 may

physiological explanation of the illness with a mythological one, whereby both cause and cure derive from the gods.[112] In the first chapters of *The Sacred Disease* the author discredits the opinion that the disease is unusually sacred. He considers the epithet "sacred" as the ignorant healer's excuse for a lack of cure. By assigning only purificatory prescriptions to the patient, such healers divert the responsibility for their own failure to cure so that it falls upon the divine will instead. The author calls such practitioners "magicians" (μάγοι), "purifiers" (καθάρται), "charlatans" (ἀγύρται), and "impostors" (ἀλαζόνες), in sum, "men who claim great piety and spiritual knowledge."[113]

4.2.2.3 Possession and Madness

Apart from the potentially beneficial divine possession manifested in prophecy, possession by a deity otherwise leads to detrimental consequences in early Greek literature, of which madness is a particularly ubiquitous form. The symptoms of madness described here often share the symptoms of later demonic possession and they warrant a closer examination to see how and by

---

contain an allusion to *Regimen on Acute Diseases*, an undisputed work by Hippocrates. This would support an early date for *The Sacred Disease*'s composition. The Hippocratic *On the Maladies of Young Women* also critiques a popular view that the "so-called sacred disease" (ἡ ἱερά νοῦσος καλεομένη), apoplexies and other terrors, were attributed to "certain hostile *daimons*" (δαίμονάς τινας δυσμενέας) (Hippocrates, *Virg.*; Littré, *Ouevres complétes d'Hippocrate*, 8.466).

[112]"and most of what they say reverts back to divinity and *daimon*" (ὅ τε πολὺς αὐτοῖς τοῦ λόγου ἐς τὸ θεῖον ἀφῆκει καὶ τὸ δαιμόνιον — Hippocrates, *Morb. sacr.* 3).

[113]The passage reads as follows: "My own view is that those who first attributed a sacred character to this malady were like the magicians, purifiers, charlatans and quacks of our own day, men who claim great piety and superior knowledge." ('Εμοὶ δὲ δοκέουσιν οἱ πρῶτοι τοῦτο τὸ νόσημα ἱερώσαντες τοιοῦτοι εἶναι ἄνθρωποι οἷοι καὶ νῦν εἰσι μάγοι τε καὶ καθάρται καὶ ἀγύρται καὶ ἀλαζόνες, οὗτοι δὲ καὶ προσποιέονται σφόδρα θεοσεβέες εἶναι καὶ πλέον τι εἰδέναι.) (Hippocrates, *Morb. sacr.* 2 [Jones, LCL]). Chapters 3–4 advance the distinction between medicine and the work of the purifier: "Yet, in my opinion their discussions show, not piety, as they think, but impiety rather, implying that the gods do not exist, and what they call piety and the divine is, as I shall prove, impious and unholy." (καίτοι ἔμοιγε οὐ περὶ εὐσεβείης τοὺς λόγους δοκέουσι ποιεῖσθαι, ὡς οἴονται, ἀλλὰ περὶ ἀσεβείης μᾶλλον, καὶ ὡς οἱ θεοὶ οὐκ εἰσί, τὸ δὲ εὐσεβὲς αὐτῶν καὶ τὸ θεῖον ἀσεβές ἐστι καὶ ἀνόσιον, ὡς ἐγὼ διδάξω.) (Hippocrates, *Morb. sacr.* 3 [Jones, LCL]). And, further down: "For if a man by magic and sacrifice will bring the moon down, eclipse the sun, and cause storm and sunshine, I shall not believe that any of these things is divine, but human, seeing that the power of godhead is overcome and enslaved by the cunning of man." (εἰ γὰρ ἄνθρωπος μαγεύων καὶ θύων σελήνην καθαιρήσει καὶ ἥλιον ἀφανιεῖ καὶ χειμῶνα καὶ εὐδίην ποιήσει, οὐκ ἂν ἔγωγέ τι θεῖον νομίσαιμι τούτων εἶναι οὐδέν, ἀλλ' ἀνθρώπινον, εἰ δὴ τοῦ θείου ἡ δύναμις ὑπὸ ἀνθρώπου γνώμης κρατεῖται καὶ δεδούλωται.) (Hippocrates, *Morb. sacr.* 4 [Jones, LCL]).

whom they may have been treated. The following section discusses madness as it appears in the literary genres of tragedy and history. The two respectively represent mythological and social-historical approaches to understanding madness. These different contexts yield different interpretations of madness, which eventually lead to different treatments of the deranged.

4.2.2.3.1 Tragedic Madness

Possession portrayed in Greek tragedy often results from some offense a god has taken at an individual, and manifests itself as an insanity or madness that leads to a destructive consequence. In reading through the Greek tragedies, one realizes that this madness often plays a central role in the development of the drama's plot, and is a means by which the tragedians explain the drastic actions committed by the leading characters. In the plays of Aeschylus, Hera brings madness to Athamas[114] and Io,[115] Apollo to Cassandra through the agency of an *alastor*,[116] Ares to Eteocles,[117] and Dionysus to Lycurgus' household,[118] Pentheus, and the daughters of Minyas.[119] Sophocles shows Oedipus maddened by some *daimon* so that he blinds himself,[120] and Ajax in a delusional rage tortures and slaughters a flock of sheep that he takes to be the Achaean army and its hated leaders.[121] We can also assume madness to have been at the centers of *Athamas 1* and *2*, *Alcmeon*, and *The Madness of Odysseus*. Nearly half of Euripides' extant plays have madness as an element central to their plot developments.[122] The *Bacchai* especially illustrates Dionysus' possession of the maenads,[123] whose epithet itself evokes the Greek word for "madness."[124] These passages offer evidence of the influence that the gods have upon human senses and actions.

---

[114]Aeschylus, *Athamas* (fragmentary).

[115]Aeschylus, *Supp.* 307–9, 562–64; *Prom.* 876–86.

[116]Aeschylus, *Ag.* 1072–1330.

[117]"Mad, inspiring to frenzy, slaying the people, defiling holiness is war" (μαινόμενος δ' ἐπιπνεῖ λαυδάμας μιαίνων εὐσέβειαν Ἄρης — Aeschylus, *Sept. c. Theb.* 343–44 [Smyth, LCL]).

[118]"Lo, the house is frenzied with the god, the roof revels, Bacchantlike" (ἐνθουσιᾷ δὴ δῶμα, βακχεύει στέγη — Aeschylus, *Edoni* frag. 28 [Smyth, LCL]).

[119]Aeschylus, *Xantriae* (fragmentary).

[120]Sophocles, *Oed. Tyr.* 1297–1330.

[121]Sophocles, *Ajax* 182–85. Sophocles calls Ajax' madness, sent by Athena, "mad sickness" (μανιάσιν νόσοις — *Ajax* 59–60), "divine sickness" (θεία νόσος — *Ajax* 185), and "divine madness" (θεία μανία — *Ajax* 611).

[122]Madness (μαινάς, μαίνομαι et al.) is central to the plots of *Medea, Hippolytus, Trojan Women, Electra, Orestes, Iphigeneia at Tauris, Bacchai*, and *Madness of Heracles*.

[123]Euripides, *Ba.* 300–1, 1122–24.

[124]Thus, μανία "madness," and μαίνομαι "to rage, to be driven mad."

The physical symptoms associated with madness in Greek tragedy tend to become somewhat standardized. Thus, Orestes in his recurrent fits of madness rolls his eyes, stands up, moves his head up and down, trembles, groans and shouts in delusion, thinking that the Erinyes are upon him.[125] Agave's lips foam and her eyes roll wildly in her bacchic possession,[126] and both she and Pentheus enter into delusional states.[127] When Lyssa comes upon Heracles, his head tosses, his gorgon-like and bloodshot eyes roll, he pants and bellows like a bull, his mouth foams, and he laughs, deluded into thinking he is about to kill Eurystheus' sons instead of his own.[128]

The example of Heracles becoming bull-like shows the bestial state to which madness can reduce one. This is literally the punishment to which Hera subjects Io who, transformed into a heifer, is driven about the eastern Mediterranean by a gadfly.[129] In *Iphigeneia at Tauris* Euripides appears to pattern Orestes after the gadfly-plagued Io. Guilty of matricide, Orestes is driven from Argos by the stinging of the Erinyes.[130] He describes the pursuit that has led him to the northern region of Thracian Tauris, as their striving to place a "bloody bridle" in his mouth.[131] Also goaded in their madnesses are the maenads[132] and Heracles.[133]

Most of the examples from tragedy show how the gods bring madness upon an individual by some external force, such as Io's gadfly or the Erinyes who pursue Orestes. But there are also instances in which the onset of frenzy or madness comes from an internal force. Such is the case with the *alastor* that has worked through Clytemnaestra to murder Agamemnon,[134] or when Dionysus stirs the maenads to frenzy.[135] Aeschylus also has the spirit of

---

[125]Euripides, *Or.* 253–61; *Iph. Taur.* 281–84.

[126]Euripides, *Ba.* 1122–24.

[127]Euripides, *Ba.* 918–22, 1264–84.

[128]Euripides, *Herc. fur.* 858–74, 930–35, 990.

[129]οἶστρος (Aeschylus, *Prom.* 566).

[130]Euripides, *Iph. Taur.* 77–84, 931–35, 1455–56; cf. the chorus' reference to Io goaded by a "gadfly" (οἶστρος) at 392–98.

[131]αἱματηρὰ στόμια (Euripides, *Iph. Taur.* 931–35).

[132]Euripides, *Ba.* 665, 1227–29.

[133]Euripides, *Herc. fur.* 1144. Madness involving dehumanization also occurs in Jewish literature, where king Nebuchadnezzar "... was driven away from human society, ate grass like an ox, and his body was bathed with the dew of heaven, until his hair grew as long as eagles' feathers and his nails became like birds' claws." (... καὶ ἀπὸ τῶν ἀνθρώπων ἐξεδιώχθη καὶ χόρτον ὡς βοῦς ἤσθιεν, καὶ ἀπὸ τῆς δρόσου τοῦ οὐρανοῦ τὸ σῶμα αὐτοῦ ἐβάφη, ἕως οὗ αἱ τρίχες αὐτοῦ ὡς λεόντων ἐμεγαλύνθησαν καὶ οἱ ὄνυχες αὐτοῦ ὡς ὀρνέων.) (LXX [θ´] Dan 4:33). One can also compare the terminology "to silence" or "muzzle" as an ox (φιμόειν), as it appears with reference to the demonically possessed in the New Testament. Φιμόειν is used in exorcistic contexts at Mark 1:25 and its parallel Luke 4:35.

[134]Aeschylus, *Ag.* 1497–1504. The passage is partially quoted in this chapter, note 55.

[135]Euripides, *Ba.* 300–1, 1122–24.

Darius say that some *daimon* must have led Xerxes to build a bridge across the Hellespont, and so to try to master not only mortals but also the realms of the gods.[136]

Despite similarities of anti-social, self-abusive, or outwardly aggressive symptoms, the fact that the gods have caused the madness gives a different significance to the hostile possession found in early Greek literature compared to the demonic possession of the New Testament. To attribute such possessions to a divinity rather than to a malicious demon suggests that the Greeks identified such afflictions with divine judgment against the sufferers, either for crimes they have committed, or for offenses that they have given to a particular god.[137] For this reason the actions of the avenging gods and spirits carry the significance of divine judgment or retribution even should the tragedian interpret the punishment to be unjustified.[138]

4.2.2.3.2 Madness in History

To see more clearly the implications that divine intervention brings to madness, it will help to compare its treatment by the tragedians with the historical work of Herodotus. Herodotus, too, describes the madnesses of both his historical and mythological subjects in ways that resemble the symptoms of demonic possession found in the New Testament. Herodotus, however, favors a different rationale for the maniae of each. Of the historical figures, Herodotus describes Cambyses and Cleomenes as maniacal.[139] Of the mythical persons, he retells the story of the Proetides. It is worth looking at

---

[136]   Alas, what great daimon came so that he did not think soundly?

...

... How is this? Does not a sickness of the mind possess my child?

(φεῦ, μέγας τις ἦλθε δαίμων, ὥστε μὴ φρονεῖν καλῶς

...

... πῶς τάδ᾽ οὐ νόσος φρενῶν
εἶχε παῖδ᾽ ἐμόν;)

(Aeschylus, *Pers.* 725, 750–51).

[137]Lycurgus writes in one of his speeches: "For the first step taken by the gods in the case of wicked men is to unhinge their reason ..." (οἱ γὰρ θεοὶ οὐδὲν πρότερον ποιοῦσιν ἢ τῶν πονηρῶν ἀνθρώπων τὴν διάνοιαν παράγουσι ...) (Lycurgus, *In Leocratem* 92 [Burtt, LCL]). To this, compare a passage from Aeschines, where he attributes human wrongdoing to individual responsibility rather than to a foreign spiritual influence (Aeschines, *In Timarchum* 190–91).

[138]Thus, Heracles appears to be innocent (Euripides, *Herc. fur.* 822–73), and Prometheus and Io consider themselves innocent (Aeschylus, *Prom.* 578–82). Compare also how the chorus considers Philoctetes to suffer innocently from his foot infection (Sophocles, *Phil.* 676–722), though Neoptolemos attributes it to the will of the gods and the curse of Chryses (Sophocles, *Phil.* 191–200).

[139]Cf. also Charilaus (Herodotus 3.145), whom Herodotus describes as "somewhat mad" (ὑπομαργότερος), a term he also use of Cambyses (Herodotus 3.29).

each individually for behavior that labels them as insane and for any treatment that they receive from those around them.

The son of Cyrus and king of the Persian Empire, Cambyses revealed his madness through a variety of rash and impious actions. The first mentioned by Herodotus are two uncalculated military offensives. In an "act of rage" (ὀργὴν ποιησάμενος), and while "he was mad and not of sound mind" (ἐμμανής τε ἐὼν καὶ οὐ φρενήρης), Cambyses first sent forth an ill-provisioned expedition against the Ethiopians.[140] The mission was aborted once his starving troops began drawing lots and eating every tenth man. The mission sent against Ammon ended in disaster when a sandstorm buried the troops.[141] On another occasion, Cambyses became "nearly mad" (ὑπομαργότερος) when the Egyptian priests led a calf into his presence as their god Apis. Affronted by the crudeness of a god envisioned as an animal, he mortally stabbed the calf and had the priests flogged.[142] He is also said to have committed acts of impiety in the lands of his allies,[143] and outrages against his own people which included having them arrested and put to death without charge.[144]

Herodotus accepts Cambyses' condition as madness,[145] and he offers several reasons for why he was so. The Egyptians, he says, attributed it to divine judgment for his having killed the Apis calf and flogging the priests.[146] Herodotus himself dismisses this, as Cambyses showed himself to be out of his wits even earlier.[147] Cambyses' fellow Persians considered his irrational acts to be the result of excessive drinking habits (θυμωθέντα), a charge that enraged Cambyses himself.[148] The view Herodotus appears to support is that Cambyses was the victim from birth of the "sacred disease,"[149] of which he says: "It would indeed not be unnatural for one whose body suffered a great sickness to have his wits diseased also."[150]

Herodotus first refers to the madness of Cleomenes, king of the Lakedaemonians, in Book 5, where he is said to be "not quite right in his head and was, indeed, a little mad."[151] Cleomenes displayed his madness by striking

---

[140]Herodotus 3.25.

[141]Herodotus 3.26.

[142]Herodotus 3.29.

[143]Herodotus 3.37.

[144]Herodotus 3.34–38.

[145]ἐμάνη (Herodotus 3.30, 38).

[146]Herodotus 3.28–30.

[147]Herodotus 3.30.

[148]Herodotus 3.34.

[149]"A certain great sickness which some call sacred" (τινὰ ... νοῦσον μεγάλην ... τὴν ἱρὴν ὀνομάζουσι τινές) (Herodotus 3.33).

[150]οὔ νύν τοι ἀεικὲς οὐδὲν ἦν τοῦ σώματος νοῦσον μεγάλην νοσέοντος μηδὲ τὰς φρένας ὑγιαίνειν (Herodotus 3.33; trans. Grene).

[151]τε οὐ φρενήρης ἀκρομανής τε (Herodotus 5.42; trans. Grene).

his fellow Spartans in the face with a stick. The problem became so severe that his family eventually had to place him in stocks.[152] While in bondage, he coerced a guard to give him a knife and with it committed suicide by slashing himself from his shins to his belly.[153]

Herodotus says that outsiders attributed the cause of Cleomenes' violent behavior to divine judgment wrought for some impiety on his part: most Greeks believed that his impiety was corrupting the Pythia; the Athenians attributed it to his ravaging the Eleusinian sanctuary of Demeter and Kore; the Argives to his destroying the sacred grove of Argos and the many of their own citizens who had sought refuge there during their conflict with Sparta.[154] The Spartans themselves considered his madness due not to a spiritual influence,[155] but to the fact that he had picked up bad drinking habits from the Scythians.[156] Herodotus himself describes it as a "maniacal illness" (μανίη νοῦσος) to which Cleomenes was predisposed, even though it came to fruition only late in his life.[157]

The symptoms of both of these men include a varied range of anti-social and self-abusive behaviors that in Cleomenes' case required imprisonment and bondage. In the cases of both, the madnesses were believed by those who suffered most from their actions to be the result of divine judgment for impiety, while those whom they ruled and so represented, more respectfully attributed it to the human weakness of a problem drinker. Herodotus himself tends to favor physiological explanations for both men, so that an illness has predisposed them to their eventual disintegrations.[158]

An alternative view to that of these historical figures comes when Herodotus retells the story of the Argive women.[159] Herodotus' account revolves around the myth of the Proetides: Lysippe, Iphinoe and Iphianassa, the three daughters of Proetus, King of Tiryns. The story of the Proetides is preserved in several ancient versions, but finds its fullest account in the *Bibliotheca* attributed to Apollodorus, though it is likely of the first centuries

---

[152]ἔδησαν οἱ προσήκοντες ἐν ξύλῳ (Herodotus 6.75).

[153]Herodotus 6.75.

[154]Herodotus 6.75.

[155]ἐκ δαιμονίου μὲν οὐδενὸς μανῆναι (Herodotus 6.84).

[156]μαθεῖν τὴν ἀκρητοποσίην παρ' αὐτῶν (Herodotus 6.84). Hence, the origin of a Spartan proverb "Scythian cup" (ἐπισκύθισον) for taking pleasure in strong drink.

[157]Herodotus 6.75.

[158]Plato in the *Timaeus* also favors a physiological explanation to madness (μανία) as well as ignorance (ἀμαθία). Both are a "disease of the soul" (νόσος ψυχῆς). Excessive pleasure or pain prohibit clear reasoning, which brings on what is popularly referred to as being "willingly evil" (ἐκὼν κακός), but is actually just another form of illness (Plato, *Tim.* 86A–E).

[159]Herodotus 9.34.

Common Era.[160] According to the *Bibliotheca* the daughters of Proetus go mad (ἐμάνησαν), driven so either by Dionysus for having shunned his mysteries,[161] or for their having insulted a statue of Hera.[162] The sisters show their madness by wandering throughout the wilderness of Argos, Arcadia, and all the Peloponnesus (γενόμεναι ... ἐμμανεῖς ἐπλανῶντο). Proetus summons for help the seer Melampus, "the first who found the treatment through drugs and purifications."[163] During the course of treatment, the eldest daughter Iphinoe dies, but the other two survive, and through Melampus' purifications (καθαρμοί) regain their sanity (σωφρονῆσαι).[164] As further reward, Proetus gives his two surviving daughters, now fully restored to health, to Melampus and his brother Bias as wives. Thus, Melampus heals the women so completely as to restore their good standing both with regard to the offended deity and to the city-state.

It is significant that Proetus calls upon a seer rather than a physician to treat the problem. Although Herodotus also calls the Proetides' "madness" (μανεισέων) an "illness" (νούσου), as he does for Cambyses and Cleomenes, he does not offer a physiological explanation of their disease, but accepts a cause of divine retribution as alone satisfactory. Here we see how context dictates the cure: with the Proetides we tread on the same mythological ground worked by the tragedians for whom divinely wrought causes necessitate divinely inspired relief. Since we are dealing with mythical rather than historical tradition, divine judgment is the accepted cause of the women's madness, and Melampus, the diviner with knowledge of drugs and purifications, is the appropriate healer for this interpretation.

4.3 Treatment of the Possessed

Beneficent and maleficent spiritual possessions are distinguishable by their treatments. Since the consequences of beneficent possession are useful to the individual or community, the entities that cause them are not driven out. In contrast, those who are subjected to the undesirable effects of maleficent possession undergo various treatments. Chapter 4 concludes with a discussion of four methods by which the ancient Greeks sought to treat the symptoms of

---

[160]Apollodorus, *Bibliotheca* 2.2. Herodotus' own reference likely draws from Aeschylus' *Xantriae*, which deals with the Argive women generally and not the daughters of Proetus specifically.

[161]Hesiod, *Fr.* 131.

[162]Acusilaus, *FGrH* 2F28.

[163]μάντις ὢν καὶ τὴν διὰ φαρμάκων καὶ καθαρμῶν θεραπείαν πρῶτος εὑρηκώς (Apollodorus, *Bibliotheca* 2.2.2).

[164]By some literary traditions the healings take place at a spring, where the sisters bathe as part of their atonement (Pausanias 8.18.7; Ovid, *Met.* 15.322–28).

maleficent possession with an interest in the relevance of such treatments to exorcism. The first section, "Binding the Possessed," concerns a means by which the symptoms of maleficent possession were dealt with rather than the cause of the possessing spirit itself. The second, "Medicine and Possession," discusses the treatment of the symptoms of a malady by attending to its physiological cause. "Possession and Cultic Healing" discusses physiological illnesses that derive their cures from the spiritual world. "Purification and Possession" concerns treatments of maladies attributed to spiritual causes.

4.3.1 Binding the Possessed

An initial treatment of madness is to control the disturbed individual. Thus, we find many cases in Greek literature in which the possessed are bound or imprisoned: Cleomenes was imprisoned and chained; Dionysus and the maenads are bound and imprisoned for their threat to the *polis*;[165] Heracles is bound after his fit of madness for fear that he will do more harm.[166] Binding and releasing are also integral to the terminology and symbolism of demonic possession and exorcism in the Jewish and Christian traditions. Conceptually, however, the intention of the exorcist works in a way opposite to the social treatment of those believed to be possessed. Whereas society bound the possessed person, the exorcist aimed at restraining the hostile spirit that possesses him or her. In this scenario exorcism constrains the foreign spirit, while it releases the victim of possession.

4.3.2 Medicine and Possession

Epilepsy is one form of *daimonic* possession that fell within the realm of ancient medical treatment. According to the medical view expounded in *The Sacred Disease*, the pseudo-healers drew from the Greek pantheon to account for epileptic possession, and they discerned which god had possession through the patient's symptoms.[167] This diagnosis of divine cause has a

---

[165]Euripides, *Ba.* 432–50, 509–18.

[166]Euripides, *Herc. fur.* 1035–38. Compare also the figurative binding and releasing of Orestes in Aeschylus' *Eumenides* where, urged on by the ghost of Clytemnaestra, the Erinyes seek to bind Orestes by a spell of derangement (δέσμιος φρενῶν — Aeschylus, *Eum.* 332).

[167]The passage reads in full: "If the patient imitate a goat, if he roar, or suffer convulsions in the right side, they say that the Mother of the Gods is to blame. If he utter a piercing and loud cry, they liken him to a horse and blame Poseidon. Should he pass some excrement, as often happens under the stress of the disease, the surname Enodia is applied. If it be more frequent and thinner, like that of birds, it is Apollo Nomius. If he foam at the mouth and kick, Ares has the blame. When at night occur fears and terrors, delirium, jumpings from the bed and rushings out of doors, they say that Hecate is attacking or that heroes are assaulting." (καὶ ἢν μὲν γὰρ αἶγα μιμῶνται, καὶ ἢν βρύχωνται, ἢ τὰ δεξιὰ σπῶνται, μητέρα θεῶν φασὶν αἰτίην εἶναι. ἢν δὲ ὀξύτερον καὶ εὐτονώτερον φθέγγηται, ἵππῳ εἰκάζουσι, καὶ φασὶ Ποσειδῶνα αἴτιον εἶναι. ἢν δὲ καὶ τῆς κόπρου τι παρῇ, ὅσα πολλάκις γίνεται ὑπὸ τῆς

parallel in Greek tragedy, where, becoming distressed at Phaedra's failing health and strange desire to go to the hills, her nurse says:

All this calls for a skillful diviner
to say which of the gods is making you swerve from the course, my child,
and striking your wits awry.[168]

Contrary to the dualism one finds in New Testament theology, the deities themselves are suspect, and a diagnostic process is used to determine which god is responsible in a given case.

The author of *The Sacred Disease* considers epilepsy an hereditary illness to which those of a phlegmatic constitution are most susceptible.[169] Chapters 6–10 of the treatise explain the physiological causes of the illness. Human emotions, perceptions, and feelings that include madness and deliriousness (μαινόμεθα καὶ παραφρονέομεν) are said to originate in the brain.[170] The illness comes from an excessive deliquescence or "melting" of the brain into phlegm[171] which, instead of departing the body through normal channels such as through the eyes and nose, descends through the veins where it cools the blood and settles in the heart or lungs. The extreme cooling of the circulatory system causes the blood to slow and even to cease in fatal cases, but otherwise produces the following symptoms:

If the phlegm (φλέγμα) be cut off from these passages, but makes its descent into the veins ... the patient becomes speechless and chokes; froth flows from the mouth; he gnashes his teeth and twists his hands [later in the chapter described as "convulsion" (σπάσμον)]; the eyes roll and intelligence fails, and in some cases excrement is discharged.[172]

νούσου βιαζομένοισιν, Ἐνοδίη πρόσκειται ἡ ἐπωνυμίη· ἢν δὲ πυκνότερον καὶ λεπτότερον, οἶον ὄρνιθες, Ἀπόλλων νόμιος. ἢν δὲ ἀφρὸν ἐκ τοῦ στόματος ἀφίη καὶ τοῖσι ποσὶ λακτίζῃ, Ἄρης τὴν αἰτίην ἔχει. οἶσι δὲ νυκτὸς δείματα παρίσταται καὶ φόβοι καὶ παράνοιαι καὶ ἀναπηδήσιες ἐκ τῆς κλίνης καὶ φεύξιες ἔξω, Ἑκάτης φασὶν εἶναι ἐπιβολὰς καὶ ἡρώων ἐφόδους.) (Hippocrates, *Morb. sacr.* 4 [Jones, LCL]).

[168] τάδε μαντείας ἄξια πολλῆς,
ὅστις σε θεῶν ἀνασειράζει
καὶ παρακόπτει φρένας, ὦ παῖ.

(Euripides, *Hipp.* 236–38. English translation in *Euripides*, translated by David Kovacs [4 vols. LCL; Cambridge: Harvard University Press, 1994–1999]).

[169] Hippocrates, *Morb. sacr.* 5.8.

[170] Hippocrates, *Morb. sacr.* 17.

[171] Thus, "we are driven mad by moisture" (καὶ μαινόμεθα μὲν ὑπὸ ὑγρότητος — Hippocrates, *Morb. sacr.* 17).

[172] "Ἢν δὲ τούτων μὲν τῶν ὁδῶν ἀποκλεισθῇ, ἐς δὲ τὰς φλέβας, ... ἄφωνος γίνεται καὶ πνίγεται, καὶ ἀφρὸς ἐκ τοῦ στόματος ἐκρεῖ, καὶ οἱ ὀδόντες συνηρείκασι, καὶ αἱ χεῖρες συσπῶνται, καὶ τὰ ὄμματα

The author of the treatise describes epilepsy as a childhood illness,[173] which can grow progressively worse if left untreated. This worsening can manifest itself in a greater frequency of occurrences,[174] incurability,[175] and even threat of death.[176] The author, however, also offers a method of treatment. By noting the form of the illness,[177] and the season of the year in which it occurs, one can counter the causes by introducing the body to the opposite influences.[178]

In the New Testament, the story of the possessed boy provides a direct point of comparison with the Hippocratic medical record.[179] Instead of the expressions "the sacred disease" (ἡ ἱερὰ νοῦσος), and "epilepsy" (ἐπιληψία) which occur in the medical treatise, Mark describes his subject as "having a speechless spirit" (ἔχοντα πνεῦμα ἄλαλον),[180] and Matthew calls the boy "moonstruck" (σεληνάζομαι).[181] Though the naming of the malady differs in the Hippocratic work and the synoptic gospels, the Table 5 shows that Mark and *The Sacred Disease* record essentially the same symptoms.

Mark also mentions other similarities: the boy has been possessed since childhood;[182] there is a frequency of occurrence;[183] the boy is left in a death-like state after the demon's expulsion.[184]

διαστρέφονται, καὶ οὐδὲν φρονέουσιν, ἐνίοισι δὲ καὶ ὑποχωρεῖ ἡ κόπρος κάτω. (Hippocrates, *Morb. sacr.* 10 [Jones, LCL]). Compare a similar understanding of how the human body works in Herodotus 4.187.

[173]*Morb. sacr.* 11, 14.1–11, and 15.8–14 are among several references in the tractate to epilepsy as a childhood illness.

[174]*Morb. sacr.* 14.1–27 refers to the increasing frequency of seizures in chronic cases of epilepsy.

[175]For example, Hippocrates, *Morb. sacr.* 11, 14; cf. 21.

[176]*Morb. sacr.* 11.1–3 refers to cases where the illness is fatal to children; 12.11–13 refers to cases where the illness is fatal to the aged.

[177]The author distinguishes madness caused by excessive phlegm from that caused by excessive bile: "Those who are mad through phlegm are quiet, and neither shout nor make a disturbance; those maddened through bile are noisy, evil-doers and restless, always doing something inopportune. These are the causes of continued madness." (οἱ μὲν ὑπὸ φλέγματος μαινόμενοι ἥσυχοί τέ εἰσι καὶ οὐ βοηταὶ οὐδὲ θορυβώδεες, οἱ δὲ ὑπὸ χολῆς κεκράκται τε καὶ κακοῦργοι καὶ οὐκ ἀτρεμαῖοι, ἀλλ᾽ αἰεί τι ἄκαιρον δρῶντες.) (Hippocrates, *Morb. sacr.* 18 [Jones, LCL]).

[178]Hippocrates, *Morb. sacr.* 21.

[179]Mark 9:14–29//Matt 17:14–21//Luke 9:37–42.

[180]Mark 9:17; cf. Luke 9:39.

[181]Matt 17:15; cf. Latin *lunaticus*.

[182]ἐκ παιδιόθεν (Mark 9:21).

[183]πολλάκις (Mark 9:22).

[184]ἐγένετο ὡσεὶ νεκρός (Mark 9:26).

Table 5: Comparison of "Epileptic" Symptoms in Mark
and *The Sacred Disease*

Mark 9:14–29	*The Sacred Disease* Ch.10
foaming (ἀφρίζει)	foaming (ἄφρος)
body becoming stiff or dry (ξηραίνεται)*	hands without strength (ἀκρατεῖς), and twisted (συσπῶνται)
speechless (ἄλαλον)	speechless (ἄφωνον)
falling (πεσών) convulsing (συνεσπάραξεν)	kicking with the feet (λακτίζει) senseless (ἄφρονα)

*Dieter Lührmann notes that ξηραίνεται, translated "dryness", is important in the doctrine of the humours, which was fundamental for ancient medicine (Dieter Lührmann, "Neutestamentliche Wundergeschichten und antike Medizin," in *Religious Propoganda and Missionary Competition in the New Testament World: Essays Honoring Dieter Georgi*, Lukas Bormann et al., eds. [New York: Brill, 1994] 201). The author of *The Sacred Disease* remarks that it is the phlegmatic who are most susceptible to epilepsy (*Morb. sacr.* 5). If one follows the medical opinion of *The Sacred Disease* this would suggest "becoming stiff" as the better sense, since the boy's foaming reflects more a phlegmatic constitution. If one dismisses the opinion of the treatise, this suggests that while Mark's use of the term coincides with medical terminology, it is not likely based upon such.

Though the symptoms of possession might lend themselves to medical definition and treatment, the Synoptic Gospels distinguish them from such by attributing to them spiritual agencies subject to the non-medical method of exorcism. On the one hand, the author of the treatise is eager to point out the need for interpreting the disease in material rather than in spiritual terms, and to prescribe for it a material treatment.[185] On the other hand, the synoptics describe the illness in terms of spiritual possession, cured when the spirit departs from the body. Again, interpretation dictates the method of treatment.

4.3.3 Cultic Healing and Possession

The Sacred Disease reveals a tension that existed between the physician's craft and the healings attributed to myth and cult as early as the Classical period when medicine was coming into its own in the Greek world. The two methodologies are distinguished by their potential for healing and the frameworks within which they operated. On the one hand, medicine operated within the limitations of the physical environment by which it explained the cause and cure of ailments. The prognostic method of Hippocratic medicine attempted to predict the logical outcome of a disease; by doing so, the doctor did not raise the patient's hopes without reason and, in fact, even stood to gain public confidence if a patient died when predicted. On the other hand, the cures which took place in the healing sanctuaries operated within a spiritual rather than a material framework and found their greatest advantage over

---

[185]E.g., Hippocrates, *Morb. sacr.* 21, quoted in footnote 8 of Chapter 1, above.

medicine in the provision they made for the miraculous cure.[186] It was typical of the Asclepius cult, for example, that the god would prescribe a treatment for a malady through a dream, or would himself often accomplish the healing by means of some activity within the dream. These prescriptions or activities often defied the rational explanation expected of the medical practitioner,[187] and their inexplicability added to the miraculous quality of the cures. Hence, the method of healing and the very impossibility of curing some of the maladies qualified such successes as miraculous.[188]

Whatever jealousies the healing cults and medical professions may have harbored against each other, they were generally compatible enough to operate within the same sanctuaries. It is easy to understand the continued need for religious healing alongside of the medical profession when the patient encountered the limitations of a doctor's skill; it was through the possibility of cultic healing that hope could continue in the face of the untreatable disease or fatal prognosis. Although the locus for cultic healing in the Greek world lay in the spiritual realm with divinity as the source of healing, the nature of the causes do not reflect the source of the cures. People flocked to the Asclepieia for every sort of physical ailment, none of which prior to the Common Era

---

[186]The ancient testimonies about Asclepius have been collected by Emma and Ludwig Edelstein (Emma J. Edelstein and Ludwig Edelstein, *Asclepius: A Collection and Interpretation of the Testimonies*, vol. I: *Testimonies* [New York: Arno Press, 1975]). A second volume provides commentary on the primary texts gathered in the first volume. The numbered references in my paper preceded by a "T." correspond to the "Testimony" as it occurs in the Edelsteins' collection. The frustration with medicine appears in the New Testament's account of the woman healed of her hemorrhage. We find this story in Mark 5:25–34//Luke 8:43–48. Of the two accounts, Mark more critically portrays the medical profession: "Now there was a woman who had been suffering from hemorrhages (οὖσα ἐν ῥύσει αἵματος) for twelve years. She had endured much under many physicians (ἰατρῶν), and had spent all that she had; and she was no better, but rather grew worse" (Mark 5:25–26).

[187]For example, in an inscription from the second half of the fourth century B.C.E. we read of patients' heads being removed, the cause of illness withdrawn, and the heads then replaced (*IG* 4².1 nos. 121–122.21, 23 [T. 423.21 and T. 423.23]). The maladies treated at the Asklepieia are also often otherwise incurable, so that a man is healed of blindness, even though one of his eyes is missing (ibid. [T. 423.9]). Rivalry between medicine and religious healing manifested itself in the conflict between medicine's elucidation of how healing takes place and the mystery surrounding the process fostered by the cults. See, for example, Aelianus, *Fr.* 100 [T. 405], where a doctor de-mystifies the remedy Asclepius has assigned to a patient in a dream. This example shows how medicine could be construed as a threat to religious healing, as it at times encroached upon what the latter held as wondrous; to a degree it could rationalize what religion called miraculous.

[188]Aristides says: "Indeed it is the paradoxical which lies paramount in the cures of the gods ..." (καὶ μὴν τό γε παράδοξον πλεῖστον ἐν τοῖς ἰάμασι τοῦ θεοῦ ... — Aristides, *Or.* 42.8 [T. 317]). Compare also Aristides, *Or.* 47.65 (T. 408).

appears to have been attributed to *daimonic* affliction.[189] In the early Greek world, to attribute cause to divine agency was to turn the affliction into a judgment against the individual. For this, relief came through rituals of purification.

4.3.4 Purification and Possession

The concern for boundaries that typifies the exorcist's craft finds its closest early Greek analogy in those purification rituals that relate both the causes of maladies and their cures to the spiritual world.[190] *Miasma* (μίασμα) is the Greek term for pollution or defilement generally, compared to the more specific *agos* (ἄγος), which describes that type of defilement that solicits divine anger and retribution typical of most of the cases of possession discussed so far. In his monograph on pollution and purification in early Greek religion, Robert Parker says of the two:

> To *miasma* gods seem irrelevant; it is a dangerous dirtiness that individuals rub off on one another like a physical taint. *Agos* by contrast has its source in a sacrilegious act, and the *enages* [the one who has committed sacrilege], as the attached genitive suggests, is in the grip of an avenging power; the reason for avoiding him is not fear of contamination but to escape being engulfed in the divine punishment that awaits him.[191]

Parker considers the Greeks to have thought of pollutions as "by-products of an ideal order; that is, the pollution being an aberration from that ideal order."[192] These aberrations manifested themselves for the early Greeks in physical flaws, social disruptions — such as sex, birth and death — and any offences made against the "images, precincts, and ceremonies" of the gods;[193] in short, "where the barrier of respect that hedges round the sacred is violated, pollution occurs."[194] The causes of pollution reminded humanity both of its own mortality and of the immortality of the gods, and *miasma* consequently

---

[189]For examples of Asclepius and other gods assisting in exorcism, see Philostratus, *Ep.* 18; *Acts Pil.* A.1 (in 2d edition of Schneemelcher, 1.506); Lactantius, *Inst.* 4.27.12; T. 333.

[190]Jameson, *A Lex Sacra from Selinous*, 44. The authors cite as examples of such purification rituals Aeschylus, *Cho.* 74 (φόνον καθαίροντες), Herodotus 1.43 (ὁ καθαρθεὶς τὸν φόνον), and Timaeus Locr. p. 224 line 8 Marg (ἀποκαθαράμεναι ψευδέας δόξας).

[191]Robert Parker, *Miasma: Pollution and Purification in Early Greek Religion* (Oxford: Clarendon Press, 1983) 8–9. *Agos* is located in the realm of sacrilege and public curse (Parker, *Miasma*, 191), where the curse characteristically functions to support the structures of authority. Parker draws out the characteristics of *agos* that distinguish it as a subcategory within *miasma* in his introduction (Parker, *Miasma*, 1–17).

[192]Parker, *Miasma*, 325–26.

[193]Parker, *Miasma*, 326–27.

[194]Parker, *Miasma*, 150.

emphasized the barrier between the two.[195] The sacrilegious act that resulted in the offender's pollution necessitated his reconciliation to the offended deity, with the effects of such a reconcilliation extending also to his restoration to his own community.

Ritual laws (*leges sacratae*) provide testimony for how spirits were thought to interact with mortals in real-life situations, and how they were dealt with by a given society in practical ways. One such law comes from a lead tablet excavated at Selinous, a Greek colony in southwestern Sicily. The editors of the text, who date the tablet to ca. 460–450 B.C.E., describe its contents as including "rites of purification and the treatment of dangerous spirits. Except for incidental references in literature, it is the earliest evidence known on this subject."[196] The Selinous *lex sacra* is a publicly sanctioned ritual. As such, it is distinguished from the magical practices that lacked public sanction, and against which the ritual may respond.[197] The deities to be placated are Zeus Eumenes, the Eumenides, Zeus Meilichios, the Tritopatores (ancestral spirits), and the *elasteroi* (a variant of *alastores*), all of whom share a common role in avenging familial bloodshed.[198] Following the propitiatory sacrifices and libations in Column A, Column B gives instructions for the suppliant then to purify himself (καθαιρέσθο) from *elasteroi*.[199] Apart

---

[195]"... exclusion from the sacred is no doubt in origin ... simply an exclusion from social life in its festive forms; there is no celebration, no feeling of community, without sacrifice. It certainly comes to seem, however, as if the real barrier that pollution sets up is not between man and man but between man and gods. By banning birth, death, and also sexuality from sacred places, the Greeks emphasize the gulf that separates the nature of god and man" (Parker, *Miasma*, 66).

[196]Jameson, *A Lex Sacra from Selinous*, ix.

[197]The editors of the inscription consider this ritual to address in part the afflictions that could have been inflicted by harmful curses and binding spells: "One of the purposes of the new *lex sacra*, we believe, was to deal with comparable miasma arising from deaths and perhaps from ineffective funerary rites for those dead (*cf.* the *miaroi* Tritopatores of Column A) and to provide ritual cleansing from the pollution of hostile spirits (Column B), similar to those instigated by curse tablets. While curse tablets are not mentioned in the *lex sacra*, their quantity at Selinous, and in particular in the *Campo di Stele*, suggests that the deliberative manipulation of miasma by means of them may have been one of the reasons why the law was written" (Jameson, *A Lex Sacra from Selinous*, 131).

[198]Jameson, *A Lex Sacra from Selinous*, 103. The two forms of Zeus we see here have connection with avengers: Zeus "Eumenes" ties him to the Eumenides, and Zeus "Meilichios" has a role similar to Zeus Alastor, Elasteros and the Erinyes as an avenger of familial bloodshed (Jameson, *A Lex Sacra from Selinous*, 103). The name Zeus Eumenes (ὁ Ζεὺς ὁ 'Ευμενής) has no attestation outside of this inscription (Jameson, *A Lex Sacra from Selinous*, 52, 77). The Tritopatores refer to ghosts of ancestors (Jameson, *A Lex Sacra from Selinous*, 57). The editors consider the *elastoroi* to be a variant of the *alastores* (so, also Fritz Graf, "Alastor," *DNP* 1.434–35).

[199]The inscription reads: "If a man [wishes] to be purified from *elasteroi* ..." (... ἄνθροπος ... [ἐλ]αστέρον ἀποκα[θαίρεσθ]-[αι]) (Column B.1). "If anyone wishes to

from the cult's role in establishing the guidelines, there is no human intermediary or authority figure who intercedes on the guilty party's behalf. In this regard the text lacks the exorcist of later demonic cleansings.

Another inscription, found on a marble stele from the Dorian Greek colony of Cyrene, records purification rituals of the fourth century B.C.E.[200] The rites for "purification, holy acts and services" (καθαρμοῖς καὶ ἀγνηίαις κα[ὶ θεραπ]ηίαις) have been set forth by an oracle of Apollo (A.1-3) which puts this inscription, like that from Selinous, in the category of ritual purification sanctioned and regulated by an official cult. The stele bears two columns of text, of which Column B, lines 28–59, preserves the rituals necessary for dealing with *hikesioi* (ἱκέσιοι), or spiritual "visitants."[201]

The passage is divided into three sections, each devoted to a particular type of spiritual visitant. The first involves the "foreign *hikesios*" (ἱκέσιος ἐπακτός) that invades a private residence and must be removed by the householder.[202] The ritual shows an interest in discerning the name and gender of the *hikesios* or its sender, and in playing host to it, albeit by accomodating it elsewhere. The ritual advises the householder to make two figurines, male and female, of wood or clay, and to set these in a virgin forest along with food and drink.[203] Thus, the case of the foreign *hikesios* at Cyrene is similar to the

---

purify himself, with respect to a foreign or ancestral one (*sc. elastores*), either one that has been heard or one that has been seen, or anyone at all, let him purify himself in the same way as the *autorektas* (homicide?) does when he is purified of an *elasteros*." (... αἴ τίς κα λεῖ ξενικὸν ἒ πατροῖον, ἒ 'πακουστὸν ἒ 'φορατὸν ἒ καὶ χόντινα καθαίρεσθαι, τὸν αὐτὸν τρόπον καθαιρέσθο ϟόνπερ ϟοὐτορέκτας ἐπεί κ ' ἐλαστέρο ἀποκαθάρεται.) (Column B.7–9). (Jameson, *A Lex Sacra from Selinous*, 16–17).

[200]The inscription corresponds to *LSSupp.* 115 (*SEG* 9.72). Carl Darling Buck discusses the text and provides an English translation in *The Greek Dialects: Grammar, Selected Inscriptions, Glossary* (Chicago: University of Chicago Press, 1955) 307–13. Likewise, Robert Parker gives commentary and translation in an appendix to his work (Parker, *Miasma*, "Appendix 2: The Cyrene Cathartic Law," 332–51). Cyrene was founded by Aristoteles Battos and his fellow Theran colonists in ca. 630 B.C.E.

[201]The identification of the *hikesioi* has been the subject of debate. The original interpreters of the text took it to refer to human "suppliants"; however, Harold Stukey proposed that the term in this context refers to *daimonic* entities from which one seeks to be purified ([H.] J. Stukey, "The Cyrenean *hikesioi*," *CPL* 32 [1937] 32–43). After its initial rejection, Stukey's view has gained support from eminent scholars in the field (thus, Parker and Burkert, as well as Jameson, Jordan and Kotansky. See the discussion in Jameson, *A Lex Sacra from Selinous*, 119–20). In their recent study, Jameson, Jordan, and Kotansky translate the term as spiritual "visitants," and they equate it with the *elastoros* of Selinous (Jameson, *A Lex Sacra from Selinous*, 119).

[202]B.29–39.

[203]The identity of the effigies is subject to debate. Harold Stukey says that "there can be little doubt that the rite of the images is a banquet at which the images represent the sender of the hikesios" (Stukey, "The Cyrenean *hikesioi*," 36, following Gaetano De Sanctis). Burkert identifies the effigies with the evil spirit itself which has been prompted by the maliciousness

conceptual framework of the New Testament's exorcisms in that it establishes a spatial separation between the place of human residence and the wilderness into which the *hikesios* is cast.[204] The second section concerns the "initiated or uninitiated" *hikesios*,[205] a *daimon* who apparently takes up residence at a public shrine in protest over a debt, apparently of funerary obligations. Compensation is to be determined by a priest of Apollo, and until such satisfaction is made the spirit will continue to haunt the site.[206] The inscription's third and most damaged section concerns the *hikesios* that is a suicide or murderer.[207] This one is seated on a white fleece (in effigy?), and is washed and anointed. In each of these cases, the strategy employed seeks to appease the *hikesios* rather than to overpower it and cast it out.

The ritual laws found at Selinous and Cyrene express the perceived need for purification and reconciliation, and they show how these processes were accomplished in daily life. Their discoveries in temple contexts, or internal evidence in the inscriptions themselves, indicate that these ritual laws came from the temple cults, and they appear to have been performed by the afflicted upon themselves under the advisement of attendant priests. Although these two examples do not portray the demons as possessing human bodies,[208] they do reveal how two Greek communities publicly responded to

---

of a sorcerer (Walter Burkert, *Orientalizing Revolution*, 69–70). It seems equally possible that the *hikesios* has come at the urging of a person who has died. Granted, the householder addresses the visitant (or the one who has sent it) as a human (ὦ ἄνθρωπε — B.34), but earlier in the inscription the human is described as dead (τεθνάκηι — B.32), and *anthropos* is also used to refer to the dead ancestors (A.22–24). For an illustration of this scenario, compare the ghost of Clytemnaestra urging on the Erinyes in their pursuit of Orestes (Aeschylus, *Eum.* 306–96).

[204]From the New Testament, compare the demons of the Gerasene demoniac, who beg Jesus not to send them to the abyss (Luke 8:31). Compare also the parable of the returning demon, which, prior to its return, wanders through waterless places (Matt 12:43–44//Luke 11:24–25). Burkert finds convergence between the Cyrenean purification ritual and one from Akkadian magic that also relocates the demonic pollution to an uninhabited place (Walter Burkert, *The Orientalizing Revolution: Near Eastern Influence on Greek Culture in the Early Archaic Age* [Cambridge: Harvard University Press, 1992] 69–70). Shrines to hostile spirits do appear within Greek communities. Compare, for example, the Erinyes, whom Aeschylus grants a shrine at the foot of the Athenian acropolis (Aeschylus, *Eum.* 916–25). Here, however, they are accepted into the city as venerable rather than hostile residents.

[205]ἱκέσιος ... τετελεσμένος ἢ ἀτελής (B.40–49).

[206]"If he presents himself anew, then twice as much" (αἰ δέ κα παρῆι ἐ[ς] νέω, δὶς τόσσα — B.44–45).

[207]ἱκέσιος ... αὐτοφόνος (B.50–59).

[208]Although the wording "Zeus Meilichios in Myskos" (τοῖ Διὶ τοῖ Μιλιχίοι τοῖ ἐν Μύσϙο — A.9) and "(Zeus) Meilichios in Euthydamos" (τοῖ ἐν Εὐθυδάμο Μιλιχίοι — A.17) is suggestive of possession, the editors note that Myskos and Euthydamos were important ancestral figures at Selinous, whose graves remained the objects

aggressive spirits with supplications. The ritual laws of the Greek world reveal a cultural environment at home with the idea of purification from demonic oppressors, and thus receptive to analogous Christian ideas.

The Ionian scapegoat ritual of renewal, the *pharmakos*, also has relevance to state-sanctioned purification.[209] In ancient Greek society the "scapegoat" (φάρμακος), served to purify the community at large.[210] Unlike the scapegoat of the Hebrew Bible, the Greek *pharmakos* was a human being, who came actually to personify the city's defilements.[211] In Athens the *pharmakos* ritual took place on the first day of the Thargelia.[212] On this occasion, two men of noteworthy repulsiveness were chosen on behalf of the male and female populations. In a pattern similar to the treatment of the foreign *hikesios* in the Cyrene inscription, who is first shown hospitality and

---

of commemorative attentions. As such, the editors interpret the phrase as Zeus Meilichios "in the plot of" Myskos or Euthydamos (Jameson, *A Lex Sacra from Selinous*, 15).

[209]See Dennis D. Hughes, *Human Sacrifice in Ancient Greece* (London: Routledge, 1991) 139–65; W. Ruge, "Pharmakos," *PW* 38 (1938) 1841–42; J. N. Bremmer, "Scapegoat Rituals in Ancient Greece," *HSCP* 87 (1983) 299–320; Burkert, *Greek Religion*, 82–84; Parker, *Miasma*, 24–26, 257–80. Concerning the ritual as performed at Athens, see references in Aristophanes, *Eq.* 1405, *Ra.* 733, frag. 655; *Pl.* 454; Eupolis, frag. 384.8 (Hughes, *Human Sacrifice*, 149–56). Concerning the ritual as practiced at Abdera, see Callimachus, *Diegeseis* 2.29–40 (frag. 90); cf. Ovid, *Ib.* 467–68. Burkert considers the *pharmakos* and other scapegoat rituals of early Greece to have bearing upon human sacrifice (Burkert, *Greek Religion*, 82–84). Parker also refers to the driving out of sycophants, the useless in society, as a way of keeping the city pure (Parker, *Miasma*, 263). Adela Yarbro Collins has studied the *pharmakos* ritual to see how it relates to the treatment of Jesus in the Gospel of Mark (Adela Yarbro Collins, "Finding Meaning in the Death of Jesus," *JR* 78 [1998] 175–96, see especially 182–87, 195–96). Collins puts the *pharmakos* ritual into the context of the Greek idea of the "noble death" — in which a person takes death upon him or herself in order to save others — that merges with rituals of substitution that one also finds in the ancient Near East. Collins sees the soldiers' mocking of Jesus to most resemble the *pharmakos* ritual (Collins, "Finding Meaning," *JR* 78 [1998] 186–87), but she also notes the following significant differences between the *pharmakos* and Jesus: the *pharmakos* was not a noble individual (though the community treated them as such for the day), he was not killed, and his sacrifice was not voluntary.

[210]The *pharmakos* is also called *katharma* (κάθαρμα), i.e. "offscouring." Robert Parker observes that: "... there was, in Greek belief, no such thing as non-contagious religious danger. ... Every member of any community, therefore, in principle lived under threat of suffering for his neighbours' offences" (Parker, *Miasma*, 257).

[211]In Greek society, Parker adds, "... the *pharmakos* ceases to be a mere vehicle on to which, like the original scapegoat of the Old Testament, the ills of the community are loaded by a mechanical process of transference, and becomes instead, through his crime, the actual cause of whatever affliction is being suffered" (Parker, *Miasma*, 259). For the scapegoat of the Hebrew Bible, see Lev 16:1–34.

[212]The Thargelia, held in the late spring or early summer month of the same name, was a festival of first fruits that honored Apollo. Burkert sees the significance of the season to lie in "purification as a prerequisite of the new beginning" (Burkert, *Greek Religion*, 83).

then removed from the house, the *pharmakoi* were first feted at city expense and then paraded around the city walls before their brutal expulsion.[213]

By analogy, the *pharmakos* ritual has bearing upon later exorcisms, though, rather than an unclean spirit cast out of an individual, the *pharmakos* ritual drives an unwanted presence out of the society as a whole. By so doing, the ritual establishes a boundary between the community and that from which the community wants to purge itself. Both the *pharmakos* ritual and exorcism begin with the idea that well-being is restored by driving away an unwanted presence. Though the demons of the New Testament and early Christian traditions do not receive the same aggrandizement seen for the *pharmakos*, the harsh treatment the *pharmakos* eventually receives does offer a point of comparison. Greek society's treatment of the *pharmakos* and Christianity's treatment of the demon also share a common understanding that neither unwanted entity willingly departs its chosen place of residence.

The differences between purification and exorcism, however, are significant, and derive from differences in the interpretation of what caused one to become impure or possessed. Contrary to the confrontation between Jesus and his disciples with the demons who opposed them, earlier Greek society attempted to pacify the gods through supplication and sacrifice. Because the victim of divine anger was judged culpable of some wrongdoing, exorcism in the New Testament sense of gaining authority over and casting out the plaguing spirit was an inappropriate means by which to bring an end to the affliction. This held true also for lesser spirits. Avenging spirits that served as mediators of the divine anger toward mortals were not exorcized in those instances where they do possess. Rather, their vengeance abated when the deity or spirit they represented, or even they themselves, had been appeased and the pollution erased.

In contrast to the public rituals, it would be worthwhile to see how things differed in private practice. Unfortunately, the sources become more limited in this less-documented realm of magic. Although curse tablets and binding spells fall into the category of private usage, they are basically contradictory in

---

[213]The terms used to describe the final driving off are: ἄγω (for Ionia and Athens, Hipponax, frag. 10), πέμπω (for Ionia and Athens, Hipponax fr. 153), ἀγινέω (Callimachus, frag. 90), ἐξελαύνω (*Diegeseis* 2.39 on Callimachus, frag. 90; Plutarch, *Quaest. conv.* 693E–F), ἐκβάλλω (Dio Chrysostom, *Or.* 8.14), *proicio* (Servius on Vergil, *Aen.* 3.57). Hughes concludes that putting the *pharmakos* to death at the end of the ritual has no solid corroboration in contemporary sources, and derives from the imaginations of later scholiasts or commentators at work upon a ceremony "of antiquarian and lexicographical curiosity, the customs having long passed into disuse" (Hughes, *Human Sacrifice*, 165). He elsewhere says: "The origin of the tradition that they were killed is obscure, but it seems possible that details from an aetiological myth attached to the ritual — the myth of Pharmakos or a similar story — were taken as historical by later authors" (Hughes, *Human Sacrifice*, 155).

nature to exorcism.[214] The itinerant magicians, at least in their capacity as manufacturers of curse tablets, do not release one from spiritual powers but effect hostile or coercive securement by them.[215] The *defixiones* are analogous to later exorcisms, however, in that they show an aggressiveness in dealing with spirits that is otherwise lacking in the literary and public sources. Euripides may provide a glimpse of practices that cater to the needs of the

---

[214]Christopher Faraone has written about binding spells (κατάδεσμοι; Latin *defixiones*) in Greek antiquity (Christopher A. Faraone, "The Agonistic Context of Early Greek Binding Spells," in Christopher A. Faraone and Dirk Obbink, eds., *Magika Hiera: Ancient Greek Magic and Religion* [New York: Oxford University Press, 1991] 3–32). Faraone finds that curses of this sort were employed in such competitive social contexts as athletic and musical competitions, judicial and rhetorical endeavors, love and war. He finds that the spells generally were sought after by the underdog to serve as "preemptive strikes" against superior competitors (Faraone, "Agonistic Context," 3–4). Faraone emphasizes that the evidence from the extant curses shows that they were intended to disable rather than to kill the opponent. *Defixiones* became popular in the Mediterranean world in the early fifth century B.C.E., and continued to at least the sixth century C.E., with heaviest concentrations of finds dating to the fourth and third centuries B.C.E., and to the third century C.E. (David Randolph Jordan, *Contributions to the Study of Greek* Defixiones [Ph.D. diss., Brown University, 1982] 4, 97). David Jordan notes that the examples of the earlier concentration of *defixiones* tend to be simple in form compared to the elaborate ones from the later concentration (Jordan, *Contributions*, 206). It may be inferred from their formulaic character that these later examples were copied from magical templates, such as the *Greek Magical Papyri* offered. He cites known *defixiones* that converge closely with the *PGM* as: *PGM* 4.336–406 for *SEG* 8.574 (third century C.E.), Wortmann 1 and 2 (third to fourth centuries C.E.), and *SEG* 26.1717 (third to fourth centuries C.E.); *PGM* 58.1–16 for Audollent 118 (fourth to fifth centuries C.E.) (Jordan, *Contributions*, 162). For the elaboration of magical formulae, compare the use of *historiolae* in magical incantations that draw upon mythical antecedents and that link the magician's work with authoritative prototypes (Jacques van der Vliet, "Satan's Fall in Coptic Magic," in Marvin Meyer and Paul Mirecki, eds., *Ancient Magic and Ritual Power* [Religions in the Graeco-Roman World 129; New York: Brill, 1995] 401). David Frankfurter describes such recitations of mythical events as "authoritative symbol systems" (David Frankfurter, "Narrating Power: The Theory of Magical *Historiola* in Ritual Spells," in *Ancient Magic and Ritual Power*, 461).

[215]For example, John Gager includes the following two pre-Christian invocations in his collection of curse tablets and binding spells: #104 (IV B.C.E. Athens; original location unknown) "I am sending a letter to the *daimones* and to Persephone, and deliver (to them) Tribitis, (daughter of) Choirinê, who did me wrong ... May Persephone restrain all of her. Hermes and Hades, may you restrain all of these. *Daimon* (may you restrain) Galênê, daughter of Pulukleia, by your side" (Gager, *Curse Tablets and Binding Spells*, 201–2). #134 (mid I B.C.E. Rome; exact location unknown) "God and beautiful Proserpina or Salvia ... snatch away the health, the body, the complexion, the strength, and the faculties of Plotinus. Hand him over to Pluto, your husband. May he not be able to escape this (curse) by his wits. Hand him over to fevers — quartan, tertian and daily — so that they may wrestle and struggle with him. Let them overcome him to the point where they snatch away his soul" (Gager, *Curse Tablets and Binding Spells*, 241–42). Compare also the words of a curse from the fourth century B.C.E.: "I bind ... and I will not release" (καταδῶ ... καὶ οὐκ ἀναλύσω) (Jordan, *Contributions*, #18).

individual when Phaedra's nurse refers to incantations and enchantments that can counter the Aphroditic passion of her mistress.[216] In contrast to the public curses that invoked *agos* upon an offender, and for which public rituals of purification were prescribed, the private remedies suggested by the nurse may anticipate the practices of the Christian exorcist for their easing of spirit-caused afflictions through the power of words.

With the *Greek Magical Papyri*[217] evidence appears for the human intermediary at work both in the manufacture of phylacteries that protect one from evil spirits,[218] and also in the actual casting out of demonic presences.[219] In their compulsion of the spirits, the exorcistic formulae also manifest a similar aggressiveness to that seen for New Testament exorcists. The papyri, however, date at earliest from the first century Common Era, and those which describe exorcism per se range in dates from the third to fifth centuries.[220]

---

[216]"There are charms and soothing words; some remedy will appear for this disease." (εἰσὶν δ᾿ ἐπῳδαὶ καὶ λόγοι θελκτήριοι· φανήσεταί τι τῆσδε φάρμακον νόσου.) (Euripides, *Hipp.* 478–79). The nurse herself offers to make an antidote (φίλτρα) from a token of Phaedra's beloved Hippolytus (Euripides, *Hipp.* 507–15).

[217]The *Greek Magical Papyri* comes from the priestly class of Greco-Roman Egypt. Fritz Graf compares the *PGM*'s importance for our understanding of Greco-Roman religion with the Dead Sea Scrolls' for Judaism, and Nag Hammadi's for Christian Gnosticism (Graf, *Magic in the Ancient World*, 4). The papyri can be found in English translation in Hans Dieter Betz, ed., *The Greek Magical Papyri in Translation, Including the Demotic Spells* (2d ed; Chicago: University of Chicago Press, 1992). The cultural origins of the magical formulae, and whether they can be traced back to a context dating prior to the period of syncretism, are in dispute. Robert Ritner argues for their origin in Egyptian myth and religious practice, and sees evidence for such among the earliest spells (see *PGM* 117 with note in Betz, *Greek Magical Papyri*, 314). Fritz Graf argues that the Egyptian allusions can be attributed to the sweeping cultural syncretism of the time: "… Egyptian religion is part of the vast fabric of Greco-Roman paganism" (Graf, *Magic in the Ancient World*, 6). Graf offers as evidence for this that Egyptian gods are also inscribed on *defixiones* that have been found outside of Egypt (Graf, *Magic in the Ancient World*, 5). The syncretistic view has also been accepted by Betz (Betz, *Greek Magical Papyri*, xlvi).

[218]See especially *PGM* 4.86–87; 7.579–90; 12.270–350. Concerning early evidence for such itinerant magicians who make curse tablets, see Plato, *Resp.* 364C (referred to by Faraone, *Magika Hiera*, 4). John Gager notes that "… in most cultures the business of making spells has been an activity entrusted to specialists" (Gager, *Curse Tablets and Binding Spells*, 4). See also Jordan, *Contributions*, 4.

[219]See especially *PGM* 4.1227–64, 3007–86; 5.96–172; 13.1–343; 94.17–21. *PGM* 4.1227–64 has an exorcism followed by the recommendation of a phylactery to prevent future demonic visitations. *PGM* 7.429–58 has a formula for controlling demons, which includes sending them into a person or thing.

[220]The *PGM* shows the interest among exorcists themselves of passing on the formulae they had inherited and developed. See especially the exorcistic passages in *PGM* 4.86–87; 1227–64; 3007–86; 5.96–172; 7.429–58; 579–90; 12.270–350; 13.1–343 (242–44); 94.17–21; 114.1–14. Although this suggests that the formulae existed in an earlier form than

Thus, they serve as contemporary evidence for exorcism in early Christianity rather than its prototype, and so anticipate some of the discussion in Chapter 6.

4.4 Conclusion

It is important to note that if exorcism demonstrably proliferates in the Greco-Roman world during the Common Era, possession does not. Possession has always been present, and is well attested throughout the Greek literary heritage. Although there appears to be no single correspondent in the early Greek world for the exorcism of Jewish and Christian traditions, some of the components of exorcism are in place, if not yet merged: indwelling possession with harmful consequences, and an appeal to the spiritual world for alleviation of afflictions. What discourages exorcism per se in early Greece is the non-dualistic world-view in which harmful agents such as the *alastor* and Erinyes operate under divine jurisdiction, and are occasionally considered deities in their own right. In the Greek tradition the *daimon* resembles more the Jewish and Christian *angelos* both in its status between humanity and divinity, and in its active role as the mediator of the divine will to humanity. As such, they are appeased by means of sacrifice and petition. Exorcism, in contrast, is a practice well-suited to the dualistic systems of Near Eastern origin as a means that essentially maintains a boundary between a divinely favored humanity and its hostile spiritual aggressors. An implication for this is that the exorcist would remain virtually irrelevant to Greek and Roman societies until those societies began both to disengage themselves from a sense of the demonic aggressor's rightful impingement upon human vitality, and to redefine their relationships to the demonic world not in terms of appeasement, but of separation and rejection.

---

when they were written down on the extant rolls, it is difficult to reconstruct the history of a given formula without more evidence than that supplied by the current papyri collections.

Chapter 5

Possession and Exorcism in the New Testament

5.1 Introduction: Demons and Demonic Possession in the New Testament

Before the Common Era the people of the ancient Near East tended to view humanity's engagement with the demonic spiritual world as an outward tormenting of the body. The Mesopotamian writings show spiritual affliction to affect the body's physiology with illnesses that could as well have been treated by the medical practitioners of the day as by those who mediated spiritual aid. What appears to have motivated a shift from the perception of demonic aggressors as outside tormentors to indwelling presences is the association of evil with human intention and desire. Zoroastrianism's ethical dualism, in which the human being makes a conscious decision to side with what is wise and good, or with what is deceitful and evil, is a likely forerunner to this. Zoroastrianism viewed one's allegiance to good or evil as all-pervasive, so that one became identified with the good of Ahura Mazda, or the evil of Angra Mainyu. Good or evil people consequently allied themselves to these corresponding spiritual forces.

Indwelling possession also appears in the intertestamental Jewish writings, where it both influences the human ability to make ethical decisions and adversely affects human physiology. The dualism present in Judaism, as in Zoroastrianism, draws a clear boundary between two opposing hierarchies of power. This provides an environment well-suited to the practice of exorcism, which maintains this boundary by restoring the victim to well-being and returning the demon to its proper abode. Although the Greeks viewed the engagement between divinities and human beings as at times an interior experience in which foreign spiritual presences affected the human body from within, when possession appears in earlier Greek society it does so within the context of a single hierarchy of gods and spirits. In this context appeasement rather than confrontation with and domination over the intrusive force is the norm.

The New Testament writings presuppose the Jewish demonology of the intertestamental period. The New Testament also follows the intertestamental literature in painting a cosmology of two opposing powers, which the synoptics identify as the kingdom of God and the rule of Satan.[1] In the New Testament the dualistic features of the Near East combine with an interest in the interiority of possession. It is in the New Testament literature that the notion of indwelling possession begins to dominate the perception of humanity's interaction with demonic and divine spiritual forces. Although demons are occasionally portrayed as exterior persecutors in the synoptic gospels,[2] they most often appear as interior inhabitants of the human body, and it is as indwelling possessors who adversely affect human physiology that they are subject to exorcism.[3] Though hierarchy structures the demonic spiritual world, so that lesser demons are held accountable to Satan, the New Testament allocates enough individuality and personality to the demons to warrant treating them as separate entities. From the least to the greatest, demonic entities in the New Testament exhibit the potential to possess the human being. Indeed, in the historical practice of exorcism the technique of

---

[1]"Kingdom of God" (βασιλεία τοῦ θεοῦ) occurs sixty-three times in the New Testament, fifty-two times in the synoptic gospels alone. Matthew prefers "kingdom of heaven" (βασιλεία τῶν οὐρανῶν), which appears thirty-three times in this gospel and only there. The dominion of Satan does not have a comparable epithet, but is recognizable through its leadership in such phrases as "the ruler of this world" (ὁ ἄρχων τοῦ κόσμου τούτου — John 12:31; 14:30; 16:11), "ruler of the demons" (ἄρχων τῶν δαιμονίων — Mark 3:22 [//Matt 9:34//Luke 11:15]; Matt 12:24), "ruler of the power of the air" (ἄρχων τῆς ἐξουσίας τοῦ ἀέρος — Eph 2:2; cf. *Jub.* 10:4–11; *1 En.* 6–10), "the god of this world" (ὁ θεὸς τοῦ αἰῶνος τούτου — 2 Cor 4:4), or in the contrast between the "present age" (νῦν αἰών) and the age to come (Matt 12:32; Mark 10:30; Luke 16:8; 18:30; 20:34; 1 Tim 6:17–19; cf. also Gal 4:3, 9; Eph 1:20–21; 6:12; Col 1:13–14; 2:15).

[2]External assault is best attested by to "be harrassed (by unclean spirits)" ([ἐν] ὀχλούμενος [ἀπὸ πνευμάτων ἀκαθάρτων] — Luke 6:18; Acts 5:16), to "become enslaved being oppressed (by the devil)" (καταδυναστευόμενος [ὑπὸ τοῦ διαβόλου] δουλεύω — Acts 10:38), and "(the spirit) seizes (him)" ([πνεῦμα] λαμβάνει [αὐτόν] — Luke 9:39). Other terms descriptive of demonic possession are to "be demonized" (δαιμονιζόμενος — Matt 4:24; 8:16, 28, 33; 9:32; 12:22; 15:22; Mark 1:32; 5:14–18; Luke 8:36; John 10:21), to "become maddened" (μαίνομαι — John 10:20; cf. 1 Cor 14:23), and to "be moonstruck" (σεληνιάζεται — Matt 17:15; cf. Matt 4:24), a term that derives its significance from the sublunar realm as the haunt of spirits (see above, Section 4.2.1.2). Compare also the image of Satan's intention to sift Simon like wheat (Luke 22:31).

[3]Terms and phrases that describe the interaction of the spiritual world with human beings as an internal presence include "send into" (ἀποστέλλω εἰς — Matt 8:31), "enter into" (εἰσέρχομαι — Mark 5:12–13; Luke 8:32–33; 22:3; John 13:27), to "dwell having entered into" (εἰσέλθων κατοικέω — Matt 12:45; Luke 11:26), and perhaps to "fill" (πληρόω — Acts 5:3). Compare also the phrases "having (a spirit, demon, Beelzeboul)" (ἔχων [πνεῦμα, δαιμόνιον, Βεελζεβούλ] — Matt 11:18; Mark 3:22; 9:17; Luke 4:33; 7:33; 8:27; 13:11; Acts 8:7; 16:16; 19:13; cf. John 7:19; 8:48–49, 52; 10:20), "with an (unclean, etc.) spirit" (ἐν πνεύματι [ἀκαθάρτῳ, etc.] — Mark 1:23), "in whom the (evil, etc.) spirit is" (ἐν ᾧ εἶναι τὸ πνεῦμα [τὸ πονηρόν, etc.] — Acts 19:16).

discerning a spirit's identity, often by discovering its name, is a first step in the exorcist's efforts to exert authority over it.[4]

Past research has provided lists of demons mentioned in the New Testament,[5] but for purposes of this study it will be worthwhile to mention

---

[4]For the use of names in exorcism and control over demons, see *PGM* 4.3037–3045 and Solomon's interrogation of the demons in the *Testament of Solomon* (*OTP* 1.960–87). Jesus' inquiry into the name of "Legion" in Mark 5:1–20//Luke 8:26–39 may also reflect the name-discovery found elsewhere in exorcistic practice (Otto Bauernfeind, *Die Worte der Dämonen im Markusevangelium* [BWANT, 44; Stuttgart: Kohlhammer, 1927] 36–37, and Edward Langton, *Essentials of Demonology: A Study of Jewish and Christian Doctrine, Its Origins and Development* [London: Epworth Press, 1949] 157). The importance of names extends to wisdom in general. A. Leo Oppenheim says of Genesis 1:26 and 2:19: "The relationship between man and nature in the ancient Near East is nowhere as pointedly formulated ... While it was thus man's privilege as the lord of creation to give names to the animals, the knowledge of all their names and their individual features and behavior was considered the privilege of the sage" (Oppenheim, "Man and Nature in Mesopotamian Civilization" [*Dictionary of Scientific Biography* 15 Supp. 1:634). In a contrasting opinion, Simon Pulleyn has offered a thoughtful critique of the power considered inherent in a deity's name. He concludes that having power over gods by knowing their names enters Greek religion only in the *defixiones* and magical papyri of later antiquity. Pulleyn says that prior to this: "Knowledge of the name is an essential prerequisite to any form of communication. There need not necessarily be anything magical about it" (Simon Pulleyn, "The Power of Names in Classical Greek Religion," *CQ* 44 [1994] 18). The importance of the name even in early Greece, however, is demonstrable as a method of "diagnosis" to determine the agent of affliction (e.g., *The Sacred Disease*).

[5]Catalogues and interpretations of demons in the New Testament may be found in Heinrich Schlier, *Principalities and Powers in the New Testament* (QD 3; New York: Herder & Herder, 1961) 11–12, and Samson Eitrem, *Some Notes on Demonology in the New Testament* (Symbolae osloensis Fasc. Supplet. 20; 2d ed.; Oslo: Universitetsforlaget, 1966). Studies concerning demons as possessing agents include Otto Everling, *Die paulinische Angelologie und Dämonologie: Ein biblisch-theologischer Versuch* (Gottingen: Vandenhoeck & Ruprecht, 1888), in which he presents the first extensive study of the subject in light of its historical context; William Menzies Alexander, *Demonic Possession in the New Testament: Its Historical, Medical, and Theological Aspects* (Grand Rapids, Mich.: Baker Book House, 1980), an informative work that draws its doctrinally driven conclusions from the fields of history, medicine, and theology; and several works by Otto Böcher, *Das Neue Testament und die dämonischen Mächte* (SBS 58; Stuttgart: KBW, 1972), a summary of the author's views on demonology; *Dämonenfurcht und Dämonenabwehr: Ein Beitrag zur Vorgeschichte der christlichen Taufe* (BWANT 90; Stuttgart: Kohlhammer, 1970), in which Böcher offers history-of-religions precedents for demonology and exorcism in the New Testament, and its companion piece, *Christus Exorcista: Dämonismus und Taufe im Neuen Testament* (BWANT 16; Stuttgart: Kohlhammer, 1972), which looks to the origins of Christian baptism in earlier Jewish and pagan apotropaic water rituals to ward off demons. Böcher's writings have the advantage of bringing Pauline thought into his interpretation of possession, but his definitions of possession and exorcism appear so broad as to include evidence for exorcism where more rigorous definitions hesitate to find them, whether in the New Testament (e.g., 1 Cor 12:30's χαρίσματα ἰαμάτων = "Heilungsexorzismus" [*Christus Exorcista*, 170]), or in earlier Greek antiquity generally. Other general studies on the origins

those demons actually said to dwell within their hosts, some of whom are also explicitly subject to exorcism.[6] The synoptic gospels refer to the head of the demonic hierarchy as an indwelling presence under the names of "Beelzeboul"[7] and "Satan,"[8] while the Gospel of John refers to him as the "devil"[9] and "the ruler of the world."[10] *Daimon*[11] and *daimonion*,[12] familiar from earlier Greek literature, now constitute exclusively evil agents in the New Testament. *Pneuma* instead serves as the generic designation always in need of a qualifying word or context to indicate whether the spirit is demonic or divine.[13] Also distinct from earlier Greek literature, the New Testament does not equate demons with the spirits of the dead, nor does it view them as intermediaries between God and humanity, a position delegated instead to their angelic counterparts.[14] Of the lesser demons only the "Legion" of the Gerasene demoniac receives a proper name.[15] Otherwise, the qualities attributed to these latter generic terms occasionally identify the demonic

---

and development of New Testament demonology include Everett Ferguson, *Demonology of the Early Christian World* (Symposium Series 12; New York: Edwin Mellen Press, 1984), who includes chapters on the Greek background and the continuation of New Testament demonology in early patristic writings; and Edward Langton, *Essentials of Demonology*, for his interest in the ancient Near Eastern and Greek backgrounds in addition to the Hebrew biblical and early Jewish influences.

[6]The references have been arranged with Mark listed first of the synoptic gospels as the historically earlier document. References to other books in the New Testament follow in their canonical order. Where the context permits, possessing entities have been classified under the first heading "exorcism" rather than the second heading "possession" as exorcism assumes a prior state of possession. Synoptic parallels are indicated by the symbol //. References that are only suggestive of exorcism or possession are preceded by the symbol ≈.

[7]Βεελζεβούλ — Exorcism: Mark 3:22 (//Matt 12:24, 27). Possession: Matt 10:25b.

[8]σατανᾶς — Exorcism: Mark 3:26 (//Matt 12:26). Possession: Luke 13:16; 22:3; John 13:27; Acts 5:3; 2 Thess 2:9; ≈1 Tim 1:20; Rev 2:9; 3:9.

[9]διάβολος — Exorcism: ≈Acts 10:38. Possession: ≈John 6:70; ≈John 8:44; John 13:2; ≈Acts 13:10; ≈1 Tim 3:6–7; ≈2 Tim 2:26; ≈Titus 2:3; ≈Heb 2:14–15; ≈1 Pet 5:8; ≈1 John 3:7–10.

[10]ὁ τοῦ κόσμου ἄρχων — Exorcism: ≈John 12:31. Possession: John 14:30.

[11]δαίμων — Exorcism: Matt 8:31, occurs here in the plural.

[12]δαιμόνιον — Exorcism: Mark 1:34 (//Luke 4:41), 39; 3:15; 3:22 (//Matt 12:24, 27–28//Luke 11:14–20); 6:13 (//Matt10:8//Luke 9:1); 7:26–30; 9:38 (//Luke 9:49); [16:9, 17]; Matt 7:22; 9:32–34 (//Luke 11:14); 17:18 (Luke 9:42); Luke 8:2, 26–39; 10:17; 13:32. Possession: Matt 11:18 (//Luke 7:33); John 7:19; 8:48–52; 10:20–21; ≈Rev 18:2.

[13]πνεῦμα — Exorcism: Matt 8:16. πνεῦμα ἀκάθαρτον — Exorcism: Mark 1:23–28 (//Luke 4:33–37); 3:11 (//Luke 6:18); 5:1–17 (//Luke 8:29); 6:7 (//Matt 10:1); 7:25; 9:25 (//Luke 9:42); Acts 5:16; 8:7. Possession: Matt 12:43 (//Luke 11:24); ≈Rev 18:2. πνεῦμα πονηρόν — Exorcism: Luke 7:21; 8:2; Acts 19:11–16. Possession: Matt 12:45 (//Luke 11:26); 1 John 5:18–19. πνεῦμα δαιμονίου ἀκαθάρτου — Exorcism: Luke 4:33.

[14]Foerster, "δαίμων et al.," *TDNT* 2:16.

[15]Λεγιών — Exorcism: Mark 5:9 (//Luke 8:30).

possessors by what they accomplish within the individual.[16] Paul's writings add "sin,"[17] the "angel of Satan,"[18] and possibly the "elements of the world" that enslave humanity as possessing entities.[19]

The story is the preferred genre for the literary presentation of exorcism in the New Testament, where it appears only in the narrative books, and only then in the writings of the synoptic authors. Stories of Jesus and his disciples having performed exorcisms permeate the synoptic traditions to their earliest written stages.[20] References occur in two miracle catenae preserved by Mark,[21] and, although most of the references in Matthew and Luke can be attributed to their use of Mark, several passages derive from the sayings passages common to Matthew and Luke (Q), or from special Matthean or Lukan sources. There are approximately four dozen references to exorcism in the synoptic gospels and Acts. The number is reduced by half when considerations of borrowing between the gospels and doublets are taken into account. The passages range from brief references to stories that provide enough detail to identify the person possessed, the form of possession, the exorcist, and the manner of exorcism.

Argument can be made for at least eight passages that satisfy the genre requirements for the exorcism story on form-critical grounds.[22] Mark records

---

[16]In such instances the human body outwardly manifests the invasive spiritual presence: e.g. πνεῦμα ἄλαλον, πνεῦμα ἄλαλον καὶ κωφόν — Exorcism: Mark 9:17, 25; πνεῦμα ἀσθενείας — Exorcism: Luke 13:11–12; πνεῦμα πύθωνα — Exorcism: Acts 16:16; πνεῦμα κατανύξεως — Possession: ≈Rom 11:8. Cf. "fever" (τὸ πυρετός) in the treatment of Peter's mother-in-law, which Luke more explicitly portrays as an exorcism than does Matthew or Mark — Exorcism: ≈Luke 4:38–39 (cf. Matt 8:14–15; Mark 1:29–31; Acts 28:8).

[17]ἁμαρτία — Possession: Rom 7:14–25.

[18]ἄγγελος σατανᾶ — Possession: 2 Cor 12:7.

[19]τὰ στοιχεῖα τοῦ κόσμου — Possession: ≈Gal 4:3, 9.

[20]Howard Clark Kee follows Geza Vermes, who considers Jesus' activity as healer and exorcist to be compatible with intertestamental and rabbinic Judaism, and places healing and exorcism at the center of Jesus' ministry. Contrary to the conclusions of earlier form critics, these stories come from the earliest traditions about Jesus rather than being later addenda designed to appeal to hellenistic culture (Howard Clark Kee, *Medicine, Miracle and Magic in New Testament Times* [SNTSMS 55; Cambridge: Cambridge University Press, 1986] 75–76, 124).

[21]Paul J. Achtemeier, "Toward the Isolation of Pre-Markan Miracle Catenae," *JBL* 89 (1970) 265–91. The first catena is found in Mark 4–6: Stilling of the Storm (4:35–41), Gerasene Demoniac (5:1–20), Jairus' Daughter and Woman with the Hemorrhage (5:21–43), Feeding of the 5,000 (6:34–44). The second catena is found in Mark 6–8: Jesus Walks on the Sea (6:45–52), Jesus Heals the Sick (6:54–56), the Blind Man of Bethsaida (8:22–26), the Syrophoenician Woman in which Jesus exorcizes the woman's daughter of a demon (7:24–31), the Deaf-Mute (7:32–37), Feeding of the 4,000 (8:1–10).

[22]Rudolf Bultmann classifies exorcisms within the larger category of healing miracles. He finds the Gerasene Demoniac to exhibit the typical features of this story form in their

four such exorcism stories, each of which finds duplication in one or both of the other synoptic gospels: the demoniac in the synagogue,[23] Gerasene demoniac,[24] Syrophoenician woman's daughter,[25] and the possessed boy.[26] The passages assigned to Q add another one, if not two exorcism stories, with the exorcism of the dumb demoniac.[27] To this, Luke adds an additional story with the healing of the woman possessed of a crippling spirit that causes her to be bent double.[28] Exorcism stories appear twice in Acts: once successfully (Paul and the slave girl),[29] and once unsuccessfully (the sons of Sceva).[30]

Less detailed references to exorcism appear in Mark's and Matthew's commissioning of the Twelve[31] and in Mark's, Matthew's, and Luke's sending of them forth,[32] in the longer ending of Mark,[33] in Mark's and Q's versions of the Beelzebub controversy,[34] in Matthew's reference to the

---

characteristic order: 1) meeting with the demons, 2) description of the dangerous characteristics of the affliction, 3) the demons recognize the exorcist and put up a struggle, 4) the exorcism, 5) the demons demonstrably depart, 6) an impression is made upon the spectators (Bultmann, *The History of the Synoptic Tradition*, 209–10). Gerd Theissen draws attention to the following characteristics of the exorcism stories that distinguish them from the other miracle stories:

A) the person must be in the power of the demon
    a) description of the distress
    b) departure of the demon
B) the battle between the demon and the exorcist
    a) possession
        victim possessed by a demon
        exorcist possessed by the divine Spirit
    b) both antagonists (demon and exorcist) possess miraculous knowledge
    c) both antagonists use same technique of adjuration
    d) violence a feature on both sides
C) the destructive activity of the demon
    a) exorcism in the New Testament is of people not places

(Gerd Theissen, *The Miracle Stories of the Early Christian Tradition*, trans. Francis McDonah [Philadelphia: Fortress, 1983] 87–90).

[23]Mark 1:23–28//Luke 4:33–37.
[24]Mark 5:1–20//Matt 8:28–34//Luke 8:26–39.
[25]Mark 7:24–30//Matt 15:21–28.
[26]Mark 9:14–29//Matt 17:14–21//Luke 9:37–42.
[27]Matt 9:32–34//Luke 11:14. This is possibly an earlier form of the exorcism of the blind and dumb demoniac found in Matthew 12:22–23.
[28]Luke 13:10–17.
[29]Acts 16:16–18.
[30]Acts 19:13–20.
[31]Mark 3:13–15//Matt 10:1–4.
[32]Mark 6:6b–13//Matt 10:7–11//Luke 9:1–6.
[33]Mark 16:17–18.
[34]Mark 3:22–30; Matt 12:22–30//Luke 11:14–23.

criteria for entering the Kingdom of God,[35] and in three passages unique to Luke: Jesus' response to John the Baptist's disciples who question whether Jesus is the messiah,[36] the report to Jesus by the 70 (72) of their accomplishments which have included exorcisms,[37] and Jesus' warning to Herod.[38] Luke also makes the healing of Peter's mother-in-law more explicitly an exorcism than either Mark or Matthew.[39] To this list we may also append the parable of the unclean spirit, who is cast out of an individual only to return again to find his "house" swept and clean.[40]

In the New Testament demonic afflictions are described as physiological ailments or as self-destructive and isolating behaviors that often appear as the subjects of medical treatment in the Greco-Roman world.[41] Sometimes the conditions are longstanding, such as the cases of deafness and dumbness,[42] and a woman bent double.[43] Others appear as sudden outbursts of erratic activity, such as a boy who periodically shouts, falls to the ground and rolls about, foams at the mouth, grinds his teeth, and becomes stiff.[44] There are also problems which appear to be more symptomatic of emotional or mental disturbances. For example, John the Baptist's neither eating nor drinking cause the authorities to consider him possessed;[45] the authorities also accuse Jesus of demonic possession because of his unusual teachings and because of his alleged paranoid conviction that they seek to kill him.[46]

Madness, with its physiological complications, emotional disturbances, and the irrational actions it evokes, appears frequently in earlier Greek literature (see Chapter 4). In the New Testament several cases of demonic possession resemble such derangements. What distinguishes the demoniac in the

---

[35]Matt 7:21–23.

[36]Luke 7:18–23; cf. Matt 11:2–6.

[37]Luke 10:17–20; cf. Luke 13:22–27.

[38]Luke 13:31–33.

[39]Luke 4:38–39; cf. Mark 1:29–31//Matt 8:14–15.

[40]Matt 12:43–45//Luke 11:24–26; cf. Mark 9:25.

[41]The description of the Syrophonecian woman's daughter is suggestive of a physical illness, as the demon has left her bedridden (Mark 7:30), but the affliction otherwise remains undescribed. The story does not appear in Luke, but Matthew calls the exorcism a healing (ἰάθη — Matt 15:28). The case of the boy with the deaf and dumb spirit concerns physical disabilities, the exorcism of which Matthew describes by the verbs to "heal" (ἐθεραπεύθη) and to "cast out" (ἐκβαλεῖν), and which Luke describes as a "healing" (ἰάσατο — Luke 9:42). These physiological symptoms, and their common perception as healings, argue against a simple equivalence of demonic possession with mental illness (as seen, for example, in Selby Vernon McCasland, *By the Finger of God: Demon Possession and Exorcism in the Light of Modern Views of Mental Illness* [New York: MacMillan, 1951]).

[42]Matt 9:32–34//Matt 12:22–24//Luke 11:14–15.

[43]Luke 13:10–17.

[44]Mark 9:14–29//Matt 17:14–21//Luke 9:37–43a.

[45]Matt 17:18//Luke 7:33.

[46]John 7:20.

Capernaum synagogue from those around him is his "shouting out with a great voice" (ἀνέκραξεν φωνῇ μεγάλῃ) that disrupts the assembly of those present.[47] The Gerasene demoniac lives naked among the tombs and strikes himself with stones;[48] after the demons are cast out, the man is described as "clothed and of sound mind" (ἱματισμένον καὶ σωφρονοῦντα).[49] In Acts, a demoniac in Ephesus overpowers his would-be exorcists, the seven sons of Sceva, a deed that shows the violent physical power that accompanies his possession.[50] The Gospel of John explicitly joins madness and demonic possession when the Jews say of Jesus, "He has a demon and is out of his mind" (δαιμόνιον ἔχει καὶ μαίνεται).[51] These manifold symptoms have the common cause of demonic possession, and it is this interpretation of their cause that determines their treatment by exorcism over against other healing options.

The evangelists have composed their stories in a manner that reveals their primary interest in the exorcist, and to some extent also in the possessing demon,[52] rather than in the demoniac. They serve primarily both to exalt those who perform the exorcisms and to proclaim the divinity from which they draw their authority.[53] The exorcism stories as a genre typically end with the exorcist's departure and the crowd's reaction to the work of the exorcist rather than to the one who has been made well. With few exceptions any biographical information about the possessed prior to or after their exorcisms is given for the sake of highlighting the severity of the possession, not for the character development of the victims as individuals.[54] Since the one possessed

---

[47]Luke 4:31–37// Mark 1:23–28 (ἀνέκραξεν).

[48]Mark 5:1–17//Matt 8:28–34//Luke 8:26–37.

[49]Mark 5:15//Luke 8:35.

[50]Acts 19:13–20.

[51]John 10:19–21.

[52]Theissen argues that the possessing demon requires equal attention to the exorcist: "An exorcism can take place only when a person is not simply impeded in one function by a demon, but has lost his autonomy to the demon. ... In form-critical terms, the demon must be an opposite number, not just a subsidiary character hidden in the background" (Thiessen, *The Miracle Stories of the Early Christian Tradition*, 87). This balanced emphasis of exorcist and demonic invader highlights the eschatological implications of exorcism as part of a larger cosmic struggle. The equality given to exorcist and demon does not extend to character development, however. Except in the case of "Legion," the demons in the New Testament are only generic representatives of a hostile power.

[53]Barrett-Lennard says of the historical Jesus in the Beelzeboul controversy: "Jesus understood his exorcisms to be not merely individual acts of assistance to afflicted people ... They were a sign ... that the harmful spiritual powers were now being challenged and their dominance broken as a new era in the reign of God manifested itself" (Barrett-Lennard, *Christian Healing after the New Testament*, 142).

[54]For example, see the biographies of the Gerasene demoniac (Mark 5:3–5) and the speechless boy (Mark 9:21–22). The story of the Gerasene demoniac provides the fullest post-exorcism description of the healed person (Mark 5:15//Luke 8:35).

serves as a means for the exorcist's public display of power and authority, it is, in fact, because they are possessed that we encounter them.

The gospels say little with regard to how one becomes possessed.[55] We consistently encounter the demoniacs already in a state of possession, with no explanation of how they have come so to be. The stories offer no evidence that demonic possession is the result of the hostile conjuring of demons through witchcraft. On the contrary, the curses that do occur in the New Testament come from those who invoke or are identified with divine power.[56] Among the synoptic authors there is also no indication that people are born into a state of possession.[57] As a whole the character of the person possessed is also never at issue. Although some passages reveal that a connection between personal failings and ill health or misfortune existed in the consciousness of the day,[58] this does not appear to be the train of thought that motivates the presentation of demonic possession in the synoptics. The exorcism stories of the New Testament appear to minimize any such impiety or sinfulness on the part of their demoniacs in favor of showing the aggressive hostility of the demons who possess them. Where biographical details of the possessed do occur, they tend to corroborate the demoniacs as the innocent and passive victims of malicious spirits. An example of such is Luke's account of the woman with a crippling spirit that has afflicted her for eighteen years.[59] There is nothing to indicate any crime or guilt on her part that has led to her possession and, in fact, before he releases her from her condition Jesus describes the woman as a daughter of Abraham whom Satan has bound. Contrary to the earlier Greek perception, the demons in the New Testament who bring physiological affliction do so not out of divine judgment against their victims, but in rebellion against divinity.

---

[55]Two passages, however, give us an insight into a perception of the demons' own motivations. One is the story of the Gerasene demoniac, in which the demons fear being sent back to the abyss (Luke 8:31). The other is the parable of the demon who returns to his former abode, and for whom possession means rest from wandering through waterless places (Matt 12:43–45//Luke 11:24–26).

[56]For example, Jesus and the fig tree (Matt 21:18–19//Mark 11:12–14), and Paul and Elymas (Acts 13:4–12).

[57]Compare the boy possessed "since childhood" (ἐκ παιδιόθεν — Mark 9:21). Outside of the New Testament, the *Testament of Solomon* attributes blindness, deafness, and dumbness at the fetal stage to the demon "Head of Dragons" (*T. Sol.* 12.2).

[58]The healing of the paralytic is an example where forgiveness of sins appears to be an event closely related to healing (Matt 9:1–8//Mark 2:1–12//Luke 5:17–26). Luke also reports about the misfortunes of the Galileans who were killed by Pilate's authority as they were performing sacrifices, and the collapse of the tower at Siloam in which eighteen people were killed (Luke 13:1–5). However, in both cases Jesus warns the people not to assume that these misfortunes resulted from a greater degree of sinfulness on the part of the victims.

[59]Luke 13:10-17.

Faith also is not an aspect of the demoniac's character. Whereas a display or gesture of faith on the part of the afflicted is a typical feature of other healing miracles, in the cases of demonic possession the condition tends to leave the victim powerless to appeal to Jesus or to the disciples personally for healing. When faith does play a role, it is on the part of those who seek help on the demoniac's behalf, such as the father of the deaf and dumb boy[60] or the Syrophonecian woman on behalf of her daughter.[61] The irrelevance of faith in the portrayal of demoniacs lends further support to seeing the possessed as innocents entrapped by demonic forces.

5.2 Purity and Physiological Possession

Despite the synoptic authors' emphasis upon exorcists, the demoniacs' separation from their communities emerges as a distinctive and common theme in the various portrayals of demoniacs in the New Testament. As an example of separation from one's civic community, compare the Gerasene demoniac who lives outside the city among the tombs and in the hills.[62] Compare also in John, where a lengthy argument between Jesus and the Jews results in their attempt to stone him. During the dispute the Jews thrice accuse Jesus of having a demon, one time of which they label him a "Samaritan" and "demoniac," terms complementary in their reference to foreignness and exclusion.[63] When Satan enters Judas during the Last Supper, John says that Judas parted company to carry out his scheme of betrayal.[64] In the early church Ananias and Sapphira forsake the church by accepting Satan into their hearts.[65]

Exorcism conveys a broadly soteriological message with respect to the demonically possessed by which their physiological restoration allows for their social reintegration.[66] Separation and reintegration may also be phrased in

---

[60]Mark 9:23–24.

[61]Matt 15:28.

[62]Mark 5:2–5//Matt 8:28//Luke 8:27.

[63]John 8:48.

[64]John 13:26–31.

[65]Acts 5:1–11. Compare also Paul's recommendation that the Corinthian church excommunicate Hymenaius and Alexander that through their delivery to Satan they may be disciplined for their blasphemy (1 Tim 1:19–20; cf. 1 Cor 5:5).

[66]Kee finds the healing and exorcism stories foundational to the gospels. He sees the purpose of Jesus' ministry to restore participation in the covenant to those otherwise excluded by occupation, illness, or impurity, the latter two of which Jesus addresses directly through healings and exorcisms (Kee, *Medicine, Miracle and Magic in New Testament Times*, 78–79). For Irenaeus in the second century, and Athanasius in the fourth, the theological implications of healing, including exorcism, were soteriological: "the work of God in Christ renewing the Creation" (Barrett-Lennard, *Christian Healing after the New Testament*, 228).

terms of impurity and purity, respectively, so that by restoring the body to wellness exorcism also restores the victim of possession to a state of purity.[67] Demonic possession as an impurity is perhaps most evidently seen in those spirits exorcized in the synoptic gospels and Acts that are called "unclean" (ἀκάθαρτον),[68] an attribute that they consequently transfer to their victims. In fact, all nineteen occurrences of ἀκάθαρτον in the synoptic gospels, and two of the five that occur in Acts, refer specifically to unclean spirits.[69]

5.3 The Significance of Exorcism

Theology is inextricably woven into the act of exorcism as the synoptic authors portray it. Chapter 4 showed how interpretation of an illness dictates its cure and how certain cures are accepted as reasonable by the author depending upon the context in which they are portrayed. Similarly, the evangelists have adapted the historical referents in their exorcism stories to accommodate their theologies. The apocalyptic perspective of Mark allows for exorcism as an appropriate response to the illnesses and afflictions attributed to demons, and Mark's presentation of a cosmos in which spirits and demons are active contributes to the expectation of exorcism among the readers. Exorcisms serve as visible signs that accompany the spoken word[70] of

---

[67]Compare the Greek concept of *miasma* as an impurity acquired through circumstances other than personal fault (see Chapter 4). According to Hans Hübner, Mark portrays Jesus as one who reenvisions purity from the cultic realm of Mosaic Law to the ethical motivations of the human heart (Hans Hübner, "Unclean and Clean [NT]," trans. Ronald B. Thomas, Jr., *ABD* 6.742). Thus, Jesus abolishes the traditional cultic means of distinguishing between the clean and unclean with respect to food (Mark 7:14–23//Matt 15:10–20), and challenges social conventions by associating with tax collectors and sinners (Mark 2:15–17; Luke 15:1–2). Exorcism fits into this revised scheme as an act of purification that restores the possessed to well-being and reintegrates them into society.

[68]Mark 1:23–28 (//Luke 4:33–37); 3:10–12 (//Luke 6:18–19); 5:1–20 (//Luke 8:26–39); 6:6b–13 (//Matt 10:1); Acts 5:12–16; 8:4–8. Compare where the synoptics explicitly equate illness with impurity, as in the cases of leprosy in which Jesus commands the lepers to visit the priest to verify their purity (Mark 1:40–44//Matt 8:1–4//Luke 5:12–14; 17:11–19; cf. καθαρίζειν at Matt 10:8).

[69]Hübner, "Unclean and Clean (NT)," *ABD* 6:743.

[70]Exorcism accompanies preaching at Mark 1:39; 3:13–15; 6:7–13; cf. Matt 10:1; Luke 4:40–41; Acts 8:4–25. Steven Davies argues for a shift away from scholarship's current emphasis upon Jesus' teachings as primary to his historical activity, which he considers to have developed later in Christian reflection, to an emphasis upon Jesus as a "spirit possessed healer" (Steven L. Davies, *Jesus the Healer: Possession, Trance, and the Origins of Christianity* [New York: Continuum, 1995] 21). As such, healing was Jesus' primary objective to which his words served a supporting therapeutic role (Davies, *Jesus the Healer*, 137–50).

the eschatological overthrow of the kingdom of Satan.[71] Demonic possession and exorcism assume a cosmological significance in the New Testament that is in keeping with the apocalyptic environment of first century Palestine.[72] What we see in many of the apocalyptic writings, both in the New Testament book of Revelation and in its Jewish counterparts, are battles between these opposing forces on an extra-mundane level.[73] The New Testament stories of exorcism individualize this warfare to make the body of the possessed a battleground within which the demonic and divine forces engage.

The story of the Gerasene demoniac illustrates well how the exorcism stories may simultaneously address several issues. Only here in the New Testament does the exorcist seek the demon's name.[74] Since the gospel writers otherwise use generic terms such as "demon" and "spirit" to describe demons, efforts have been made to understand the significance of "Legion" (Λεγιών) here. Most simply, and for the immediate purposes of the story, "Legion" indicates a large number.[75] Samson Eitrem, however, has also interpreted the

---

[71]This is seen most clearly in Jesus' response to the 70's (72's) report that they have successfully performed exorcisms in his name (Luke 10:17–18). Susan Garrett refers to this passage as "unabashadly apocalyptic" (Susan R. Garrett, *The Demise of the Devil: Magic and the Demonic in Luke's Writings* [Minneapolis: Fortress, 1989] 46), and she considers all exorcisms and healings in Luke's writings to serve as visible signs of the cosmic defeat of Satan (Garrett, *The Demise of the Devil*, 59). Graham Twelftree situates eschatology within Jesus' own understanding of his exorcistic activity as the initial binding of Satan who would meet destruction in the eschaton (Graham H. Twelftree, *Jesus the Exorcist: A Contribution to the Study of the Historical Jesus* [WUNT 2.54; Tübingen: Mohr, 1993] 173, 224).

[72]The mission of the 70 (72), for example, identifies exorcism as an apocalyptic and eschatological event through which "the enemy" (ὁ ἐχθρός) is overthrown and the name of Jesus is exalted at Satan's expense (Luke 10:17–20). Concerning the apocalyptic environment of first century Palestine, see Adela Yarbro Collins, "Apocalypses and Apocalypticism (Early Christian)," *ABD* 1:288–92. Concerning the apocalyptic eschatological context of exorcism, and how Mark uses it to portray Jesus as an apocalyptic prophet, see James E. Lanpher, *The Miraculous in Mark: Its Eschatological Background and Christological Function* (Ph.D. diss., University of Notre Dame 1994), especially pages 121–42, 170–86, 223–26.

[73]Cf. also the Stilling of the Storm, which evokes a power struggle between Jesus and the natural world (Mark 4:35–41//Matt 8:23–27//Luke 8:22–25).

[74]Mark 5:1–20//Luke 8:26–39. Matthew, who records two demoniacs rather than one, otherwise trims the passage at several points, and does not include the naming of Legion (Matt 8:28–34).

[75]In Mark's and Luke's versions, the possessing entities call themselves "Legion," which the authors themselves explain as descriptive of the vast number of demons that inhabit the man (Mark 5:9; Luke 8:30; cf. *T. Sol.* 11). A legion is literally the largest unit of a Roman army (*legio*), and consists of 4,200–6,000 men with some cavalry. In Latin literature the term also appears figuratively to refer to a vast number, similar to the Greek *myriad* (Hans Dieter Betz, "Legion Λεγιών," *DDD*[2] 507–8). We see this sense also in the term's only other occurrence in the New Testament, where Matthew describes God's angelic hosts as arranged in "legions" (Matt 26:53). Herbert Preisker says of "legion's" exclusive reference to supernatural powers in the New Testament: "In the NT the word λεγιών is not used for the

name in a way that reflects the first century political and social situation, so that "Legion" symbolizes the Roman occupation of Judaea and its environs.[76] The story read in this way equates demonic possession with the local populations' discontent with their Roman overlords, who in the story are driven out and destroyed. Legion's being sent into the swine, an unclean animal in Judaism (cf. Lev 11:1–8), would serve as a final insult to the occupying force. The story may also be seen to transcend the earthly conflict to reflect a cosmic one in which the forces of God and evil clash. The pericope's references to the abyss where the demons are to be cast (Luke), and the change of era suggested by the demons' complaint that Jesus has come "before the time" (πρὸ καιροῦ — Matthew) do, in fact, suggest both a cosmological struggle and the ensuing victory of the kingdom of God over the

---

military world ... It is used to denote transcendent forces. It thus shows us where the Church militant has to fight its war, namely, where the struggle is between the kingdom of God and demonic powers" (Herbert Preisker, "λεγιών," *TDNT* 4:68–69; cf. Eph 6:12).

[76]Eitrem, *Notes on Demonology*, 71. Betz supports Eitrem's interpretation with the papyrological evidence found in *PGM* 22.b.35 and 35.15 (Betz, "Legion," 508). Richard Horsley also sees the intention behind the exorcism stories to frame the contemporary political situation of Rome's occupation of Palestine in terms of cosmic conflict (Richard A. Horsley, *Jesus and the Spiral of Violence: Popular Jewish Resistance in Roman Palestine* [San Francisco: Harper & Row, 1987] 184–90). Ched Myers' socio-literary reading of Mark also leads him to see Jesus' exorcism of the Gerasene demoniac as a symbolic act of liberation from a "collective anxiety over Roman imperialism" (Ched Myers, *Binding the Strong Man: A Political Reading of Mark's Story of Jesus* [Maryknoll, N.Y.: Orbis Books, 1988] 193). Myers contends that Mark's contemporary audience would have drawn such militaristic implications from the exorcism not only from the term "Legion" and from several other words in the passage that bear such a connotation in Greek, but also from the community's awareness of Roman autrocities perpetrated in the vicinity of Gerasa (Josephus, *Bell.* 4.9.1) (Myers, *Binding the Strong Man*, 190–94). John Dominic Crossan also relates the story to Roman imperialism, and interprets demonic possession as an internalization of political oppression by suppressed colonials, for which exorcism is tantamount to "individuated symbolic revolution" (John Dominic Crossan, *The Historical Jesus: The Life of a Mediterranean Jewish Peasant* [San Francisco: HarperSanFrancisco, 1991] 313–18). The anthropological studies upon which Crossan and Horsley rely do make compelling their own analogies to the social-political situation in first century Common Era Palestine, especially given the inherently political nature of apocalyptic movements generally. Such an anti-Roman reading, however, reflects a political conflict between Rome and its conquered territories that is otherwise not an issue for the evangelist. Contrary to Crossan's (*Historical Jesus*, 313–20) and Horsley's (*Jesus and the Spiral of Violence*, 184–90) arguments that demonic possession among the Palestinian population is tied to the occupation by the Roman army and heavy taxation, Davies notes that Galilee was not an occupied territory during the time of Jesus, and that there is no evidence for a higher taxation there than elsewhere (Davies, *Jesus the Healer*, 78–80). Compare Marten Stol's interpretation, which traces back the ritualistic precedent for Jesus' casting out Legion into the herd of swine to the Babylonian practice of marrying off diseases to unclean animals (Stol, *Epilepsy in Babylonia*, 99–101).

forces of evil. Read in this way the story now has eschatological bearing upon the kerygmatic message of Satan's overthrow that one finds in the other exorcisms. The exorcism stories, then, invite complementary interpretations that range from soteriological issues of personal healing and social reintegration, to larger political struggles, to the eschatological context of cosmic conflict.[77]

5.4 The Terminology of Exorcism

In the New Testament those who perform exorcisms are Jesus,[78] the Twelve apostles,[79] the disciples generally,[80] Philip,[81] Paul,[82] one outside of Jesus' circle who nevertheless employs Jesus' name successfully in exorcism,[83] Jews outside of Jesus' followers in Palestine (the sons of Pharisees),[84] and Jewish "exorcists" outside of Jesus' followers in the Diaspora (among whom are the sons of Sceva at Ephesus, whose attempt to exorcize in Jesus' name fails).[85] Thus, the New Testament suggests that exorcism was an accepted practice not only for Jesus and his followers, but also for their Jewish contemporaries.[86]

---

[77]Horsley, who recognizes therapeutic, political, and cosmological implications of exorcism generally, downplays the relevance of the exorcism stories per se to healings. He considers the evangelists to have recorded exorcism stories that are true to Jesus' historical character as an exorcist, but which are divorced from specific historical healings (Horsley, *Jesus and the Spiral of Violence*, 181). Horsley's point is well taken, yet even if the New Testament exorcism stories do not portray historical events, it is important to allow for other readings that could also have had value for first century audiences. In comparison, Twelftree attributes four original stories and the Beelzeboul controversy to actual events in the life of the historical Jesus, which the early church perpetuated and augmented (Twelftree, *Jesus the Exorcist*, 138–39).

[78]Mark 1:23–28 (//Luke 4:33–37); 1:32–34 (//Matt 8:16–17//Luke 4:40–41); 1:39; 3:22 (//Matt 9:32–34; 12:22–30//Luke 11:19–23); 5:1–20 (//Matt 8:28–34//Luke 8:26–39); 7:24–30 (//Matt 15:21–28); 9:14–29 (//Matt 17:14–21//Luke 9:37–43); 16:9; Matt 4:24; Luke 11:14–23; 13:31–33; Acts 10:36–43.

[79]Mark 3:13–15 (//Matt 10:1–15); 6:7–13 (//Luke 9:1–2); 9:14–29 (//Matt 17:14–21//Luke 9:37–43) (failed attempt); 16:17.

[80]Luke 10:17–20; ≈Matt 7:22; 10:1, 5–15.

[81]Acts 8:4–8.

[82]Acts 16:16–18; 19:8–12.

[83]Mark 9:38–40//Luke 9:49–50.

[84]Luke 11:14–23.

[85]Acts 19:13–20.

[86]The exorcism stories of the synoptic tradition portray Jesus as having acted in accordance with his audiences' expectations and, consequently, in a manner consistent with his society's realm of belief. We see this, for example, in Mark 9:14–29 (//Matt 17:14–21//Luke 9:37–42) where a father interprets his son's ailment as possession and brings him to the disciples and Jesus with the expectation that they will exorcize him. Again, the

The practice of exorcism requires no defense in Mark. Even in the Matthean and Lucan versions of the Beelzeboul controversy the fact that the sons of the Jews also perform exorcisms shows that the challenge is not directed toward the practice of exorcism per se, only toward the authority from which that practice is drawn.

In the New Testament, the followers of Jesus who cast out demons do so as but one part of a larger ministry to make known the kingdom of God that also included preaching, healing, and other forms of wonder-working. As such, this community of followers does not yet appear to identify the practice of exorcism as a specialized profession.[87] "Exorcism" itself does not appear to have attained a technical designation in Greek by the middle of the first-century Common Era. An important term in later magical texts, ὁρκίζω refers to the swearing of an oath, or putting one under the obligation to say or to do something. It appears, however, only once in the New Testament, in the sons of Sceva episode.[88] When ὁρκίζω receives the intensifying prefix ἐξ-[89] we arrive at the basis for our own familiar terminology for "exorcism." It is a compound, however, that also very nearly eludes the New Testament, with one occurrence of a substantive form (ἐξορκιστής), also found in the story of the sons of Sceva,[90] and a single occurrence of the verbal form which appears in a non-exorcistic context.[91] The verbal form, "to exorcize" (ἐξορκίζειν) only begins to gain currency with reference to the removal of evil spirits during the second and third centuries of the Common Era, when *exorcismus* also entered as a loan word into the Latin language through the influence of Christian writers.[92] Its use in this context in ecclesiological

---

interpretation of a malady dictates its method of treatment. (Compare "Madness in History" in Chapter 4, above).

[87]The professional exorcist may, however, be present outside of this community. The account of the anonymous exorcist who manipulates demons in Jesus' name suggests this, as we hear of no other activity in which he engaged (Mark 9:38–41//Luke 9:49–50). The reference to certain itinerant Jews that included the sons of Sceva as *exorkistai* (Acts 19:13–14) also suggests their practice to be a recognizably distinct profession.

[88]Acts 19:13.

[89]Herbert Weir Smyth, *Greek Grammar* (Cambridge: Harvard University Press, 1984) §§1648, 1688.2.

[90]Acts 19:13.

[91]The verbal form appears in Jesus' trial before the Jewish authorities (Matt 26:63). Although this is not an exorcism, it does present a similar context of control and assertion of authority. Like the exorcism stories in which the demons are interrogated and their identities sought out, so, too, does Caiaphas interrogate Jesus and demand to know his identity. In the Western manuscript tradition 𝔓38 (ca. 300) twice uses the verb ἐξορκίζω in its rewriting of Acts 19:13–14 (Bruce M. Metzger, *A Textual Commentary on the Greek New Testament* [Stuttgart: United Bible Societies, 1975] 470–71).

[92]Of the Latin authors, Tertullian (*ca.* 160–240) uses *exorcismus* in *De corona* 11. Among non-Christians, Ulpian (d. 228) uses the verb *exorcizo* at *Dig.* 50.13.1.3.

writings from the second century of the Common Era onwards led to its eventual adoption also into English, where it conveys the sense of casting out demons from its earliest occurrences.[93]

Instead of a single technical term, the synoptic authors use a handful of terms to describe the activity of exorcism which, taken as a whole, generate a composite of demonic possession and exorcism as a struggle to establish authority and to exert control. By far the most common terms are ἐξέρχομαι[94] and ἐκβάλλω,[95] and these are the principal terms employed by Mark. These terms underscore the "locative" aspect of exorcism: the removal (and relocation) of the possessing agent. Ἐκπορεύομαι,[96] πέμπτω,[97] ἀποστέλλω,[98] and ὑπάγω,[99] each of which occur only once in exorcistic contexts, also convey the dismissal of the demon from its host. The seizing or binding by a demonic agent from which one seeks release, an image for possession so prominent in ancient Near Eastern literature, appears in exorcistic contexts in the New Testament only where Jesus "releases" ([ἀπο]λύω) the woman from her crippling condition caused by Satan,[100] and in Jesus' parable of "binding" (δέω) the strong man (=Satan).[101] Binding and releasing would, however, become integral to the terminology and symbolism of demonic possession and exorcism in late antique and medieval Christian iconography, where fetters and straightjackets became attributes of the demoniac.[102]

---

[93]"exorcism," *OED²* (1989) 5.549–50.

[94]Mark 1:25–28 (//Luke 4:35–36); 5:8, 13; 7:29–30; Matt 8:31–32; Luke 4:41; 8:29, 33–35; Acts 16:18.

[95]Mark 1:34 (//Matt 8:16), 39; 3:15 (//Matt 10:1); 3:22 (//Matt 9:33–34; 12:24–28//Luke 11:14–20); 6:13; 7:26; 9:18, 28 (//Matt 17:19//Luke 9:40) 9:38 (//Luke 9:49); 16:9, 17; Matt 7:22; 10:8; Luke 9:49; 13:32.

[96]Acts 19:8–12.

[97]Mark 5:12.

[98]Mark 5:10.

[99]Matt 8:31.

[100]Luke 13:10–17. For the idea of possession as being seized or bound by demonic forces, cf. also the image of the "snare of the devil" (παγίδα τοῦ διαβόλου — 1 Tim 3:7), and images of being "handed over" to Satan (παραδίδωμαι — 1 Cor 5:5; 1 Tim 1:20), or being "enslaved" (δουλεύω) to the elements of the world (Gal 4:8–11) or to sin (Rom 7:1–25).

[101]Mark 3:27//Matt 12:29. Compare also Satan's "release" (λυθήσεται) from his thousand years of imprisonment in Revelation 20:7.

[102]In an illuminated manuscript dated to 586 Jesus exorcizes two demoniacs whose possession is illustrated by distressed looks, lack of clothing, and bondage (Florence: Lib., Bibl. Laurenziana, Plut. I.56; see, Raffaele Garrucci, *Storia della arte cristiana nei primi otto secoli della chiesa* [6 vols.; Prato: G. Guasti, 1872–1881] vol. 3, pl. 134 [2]; Carlo Cecchelli et al., eds., *The Rabbula Gospels* [Monumenta occidentis 1; Olten: Urs Graf-Verlag, 1959] pl. 8b). An ivory plaque from a book cover (pre 700 C.E.) portrays on its left side in the second panel Christ holding a cross and healing a demoniac. The demoniac

In addition to these terms that actually describe the removal of a possessing spirit, other terms occur in the New Testament exorcism passages that further inform of exorcism's significance and implications. Such terms as to "muzzle" (φιμόω),[103] to "silence" (σιώπα),[104] "by no means permit" (οὐκ ἀφίημι),[105] "to have authority" ([ἔχειν] ἐξουσίαν),[106] "power over" (δύναμις [ἐπί]),[107] to "conquer" (νικάω),[108] and words of command such as ἐπιτιμάω,[109] παραγγέλω,[110] ἐπιτάσσω[111] (with the demon's "being subjected" [ὑποτάσσομαι][112]), assert the exorcist's authority, and his intention to dominate the demon.

The language of exorcism also occurs in non-exorcistic accounts. In the synoptic gospels Jesus "muzzles" (φιμόω) and "rebukes" (ἐπιτιμάω) the wind to still the storm.[113] Although the Gospel of John makes no reference to exorcism, demonic possession is prominent at several points, and in John 12:31 Jesus uses the vocabulary of exorcism to describe the overthrow

---

himself wears chains about his neck, wrists, and ankles, and the small figure of the exorcized demon appears above his head (see, Louis Bréhier, *La sculpture et les arts mineurs byzantins* [Histoire de l'art byzantin; Paris: Les Éditions d'art et d'histoire, 1936] pl. 26). The motif appears regularly in Medieval iconography. Because no demoniac is brought before Jesus or the disciples in bonds or chains (cf. the Gerasene demoniac who had earlier broken free from his constraints [Mark 5:3–4; Luke 8:29]), the bonds in these illustrations appear to signify the demoniacs' captivity by Satanic powers.

[103]Mark 1:23–28//Luke 4:33–37; cf. Mark 4:35–41.

[104]Mark 4:39.

[105]Mark 1:34.

[106]Mark 1:27 (//Luke 4:36); 3:15 (//Matt 10:1); 6:7; Luke 9:1; 10:19.

[107]Luke 4:36; 6:19; 9:1.

[108]Luke 11:22. Compare the demon's fear of being "destroyed" (ἀπόλλυμι — Mark 1:24//Luke 4:34) and "tormented" (βασανίζομαι — Matt 8:29//Mark 5:7//Luke 8:28).

[109]Mark 9:14–29 (//Matt 17:14–21//Luke 9:37–43); Luke 4:33–37; 4:40–41.

[110]Acts 16:16–18.

[111]Luke 8:26–39.

[112]Luke 10:17–20; cf. ἐπιτρέπω in Luke 8:26–39.

[113]Mark 4:35–41//Matt 8:23–27//Luke 8:22–25. The winds were commonly personified in antiquity. Note, for example, the cult for Boreas set up by the Athenians after the north wind devastated the Persian fleet off Artemision (Herodotus 7.189). Early Christian artists likewise personified the wind(s) to depict the "Stilling of the Storm." From a later example, an illustrated manuscript of the tenth to eleventh centuries is particularly illustrative of the relationship between stilling and exorcism as they were interpreted by the church. In its upper and lower registers of folio 103 verso, the Gospel Book of Otto III portrays the Stilling of the Storm and the Gerasene Demoniac respectively. Both illustrations show Jesus making the same hand gesture to silence the personified winds as to cast out the demons (see, Georg Leidinger, *Miniaturen aus Handschriften der Kgl. Hof- und Staatsbibliothek in München. Heft 1: Das sogenannte Evangeliarium Kaiser Ottos III* [Munich: Riehn & Tietze, 1912] pl. 27).

(ἐκβληθήσεται ἔξω) of the demonic ruler of this world.[114] Revelation uses exorcistic language to describe the cosmomachy between the powers of God and Satan. For example, Revelation 9:11 mentions the Destroyer ('Αβαδδών, 'Απολλύων), and 20:7–10 mentions Satan (ὁ σατανᾶς), the latter of whom will go forth and lead astray the nations after his release (λυθήσεται) from a thousand years of imprisonment. He and his forces will be defeated in battle, and the devil (ὁ διάβολος) will himself be cast (ἐβλήθη) into the lake of fire and sulfur as were earlier cast (ἐβλήθησαν — Rev 19:20) the beast and false prophet.

In Mark, exorcisms frequently occur in the same episodes as healings, and the two can overlap in their symptoms. The gospel, however, virtually always distinguishes the two by the use of separate verbs.[115] This may reflect a perceived distinction on Mark's part between exorcism and healing that subsequent authors either failed to recognize or sought to blur. In contrast, Matthew and Luke-Acts occasionally use verbs of healing (θεραπεύω and ἰάομαι) to describe the activity of expelling demons.[116] By classifying

---

[114]References to demonic possession occur when the Jews consider Jesus demon-possessed (John 7:20; 8:48–53; 10:19–21) and in the critical denouement of the gospel itself when Satan's possession of Judas leads to his act of betrayal (John 13:26–31). William Menzies Alexander remarks on the lack of exorcism in John's gospel: "The omission in itself is not surprising, as John does not attempt to exhaust the types of miracles wrought by our Lord. He has no mention of deafness, dropsy, dumbness, fever, lameness, leprosy, or paralysis. Silence, therefore, cannot be construed into dissent from the other Evangelists. Indeed, John is entirely at one with Luke in regarding Judas as possessed of Satan. That is a specific point of contact which may import agreement elsewhere" (Alexander, *Demonic Possession in the New Testament*, 252–53). Alexander's argument from silence, however, is not entirely satisfactory. John's use of the language of possession and exorcism, and his interest in other miracles makes this apparent omission all the more puzzling. Twelftree offers a more compelling series of theological solutions. He considers John to have known of traditions of Jesus as exorcist, but to have suppressed them for the following reasons: 1) John uses miracles to show Jesus' identity as Christ. He chooses spectacular miracles, rather than the mundane exorcisms. 2) John also excludes the idea of the Kingdom of God, which has implications for exorcism. 3) For John, the defeat of Satan comes at the cross, whereas for the synoptic authors it is linked with exorcism (Twelftree, *Jesus the Exorcist*, 141–42). The first of these positions is least substantiated in the synoptic gospels themselves, as they portray exorcisms as spectacles that do attract crowds and evoke their amazement. The second explanation shifts the question from why John omits exorcisms to why he omits references to the Kingdom of God. The third offers the most satisfactory explanation, though even here it is not apparent why John cannot use exorcism to complement rather than replace the significance he gives to the cross.

[115]See Mark 3:7–12 as the possible exception.

[116]Θεραπεύω is used for relief from demonic possession in Matt 4:24; 8:16–17; 12:22–30; 17:14–21; Luke 6:17–19; 7:18–23; 8:1–3.'Ιάομαι occurs at Matt 15:21–28 and Luke 9:37–43. Luke's choice of vocabulary belies W. G. Marx's assertion that Luke's demoniacs are never healed per se, but their demons driven out (W. G. Marx, "Luke, the

exorcism as a form of healing both Matthew and Luke gain the practical advantage of connecting Jesus' activity to the biblical prophetic tradition about the works that identify the true messiah which otherwise did not mention exorcism.[117] That the evangelists were compelled to include exorcism among Jesus' messianic acts, even though it was not prescribed by prophecy, also lends support to seeing exorcism as an activity engaged in by the historical Jesus.

5.5 The Authority of the Exorcist

As the earliest extant written evidence for exorcism in the Christian tradition, the Gospel of Mark offers an opportunity to establish a point of comparison between its description of exorcism and the analogous practices that preceded it (as set forth in Chapters 2, 3, and 4), and how it would come to be used as Christianity interacted with the Greco-Roman world (the subject of Chapter 6). For the author of Mark, however, it is less important to portray how Jesus performs exorcisms than that he does perform them, and so to underscore the divine authority behind his ministry. In contrast to the Marcan healings which can employ several distinct actions, the exorcisms in Mark are simply wrought, often performed only through a command or rebuke.[118] What the Gospel more clearly lacks, however, is prescription, and, thus, an intention to preserve the procedures of exorcism in a way to be practiced by others.[119] For this reason the Gospel of Mark can immediately be distinguished from the Mesopotamian ritual manuals *Šurpu*, *Udug-hul*, and *Maqlû*. Further, Mark's austere descriptions set Jesus' technique in contrast, perhaps deliberately so, with the elaborate methods known to have existed for other exorcists outside of the New Testament.[120]

Physician, Re-examined," *ExpTim* 91 [1979–80] 169–72; cited by Barrett-Lennard, *Christian Healing after the New Testament*, 145 n. 48).

[117]Matt 11:2–6 (citing Isa 53:4); Luke 7:18–23 (cf. Isa 29:18–19; 35:5–6; 61:1).

[118]The technique of exorcism that can be gathered from Mark comes primarily from three of the exorcism stories: the exorcism of the man in the synagogue (Mark 1:23–28); the story of the Gerasene demoniac, which includes discovery of the demon's name (Mark 5:9); and the story of the speechless boy, which includes an interest in the history of the boy's symptoms, and concludes with Jesus telling his disciples that this kind of spirit is only driven out by prayer (Mark 9:21, 29).

[119]Although prescription may be seen in Jesus' teaching that prayer is essential to relieve severe forms of demonic possession (Mark 9:29), even here Mark leaves unspecified the words of such a prayer.

[120]A single formula in the *Greek Magical Papyri*, for example, can contain ritualistic elements scattered throughout the Markan narrative. Compare *PGM* 4.3007–86 (IV C.E.), which prescribes a combined manual and verbal formula that includes such features as invocation of a deity, *rhesis barbarike*, and discovery of the demon's name. Of these, only

Although words of command to cast out demons are a common feature of the exorcism stories throughout the synoptics, a comparison of the words used in these confrontations reveals little interest in or adherence to formula.[121] The following tables provide the words Mark attributes to Jesus in the three of the four exorcism stories where Jesus addresses the demons directly. These are followed by their Lucan and Matthaean parallels. A single underline indicates a precise correspondence between the parallel passages. A single dotted underline indicates common words in different word order between parallel passages. A double underline indicates common words found in different pericopes.

Table 6: The Demoniac in the Synagogue

Mark 1:23–28	Luke 4:33–37	
φιμώθητι καὶ ἔξελθε ἐξ αὐτοῦ	φιμώθητι καὶ ἔξελθε ἀπ᾽ αὐτοῦ	

---

the discovery of the demon's name appears in Mark in an exorcistic context (Mark 5:1–20). The austerity of Mark's exorcisms comes into relief when compared to some of his healings. Jesus' healing of the deaf and dumb man (Mark 7:31–37), for example, is quite ritualistic in its sequential interconnected use of words and acts: 1) *rhesis barbarike* (at least to Mark's Greek readers if not to Jesus himself whose native language was likely Aramaic), 2) sympathetic touch, 3) glance to heaven (perhaps as source of authority), 4) sigh (as inspiration of that authority; cf. Jesus' transfer of power to his disciples by breathing the Holy Spirit upon them in John 20:22). Although this story in part uses words to cure the malady, it nowhere explicitly personifies the illness or equates it with a demon. By definition, then, this, is a healing distinct from an exorcism.

[121] A general distinction between methods of exorcism and healing in Mark is that the former tend to rely upon the power of speech, while the latter most often employ touch. These standards waver only slightly in Mark, where Jesus grabs the hand of the demoniac boy to revive him, though he does so only after the demon has been cast out (Mark 9:27), and where the multitude that included demoniacs sought to heal their afflictions by touching Jesus (Mark 3:10–11). The distinction between exorcism and healing disappears, however, in Luke's writings (Luke 6:19; 11:20; 13:13; cf. 4:40–41, and Acts 5:12–16; 19:11–12). In his unique story of the woman bent double, Luke thoroughly blends exorcism and healing with regard to both the interpretation of an ailment and its method of cure. Here, he describes the woman's physiological condition in terms of possession by a "crippling spirit" (πνεῦμα ἔχουσα ἀσθενείας), which Jesus heals (ἐθεράπευσεν) by both word and touch: "When Jesus saw her, he called her over and said, 'Woman, you are set free from your ailment' (γύναι, ἀπολέλυσαι τῆς ἀσθενείας σου). When he laid his hands on her (ἐπέθηκεν αὐτῇ τὰς χεῖρας), immediately she stood up straight and began praising God" (Luke 13:12–13). Compare also Luke's version of the Beelzeboul controversy, where he figuratively describes Jesus' exorcisms as done "by the finger of God" (Luke 11:20).

Table 7: The Gerasene Demoniac

Mark 5:1–20	Luke 8:26–39	Matthew 8:28–34
ἔξελθε τὸ πνεῦμα τὸ ἀκάθαρτον ἐκ τοῦ ἀνθρώπου ... τί ὄνομά σοι;	τί σοι ὄνομά ἐστιν;	ὑπάγετε

Table 8: The Possessed Boy

Mark 9:14–29	Luke 9:37–42	Matthew 17:14–21
τὸ ἄλαλον καὶ κωφὸν πνεῦμα, ἐγὼ ἐπιτάσσω σοι, ἔξελθε ἐξ αὐτοῦ καὶ μηκέτι εἰσέλθῃς εἰς αὐτόν.	[none]	[none]

All three of these exorcisms share the imperative mood that asserts Jesus' authority and forcefulness in communicating with the demons. The two longer examples also include an identification of the spirit's characteristics — "unclean" and "speechless and deaf" — and, in the former of these, an interest in the discovery of the demon's name. Yet, even though they consistently employ verbal techniques, these exorcisms offer little consistency in the choice of the words themselves. If the words of Jesus are meant to be reused this has escaped the notice of the other synoptic authors. Luke changes the wording and Matthew only records direct speech once in the exorcisms, where he uses the unparalleled ὑπάγετε. Even within Mark itself the author brings variety to the core exorcistic phrase "depart from" (ἔξελθε ἐκ). Mark offers descriptions of exorcism as it was practiced by Jesus and a mandate for the apostles to do likewise, but the gospel provides no prescription of the technique to do so. Instead, the exorcist operates through a direct relationship with the empowering deity in a way that is not reliant upon ritualistic or formulaic practice.

In relating their exorcism stories the synoptic authors show an interest in displaying the source of power by which they are performed. Aggressiveness pervades Jesus' and the disciples' interactions with the hostile demonic world.[122] The synoptic authors work on the assumption that exorcism reveals the exorcist as a mediator of divine power that constrains and overthrows an equally aggressive evil that has willfully caused innocent people to suffer. As such, exorcism conveys a message that addresses the exorcist's power and authority over the demons, and it asserts the exorcist's relationship to the

---

[122]This finds its only qualification in the case of the Gerasene demoniac, where Jesus does entertain a negotiation with the demons by granting them their request to enter into the swine rather than to depart the region (Mark 5:10–13) or return to the abyss (Luke 8:31–32; cf. Matt 8:31–32). To this compare the uncompromising exorcism of the possessed boy, whose demon Jesus not only casts out but commands never to return again (Mark 9:25).

divine spiritual source through which he both coerces the demons and mediates its restorative powers to the victims of possession.

As representatives of divine power, the exorcists' faith in that power regularly plays a role in the effectiveness of their exorcisms. This is seen inversely, both where Matthew and Luke attribute a lack of faith to the disciples' inability to exorcize the deaf and dumb boy,[123] and in the failure of the sons of Sceva in Acts.[124] Positively, the exorcists' faithfulness receives validation through their ability to perform exorcisms and other miracles, which in turn become visible signs to others of their divine support.[125] By this means, exorcism enhances the reputation of the exorcist[126] and creates certain expectations of them among those who witness their acts.[127]

---

[123]Matt 17:14–21//Luke 9:37–43a; cf. Mark 9:14–29. Matthew's critique of the disciples' poverty of faith in this episode is particularly relentless, and includes their "little faith" (διὰ τὴν ὀλιγοπιστίαν ὑμῶν) as the summary reason for their failure, followed by the lesson that even a small amount of faith can do much. Luke also closes his pericope with this lesson. Mark, however, includes it later in his gospel (11:22–23) and further minimizes the disciples' failure to exorcize by saying that this kind of demon requires also prayer to drive it out (Mark 9:29).

[124]Acts 19:13–20.

[125]In Luke the exorcisms performed by Jesus evoke from their audiences a recognition of the divine authority necessary to do them. This is attested in the praise they give to God upon witnessing the miracles. Such praise shows the intimate connection between the exorcists' work and their source of power: the performance of an exorcism not only enhances their own reputations, but also magnifies their divine sponsors. Recognition of this relationship in Mark is assumed of the reader and is evident among the demons who are subject to exorcism, but is less evident for those in the narrative who witness the exorcisms (cf. the longer ending of Mark which makes the connection explicit [Mark 16:17]). Although Mark is the most unflinching of the synoptic gospels in support of exorcism, the subdued, sometimes ambiguous responses its exorcisms evoke from the crowds suggest the author's awareness of a bias harbored by some of his contemporaries against exorcism and other miraculous acts.

[126]In the case of the exorcism of the demoniac in the synagogue, the report circulates throughout Galilee and establishes Jesus as an authoritative figure (Mark 1:23–28//Luke 4:33–37). In the exorcism of the woman bent double she directs her praise to God while the crowd rejoices over Jesus (Luke 13:10–17).

[127]Jesus' exorcism of the deaf and dumb demoniac evokes from the crowd a connection of Jesus with the son of David (Matt 12:22–24). Also in Matthew, the Syrophoenician woman appeals to Jesus as "Lord, Son of David" in her petition for him to heal her daughter (Matt 15:6). In Luke, Jesus tells the followers of John the Baptist that his own ability to perform exorcisms is part of a larger ministry that serves as proof that he is the one to come, whom John's own ministry has anticipated (Luke 7:18–23). Given their exorcistic contexts, the two Matthaean passages could well be a reference to Jesus' activity in keeping with the tradition of Solomon as the exorcist *par excellence* rather than to messiahship. For discussion, see Dennis Duling's article in which he concludes "Solomon-as-exorcist" to be an aspect of Mark's Son of David Christology (Dennis C. Duling, "Solomon, Exorcism, and the Son of David," *HTR* 68 [1975] 235–52). Note, however, that the use of "Son of David"

The message of divine sponsorship that exorcism intends to convey is, however, subject to misinterpretation. In the Beelzeboul controversy the Jewish authorities challenge the authority by which Jesus exorcizes.[128] The scribes raise a twofold accusation in Mark's version of the controversy, both of which essentially question the authority from which Jesus draws his power to exorcize: that Jesus is possessed by Beelzeboul (Βεελζεβοὺλ ἔχει),[129] and that it is by Beelzeboul, the ruler of the demons, that he casts out demons.[130] According to Mark, Jesus defends himself on the premise of the exorcist's divine authority. Jesus begins his response by rephrasing the scribes' accusation in the form of a rhetorical question: "How is Satan able to cast out Satan?" This triggers a series of illustrations intended to display the flaw in their assumption, as he asks how a kingdom, a house, and finally Satan himself can remain intact if they suffer from division. The illustrations culminate with the parable of the binding of the strong man drawn from scripture. Isaiah 49:24–25 reads in the Septuagint:

> Would someone take spoils from a giant (παρὰ γίγαντος σκῦλα)? And if someone should unjustly take captive, would (the captive) be rescued? Thus says the Lord: "If even someone should capture (αἰχμαλωτεύσῃ) a giant, he would take his spoils; and the one who takes them from the strong man (ἰσχύοντος) will be rescued; I will decide your judgment, and I will free your sons.[131]

---

for Jesus also in a non-exorcistic context (Mark 12:35–37) appears to confirm it as a messianic title.

[128]Mark 3:22–30; cf. Matt 12:22–37//Luke 11:14–15, 17–27; 12:10. The Beelzeboul controversy is thought to derive from an early stratum of the Gospels' literary history, with representations in both Mark and the Q source. Though there is some overlap between Mark and the other synoptic gospels, the agreement between Matthew and Luke against Mark on several counts justifies treating the Beelzeboul controversy as having found expression through two independent witnesses (John S. Kloppenborg, *Q. Parallels: Synopsis, Critical Notes and Concordance* [Sonoma, Calif.: Polebridge Press, 1988] 92).

[129]This charge in Mark 3:22 is reiterated in verse 30's, "he possesses an unclean spirit" (πνεῦμα ἀκάθαρτον ἔχει), so as to bracket the pericope.

[130]Mark 3:22.

[131]Compare from the Hebrew:

Can spoil (מלקוֹח) be taken from a warrior (מגבוֹר),
Or captives retrieved from a victor (צדיק)?
Yet thus said the Lord:
Captives shall be taken from a warrior
And spoil shall be retrieved from a tyrant (עריץ);
For I will contend with your adversaries (ואת־יריבך אנכי אריב),
And I will deliver (אושיע) your children.

Luke's version of the parable comes closest to the LXX: "When a strong man (ὁ ἰσχυρός), fully armed, guards his castle, his property is safe. But when one stronger than he attacks him and overpowers him, he takes away his armor in which he trusted and divides his plunder (τὰ σκῦλα)" (Luke 11:21–22). Compare the *Testament of Zebulun*, where the

The passage occurs in the context of Second Isaiah (Isaiah 40–55), in which the prophet encourages the exiled Judean nation to return home, and for which the historical referent is considered to be Judea's liberation from Babylonian tyranny (="the strong man") through the Persians under Cyrus the Great.[132]

This passage from Isaiah undergoes significant conceptual changes when put into the contexts of possession and exorcism. In part, the image lends itself to the conceptual world of these contexts, in which "binding" (δέω) converges with the constraints placed upon the possessed by their demonic aggressors and upon the aggressors themselves by the exorcist.[133] In Mark, the parable of the strong man draws its literal referent from the exorcism of demonic possessors.[134] On one level this internalizes the idea of conquest otherwise conceived of as an external political event in Isaiah. But Mark additionally elevates the exorcistic binding from the earthly immediacy of individual possession subject to exorcism to the event as a cosmic struggle in which Beelzeboul's kingdom is now subjected.[135] The strong man of Isaiah now represents Beelzeboul (Satan),[136] with Jesus the most likely counterpart

---

possessed are described as prisoners of war (αἰχμαλωσίαν) whom the Lord will ransom from Beliar, and all spirits of deceit will be trampled (*T. Zeb.* 9.8).

[132]Richard J. Clifford, "Isaiah, Book of [Second Isaiah]," *ABD* 3:492–94.

[133]Cf. Mark 5:2–4; Luke 13:16.

[134]Here again the evangelists are able to use Isaiah to validate the practice of exorcism (cf. Matt 11:2–6; Luke 7:18–23). Although σκεῦος in the plural often has the generic connotation of "property" (see "σκεῦος," BDAG³, 927–28), the exorcistic context of this passage suggests "vessels" as a possible interpretation. Commentaries interpret the σκεύη in the house (= the "spoils" taken from Isaiah's strong man-warrior) as diversely as the possessed and the demons of possession. Robert Guelich takes the former view, with the plundering as a reference to Jesus' exorcism of them (Robert Guelich, *Mark 1–8:26* [WBC 34A; Dallas, Tex.: Word Books, 1989] 176). Ezra Gould takes the latter view, and considers the vessels to denote "the demons as Satan's instruments, or tools" (Ezra P. Gould, *A Critical and Exegetical Commentary on the Gospel According to St. Mark* [ICC; Edinburgh: T&T Clark, 1955] 64. For a parallel to Gould's use of σκεύη, cf. 2 Tim 2:20–21). The vessels or spoils, however, are of value as booty both in the context of Isaiah and the synoptics. For this reason they likely represent the possessed in the exorcistic scenario of the gospels. The "vessel" as a metaphor of the demonically possessed is otherwise unprecedented, though it appears in later Christian writings as an object of both divine and demonic possession (e.g., *Herm.* Mandate 5.1–3; cf. the late antique Christian magical text *Cod. Marc. gr. app.* II 163, found in *RVV* 3.3 [1907] 9.11–16). In early Christian exegesis, Irenaeus interpreted the house and vessels to represent humanity in a state of apostasy and bound by sin (Irenaeus, *Haer.* 3.8.2; 5.21.3).

[135]Compare Revelation 20:2–3, where the devil (Satan) is subject to bondage.

[136]This is explicit, however, only in Matthew 10:25b, which foreshadows the Beelzeboul controversy of 12:22–37. The verse reads: "If they have called the master of the house Beelzeboul, how much more its residents!" (εἰ τὸν οἰκοδεσπότην Βεελζεβοὺλ ἐπεκάλεσαν, πόσῳ μᾶλλον τοὺς οἰκιακοὺς αὐτοῦ). Prior verses show that slander against the householder and household is responded to here, which the final clause echoes as "how much more will they malign his household" (Matt 10:25c). The content of Matthew

who binds him.[137] The image of binding introduces the exorcist and his source of power into the discussion. Contrary to the scribes' accusations, Jesus' response suggests that his ability to exorcize indicates a hostile relationship with the demonic powers and the subjugation of Beelzeboul's kingdom. This anticipates the reference to possession of the Holy Spirit implied in Mark 3:30, where Mark equates the accusation of Jesus' possession by Beelzeboul with blasphemy against that Spirit.[138] For the gospel of Mark the authority to exorcize is not something external to the exorcist, but a spiritual presence which he possesses.[139]

The accusation that the Jewish authorities raise against Jesus in the Beelzeboul controversy may reflect a genuine critique of exorcism current in Jesus' time and place, but it is a criticism that Mark rejects. For Mark, the success of an exorcist argues for his legitimate authority to exorcize.[140] This is also seen in the story of the anonymous exorcist who casts out demons in Jesus' name and receives Jesus' sanction to do so.[141] Mark grants some latitude toward such exorcists on the assumption that those who successfully perform miracles in Jesus' name, but do so out of context of his cause, will soon gain an appreciation for both.

Although this attitude finds some support elsewhere in the New Testament,[142] an opposite view also arises. Luke includes a version of the

---

10:25b thus reflects the same controversy as found in the parallel passages: namely, the slander that comes from identifying the divine presence with Beelzeboul.

[137]Werner Foerster suggests that the actual binding of the strong man has its corollary in Jesus' earlier victory over Satan during the temptation in the wilderness (Werner Foerster, "σατανᾶς," *TDNT* 7:159).

[138]Mark 3:28–29.

[139]Matthew's and Luke's versions of the Beelzeboul controversy make Jesus' divine authority clear where they identify his power as the "spirit of God" (ἐν πνεύματι θεοῦ [Matt 12:27–28]) and the "finger of God" (ἐν δακτύλῳ θεοῦ [Luke 11:19–20]) respectively. Unlike Mark, however, they neither specify this as an indwelling power, nor do they include the charge that Jesus is demonically possessed.

[140]Compare the passages in Matthew and Luke where Jesus calls attention to the scribes' own sons who practice exorcism without their authority being questioned (Matt 12:27//Luke 11:19).

[141]Mark 9:38–41//Luke 9:49–50. These stories conclude with Jesus' words to the disciples: "Who is not against us is for us" (ὃς γὰρ οὐκ ἔστιν καθ᾽ ἡμῶν, ὑπὲρ ἡμῶν ἐστιν — Mark 9:40). Matthew and Luke have also incorporated a similar moral into the conclusions of their Beelzeboul controversies (Matt 12:30; Luke 11:23).

[142]Compare similar sentiments in 1 Corinthians 12:3, where the Holy Spirit inspires one to say "Jesus is Lord," and in Philippians 1:15–18, where Paul considers the proclamation of Christ to outweigh the motivation for the proclamation. Compare also 1 John 4:2–3, where "every spirit" (πᾶν πνεῦμα) which confesses Jesus Christ in the flesh is from God, and every spirit which does not so confess is not from God.

anonymous exorcist in his gospel,[143] but in Acts he critiques such a practice with the story of the sons of Sceva. Matthew displays an even greater awareness of exorcism's shortcomings as an unambiguous indicator of divine sponsorship. The accusation of casting out demons by the ruler of the demons appears twice in Matthew, whereas it appears only once in each of the other two synoptic gospels.[144] Further, in a passage not found in Mark, Matthew subordinates exorcism and other deeds of power to doing the will of God, so that neither prophecy, casting out demons in Jesus' name, nor other miracles will secure one's entry into the kingdom of Heaven.[145] Thus, the question of authority that the Jews raise against Jesus in the Beelzeboul controversy, and that Jesus dismisses, would become a question the early Christian authorities could suspect of those who practiced exorcism outside of Christianity.[146]

Jesus performs exorcism by divine sanction implicitly, but when his ministry shifts over to the disciples their own practices will draw explicitly upon Jesus' name. Perhaps initially Jesus represented the favored mediator of divine power to the disciples.[147] He would soon, however, become identified with the divine power itself. The invocation of Jesus' name would become the most important technique for exorcism in early Christianity, where it both promoted the religious founder figure to the uninitiated and validated the exorcist's sponsorship by that figure before the community of believers. This prescription, however, only enters into the gospel of Mark late, in its longer

---

[143]Luke's version of the story includes the moral "who is not against you is for you" (Luke 9:50), but lacks the explanation found in Mark 9:39 that the ability to work a miracle in Jesus' name will lead to the miracle worker's respect for Jesus.

[144]Matt 9:32–34; 12:22–32. The accusation does, however, receive a refutation in the second passage much along the lines of Luke's response, and it also makes an uncritical reference to other Jews who perform exorcisms.

[145]Matt 7:21–23. Luke offers a similar but less qualified critique, where Jesus is pleased with the 70's (72's) success at exorcism, but reminds them that their place in heaven is more important (Luke 10:17–20). Contrary to Matthew, Luke appears to suggest here that the ability to exorcize does presuppose one's election into heaven. Although Matthew is more reserved in his endorsement of exorcism than Mark (and Luke), he does include it in a passage not mentioned by either of the other gospels (Matt 4:24; cf. also Matt 12:22–23), and he, as does Luke, associates it with Isaiah's prophecy (Matt 11:2–6; Luke 7:18–23).

[146]E.g., Irenaeus, *Haer.* 2.31.2–3; 3.12.12; Pseudo-Clement, *Recogn.* 3.60; *Hom.* 2.33 (see below, Chapter 6). Comparison can be made to the Greek magical spells that invoke the names of Jesus and of others from the biblical tradition without necessarily having regard for the cultic contexts of Christianity and Judaism from which they derive.

[147]Compare the story of Eleazar's exorcism before Vespasian, in which Josephus reveals the dependence of later Jewish exorcists upon Solomon (Josephus, *Ant.* 8.42–49). The relationship between Eleazar and Solomon offers one interpretation for the significance of Jesus' name in the New Testament and early Christianity according to which Jesus is the original recipient of divine favor, and his followers use his name to achieve similar results in exorcism. In addition, their effective use of Jesus' name continues to demonstrate his favored status with God.

ending, where it serves as a sign for believers and as a proof of the authority of their message in their effort to preach the gospel throughout the world.[148]

Although the use of Jesus' name in exorcism is only prescribed in this secondary addition to the gospel, it is in unprescribed use earlier with the anonymous exorcist,[149] in Luke's mission of the 70 (72), and in the commissioning and sending forth of the Twelve found in all of the synoptic gospels.[150] These passages show not only the power of Jesus' name over the demons, but the successful transfer of his exorcistic ability to the disciples.[151] This confidence in the successful transference of Jesus' authority and power to the new apostolic leaders of the Christian movement is also apparent in Acts, where people come from the cities near Jerusalem to experience for themselves the signs and wonders performed by the followers of Christ, which include healing (θεραπεύω) from demonic possession.[152]

5.6 The Deity and Divine Possession

Like the demonic world the divine spiritual world is also hierarchically structured, with regiments of angelic figures subject to God. These lesser divine beings, however, tend not to possess the individual.[153] Instead, divine

---

[148]ἐν τῷ ὀνόματί μου δαιμόνια ἐκβαλοῦσιν (Mark 16:17). There is no mention of the disciples exorcizing in Jesus' name in those passages where Jesus has commissioned them to exorcize (Mark 3:13–19; 6:7–11). Due to its non-Markan vocabulary and style and its awkward connection to the foregoing verses, Mark 16:9–20 is considered a secondary, albeit early appendage to the gospel. Bruce Metzger has estimated its date to the first half of the second century (Metzger, *A Textual Commentary on the Greek New Testament*, 122–26). For a discussion of literary dependence and a refinement of the date of the longer ending to ca. 120–140 C.E., see James A. Kelhoffer's recent and detailed study, *Miracle and Mission: The Authentication of Missionaries and Their Message in the Longer Ending of Mark* (WUNT 2.112; Tübingen: Mohr [Siebeck], 2000), especially pages 169–77.

[149]Mark 9:38–40//Luke 9:49–50. Independent of exorcism, compare the importance of Jesus' name to the early Christian communities apparent in the "Christ Hymn" of Philippians 2:5–11. Although the hymn does not actually state the "name" referred to in verse 9 or what it signifies, the importance of the name "Jesus" in exorcism within and outside of Christianity in the first centuries of the Common Era argues for this as the implied correlative of ὄνομα in verse 9, and placed in complementary relationship to the honorific title κύριος. (Compare, R. P. Martin, *Carmen Christi: Philippians ii.5–11 in Recent Interpretation and in the Setting of Early Christian Worship* [Cambridge: Cambridge University Press, 1967] 235–47).

[150]Mark 3:13–15; 6:6b–13//Matt 10:1–15//Luke 9:1–6.

[151]The transference is not absolute in the synoptics, as shown by the inability of the disciples to exorcize the possessed boy (Mark 9:14–29//Matt 17:14–21//Luke 9:37–43a).

[152]Acts 5:12–16.

[153]For instances of angels encountering individuals compare, for example, Gabriel's annunciations to Zechariah (Luke 1:8–23) and Mary (Luke 1:26–38), and an angel's attending to John in the Apocalypse (Rev 17:1–2). The spirit of Elijah upon John the Baptist is a

possession is the prerogative of the godhead.[154] References to divine possession are found throughout the New Testament writings to such an extent and significance that it becomes a defining feature of Christian identity. To some extent the terms for divine possession reflect those for demonic possession, such as "dwelling in" (οἰκεούμενον ἐν),[155] "coming upon" (ἐρχόμενον ἐπί),[156] and "working within" (ἐνεργουμένην ἐν).[157] A distinctive feature of divine possession, however, lies in the fluidity and

---

possible exception, where an angel of the Lord tells Zechariah that the spirit of Elijah will assist his son: "With the spirit and power of Elijah he will go before him, to turn the hearts of parents to their children, and the disobedient to the wisdom of the righteous, to make ready a people prepared for the Lord." (Luke 1:17). Although Luke here relates the Baptist's future activity in the spirit to Malachi 4:5, the tradition originates in 2 Kings with Elisha's request to inherit a double share of Elijah's spirit (2 Kings 2:9–15). The reference to a "double share" derives from the legal inheritance owed to the eldest son (Deut 12:17), and so indicates Elisha's desire for recognition as his master's true heir (see, John Gray, *1 and 2 Kings: A Commentary* [Philadelphia: Westminster Press, 1970] 475). It is unclear in 2 Kings, however, whether the "spirit of Elijah" refers to Elijah's personal spirit or to the divine spirit which he possesses. In its Hebrew Biblical context, Ze'ev Weisman takes the former view, and argues that "not only is the spirit not in any way attributed to God, but God does not fulfill any task in its transference" (Ze'ev Weisman, "The Personal Spirit as Imparting Authority," *ZAW* 93 [1981] 227). Yet Elisha's re-crossing of the Jordan could be just such a show of divine transference: Elisha cannot part the Jordan only by striking its waters with Elijah's mantel, but must also call out "Where is the Lord, the God of Elijah?" Mordechai Cogan and Hayim Tadmor instead take the "spirit of Elijah" as transcendent of Elijah: "… Elijah, like Moses, enjoyed a special relationship with YHWH, described in terms of spirit transferable to others (cf. Num 11:16–17, 24–26)" (Mordechai Cogan and Hayim Tadmor, *2 Kings* [AB 11; New York: Doubleday, 1988] 32). The parallel with Moses is significant here, as Kings throughout has patterned Elijah after him. Although Weisman also finds the transference of spirit in Numbers to signify a personal rather than transcendent spirit, that is, Moses' personal authority given to the seventy elders, the spirit here is even less explicitly Moses' own than we find for Elijah. That it is not Moses' personal spirit is evident in its ability to be distributed: Moses and the seventy share simultaneously in the same spirit. Given the New Testament context, a transcendent spirit appears intended by Luke as well. Such is not only consistent with divine possession found elsewhere in the New Testament, but Luke's coupling of "the power" with "the spirit of Elijah" identifies the transcendent force at work in him.

[154]The divine presence as a possessing entity finds expression through a multiplicity of names, which revolve around different aspects of the single godhead. The notion of a unified Spirit despite its diversity of names finds its clearest articulation in the writings of Paul, where it becomes at times a central issue, and which finds its most extensive discussion in 1 Corinthians. In 1 Corinthians 6:17, Paul says that the person united with the Lord "is one Spirit" (ἓν πνεῦμά ἐστιν). In 1 Corinthians 12:13, Paul says that all are baptized with one Spirit into one body, a process which he describes as "all drinking in the one Spirit" (πάντες ἓν πνεῦμα ἐποτίσθημεν).

[155]Rom 8:9; 1 Cor 3:16; Eph 3:17; Col 3:16; 2 Tim 1:14; cf. James 4:5.

[156]Matt 3:16; Acts 11:15; 19:6.

[157]Eph 3:20; Col 1:29.

abundance of the Holy Spirit: the Holy Spirit is "poured out upon" one (ἐκχέω ἐπί);[158] one "drinks in" (ἐποτίσθημεν),[159] "imbibes" (μεθύσκεσθε),[160] "boils with" (ζέων),[161] is "anointed" (ἔχρισεν)[162] or "baptized" with (βαπτισθήσεσθε),[163] is "filled" or "abounds with" (περισσεύειν and πληρωθῆτε)[164] this Spirit.

The same people who perform exorcisms also invoke the divine Spirit.[165] Contrary to the harmful experiences of demonic possession, the manifestations of divine possession in the New Testament are generally beneficent to the possessed individual, and can have advantages to those around them who might benefit from healing or enlightenment.[166] The manifestations of divine possession are to some degree antithetical to symptoms of demonic possession: divine possession can enable one to heal ailments often attributed to demonic possession;[167] whereas demonic possession is debilitating, divine possession counters weakness;[168] divine possession also restores life,[169] while demons are occasionally described as trying to destroy their hosts; whereas demonic possession causes social separation in the synoptic gospels, possession of the Holy Spirit establishes community in Acts and the Pauline letters.

The New Testament portrays the reception of divine possession as a positive experience that comes through preaching,[170] prayer,[171] breathing

---

[158]Acts 2:1–41; 10:44–48; Rom 5:5; Tit 3:4–7 (πλουσίως).

[159]1 Cor 12:13.

[160]Eph 5:18. Compare this with the apparent intoxication of the apostles with the Holy Spirit during Pentecost (Acts 2:1–13). See also Philo's use of the image of intoxication when he speaks of the *therapeutae* having "drawn in" (σπάσαντες) the divine love during their banquets in favorable contrast to the bacchic character of pagan symposia (Philo, *Contempl.* 9 [§85]).

[161]Acts 18:25; Rom 12:11.

[162]Acts 10:38; 2 Cor 1:21–22.

[163]Acts 1:5; 11:16; 19:1–7.

[164]Rom 15:13; Eph 3:19.

[165]Compare, however, the passage where Peter and John, rather than Philip, bestow the Holy Spirit upon Philip's converts in Samaria (Acts 8:14–17).

[166]Possible exceptions in the New Testament to the maleficent nature of demonic possession are the girl with a spirit of prophecy, whose possession at least brings gain to her owners (Acts 16:16), and Paul's "thorn in the flesh," which ultimately works to his advantage (cf. also the handing over of Hymenaius et al. to Satan [1 Tim 1:19b–20]). The exceptions to divine beneficent possession may be evident when the deity is invoked in a curse, e.g., Barjesus/Elymas (Acts 13:4–12).

[167]Luke 4:18; Acts 10:38; 1 Cor 12:9.

[168]Rom 8:22–27; 2 Tim 1:6–7; perhaps also Luke 1:80 if the "spirit" is the Holy Spirit rather than John's own (cf. Luke 1:15).

[169]Rev 11:11.

[170]In Acts 10:37–48, Peter gives a summary to Cornelius' household of Jesus' ministry (compare Matthew's quotation of Isaiah [Matt 12:18–21]). Therein, Jesus is said to have

upon,[172] and especially laying on of hands.[173] Regardless of method, those who bestow the Holy Spirit first possess it themselves. The many manifestations of divine possession principally serve to bring revelation of divinity to humanity: from the revelation's reception, through its proclamation and, if necessary, its proof. Particularly in the book of Revelation we see how possession of the divine Spirit makes one attentive or receptive to divine messages. Thus, being "in the Spirit" (ἐν πνεύματι) repeatedly anticipates different stages of the vision which John experiences: at the vision's trumpet-heralded outset,[174] at its escalation when he views the throne of heaven,[175] when he is taken to the desert to see the personified Babylon,[176] and before the climactic viewing of the New Jerusalem.[177] In

received the Holy Spirit from God. Through the course of Peter's speech, the Holy Spirit is poured out upon Cornelius' household (ἡ δωρεὰ τοῦ ἁγίου πνεύματος ἐκκέχυται). In Acts 11:15–18, before the disciples in Jerusalem, Peter compares the reception of the Holy Spirit at Cornelius' house to their own experience on Pentecost (Acts 15:8). In Galatians 3:1–5, Paul says that the Galatians have received the Spirit from the preaching of faith (τὸ πνεῦμα ἐλάβετε ἢ ἐξ ἀκοῆς πίστεως), and that Paul has provided it for them (ὁ ... ἐπιχορηγῶν ὑμῖν τὸ πνεῦμα).

[171]In Acts 8:15–19, Peter and John pray that the Holy Spirit may come upon the Samaritan believers.

[172]In John 20:22, Jesus transfers the Holy Spirit to his disciples by breathing on them (ἐνεφύσησεν) and saying "Receive the Holy Spirit" (λάβετε πνεῦμα ἅγιον).

[173]In Acts 8:14–25, Peter and John lay their hands on the baptized of Samaria to convey the Holy Spirit (ἐπετίθεσιν τὰς χεῖρας ἐπ᾽ αὐτοὺς καὶ ἐλάμβανον πνεῦμα ἅγιον). In Acts 9:10–19, Ananias lays hands upon Saul (ἐπιθεὶς ἐπ᾽ αὐτόν) to restore his sight (ἀναβλέψῃς) and to fill him with the Holy Spirit (πλησθῇς πνεύματος ἁγίου). In Acts 19:1–7, Paul conveys the Holy Spirit through the laying on of hands (ἐπιθέντος αὐτοῖς ... χεῖρας ἦλθε τὸ πνεῦμα τὸ ἅγιον ἐπ᾽ αὐτούς). In 2 Timothy 1:6–14, the author says that the gift of the Holy Spirit was given by God (τὸ χάρισμα τοῦ θεοῦ) through the laying on of hands (ὅ ἐστιν ἐν σοὶ διὰ τῆς ἐπιθέσεως τῶν χειρῶν μου), and it dwells within (τοῦ ἐνοικοῦντος ἐν ἡμῖν). Laying on of hands will also come to accompany the verbal technique of exorcism as a ritual in the first centuries of the church (see Chapter 6).

[174]Rev 1:10.

[175]Rev 4:2.

[176]Rev 17:3.

[177]Rev 21:10. Compare also Stephen, who, "filled with the Holy Spirit" (πλήρης πνεύματος ἁγίου), sees a vision which he then proclaims to the hostile crowd (Acts 7:54–60). In her anthropological studies of possession, Erika Bourguignon distinguishes between "possession" and "possession trance": "We shall say that a belief in *possession* exists, when the people in question hold that a given person is changed in some way through the presence in or on him of a spirit entity or power, other than his own personality, soul, self, or the like. We shall say that *possession trance* exists in a given society when we find that there is such a belief in possession and that it is used to account for alterations or discontinuity in consciousness, awareness, personality, or other aspects of psychological functioning" (Bourguignon, *Possession*, 7–8). David Aune builds upon these definitions and uses the terms "vision trance" (in which the soul leaves the body) and "possession trance" (in

addition to spectacle and sound, the divine presence also makes itself known more intimately through the teaching and counseling of the intellect. This is seen most clearly in the Johannine writings where the "Paraclete" and "spirit of truth" will doctrinally guide the disciples after Jesus' departure.[178]

5.7 Exorcism and Early Christian Mission

The reception of revelation compels the pronouncement of that revelation, so that the bounty of the Holy Spirit overflows into mission. The connections between divine possession and one's compulsion to pronounce or to bear witness to revelation are manifold, and result in the verbal forms of preaching,[179] teaching,[180] and especially prophecy,[181] and in the performances

---

which a foreign spiritual power enters into the body, as in ecstatic prophecy) as distinct categories of "revelatory trance" to identify prophetic patterns in the biblical tradition (David E. Aune, *Prophecy in Early Christianity and the Ancient Mediterranean World* [Grand Rapids, Mich.: William B. Eerdmans, 1983] 19–21, 86–87; cf. also Erika Bourguignon, ed., *Religion, Altered States of Consciousness, and Social Change* [Columbus, Ohio: Ohio State University Press, 1973], especially her introductory and summary chapters: "A Framework for the Comparative Study of Altered States of Consciousness" [pp. 3–35] and "An Assessment of Some Comparisons and Implications" [pp. 321–39]). Aune considers the former of these two terms to reflect John's state in Revelation 1:10, 4:2, and 17:3, so that the phrase being "in the spirit" (ἐν πνεύματι) refers to going into a trance, and moving somewhere "in the spirit" refers to being miraculously transported (David E. Aune, "Revelation," *HBD* 1187–1202). Even in a vision trance, however, John remains the passive agent of the divine will, as God induces and summons him to experience the revelation (Rev 1:1–2; 4:1–2; 17:1–3).

[178]According to John 14:15–17 Jesus will ask the Father to give the Holy Spirit (or Spirit of Truth) as a divine counselor to the disciples. This Spirit will teach them and cause them to remember Jesus' own teachings (John 14:26). The Counselor bears witness (μαρτυρήσει) to Jesus (John 15:26–27), and guides to the truth by showing the world its sin (ἁμαρτίας) and by making known God's righteousness and judgment (John 16:8-11). Compare Acts 20:28, where Paul reminds the church that, although he is leaving, the Holy Spirit has assigned overseers to their flock (ἔθετο ἐπισκόπους ποιμαίνειν). Compare also Romans 9:1–2, where Paul's truthfulness is supported by the Holy Spirit.

[179]E.g., Luke 3:2–3; Acts 2:1–42; 1 Thess 2:9–13; Gal 3:1–5.

[180]E.g., John 14–16 (the activity of the Paraclete); Col 3:16.

[181]E.g., Luke 1:67; Acts 11:28; 19:1–7; 21:4; 21:7–14; 2 Pet 1:20–21. The ambiguity of the oracular messages in early Greece that required discernment for its appropriate meaning differs from the lucidity of prophecy that Paul sought for the edification of his congregations (1 Cor 14:1–5). Evenso, Paul draws a similar distinction to the one made by Plato with respect to the reception and transmission of revelation through inspired prophecy (Plato, *Tim.* 71D–72B; see above, Section 4.2.1.2). Paul differentiates between the one who receives divine messages (ὁ λαλῶν γλώσσῃ) and the one who interprets them (προφήτης — 1 Cor 14:1–40), which compares favorably to the distinction Plato makes between the diviners (μάντεις) who receive messages in their belly, and the prophets (προφῆται) who decipher such encrypted messages through reason and intelligence.

of visual signs and wonders that include exorcism.[182] In the synoptic Gospels
and Acts the performance of exorcism, or the reputation of that performance,
provides new communities with their initial exposure to Jesus or the message
associated with him.[183] Chronologically in their narratives Jesus first performs
exorcisms before his immediate Jewish communities, and the mission comes
gradually to expand into the regions surrounding Galilee and Judea: the
Decapolis, Samaria, Tyre, and Sidon, and through the disciples as far to the
west as Ephesus and Philippi. As a consequence, the shift in settings from the
vicinity of first century Jewish identity at Jerusalem and Judea to the outlying
Greek and Roman cities brings exorcism before audiences of diverse cultural
backgrounds, and places it at the forefront of Christian mission. The visible
symptoms of physiological demonic possession and its equally recognizable
cure through exorcism lend themselves to the public activity otherwise
engaged in by Jesus and the disciples. These public displays contributed to
the Christian missionary efforts of the first centuries by making known the
exorcists and the sheer power of the divine source from which they drew their
authority.

Matthew's and Luke's classification of exorcism as a healing activity has
implications for how it would be received and with what institutions it would
then compete in the Greco-Roman world. Acts occasionally shows
Christianity to compete with and even to supersede existing Greek cults.[184]

---

[182]E.g., Luke 4:18 (Isa 61:1); Acts 2:17–18 (Joel 3:1–5); Rom 15:19 (Joel 3:1–5); Heb
2:4; 1 John 3:2. In addition to the mission context, preaching, teaching, prophecy, and the
performance of signs and wonders also occur in the historical context of persecution in early
Christianity, which raised the need for encouragement toward steadfastness in the faith. For
example, in Matthew 10:20, a Q passage, the "Spirit of the Father" (cf. Luke's "Holy Spirit")
will guide the disciples in their presentations to the authorities and to the nations. In the
context of Mark's apocalyptic discourse, Jesus encourages the disciples' confidence in their
witness during times of persecution, since the "Holy Spirit" will be with them (Mark
13:9–11). In 1 Peter 4:14–16 the Spirit of God rests upon Christians who suffer reproach in
the name of Christ (τὸ τοῦ θεοῦ πνεῦμα ἐφ᾽ ὑμᾶς ἀναπαύεται). The context of
persecution is also one of the motivations for Paul's occasional references to his own
sufferings on behalf of the faith (1 Cor 4:9–13; 2 Cor 5:6–10; 11:21b–33). As with the
passages found elsewhere in the New Testament, Paul makes these references to show his
commitment to the faith, and to offer encouragement to those to whom he writes should they
undergo the same. But he also sees it as evidence of one's possessing the Spirit of Christ:
one's undergoing suffering likens that person to Christ who suffered on their behalf (Phil
3:20–21; cf. Col 1:21–24).

[183]For example, early in the Gospels, news of Jesus' activity spreads to surrounding
regions, so that people from Galilee, Judea, Jerusalem, Idumea, the region across the Jordan,
Tyre, and Sidon come to experience his miracle working first hand, exorcism included (Mark
3:7–12[//Matt 4:24//Luke 6:17–19]).

[184]For example, Barnabas and Paul at Lystra, where they correct the citizens who have
mistaken them for Zeus and Hermes respectively (Acts 14:8–18), and Paul at Athens, where

The uproar over the cult of Artemis that results from Paul's successful mission at Ephesus best exemplifies this. The story nominally concerns the expansion of Christianity at the expense of the traditional cult of Artemis. It is an issue Demetrius and other artisans raise when they fear a dwindling number of worshippers to buy their votives.[185] Although their decrease in business does reflect Christianity's successful competition with the civic cult, Luke steers the emphasis away from this concern. Despite a public tumult, the city officials defend Paul's travel companions before the protesters and leave them unpunished.

Indications of competition with Greek cults elsewhere in the New Testament may be seen where Paul "demonizes" the Greek gods in 1 Corinthians 10:20–21 and in Revelation's reference to "the throne of Satan" which may refer to the Great Altar of Zeus at Pergamum.[186] The subjection of these deities through exorcism per se, however, does not appear in literature until later, unless one associates the "pythian spirit" (πνεῦμα πύθωνα) of the slave girl at Philippi with Apollo.[187] Rather than critique Greek cultic life or attack the Greek pantheon, the exorcisms of the synoptic Gospels confront the mostly nameless and generic host of evil and unclean spirits.

---

he offers his own message about the resurrected Jesus as the previously unrecognized object of Greek philosophy and cult (Acts 17:16–27).

[185]Acts 19:21–20:1.

[186]Adela Yarbro Collins has conjectured that by identifying the Great Altar of Zeus with the "throne of Satan" (Rev 2:13) the author of Revelation critiques both the literal deity to whom the altar is dedicated and the political power glorified in its outer frieze (Attalus I's victory over the Gauls), which John has contemporized to portray the expansion of imperial Rome under Domitian (Adela Yarbro Collins, "Pergamon in Early Christian Literature," in *Pergamon, Citadel of the Gods: Archaeological Record, Literary Description, and Religious Development*, Helmut Koester, ed. [HTS 46; Harrisburg, Pa.: Trinity Press International, 1998] 163–84).

[187]Acts 16:16–24. The term μαντευομένη links the girl's work securely to prophecy, and, in as much as her soothsaying activity ends with exorcism, prophecy must also be an aspect of the exorcized spirit, which has transfered this trait to its host. "Pythian," then, serves as the spirit's functional epithet, and likely draws upon associations with the python, or the mantic Pythian priestess of Apollo's oracular shrine at Delphi. J. W. van Henten notes that the name also appears in *Sib. Or.* 11:315 in a possible Delphic reference (J. W. van Henten, "Python Πυθών," *DDD*² [1999] 669–71). Werner Foerster notes the singularity of the phrase πνεῦμα πύθωνα, and favors reading it as "a spirit of python." Foerster finds its earliest appearance in the writings of the grammarian Erotian (ca. the time of Nero), who says in a comment upon Hippocrates, *Epid.* 5.63.7: "*engastrimythoi*, whom some call *pythones*; and it is only with respect to those so called" (ἐγγαστρίμυθοι· οὓς πύθωνάς τινες καλοῦσιν· ἔστι δὲ τῶν ἅπαξ εἰρημένων) (Foerster, "πύθων," *TDNT* 6:917–20; cf. Plutarch, *Def. orac.* 414E). The python eventually received an identity as an oracular spirit in late sources, for example, where Suda calls Python a *daimonion mantikos* (Henten, "Python," 670).

A more emphatic critique or competition in the New Testament is directed toward differentiating the exorcisms performed by Christian missionaries from the more entrepreneurial aspects of Greek religion, which the exorcism at Philippi more accurately represents. Paul's missionary travels, which have led him to the Roman colony of Philippi in Macedonia, serves as the general context for the expulsion of the "pythian spirit". The slave girl's talent results in private gain for her owners and, now deprived of a means of their livelihood, the girl's owners bring Paul and his companions before the Roman authorities who have them beaten and imprisoned. The charge the owners raise against them is that their work runs counter to Roman social convention: Paul the Jew has disrupted the city's affairs with "customs (ἔθη) that are not fitting for Romans to engage in or do."[188] To counter the accusation, Paul reveals to the city's officials that he is, in fact, a Roman citizen; their full acquittal of him lends credibility to his work, exorcism included, as a legitimate activity compatible with Roman culture.[189]

In Acts, the area of society against which exorcism does offer an explicit critique, and with which it does directly compete in an effort to differentiate itself, is the occult practices of the magi. The story of the seven sons of the Jewish high priest Sceva, who attempt to appropriate Jesus' name in exorcism, illustrates this well.[190] The story ends with the magicians who burn their books after they recognize the power of Jesus' name. The exorcism is seen to make "magic" (μαγεία) inefficient as currently practiced: the power of a single name renders obsolete the pedantry of the magi and makes superfluous the complexity of exorcistic formulae that their books represent. The sons of Sceva's unsuccessful attempt at exorcism also illustrates how the power to exorcize has shifted from Jesus to his followers by their ability to use his name effectively and, in contrast, it disenfranchises the Jews from access to this same power. In addition, the episode promotes the name of Jesus as authoritative, as those among the Jewish and Greek populations of Ephesus magnify his name when they hear of the events accomplished by it.

---

[188]Acts 16:20–21.

[189]Elizabeth Ann Leeper sees this story as a point of transition in the use of exorcism in Christian history from charismatic healing toward exorcism as a means of controlling aberrant thought and behavior: "Exorcism, which in all Christian accounts to this point has been for healing and helping, is here being used as a means of social control [of individual behavior] and to demonstrate Christian superiority" (Leeper, *Exorcism in Early Christianity*, 123). The soteriological aspect of exorcism is indeed wanting in this passage, though Christian superiority, or at least the superiority of the divine power as mediated through Jesus, can be argued as at least an implicit feature of all prior exorcisms. This superiority of divine power is a thesis of Garrett's study of magic in Luke-Acts, in which she sees Luke consistently to denigrate magical power compared to Christianity (Garrett, *The Demise of the Devil*, 10).

[190]Acts 19:11–20.

In addition to the book burning that follows the failed exorcism at Ephesus, magi appear in two other pericopes in Acts, both in negative comparison with the disciples. The first passage concerns Simon, who himself impressed the Samaritans with his "magical arts" (μαγεύων), but is now himself awed by the "signs" (σημεῖα) that Philip accomplishes, and by the power of the Holy Spirit that Peter and John transfer to the believers.[191] The second passage concerns Paul's rebuke and temporary blinding of the Jewish "magus" (μάγος) and false prophet Elymas. This event takes place in the presence of the Roman proconsul on Cyprus, Sergius Paulus, and the act helps the proconsul to believe in Paul's message.[192]

These confrontations, especially Paul's with Elymas, may be related to the comparable activities of Joseph, Moses, and Daniel, who perform wonders before foreign rulers. Although proscriptions against the magical arts appear in both testaments,[193] the miracle workers of the Jewish and Christian traditions not only do them, but become exemplary figures for such activities.[194]

---

[191]Acts 8:4–25.

[192]Acts 13:6–12.

[193]From the Hebrew Bible see, for example, Lev 19:26 and Deut 18:10–11. From the New Testament, compare "sorcery" (φαρμακεία), which appears as one of the works of the flesh contrary to the fruits of the spirit (Gal 5:19–21).

[194]Compare Solomon as the archetypal exorcist in the Jewish tradition as found in Josephus' account of Eleazar's performance of an exorcism before Vespasian (*Ant.* 8.42–49). Josephus sets the episode within his explanation of the divine source for Solomon's own expansive wisdom, which includes the knowledge to control demons: "And God granted him [Solomon] knowledge of the art used against demons for the benefit and healing of men. He also composed incantations by which illnesses are relieved, and left behind forms of exorcisms with which those possessed by demons drive them out, never to return. And this kind of cure is of very great power among us to this day, for I have seen a certain Eleazar, a countryman of mine, in the presence of Vespasian, his sons, tribunes and a number of other soldiers, free men possessed by demons ... [The method of exorcism follows, which includes drawing the demon out of the possessed's nostrils with a seal-ring that contains a root prescribed by Solomon, and by reciting Solomon's name and an incantation composed by him] ... And when this was done, the understanding and wisdom of Solomon were clearly revealed, on account of which we have been induced to speak of these things, in order that all men may know the greatness of his nature and how God favoured him, and that no one under the sun may be ignorant of the king's surpassing virtue of every kind." (παρέσχε δ᾽ αὐτῷ μαθεῖν ὁ θεὸς καὶ τὴν κατὰ τῶν δαιμόνων τέχνην εἰς ὠφέλειαν καὶ θεραπείαν τοῖς ἀνθρώποις· ἐπῳδάς τε συνταξάμενος αἷς παρηγορεῖται τὰ νοσήματα καὶ τρόπους ἐξορκώσεων κατέλιπεν, οἷς οἱ ἐνδούμενοι τὰ δαιμόνια ὡς μηκέτ᾽ ἐπανελθεῖν ἐκδιώκουσι. καὶ αὕτη μέχρι νῦν παρ᾽ ἡμῖν ἡ θεραπεία πλεῖστον ἰσχύει· ἱστόρησα γάρ τινα Ἐλεάζαρον τῶν ὁμοφύλων Οὐεσπασιανοῦ παρόντος καὶ τῶν υἱῶν αὐτοῦ καὶ χιλιάρχων καὶ ἄλλου στρατιωτικοῦ πλήθους τοὺς ὑπὸ τῶν δαιμονίων λαμβανομένους ἀπολύοντα τούτων. . . . γενομένου δὲ τούτου σαφὴς ἡ Σολομῶνος καθίστατο σύνεσις καὶ σοφία δι᾽ ἣν, ἵνα γνῶσιν ἅπαντες αὐτοῦ τὸ μεγαλεῖον τῆς φύσεως καὶ τὸ θεοφιλὲς καὶ λάθῃ μηδένα τῶν ὑπὸ τὸν

Whereas the Hebrew Bible appears to denigrate the cults of other nations by closely identifying them with magic, the author of Acts appears to distinguish between magic and the civic cult; it was the latter's social credibility that the early Christian movement hoped to attain for itself. In keeping with the miracle competitions of the biblical tradition, the author of Acts seeks to discredit magical practices by superseding those practices with similar though more effective ones accomplished under the authority of God. He would, however, at best attain only a pyhrric victory in the view of some of his non-Christian readers, who would recognize the effectiveness of Christian miracle workers, but would identify them with the type of magi whom both they themselves and the Christians despised.

5.8 Sanctification and Divine Possession

The exorcism stories in the New Testament present demoniacs as the innocent and passive victims of demonic possession, whose afflictions provide exorcists an opportunity to display their power publicly. In their exorcism stories the synoptic authors associate demonic possession nearly exclusively with human physiology without ethical causes or consequences. Aside from physiological suffering, however, the New Testament also describes demonic possession that affects ethical behavior, and in such literary contexts the demoniacs are indeed considered culpable for their demonic possession.[195] As

---

ἥλιον ἡ τοῦ βασιλέως περὶ πᾶν εἶδος ἀρετῆς ὑπερβολή, περὶ τούτων εἰπεῖν προήχθημεν.) (Josephus, *Ant.* 8.45–49. English translation in *Josephus*, translated by H. St. J. Thackeray et al. [9 vols. LCL; Cambridge: Harvard University Press, 1926–1965]. Cf. 1 Kgs 3:3–28). The underlying context is that Solomon received his wisdom from God (*Ant.* 8.42) in recognition of his virtuous life (*Ant.* 8.49). By following in this tradition Eleazar likewise taps into the divine favor that God originally granted to Solomon. In placing Eleazar's practice firmly within the Solomonic tradition Josephus also gives his Roman audience an appreciation for exorcism as a respected and ancient practice within Judaism.

[195]Whereas the identity of the one possessed is downplayed in the exorcism stories, it is given fuller treatment in several passages in the Gospels and Acts that mention the possessed but lack an exorcist. Judas, who becomes possessed in Luke 22:3 and John 13:27, is one for whom we have some information about his life, activity, and inclinations prior to his possession, but who is not exorcized. According to John, Jesus calls Judas the devil because he "intended to betray him" (ἔμελλεν παραδιδόναι αὐτόν — John 6:70–71). Compare Jesus calling Peter "Satan" because he considered the things of humanity rather than of God (ὅτι οὐ φρονεῖς τὰ τοῦ θεοῦ ἀλλὰ τὰ τῶν ἀνθρώπων — Matt 16:23; Mark 8:33). John especially emphasizes the argument that one's activities reveal the nature of the spirit that one has within. In the Johannine literature those who pursue truth and righteousness or falsehood and sin associate themselves with God or the devil respectively (John 8:31–47; 1 John 3:4–10). The Johannine writings understand Satan's influence as a moral affliction associated with sin, and John contrasts slavery to sin with the freedom that truth brings. Note also where 1 John contrasts the spirit of truth with the spirit of errancy (τὸ

a malady takes on a demonic persona in the cases of physiological possession, the passions and desires can also become demonized to affect moral judgment.[196] On these occasions, the culpability for possession falls upon the possessed for their allegiance with evil.[197]

Sometimes the language of demonic possession in ethical contexts is employed for rhetorical effect as a metaphor of the outsider. In such cases the intellect becomes in a figurative sense "possessed" by a spirit that misleads one into doctrinal aberrancies or intellectual disagreements.[198] The social context for intellectual possession is primarily an intimate one that tends to take place within familiar social groups.[199] We see examples of this in the New Testament with the accusations made by the Jewish authorities against Jesus in the Beelzeboul controversy,[200] Jesus' misguided teachings,[201] Jesus' alleged paranoia,[202] suspicions about John the Baptist,[203] John the Baptist's neither

---

πνεῦμα τῆς ἀληθείας καὶ τὸ πνεῦμα τῆς πλάνης — 1 John 4:1–6; cf. 1 John 2:20–27; Heb 5:14). Although John records no exorcism stories, the gospel succinctly lays out the theology and cosmology behind exorcism: "Now there is judgment of this world, now the ruler of this world is cast out (ἐκβληθήσεται ἔξω)" (John 12:31). The parable of the returning demon also suggests that its victim of possession is analogous to the "evil generation" mentioned at the conclusion of Matthew's version of the parable, and is in some way culpable for the repeated suffering (Matt 12:43–45). The closing condemnation does not appear in Luke's version of the story (Luke 11:24–26).

[196]From earlier Jewish literature, compare Qumran *11QPsalms*^{a} (11Q5) 19.15–16, and the evil "inclination" (*yetzer*) of *Jubilees* 35.9.

[197]From Jewish literature cf. *Jubilees*, which reveals Satan's (Beliar's, Mastema's) entitlement to lead astray a portion of humanity (e.g., *Jub.* 10:8) and the efforts of some to ward off such demonic influence (e.g., Abram's prayer at *Jub.* 12:20). From the New Testament, the story of Ananias and Sapphira shows how even those who receive the favor of the Holy Spirit forfeit that support as a consequence of their own actions and transfer their allegiances to Satan (Acts 5:3–9).

[198]Elaine Pagels writes in this regard: "The gospel writers want to locate and identify the specific ways in which the forces of evil act through certain people to effect violent destruction ... The subject of cosmic war serves primarily to interpret human relationships — especially all-too-human conflict — in supernatural form. The figure of Satan becomes, among other things, a way of characterizing one's actual enemies as the embodiment of transcendent forces" (Pagels, *The Origin of Satan*, 13). Pagels argues that Satan becomes the symbol for opposition in sectarian Judaism as found at Qumran, and continues as the internecine adversary for first century Christians. After the first century, however, Christians appear to apply it to any who oppose them, whether pagans, Jews, or heretics.

[199]Although Pagels concludes that this demonizing of the opponent represents a unique expression of Christians and of Jewish sectarian groups such as at Qumran, this denunciation of the opponent also appears in Zoroastrian writings (see Chapter 2) and in early Greek societies (see Chapter 4).

[200]Mark 3:22–30//Matt 12:22–30//Luke 11:14–23.

[201]John 8:48–59; 10:20.

[202]John 7:20.

[203]Matt 11:18//Luke 7:33.

eating nor drinking,[204] and Paul's accusation and curse against Elymas.[205] At a later period, this language of possession finds its place in intra-Christian polemics, frequently with respect to doctrinal issues in which supporters of heresy are subjected to accusations of demonic possession.[206] In rhetorical usage those accused of demonic possession are seen to have used their freedom of decision to commit themselves to error. Consequently, the charge of demonic possession is left at the level of accusation, with the intention to exclude the accused from the community. If there is a "therapy" for such ethical possession it lies in ostracism rather than in the reintegration achieved through exorcism.

More central, however, to the development of exorcism in early Christianity are those cases of ethical possession for which decision still lies in the balance, and possession by the Holy Spirit remains a possibility. Whereas the synoptic Gospels and Acts use their exorcism stories as a means by which the followers of Jesus are said to introduce their movement to those who do not yet believe, Paul directs his epistles to established congregations with initiated members. A difference between Paul and the synoptics lies in the perspectives which they bring to the issue of demonic possession: while the synoptics give an outside observer's view of possession to promote the miracle worker, Paul writes from the perspective of the one afflicted. What we read in Paul is the testimony of one who empathizes with the bonds and strictures of evil, and who describes possession in terms of both physiological and moral bondage. In marked contrast to the extreme otherness of the demonically possessed in the synoptics and Acts, Paul identifies such hardship as an experience applicable to his Christian communities and to humanity in general.

Paul's missionary work in Greece and Asia Minor included the performance of signs and wonders. He writes of himself having performed such before the Thessalonians,[207] Corinthians,[208] and elsewhere throughout his mission,[209] and as activities of his followers[210] and

---

[204]Matt 17:18//Luke 7:33.

[205]Acts 13:6–12.

[206]An early example of such is the exchange between Polycarp and Marcion: "And Polycarp himself, when Marcion once met him and said, 'Recognize us,' answered 'I do, I recognize the first-born of Satan.'" (καὶ αὐτὸς δὲ ὁ Πολύκαρπος Μαρκίωνί ποτε εἰς ὄψιν αὐτῷ ἐλθόντι καὶ φήσαντι ἐπιγίνωσκε ἡμᾶς ἀπεκρίθη ἐπιγινώσκω· ἐπιγινώσκω τὸν πρωτότοκον τοῦ σατανᾶ) (Irenaeus, *Haer*. 3.3; quoted in Eusebius, *Hist. eccl*. 4.14.6–7 [Lake, LCL]). Irenaeus refers to Titus 3:10–11 as justification for Polycarp's actions.

[207]1 Thess 1:5.

[208]1 Cor 2:4; 14:18–19; 2 Cor 12:12.

[209]Rom 15:17–19; cf. Gal 3:1–5. Compare the portrayal of Paul as miracle worker in Acts 16:16–18; 19:11–12; 20:7–12.

[210]1 Cor 12:8–11, 28–31.

competitors.[211] Exorcism as one of those signs and wonders, however, is virtually absent from Paul's writings. Where argument can be made for it is in 1 Corinthians 12:10 and in 2 Corinthians 12:1–5. In the latter passage Paul describes his having been taken up to paradise, and in verses 6–10 says that in order to keep himself from pride a "thorn in the flesh" (σκόλοψ τῇ σαρκί) was given to him. He describes this as an "angel of Satan" (ἄγγελος σατανᾶ) that "troubles" him (κολαφίζῃ). How this "thorn" manifests itself in Paul remains otherwise undisclosed. If it is equivalent to the "weakness of the flesh" (ἀσθένεια τῆς σαρκός) in Galatians 4:12–14, then it appears that Paul suffered from a physiological malady that he attributed to the workings of Satan, and it is as a demonic personification of this physiological affliction that his petitions to God would converge with exorcism.[212] Yet, if this is exorcistic it lacks a mediator. Three times on his own behalf Paul unsuccessfully petitions God that it might "depart" (ἀποστῇ) from him, so that he comes not only to accept his condition, but to realize a certain strength through it: because of his failings "the power of Christ dwells in him" (ἐπισκηνώσῃ ἐπ᾽ ἐμὲ ἡ δύναμις τοῦ Χριστοῦ). In this regard, the "angel of Satan" works for Paul in a way more similar to the harmful agents in the earlier biblical and Greek traditions, who serve the purposes of the deities who send them, rather than acting as self-motivated aggressors.

A stronger case for exorcism in Paul's writings can be made for the phrase "discernment of spirits" (διακρίσεις πνευμάτων) in 1 Corinthians 12:10. Paul uses the phrase in a discussion of the unity of the Holy Spirit, where it appears as one of the many gifts bestowed by that Spirit. Otherwise, he does not elaborate on the meaning of the phrase, and this lack of explanation,

---

[211]Compare "the super-apostles" (τῶν ὑπερλίαν ἀποστόλων) against whom Paul must compare his own deeds (2 Cor 11:1–13:13, especially 12:11–12).

[212]An attempt was made early on by Joseph Barber Lightfoot to connect the reference to Paul's "weakness of the flesh" in Galatians 4:12-14 with others elsewhere in the authentic epistles where Paul hints of possible physical afflictions (cf. 1 Thess 2:18, 1 Cor 2:3; 2 Cor 1:8–9 and 12:7–10; cf. also 2 Cor 10:1, 10). Lightfoot considered that they refered to the same malady, which he conjectured to have been epilepsy (Joseph Barber Lightfoot, *Saint Paul's Epistle to the Galatians* [10th ed.; Grand Rapids, Mich.: Zondervan, 1971] 190). Others have been less venturesome in seeing their connections and making a diagnosis. Alfred Plummer found the parallel between Galatians 4:13–14 and 2 Corinthians 12:7 attractive, but ultimately unsupportable. Further, he saw their parallelism to diverge: "Any acute and recurrent malady will suit 2 Cor xii.7, but for Gal. iv.13,14 we require something likely to inspire those who witness it with repulsion" (Alfred Plummer, *A Critical and Exegetical Commentary on the Second Epistle of St Paul to the Corinthians* [ICC; Edinburgh: T&T Clark, 1956] 351–52). More recently, Hans Dieter Betz has considered the "physical infirmity" (ἀσθένειαν τῆς σαρκός) of Galatians 4:13 to be a real illness the nature of which, however, is unknown (Hans Dieter Betz, *Galatians: A Commentary on Paul's Letter to the Churches in Galatia* [Hermeneia; Philadelphia: Fortress, 1979] 224; cf. 227–28).

combined with the lack of evidence for exorcism elsewhere in Paul's letters, makes its exorcistic implications uncertain. Though patristic authors interpreted the phrase differently, their commentary on and independent use of the phrase may shed some light on its possible reference here. Like Paul, Athanasius identifies "discernment of spirits" as a charisma given by the Holy Spirit, but he describes the charisma with reference to exorcistic technique. A passage from his *Life of Antony* reads:

A man has need of much prayer and self-discipline that he may receive from the Spirit the gift of discerning spirits and be able to know their characteristics — which of them are less evil, which more; what is the nature of the special pursuit of each of them, and how each of them is overcome and cast out.[213]

---

[213]Δι᾽ ὃ καὶ πολλῆς εὐχῆς, καὶ ἀσκήσεώς ἐστι χρεία· ἵνα τις, λαβὼν διὰ τοῦ Πνεύματος χάρισμα διακρίσεως πνευμάτων, γνῶναι δυνηθῇ τὰ κατ᾽ αὐτούς· καὶ τίνες μὲν αὐτῶν εἰσιν ἔλαττον φαῦλοι, τίνες δὲ ἐκείνων φαυλότεροι, καὶ περὶ ποῖον ἐπιτήδευμα ἕκαστος αὐτῶν ἔχει τὴν σπουδὴν, καὶ πῶς ἕκαστος αὐτῶν ἀνατρέπεται καὶ ἐκβάλλεται (Athanasius, *Vit. Ant.* 22, as quoted in Joseph T. Lienhard, "On 'Discernment of Spirits' in the Early Church," *TS* 41 [1980] 515. Greek text in PG 26:876). In comparing Origen and Athanasius, Joseph T. Lienhard says: "There is a notable difference between Origen's understanding of discernment of spirits and that in the *Vita Antonii*. For Origen, discernment was a gift which enabled its recipient to distinguish between good and evil spirits. For Athanasius in the *Vita*, although he mentions good spirits once or twice, discernment is essentially concerned with the various kinds of evil spirits, their distinguishing characteristics, and the proper remedy against each" (Lienhard, "On 'Discernment of Spirits' in the Early Church," 517). Lienhard also cites from the chapter on Pityrion in the *Historia monachorum in Aegypto* (anonymous, ca. 400), where the author writes of Pityrion's gifts: "… he discoursed especially about the discernment of spirits, saying that there are certain demons which accompany our passions and often turn our characters to evil. "Children," he said to us, "whoever wishes to drive out the demons, must first conquer his passions. For whichever passion he masters, he also drives out its demon." (… οὐ μὴν ἀλλὰ καὶ περὶ τῆς τῶν πνευμάτων διακρίσεως ἰσχυρῶς διελέξατο, λέγων δαίμονας εἶναί τινας τοὺς τοῖς πάθεσιν ἐπακολουθοῦντας καὶ τὰ ἤθη ἡμῶν πολλάκις ἐπὶ τὸ κακὸν μετατρέποντας. «Ὅστις οὖν, ὦ τέκνα,» πρὸς ἡμᾶς φησίν, «βούλεται τοὺς δαίμονας ἀπελαύνειν, πρότερον τὰ πάθη δουλώσῃ. οἵου γὰρ ἂν πάθους τις περιγένηται, τούτου καὶ τὸν δαίμονα ἀπελαύνει.») (Pityrion 15.2–3; *Hist. mon.* 110. Greek text from André-Jean Festugière, ed., *Historia monachorum in Aegypto* [Brussels: Société des Bollandistes, 1971] 111; English translation in Lienhard, "On 'Discernment of Spirits' in the Early Church," 518). Like Athanasius, this author has connected discernment of spirits with exorcism. Lienhard sees this passage as the beginning of a shift in patristic writings by which spirits that were once personalized as demons are now becoming depersonalized into passions (Lienhard, "On 'Discernment of Spirits' in the Early Church," 528). From the secondary literature, Eitrem considers 1 Corinthians 12:10 to refer to exorcism, and compares it to Paul's wondrous healings described in Acts 19:11–12 (Eitrem, *Notes on Demonology*, 67).

Athanasius' interpretation dovetails with the name-determination found elsewhere in exorcistic technique, and makes an exorcistic implication for "discernment of spirits" also possible for Paul.[214]

Paul's reticence with respect to exorcism, an activity of which he likely would have known,[215] can perhaps be attributed to his disinterest in signs and wonders in general within his letters. Although Paul performed such acts in his own missionary work, his letters reveal his concern for a theologically informed faith. For Paul, such signs are insignificant in and of themselves, and only gain significance in so far as they lead one to a greater awareness of the gospel's message of salvation. When his congregations begin to focus their attention and fascination upon these signs and wonders without consideration of this message, he offers correction by downplaying the importance of such acts.[216]

---

[214]Another interpretation of "discernment of spirits" consistent with the concerns of early Christian mission was over the authenticity of revelation. Friedrich Büchsel associates Paul's use of "discernment of spirits" with the distinction made between the spirits of prophetic inspiration (Friedrich Büchsel, "διάκρισις," *TDNT* 3:949–50), and in this he has good company with the eastern Patristic commentators. Lienhard notes that in the eastern Patristic tradition the phrase in 1 Corinthians 12:10 becomes associated with 1 John 4:1, so that the "spirits" were interpreted with respect to prophetic inspirations that needed to be recognized as true or false in order to authenticate their value for the community of believers (Lienhard, "On 'Discernment of Spirits' in the Early Church," 509–14. E.g., Origen, *Hom. Ex.* 3.2; Didymus the Blind, *Enarrat. ep. cath.* [1 John 4:1–2]; cf. John Chrysostom, *Hom. 1 Cor.* 29; Theodoretus of Cyrrhus, *Interpretationes in Pauli epistulas* [1 Cor 12:10]). Although in theory one cannot confess Jesus without the divine Spirit (for example 1 Cor 12:3; 1 John 2:22–23; 4:15), in practice inspired guidance proved more problematic, and the reception and transmission of prophecy through inspiration was an issue for the early Christian communities. In the New Testament itself several passages warn specifically of those who will come and mislead (Mark 13:21–22; Acts 20:28–31; 2 Cor 11:1–4; Jude 19). Consequently, a number of passages discuss how to determine authenticity, with the recurrent advice that one's words and deeds reveal the nature of the spirit one has within. This is especially evident in the Johannine writings where one's works help to identify the nature of one's spiritual influence (John 3:2; 8:29; 10:31–39; 14:8–11; 1 John 3:23–24; 2 John 9. Cf. also Acts 15:8; 2 Cor 3:2–3; Gal 3:1–5). In early Greece ambiguity of divine messages, such as the oracles from Delphi, required a keen exegesis of the prophetic words themselves (see Chapter 4). In contrast, ambiguity in early Christian prophecy lay less in the scrutiny of words than in the scrutiny of the messenger and the need to discern between the true or the false spirits who guided them.

[215]Luke even credits Paul with having performed exorcisms in Acts 16:16–18; 19:8–12.

[216]Compare Paul's anti-aretalogies in the "First Apology" (2 Cor 2:14–6:13; 7:2–4) at 2 Corinthians 6:3–10, and in the "Second Apology" or "Letter of Tears" (2 Cor 10:1–13:10) at 2 Corinthians 11:1–12:10 (Hans Dieter Betz, "Corinthians, Second Epistle to the," *ABD* 1:1148–50). The latter reference falls within Paul's "Fool's Speech," a parody of the boasting of the "super-apostles" who have fascinated his own followers. In both passages Paul intentionally contrasts his own method of self-presentation with that of his opponents', whom Dieter Georgi identifies as migrant Jewish-Christians who attempt to impress their

Paul's silence can perhaps also be attributed to the fact that exorcism is at odds with his view of the relationship between humanity and God. Paul articulates the nature and significance of this relationship as one secured through spiritual possession, so that when one is close to God one possesses God's Holy Spirit, but when other forces gain influence within the body the relationship with God becomes strained. References to Satan,[217] Beliar,[218] the demons to whom the pagans sacrifice,[219] "the elements of the world" to which one is "enslaved,"[220] the "angel of Satan,"[221] and perhaps "the tempter,"[222] and "spirit of stupefaction"[223] all reveal Paul's awareness of demonic entities. In addition to these references to demonic agents Paul juxtaposes the spirit of God with impersonal "sin" (ἁμαρτία). Although he neither associates sin

---

audience by means of signs and revelations by analogy to the "divine men" (θεῖος ἄνδρες) of Greek culture (Dieter Georgi, *The Opponents of Paul in Second Corinthians* [Philadelphia: Fortress, 1986]).

[217]Rom 16:20; 1 Cor 5:5, 7:5; 2 Cor 2:11; 11:14; 12:7; 1 Thes 2:18.

[218]2 Cor 6:15.

[219]1 Cor 10:20.

[220]ὑπὸ τὰ στοιχεῖα τοῦ κόσμου ἤμεθα δεδουλωμένοι (Gal 4:3). In Galatians 4:8–11 Paul describes the elements as weaker and inferior, not gods by nature. Given the context of Paul's admonishing the Galatians for observing days, months, seasons, and years, contemporary scholarship tends to view the elements as demonic powers that operate in the realm of fate. The "elements" likely derive from Greek thought. Eduard Schweizer considers the phrase "slavery under the elements of the world," as it occurs in Galatians and Colossians, to refer to the same concept as supported by Greco-Roman philological evidence from Empedocles to Hippolytus: "the imprisonment of the soul in the ceaseless rotation of the four elements [i.e., earth, water, air and fire]" (Eduard Schweizer, "Slaves of the Elements and Worshippers of Angels: Gal 4:3, 9 and Col 2:8, 18, 20," *JBL* 107 [1988] 466). He adds that to accept the Greek philosophical tradition for Paul's use of "elements" is also to recognize that he personifies them in keeping with that tradition (Schweizer, "Slaves of the Elements and Worshippers of Angels," 455–68, 467. See also L. J. Alderink, "Stoicheia στοιχεῖα τοῦ κόσμου," *DDD*² [1999] 817). Yarbro Collins draws attention to the "angel of the waters" (Rev 16:5), which suggests an early connection between angels and elements (Adela Yarbro Collins, "The History-of-Religions Approach to Apocalypticism and the 'Angel of the Waters' [Apoc 16:4–7]," *CBQ* 39 [1977] 367–81). Compare Betz on τὰ στοιχεῖα in Galatians 4:3: "A large number of scholarly investigations have arrived at the conclusion that these 'elements of the world' represent demonic forces which constitute and control 'this evil aeon' (1:4). The Greco-Roman (and Jewish) syncretism of the time of Paul is characterized by a very negative view of the world; the κόσμος ("world") was thought to be composed of four or five 'elements,' which are not simply material substances, but demonic entities of cosmic proportions and astral powers which were hostile towards man. In Judaism, these forces were integrated in the world of 'angelic beings'" (Betz, *Galatians*, 205). See also Clinton E. Arnold's recent discussion of τὰ στοιχεῖα as demonic powers (Clinton E. Arnold, "Returning to the Domain of the Powers: *Stoicheia* as Evil Spirits in Galatians 4:3, 9," *NovT* 38 [1996] 55–76).

[221]ἄγγελος σατανᾶ (2 Cor 12:7).

[222]ὁ πειράζων (1 Thes 3:5).

[223]πνεῦμα κατανύξεως (Rom 11:8).

with a demonic figure such as Satan, nor explicitly identifies sin itself as a demon, Paul does portray human sinfulness as an active agent at work within the human being.[224] In Romans 7, using the rhetorical technique of writing in character,[225] Paul associates sin with human desire (ἐπιθυμία),[226] which "dwells in" (ἡ οἰκοῦσα ἐν) and "enslaves the flesh" (δουλεύω ... τῇ δὲ σαρκὶ) of his gentile audience. He portrays sin as a shadow-like figure that assumes a presence only in relationship to the law of God,[227] and whose own law is at work "in their members" (ἐν τοῖς μέλεσίν μου).[228]

Ethical possession has a confidential and intimate context that is as true for the divinely possessed in their relationship to God as it is for those who are dominated by evil influences. Paul uses the language of possession to describe the believer's motivations toward sinful or appropriate behavior, and he interprets both good and evil forces as working simultaneously within the body of the believer, albeit in different realms: the sinful dominating in the "flesh" (σάρξ), and the good operating in the "mind" (νοῦς) and "inner person" (ἔσω ἄνθρωπος).[229] This simultaneous residency of the demonic

---

[224]Compare Böcher, who interprets sin as a personal demonic power overcome by baptism in Romans 6 and 7. Consequently, he also views baptism at this early stage as an exorcistic act (Böcher, *Christus Exorcista*, 178–79).

[225]Krister Stendahl has argued that Paul does not speak autobiographically here, but uses the first person as a rhetorical device to address the human condition (Krister Stendahl, "The Apostle Paul and the Introspective Consciousness of the West," in *Paul among Jews and Gentiles* [Philadelphia: Fortress, 1976] 78–96). Stendahl traces the introspective interpretation of Paul as one troubled by guilt back to Augustine, who has read his own internal conflicts back into Paul's experience. For a discussion of *prosopoiia* ("speech-in-character") as a rhetorical technique, and how early interpreters of Paul read Romans 7:7–25 as such, see Stanley Stowers, *A Rereading of Romans: Justice, Jews, and Gentiles* [New Haven: Yale University Press, 1994]) 264–72.

[226]Rom 7:7–8.

[227]Rom 7:8–11.

[228]Rom 7:23; cf. 7:5.

[229]Rom 7:1–25. Walter Burkert explores the pre-history of Paul's concept of the "inner person," which he traces in terminology back to Plato's conceptualization of human morality (Plato, *Politeia*) and rationality (Plato, *Resp.* 589A). Burkert further argues that the concept of a human sense of emotional or psychological presence within the human being and distinct from the physical body has a long history in Greek literature prior to Plato and in earlier writings from the ancient Near East (Walter Burkert, "Towards Plato and Paul: The 'Inner Human Being,'" in *Ancient and Modern Perspectives on the Bible and Culture: Essays in Honor of Hans Dieter Betz*, Adela Yarbro Collins, ed. [Atlanta: Scholars Press, 1998] 59–82). Hans Dieter Betz has published a continuation of Burkert's argument in which he explores the means by which Plato's concept came into Paul's argumentation, and how Paul used it distinctly from Plato in accordance with his own theological anthropology. The former issue has occupied much of the previous research, which has concluded that the concept circulated in a variety of expressions in the hellenistic philosophical world after Plato, and likely entered Paul's realm of thought through debates arising in his Corinthian congregation. As to the latter issue, Betz concludes that in his own use of the concept Paul

and the divine within the body distinguishes Paul's view of indwelling possession from the mutually exclusive states in the synoptics and Acts. Rather than the expulsion of the harmful demon and the consequent restoration of well-being as seen in the synoptic stories of exorcism, this struggle to act in accordance with the law of God is more similar to the internal ethical struggle seen earlier in the sectarian writings at Qumran.[230] Likewise for Paul, one's submission to sin or to the Spirit of God manifests itself in ethical actions.

For Paul, the ritual that releases one from the body of death is not exorcism or exorcistic. The resolution to this ethical struggle comes instead through the believer's adoption by God achieved through baptism.[231] Whereas exorcism restores the possessed individual to a normal state of physiological or mental well-being, and so brings one from an impure to a pure though profane

---

has removed from it the Middle Platonic anthropological dualism that saw an immortal soul imprisoned in a material body. In Paul's view, the "inner" and "outer" person constitute the body, and it is the body as a whole for which he anticipates salvation (Hans Dieter Betz, "The Concept of the 'Inner Human Being' (ὁ ἔσω ἄνθρωπος) in the Anthropology of Paul," *NTS* 46 [2000] 315–41).

[230]In the *Community Rule* the sectarians perceive a conflict between the spirit of truth and the spirit of injustice in the human heart, and a commitment by the members of the community to strive to comply with the will of God (1QS 4.20–5.1). Compare also the Lord's allotment of spirits of good and evil to all people in 1QH^a 6.11–12, which suggests that human beings are under varying degrees of positive and negative spiritual influences.

[231]For Paul, baptism is a ritual that transfers the Holy Spirit to the believer, as can be inferred from several passages in his letters. Galatians 4:1–7 uses the language of divine adoption and the process of becoming a "child of God," where it follows upon baptism as the "putting on of Christ" (Χριστὸν ἐνεδύσασθαι) (Gal 3:23–27). This passage in Galatians is interesting for the exchange of spiritual dependencies that takes place: through adoption, God sends the spirit of his Son into the Galatians' hearts, which converts them from slaves into sons, and so into heirs of the promise. The reception of the Holy Spirit at baptism is even more strongly conveyed in 1 Corinthians 12:13, where the image is one of "drinking in one spirit" (ἐν πνεῦμα ἐποτίσθημεν). Compare Romans 6:1–11, where Paul identifies baptism as the believer's commitment to death in anticipation of a resurrection accomplished through the unwavering love of God and Christ; to be a follower of Christ is to resign oneself to present suffering with the hope of a future glorification (Rom 8:18–39). Paul does speak of receiving the spirit of adoption in Romans 8:9–17, but he does not explicitly tie its reception to baptism here. The exclamation "Abba! Father!" in Romans 8:15–17 has been connected to the same phrase in Galatians 4:1–7 (cf. Gal 3:25–27), and on the greater strength of Galatians' baptismal context the same has been seen also for the context behind Romans. Alfred Seeberg and Georg Braumann, for example, both note that the two passages share a common theme of transition to sonship that is achieved through the reception of the Holy Spirit at baptism (Alfred Seeberg, *Der Katechismus der Urchristenheit* [Leipzig: Deichert, 1903] 240–44. Georg Braumann, *Vorpaulinische christliche Taufverkündigung bei Paulus* [BWANT 82; Stuttgart: Kohlhammer, 1962] 62–64. Referred to in Betz, *Galatians*, 219, n. 81). Compare the use of baptism in Acts, where the Holy Spirit is conveyed through various means other than baptism, such as preaching, prayer, and laying on of hands.

condition, the invocation of the Holy Spirit accomplished through baptism elevates one from a profane condition to a condition of sanctification (δικαιοσύνη).[232]

Where the language of possession occurs in Paul it tends to revolve around issues of "holiness" (ἁγιωσύνη, ἁγιασμός, adj. ἅγιος),[233] and it is precisely in relation to issues of maintaining holiness that Paul presents to his Corinthian congregation the metaphor of the body as a "temple" (ναός) to describe their relationship to God.[234] As a locus of divine possession the

---

[232]E. P. Sanders defines Paul's use of "righteoused by faith" (δικαιοῦσθαι) as "being transferred from the group which will be destroyed to that which will be saved" (E. P. Sanders, *Paul* [Past Masters; Oxford: Oxford University Press, 1991] 76). Sanders says of δικαιοῦσθαι: "The passive verb 'to be righteoused' in Paul's letters almost always means to be *changed*, to be *transferred* from one realm to another: from sin to obedience, from death to life, from being under the law to being under grace ... The noun 'righteousness' implies a status, while Paul's verb has more the connotation of something which happens to a person" (Sanders, *Paul*, 48). "Being righteoused" is the divine act done to the individual that motivates a reciprocal action of the believers' dedicating themselves to God.

[233]ἁγιωσύνη (Rom 1:4; 2 Cor 7:1; 1 Thess 3:13); ἁγιασμός (Rom 6:19–22; 1 Cor 1:30; 1 Thess 4:3–7). On the distinction between "holiness" and "purity" compare Christine Hayes' definitions as they occur in the Hebrew Bible's Priestly Source: "The term 'impure' denotes a state of cultic disability and is the antonym of 'pure.' The term 'holy' denotes that which has been consecrated and thus belongs to God and is the antonym of 'profane' which designates ordinary non holy entities" (Christine Hayes, "Intermarriage and Impurity in Ancient Jewish Sources," *HTR* 92 [1999] 5). Although Hayes' article deals specifically with ritual impurity with respect to intermarriage in ancient Israelite and Jewish texts, the distinction she makes between these terms has relevance to other contexts. In his article on holiness in the New Testament, Robert Hodgson defines the "holy" person (ἅγιος, Latin *sanctus*) similarly, as "one removed from the profane order of things for the service of God" (Robert Hodgson, Jr., "Holiness (NT)," *ABD* 3:250). Hodgson notes that the term appears rarely in classical Greek, but frequently in the LXX as a translation for קדשׁ (Hodgson, "Holiness (NT)," *ABD* 3:249). Hübner notes that the Old Testament writings viewed cleanness as a cultic-ritualistic issue, while the New Testament views it as an ethical-soteriological, or soteriological-sacramental one. This holds true for Paul specifically, who affirms that nothing is unclean in itself (Rom 14:14), and juxtaposes impurity (ἀκαθαρσία) and sanctity (ἁγιασμός) in 1 Thessalonians 4:7 (Hübner, "Unclean and Clean [NT]," *ABD* 6:743–44). Holiness is used in the New Testament with reference to people on several occasions. Mark describes both Jesus and John the Baptist as holy (Mark 1:24 and 6:20, respectively), and Paul uses the term prolifically to describe the believers, whether in his own congregations, or in other communities such as those at Jerusalem and Rome (e.g., Rom 1:7; 15:25–26; 1 Cor 1:2; 16:1; 2 Cor 1:1; Phil 1:1; Phlm 5).

[234]In 1 Corinthians 3:9–17 Christ is the foundation (θεμέλιος) of this temple, the superstructure of which the servants of God construct. The temple imagery highlights the concern for holiness (ἅγιος), to be preserved from corruption (φθείρειν). The motivation for the metaphor in this instance is the internal strife within the congregation that results from factional allegiances to different apostles (Paul, Apollos, Cephas) who have built up the temple-congregation (1 Cor 3:1–7; 3:18–4:21). Further along, in 1 Corinthians 6:9–20 Paul revives the metaphor in his polemic against fornication and other sinful acts. Robert Jewett

congregation becomes a type of sanctuary which requires a state of holiness. In 2 Corinthians 6:14–18, for example, Paul compares the followers of Christ to a temple of the living God (ἡμεῖς γὰρ ναὸς θεοῦ ἐσμεν ζῶντος), and he supports the analogy with scriptural passages in which God says that he will dwell and live among his people (ἐνοικήσω ἐν αὐτοῖς καὶ ἐμπεριπατήσω).[235] Here, Paul reinterprets the biblical notion of the divine presence which dwells "among" God's people now to dwell "within" the "body" (σῶμα) of the Corinthian community.[236] Rather than a tabernacle in the people's midst, the believers themselves have become the tabernacle or temple in which God dwells.[237]

---

stresses that the metaphor here as elsewhere in early Christian literature applies to the body of the church and not to the individual (Robert Jewett, *Paul's Anthropological Terms: A Study of Their Use in Conflict Settings* [AGJU 10; Leiden: Brill, 1971] 284). Hans Conzelmann notes that, "For the collective sense in Paul the link with the Hebrew Bible and Judaism should be noted ..." (Hans Conzelmann, *1 Corinthians: A Commentary on the First Epistle to the Corinthians* [Hermeneia: Philadelphia: Fortress, 1975] 77, nn. 90–91. Concerning Judaism, see Isa 28:16; 1QS 8:7f; 1QH^a 6.26; 7.9). Although Paul speaks here in terms of the actions of individuals (such as engaging with a prostitute), so that the singular ναός may here refer to the body of the individual, nevertheless these private actions have implications for the congregation as a whole. In 2 Corinthians 6:14–18, Paul introduces the temple metaphor in response to outside threats to the community's integrity. At the beginning of the passage he advises against their being "mismated" or "wrongly yoked" to unbelievers (μὴ γίνεσθε ἑτεροζυγοῦντες ἀπίστοις). To be a believer is to associate oneself with righteousness, light, and Christ, and to keep separate from lawlessness, darkness, and Beliar. The threat of contamination necessitates that the Corinthians be vigilant in the maintainance of their holiness before God (2 Cor 7:1). From the deutero-Pauline epistles, compare the temple imagery in Ephesians 2:19–22 (cf. 1 Pet 2:5). The Ephesians themselves are being built into a "holy temple (ναός) in the Lord," a "house (κατοικητήριον) of God in spirit." It is an harmoniously assembled work-in-progress, of which Christ is the cornerstone (ἀκρογωνιαῖος), and the apostles and prophets serve as the foundation (θεμέλιος). Compare also the universal church under construction in *Shepherd of Hermas* Vision 3 and Similitude 9.

[235]Lev 26:11; Isa 52:11; Ezek 20:34; 37:27; 2 Sam 7:14, 8.

[236]The body as temple has some precedent in Philo (30 BC.E.–45 C.E.), who uses it in terms of the individual's mystical union with God (e.g., *Somn.* 1.149; *Sobr.* 62f.; *Cher.* 98, 106), and a similar later usage by the Stoic philosopher Epictetus (ca. 55 C.E.–ca. 135), who applied it to the "innate divine reason" that occupies the individual (Epictetus, *Diatr.* 1.14.14f.; 2.8.11f; cf. M. Ant. 3.6.2) (Otto Michel, "ναός," *TDNT* 4.886, note 25). For the body as a house or tabernacle of the soul, cf. also Hippocrates, *Aph.* 8.18; Philo, *Somn.* 1.122 (Edward Gordon Selwyn, *The First Epistle of St. Peter* [London: MacMillan, 1946] 289–90). Plummer notes Seneca, *Ep.* 31.11, part of which asks: "What else would you call such a soul than a god dwelling as a guest in a human body?" (*Quid aliud voces hunc, quam Deum in humano corpore hospitantem?*) (Plummer, *Second Epistle of St. Paul to the Corinthians*, 209. Latin text and English translation in Seneca, *Ad Lucilium, Epistulae, Morales*; translated by Richard M. Grummere [3 vols. LCL; New York: Putnam, 1925]).

[237]For closer-to-biblical views, cf. John's prologue, which says that the Word dwelt among (ἐσκήνωσεν) humanity (John 1:14); Revelation 7:15, where the one upon the throne

In her lucid presentation of 1 Corinthians, Margaret Mitchell finds that Paul's recurrent use of the building metaphor in the epistle[238] falls within the context of political *topoi* (e.g., building, body, ship) common to deliberative rhetoric, and which serve to facilitate political unity.[239] Mitchell rightly emphasizes the exhortation toward "political" unity in the letter, and the "practical ecclesiology" that Paul offers his congregation.[240] The temple, as a subcategory of the building metaphor, also contributes to Paul's appeal to his Corinthian congregation that they pursue a policy of community building and common interest. However, the temple (*naos*) metaphor brings further nuance to the expectations of the community otherwise not required of more secular buildings, such as the "house" (*oikos*), which appeal to social unification for its own sake. Mitchell leads us in this direction herself where she notes that the temple in Jewish, Greek, and Roman literature introduces the symbolism of peace and unity into the imagery.[241] More specifically, the narrowing of the building to a temple particularizes that type of building which the Corinthians ought to emulate as one belonging to God.[242] Mitchell says:

---

will dwell with the martyrs (σκηνώσει ἐπ᾽ αὐτούς); and Revelation 21:3–4, where God will dwell with his people (σκηνώσει μετ᾽ αὐτῶν) in the new Jerusalem, and will be with them (αὐτὸς ὁ θεὸς μετ᾽ αὐτῶν ἔσται). Plummer compares the biblical citations and those given for Revelation, and notes of the former: "... the remarkable ἐνοικήσω ἐν αὐτοῖς is not in any of them. It is much stronger than 'walk among them' or 'tabernacle among them'" (Plummer, *Second Epistle of St. Paul to the Corinthians*, 209). Jewett notes that Paul inserts the newer concept of "body" (σῶμα), a term indicative of the exclusive relationship among the believers, into the older *naos* tradition in 1 Cor 6:19 (Jewett, *Paul's Anthropological Terms*, 261–62). But one should also note that in so altering the "body" image Paul thereby also alters the traditional *naos* metaphor to describe an intimate indwelling occupancy of the divine presence within the body of the believer and believing community.

[238] 1 Cor 6:19; 8:1, 10; 10:23; 14:3–5, 12, 17, 26; cf. 15:58; 16:13.

[239] Margaret M. Mitchell, *Paul and the Rhetoric of Reconciliation: An Exegetical Investigation of the Language and Composition of 1 Corinthians* (Louisville: Westminster/John Knox, 1991).

[240] Mitchell says: "In this study much attention has been devoted to the 'political' nature of 1 Corinthians. This is not to say, however, that 1 Corinthians is not a 'religious' document. Rather, 1 Corinthians represents the fundamental problem of practical ecclesiology which Paul chose to treat by employing Greco-Roman political terms and concepts for the society and the interrelationships of its members" (Mitchell, *Paul and the Rhetoric of Reconciliation*, 300).

[241] E.g., Aristides, *Or.* 27.40–41 (Mitchell, *Paul and the Rhetoric of Reconciliation*, 104, with other references on p. 101 n. 219).

[242] Mitchell, *Paul and the Rhetoric of Reconciliation*, 103. Mitchell appears to follow Philipp Vielhauer here, who sees the significance of the temple as a possession of God: "The thought is not of a house or temple with regard to architectural structure, nor is it a matter of divine dwelling as in vv. 16–17. The context implies that the community is simply being described as God's possession." (*An ein Haus oder einen Tempel hinsichtlich der architektonischen Struktur ist nicht gedacht, ebensowenig an ein Wohnen Gottes wie in V.*

... they [the Corinthian community] are θεοῦ οἰκοδομή, which has Jesus Christ as its firm and uniting θεμέλιος, forming the ναὸς τοῦ θεοῦ in which the holy spirit dwells.[243]

This, again plays into the letter's overarching theme of unity: one God, one temple, one community.

Another contribution that the temple (*naos*) metaphor makes beyond other political *topoi*, however, is the reciprocity of the relationship it establishes between the community of believers and God. In contrast to the involuntary nature of demonic possession, divine possession in Paul's writings, and in the New Testament and early Christian literature in general, represents a voluntary relationship that the believer enters into with God. In this regard, it is significant that Paul uses the term *naos* (ναός), the building that actually housed the image or essence of the deity, instead of the *hieron* (ἱερόν), or larger sanctuary complex in which the temple-proper stood.[244] The choice of *naos* not only draws attention to the indwelling occupancy of the Holy Spirit that characterizes one's inclusion within the community of believers, it also identifies the believer's possession as a voluntary relationship. More than just the ownership of the building by God — an aspect as readily addressed by the owner of a house, or farmer of a field — the fact that the Corinthian Christians represent a temple adds the further nuance of their having dedicated[245]

16f. Die Gemeinde soll dem Zusammenhang nach lediglich als Eigentum Gottes bezeichnet werden.) (Philipp Vielhauer, "Oikodome. Das Bild vom Bau in der christlichen Literatur vom Neuen Testament bis Clement Alexandrinus," in Philipp Vielhauer, *Oikodome: Aufsätze zum Neuen Testament* [vol 2; TB 65; Munich: Chr. Kaiser, 1979] 75).

[243]Mitchell, *Paul and the Rhetoric of Reconciliation*, 213.

[244]The noun ναός derives from the verb ναίειν "to dwell," "inhabit." Otto Michel unwarrantedly blurs the distinction between *naos* and *hieron* as they are used in the New Testament (O. Michel, "ναός," *TDNT* 4:882). Otherwise, Michel considers Paul to have interpreted *naos* in terms of an earlier prophecy by Jesus: "Writing to the Corinthians, Paul appeals again and again to the principle that they are the temple of God and God's Spirit dwells in them (1 C. 3:16; 6:19; 2C. 6:16f.). He does not tell us the source of the statement, but assumes that the Corinthians are familiar with it (οὐκ οἴδατε ὅτι ..., 1C. 3:16; 6:19). It may be conjectured that the apostle catechetically interprets the prophecy of Jesus in a form related to Mk. 14:58" (Michel, "ναός," *TDNT* 4:886). Assuming that Paul knew of such a prophecy by Jesus the connection with Mark 14:58 is an intriguing one.

[245]Walter Burkert draws attention to the dedicatory nature of the temple: "Each building [within a sacred precinct], especially each temple, is in the first instance an individual, constructed for its own sake and beautiful as an *agalma*" (Burkert, *Greek Religion*, 94; cf. Burkert's discussion of votive offerings generally, ibid., 68–70. See also William Henry Denham Rouse, *Greek Votive Offerings* [Cambridge: Cambridge University Press, 1902] 118–22).

themselves to God. As a temple is a dedication, the believers present themselves as a votive offering to the deity whom they host.[246]

None of the political metaphors discussed by Mitchell are static images: the body, the ship, the house, all require constant governance and maintenance to remain healthy and productive. In like manner the maintenance of the temple requires constant attention. What the dedicatory nature contributes to Paul's argument is the obligation toward maintaining the holiness to which the community of believers has committed itself. Unlike the physiological possession that causes impurity, and for which exorcism serves as a catharsis, one does not attain sanctification before God by driving a demonic Sinfulness out of the body. Ethical possession instead requires a constant vigilance to maintain the dominance of the divine presence within the individual. Consequently, Paul speaks of mitigating the force of sin in the body, and his preaching relies upon ethical exhortations to maintain one's sanctity.[247]

5.9 Conclusion: The New Testament's Legacy of Exorcism to the Early Church

The New Testament inherited its demonology from the hellenistic Jewish environment familiar to Jesus and the first generation of his followers. Although demonic possession appears throughout the New Testament literature, exorcism of demonic spirits appears explicitly only in the writings of the synoptic authors. The demonic possessions that are subject to exorcism affect human physiology and can render their victims impure. Consequently, by driving out evil spirits, exorcism restores demoniacs to a pure though profane condition, which also allows for their reintegration in society that their earlier possessions had prevented. In contrast, invocation of the divine Spirit elevates one from a profane condition to sanctification. The New Testament also made use of exorcism as a means of visualizing its eschatological message of the Kingdom of God overcoming the power of Satan, which may also have held social connotations for early Christian audiences who associated the rule of Satan with Roman imperialism. The New Testament authors also made use of exorcism in an apparently unsuccessful

---

[246]Similarly, the "body politic" metaphor takes on new connotations when that body becomes particularized as the body of Christ. As a member of Christ's body specifically, one will consequently participate in Christ's suffering and death with the hope of a future resurrection (Rom 6:1–11; 8:18–39).

[247]Paul's temple metaphor works well as a call to responsible action, but it is best not to apply the metaphor too widely. The *do ut des* ("I give that you may give") mindset of Greek religion stands in contrast with Paul's message of righteousness bestowed by faith through the grace of God. It should be noted, however, that dedications in Greek religion were given for a variety of reasons, which included thank offerings for initial divine actions.

attempt to distinguish its own exorcistic practice from that of the *magus*. In so doing, they hoped to align Christianity with the credibility that Greco-Roman society otherwise granted to its own respected cults.

The New Testament authors use the language of indwelling spiritual possession to describe humanity's relationship to both divine and demonic influences. Yet, although the New Testament juxtaposes divine and demonic possession in ethical contexts, neither Paul nor any other New Testament author connects exorcism with the ethical purification achieved through one's renunciation of demonic forces. Despite the fact that exorcism does not overtly appear in his epistles, Paul's notion of the influence of sin countered by the indwelling presence of the Holy Spirit constitutes an important primary resource for the theological development of the exorcist's role as it came to be incorporated into early Christian catechetical and baptismal practices. Thus, as the synoptic gospels and Acts would serve as literary exemplars for exorcism in early Christianity, Paul's writings would serve as an interpretive basis for what it meant to be possessed. By restoring the victim of demonic possession from an impure condition to a profane state of well-being, exorcism would serve as a preliminary act to the invocation of the Holy Spirit, which itself elevates one from a profane condition to sanctification. Such descriptions of possession as we find in Paul's accounts are, in fact, more relevant to the daily experience of the church communities: Paul's interpretation of possession as sinfulness removes it from the exorcism story's realm of "otherness," "foreignness," and the object of spectacle, to one of personal relevance to every member of the Christian community.

Chapter 6

POSSESSION AND EXORCISM
IN EARLY CHRISTIANITY

6.1 Introduction

The previous chapter identified the literary contexts in which exorcism and possession occur in the New Testament. On the one hand, the narrative writings record demonic possession as physiological disturbances subject to exorcism. In these narratives exorcism displays the exorcist's divine authority and contributes to the apocalyptic, eschatological, and broadly soteriological aspects of the gospel message. On the other hand, the most focused discussions on the meaning of possession occur in the personal testimonies of the epistles and tend to revolve around demonic and divine influences upon ethical actions. In contrast to physiological possession, demonic possession that affects ethical decision making is not subject to exorcism in the New Testament.

The New Testament places exorcism within the context of public demonstration. This context also makes exorcism well suited to early Christian missionary service, where Christians introduced their beliefs and practices to non-Christian society. Consequently, exorcism serves as a particularly useful practice by which to explore the influences Christianity and non-Christian cultures had upon one another. This final chapter will examine the transformative factors at work in the encounter of Christian exorcism with non-Christian culture as evident within Christian and non-Christian literature written before the Council of Nicaea; that is, the era before Christianity became a preferred religion within the empire, and after which societal condemnation of Christian practices, exorcism included, would have diminished.[1] From non-Christian literature this chapter will look at

---

[1] The shift toward a lasting state policy that favored Christianity can most arguably be assigned to Constantine's Edict of Milan in 313, which granted Christianity freedom from persecution. Two years earlier the Palinode of Galerius also formally ended persecution of the Christians, but this was valid only for the western half of the Roman Empire; in the eastern

representative texts that, on the one hand, reinforced magical stereotypes upon Christianity (the *Greek Magical Papyri*) and, on the other hand, offered an analogous attempt by an author to distance his own subject from such associations (Philostratus' *Life of Apollonius of Tyana*). Within Christian literature, this chapter will look at Christian apologetic writings for their efforts to facilitate cultural acceptance, heresiological writings for their theological modifications to the meaning of spiritual possession and its implications for the practice of exorcism, and pseudepigraphy and hagiography as literary realms that preserved exorcism's original charismatic quality in the face of its increasingly institutionalized status as a church office.

6.2 The Utility of Christian Exorcism: Transferal of Cult

The writings of the New Testament attempt at times to reorient the believer's perception of foreign gods as demons.[2] According to the classical Greek pantheon, however, for Christians to call the gods *daimones* would, in fact, only lower their status within the divine hierarchy. To make the gods also the object of exorcism requires an alteration of their character into evil entities, and until the Greeks and Romans revised their perceptions of the *daimon* the exorcist would remain a foreign presence in this cultural context.[3] The transfer of eastern dualistic values upon the Greek and Roman sensibilities of retribution and appeasement facilitated the reinterpretation of the existing gods from the supervisors of humanity to its malicious aggressors.[4] Although

---

half persecution continued under the Emperor Maximin (W. H. C. Frend, *The Rise of Christianity* [Philadelphia: Fortress, 1984] 479–80).

[2]For example, 1 Cor 10:20–21; Rev 2:13. The patristic writers also apply this practice to the Hebrew Bible; e.g., Justin Martyr interprets the "idols" of Ps 96.5 (95.5) as "demons" (Justin, *Dial.* 55, 73; *Res.* 5 [*ANF* 1:296]).

[3]Robin Lane Fox summarizes the apparent lack of need for exorcists in Greek and Roman societies during Christianity's second through fourth century period of expansion: "Pagans had no organized order of exorcists, because they accepted no organized 'kingdom of Satan': invasive *daimones* of ambiguous status were sometimes cast out by spells or particular lines of Homer, but the experts in this field were the Jews ..." (Robin Lane Fox, *Pagans and Christians* [New York: Knopf, 1987] 327). It was a domain, Lane Fox goes on to say, in which Christians would claim superiority for themselves despite the cultured pagan perception that "exorcism was tommy-rot" (Lane Fox, *Pagans and Christians*, 328).

[4]Dölger, *Der Exorzismus im altchristlichen Taufritual*, 19–24. Compare Klaus Thraede, who notes that Christian writers lowered the status of foreign gods not for reason of their evil character, but for their inherent weakness manifest in their being recurrently subjugated to the names of God and Jesus (Thraede, "Exorzismus," 72). Several passages from the apologists, however, portray the demons as intentionally deceptive and malicious. Justin, for example, devotes part of his *First Apology* to introducing his audience to Christian demonology by deriving its origin from the Greek pantheon. The picture he paints is one of demonic hostility toward Christianity. Through their deceptions the demons have employed human vices and

references to Near Eastern sages connected with dualistic beliefs begin to pepper the Greek philosophical writings of the first centuries of the Common Era,[5] it is through Jewish and Christian thought and practice that a dualistic sensibility begins to permeate Greco-Roman culture.[6] Consequently, whereas

---

weaknesses to persecute the Christians. Compare in the ca. fourth century pseudo-Clementine *Recognitions* (the *Clementine Romance*), where the serpent insinuates a belief in gods to distract humanity from belief in the true God (Pseudo-Clement, *Recogn.* 5.17). Compare Clement of Alexandria's statement in his *Exhortation to the Greeks* that Satan binds men to false gods as prisoners are bound to corpses (Clement, *Protr.* 1 [*ANF* 2:173]), and that the Greek gods are "unclean and impure spirits" (βδελυρὰ ὄντως καὶ πνεύματα ἀκάθαρτα) (Clement, *Protr.* 4 [PG 8:152; *ANF* 2:187–88]). In the first book of his apology, Arnobius (fl. 297–303) counters the pagan accusation that recent cultural disasters and calamities are due to the Christians by explaining that these are instead the result of an evil force at work against humanity (Arnobius, *Adv. nat.* 1.48).

[5]Frederick E. Brenk observes of the general increase in interest about demons in the late Hellenistic and early Roman periods: "... many currents — religious, philosophical, literary, ideological, visionary, emotional — contributed to a renewed interest in the world of the *daimones* [during the early imperial period]. Besides this, the involvement of the Empire with the Near East contributed to an interest and acquaintance with the demonology which had been at home there for centuries" (Brenk, "In the Light of the Moon," *ANRW* 2.16.3:2069). This renewed interest in demons manifests itself in the novel reporting of exorcism by Greek and Latin authors, which reflects a corresponding increase in the belief in hostile demonic possession among the people. Brenk identifies Plutarch (ca. 50–120 C.E.) as the author of the age who writes most fully about demonology, and who considered the *daimones* to occupy a status midway between gods and mortals. Brenk, however, places Plutarch within the "rationalistic philosophic tradition hostile to the Xenocratic or Oriental type *daimon*" (Brenk, "In the Light of the Moon," *ANRW* 2.16.3:2130). As a consequence, Brenk concludes of this tradition's treatment of demonology: "While at times entranced with the irrational and daimonic, the philosophical tradition gained control of it by shifting its meaning, subordinating it, and allegorizing it away. The gulf between philosophical and sophisticated literature and popular pseudo-scientific superstition seems to have been immense" (Brenk, "In the Light of the Moon," *ANRW* 2.16.3:2142–43). The hesitancy with which the rationalists engaged demonology also reflected their attitude toward those who engaged in the coercion of spirits through exorcism. Yet, we can see Plutarch's willingness at least to consider eastern traditions, and to discuss the teachings of Zoroaster, the Thracian Orpheus, and teachings from Egypt and Phrygia in the company of Plato, Homer, and Hesiod (Plutarch, *Def. orac.* 414F–415B). For references to eastern sages in Christian writings, compare Melito, the Bishop of Sardis from 160–177, who calls Orpheus and Zaradusht (cf. Zarathushtra) Thracian and Persian magi respectively (Melito, *Apologia* [*ANF* 8:752–53]). References to Zoroaster appear in Clement of Alexandria's writings, which refer to him as a Persian magus (Clement, *Strom.* 1.15 [*ANF* 2:316]), and as a prognosticator (Clement, *Strom.* 1.21 [*ANF* 2:330]). Clement also refers to Hystaspes (Clement, *Strom.* 6.5 [*ANF* 2:490]). Compare also the statement in the pseudo-Clementine *Recognitions* that Ham, son of Noah, was the first magician, and the father of Mesraim, the patriarch of the Egyptians, Babylonians, and Persians, of whom Zoroaster was a renowned magician (Pseudo-Clement, *Recogn.* 4.27).

[6]Compare, for example, Celsus' opposition to a belief in Satan and the dualistic system that accommodates him (Origen, *Cels.* 6.42–45). In his response to Celsus, Origen

the Greeks sacrificed with a conscious understanding of appeasing their gods, whose actions were motivated by justice, retribution, perhaps even unjustified anger, the early patristic authors sought to replace these motives with those of greed, a desire to deceive, and other forms of maliciousness so as to make the polytheists the unwitting dupes of their gods' stratagems.[7]

---

distinguishes between the Christian dualistic cosmology and the ethical ambiguity of the Greek pantheon as seen, for example, in the Christian use of "demon" as evil beings exclusively and how it can be used by polytheists also with reference to the angels (Origen, *Cels.* 4.24; 5.5). Lactantius devotes much of Book 2 of *The Divine Institutes*, "On the Origin of Error," toward educating his readers about the dualistic hierarchy of the Jewish and Christian traditions which reveals the falsehood of the polytheistic pantheon. Lactantius cites heavenly and earthly registers of demons. The heavenly register consists of the devil who, though created by God, lost his divine nature through envy (Lactantius, *Inst.* 2.9), and through his corruption reduced also those angels sent to earth by God. The earthly register consists of the mixed offspring of these fallen angels and mortal women. It is this latter group that maliciously seeks to harm humanity, and who insinuate themselves into human bodies to induce physiological maladies, and it is they who are the demons employed in magical conjurations (Lactantius, *Inst.* 2.15). Lactantius assumes a dichotomy between the earthly human body that is susceptible to such evil influences, and the loftier soul that relates to God and heaven (Lactantius, *Inst.* 2.13). In Book 6, Lactantius also distinguishes between the Christian and pagan uses of the Two Ways metaphor, for which Christianity assigns guides along both paths, while the Greeks assign a guide only along the path of goodness (see below, "Possession and Ethics: The Two Ways Doctrine"). At a later stage, Manichaeism, the religious system taught by Mani (216–277), was also influential in furthering dualistic thought. Manichaeism was universalistic in its search for a single truth that undergirded the religions of Christianity, Zoroastrianism, and Buddhism. It was a dualistic, apocalyptic system that anticipated an eventual separation of the current commingling of Light and Darkness, and Good and Evil. Mani's teachings spread quickly during his own lifetime, facilitated in part by his own extensive travels as a foreign envoy of Sapor, the Sassanid ruler, and continued on for several centuries thereafter (Samuel N. C. Lieu, *Manichaeism in the Later Roman Empire and Medieval China* [2d rev. ed.; WUNT 63; Tübingen: Mohr, 1992] 7–32). Although Manichaean dualism would appear to give it some compatibility with Christianity, the Christian apologist Archelaus (fl. 277) saw it as a more insidious threat than polytheism. In contrast to Christian dualism, Archelaus maintained that Mani's dualism offered an unbegotten evil that placed it on the same footing as the unbegotten God. It also held to a material dualism that stipulated an evil material world juxtaposed to the good spiritual world of the soul (Archelaus, *Acta disputationis cum Manete* 20 [*ANF* 6:194]).

[7]In the writings that Justin addresses to potential converts, he couches his critique of polytheism in a conciliatory argument by which the polytheists have acted unwittingly under the influence of demons (Justin, *1 Apol.* 5, 56–58). Tertullian says that demons who seek humanity's destruction at the same time receive sacrifices from deluded idol worshippers (Tertullian, *Apol.* 22). Minucious Felix says that demons enter bodies and feign illnesses, etc., in order to solicit pleasing sacrifices from their victims, and it is through exorcism that Christians reveal the demonic nature of these false gods (Minucius Felix, *Oct.* 27). In one of his treatises Cyprian says that demons afflict pagans with invented physiological problems, and adds with scorn that these demons are the very gods appealed to with sacrifices for alleviation of such afflictions (Cyprian, *Opusc.* 6.6–7). Lactantius also says that earthly

The apocalyptic and eschatological significance of exorcism in the New Testament to some extent continues on in Christian literature written during later eras of persecution. Cyprian (200–258), Bishop of Carthage from 248 until his martyrdom, conveys this apocalyptic and eschatological sense well. In his own letters Cyprian reveals a Christian community persecuted by the Roman authorities and threatened from within by such heretical voices as Novatian's (ca. 200–258). Cyprian presents his views within polemical contexts in which he demonizes his opponents, all of whom — whether heretics, Jews, or polytheists — he labels possessed by the devil.[8] On these occasions his language conveys imagery similar to what one reads in apocalyptic literature. Like the sectarian texts from Qumran, these epistles reveal an urgency that expects an imminent divine retribution against the persecutors, and which translates current earthly struggles into a cosmic battle waged between the demonic host and the company of angels.[9] For Cyprian and other patristic writers, martyrdom constitutes a culmination of this battle that has exorcistic connotations as a conquest over evil in analogy with Christ's own death on the cross.[10]

---

demons (that is, the mixed offspring of women and the fallen angels [Gen 6:1–4]) insinuate themselves into bodies and cause physiological distresses, and that their victims unwittingly then turn to them for aid (Lactantius, *Inst.* 2.15). Gregory of Nyssa ascribes to Gregory Thaumaturges a miracle performed through prayer that stops a plague sent in playful malice by Zeus upon his own worshipers after they have prayed to him to create more room in the sanctuary to accommodate their numbers. Gregory's prayer to God is thus contrasted with the foolish prayers of invocation that the pagans have made to the demon Zeus (Gregory of Nyssa, *Vita Gregorii Thaumaturgi* 99–104). The pseudo-Clementine *Recognitions* says that part of evil's deception of humanity will include the performance of exorcism and other miracles. Its useful acts for purposes of deception reveal, however, its weakened and divided condition, and indicate its approaching demise (Pseudo-Clement, *Recogn.* 3.60).

[8]Cyprian and his colleagues save their greatest vehemence for the heretics, whom Cyprian calls children of the devil (Cyprian, *Ep.* 54.2, 11). From the Seventh Council of Carthage, Rogatianus, Bishop of Nova, calls the heretics the "synagogue of Satan" (*synagoga Satanae*) (Seventh Council of Carthage [*ANF* 5:571; PL 3.1108]). In the same record Cyprian calls them adversaries and antichrists, who upon their reconciliation with the catholic church are restored to the statuses of friends and Christians (Seventh Council of Carthage [*ANF* 5:572]).

[9]For example, Cyprian, *Ep.* 1.15; 53; 77.22.

[10]Martyrdom constitutes a heavenly battle in which the tortured are armed with weapons of faith, and in which the martyrs carry on the fight prophesied by the prophets, inaugurated by Christ, and continued by the apostles (Cyprian, *Ep.* 8 [ca. 250]). Athanasius says that Christ's death casts out demons (Athanasius, *Inc.* 50.17–20). Compare Origen, who says in *Against Celsus* that martyrdom overpowers demons (Origen, *Cels.* 8.44) and derives its archetype from Jesus' own death on the cross that itself consummates the divine plan to destroy the devil and demons that plague humanity (Origen, *Cels.* 1.31). Origen also notes that freedom from the devil and demons is a sign of Christ's destruction of the devil's kingdom (Origen, *Cels.* 7.17; cf. 8.72). Eusebius compares martyrs to athletes, and he says that Christ suffers in the martyr, and through martyrdom overthrows the adversary (Eusebius, *Hist. eccl.* 5.1.19–23). The origin of the name *Christopher* lies in martyrdom, as martyrs

Whereas Cyprian wrote for a Christian community that suffered under persecutions in anticipation of a future reward for their faithfulness, other writers addressed their words to the non-Christian population, and as a result their views and presentations of exorcism differed from those directed toward the faithful. Both exorcism and the demonization of the pantheons are recurrent features in the extant Christian apologies of the ante-Nicene period, where they appear in the writings of Justin Martyr (d. 165), Tatian (110–172), Theophilus of Antioch (fl. 180), Clement of Alexandria (153–217), Tertullian (ca. 160–ca. 220), and Minucius Felix (d. ca. 250).[11] The apologists' intended audiences are at least nominally those outside of Christianity and, as a consequence, the earlier eschatological significance of exorcism intended for an elect few recedes in favor of validating Christian exorcism in the opinion of contemporary society.[12]

When viewed through the accusations of its leading critics, Christianity's rise to credibility appears as a sequence of nearly pyrrhic victories: from

---

become Christ-like through their endurance of suffering to overcome evil (Phileas, *Epistula ad Thmuitanos* [*ANF* 6:162]).

[11]Arnobius may suggest Christian exorcism where he says that the Roman pantheon trembles at the mention of Christ (Arnobius, *Adv. nat.* 1.27), but otherwise this is one of the exceptional early apologies in which exorcism has no major role. Without specifying exorcism, Quadratus, Bishop of Athens (fl. 126), says that some of the beneficiaries of Jesus' healings still lived into his own day (Eusebius, *Hist. eccl.* 4.3.1–3). Exorcism also does not appear in the surviving apologies of Athenagoras (ca. 170–80), Commodianus, Melito, and Aristides. Although certain themes recur in the apologies, none appear to be essential. The apology of Aristides (ca. 145), as it is preserved in Syriac, contains no reference to the miracles performed by Jesus or the disciples, and Robert Grant notes that the apologies of Athenagoras, Tatian, Theophilus, and Minucius Felix do not even refer to Jesus (Robert M. Grant, *Greek Apologists of the Second Century* [Philadelphia: Westminster Press, 1988] 165).

[12]Grant finds the second century Christian apologists who wrote in Greek — Aristo of Pella, Quadratus, Aristides, and Athenagoras, all of Athens, Justin Martyr, Apollinaris of Hierapolis, Melito, Tatian, Theophilus of Antioch, and Clement of Alexandria — to have fashioned their apologies with regard to the political and social struggles of their day. He observes, however, that the apologists are at the other end of the spectrum from apocalypticists and prophets. On the one hand, the apologists seek to reconcile their faith with the popular cultural perceptions of it among those outside of Christianity. On the other hand, apocalypticists eagerly anticipate an overthrow of existing power, and the realm of prophecy, outside of state-sanctioned oracles, can foster revolutionary thoughts among those subjected to Roman imperialism. For this reason, Grant contends, Christian apologists say little about the future relative to their own day (Grant, *Greek Apologists of the Second Century*, 14–15). In Justin's *Second Apology* exorcism still has the veneer of Christian eschatology. It is a prophetic act in so far as it illustrates the future event of eternal punishment, and validates the message about Jesus, which itself anticipates his return (Justin, *2 Apol.* 8).

superstition to foolish school (Galen),[13] to religion with ignoble founder (Celsus),[14] to noble founder with ignoble followers (Porphyry).[15] These criticisms reveal perceptions the broader populace held of Christians, and the issues these polemics raise dictated the responses generated by the apologists. Consequently, the earlier Christian apologists adopted a conciliatory tone in their overtures to the dominant polytheistic culture.[16] Where demonization

---

[13]Galen differed from earlier critics by referring to Christianity (and Judaism) as a philosophical school rather than a *superstitio*, the latter term having been used of Christianity by Pliny, Tacitus, and Suetonius at the beginning of the second century (Wilken, *The Christians as the Romans Saw Them*, 50, 73). Despite Galen's belief that Christian doctrine was flawed and misguided, Frend finds evidence in his admiration of Christian virtue and in his reclassification of Christianity that the persecutions of Christians during the second century elicited a modicum of respect from non-Christians (Frend, *The Rise of Christianity*, 184). Compare Lactantius' later conclusion that persecution served to increase the numbers of Christians by inspiring polytheists to convert for a number of reasons: it brings a public denouncement of gods and a proclamation of the true God; perseverance adds credibility, and the divine retribution brought against the persecutors attracts positive interest (Lactantius, *Inst.* 5.23).

[14]Celsus may have written *True Doctrine* (᾽Αληθὴς λόγος) (ca. 180) in response to Justin Martyr's apologies of some twenty years earlier (Wilken, *The Christians as the Romans Saw Them*, 101). Celsus was himself rebutted approximately eighty years later by Origen in his work *Against Celsus*, which alone preserves the remnants of Celsus' original. In *True Doctrine*, Celsus made a Jew his fictional mouthpiece, who criticizes Christianity before other Jews (Origen, *Cels.* 2.52). Wilken says of Celsus: "One of his strategies was to compare Christianity to unpopular and arcane religious movements that offended the sensibilities of the Romans" (Wilken, *The Christians as the Romans Saw Them*, 96). As Wilken observes, by elevating their founder to divine status Christians "set up a rival to the one high God who watched over the empire"; Celsus saw this elevation as threatening not only pagan polytheism, but also pagan henotheism (Wilken, *The Christians as the Romans Saw Them*, 125). Frend finds in the assumptions behind Celsus' argument evidence of Christianity having moved from the status of a sect to that of a world mission (Frend, *The Rise of Christianity*, 180).

[15]Porphyry wrote his fifteen volume work *Against the Christians* during the years 303–312. Whereas Celsus attacked the founder of Christianity, Porphyry attacked his immediate followers. He considered Jesus a wise and pious man, like Pythagoras, whose disciples erred by worshiping him (Wilken, *The Christians as the Romans Saw Them*, 152–53). In *On Philosophy from Oracles* he likewise sought to place Jesus in the context of pagan religion. Like Galen, Porphyry advocated henotheism, and he considered Christianity misguided by not worshiping the same one God worshipped by others.

[16]Justin Martyr's authentic works — the *First Apology* (ca. 156), perhaps inspired by the martyrdom of Polycarp in 155/56, the *Second Apology*, and the *Dialogue with Trypho* — constitute the earliest surviving Christian apologetic writings, and they raise themes that would recur in the writings of subsequent apologists. Justin attempts to bring respectability to the terms "Christ" and "Christian" as they are perceived by his polytheistic audiences. Justin, for example, does not demonize the Jews and pagans so much as he finds them guilty of the same abuse of free will as was committed by the demons (Justin, *Dial.* 140–41). By attacking the demonic pantheon Justin only indirectly critiques the polytheists themselves; the demons are the real object of his assault and by exposing their deceit he hopes to raise his

occurs it is of the pantheons rather than of the pagans themselves. In contrast to the apocalyptic and eschatological aspects of exorcism found in intra-Christian writings, the apologies draw more upon exorcism's broadly soteriological aspects.[17] By portraying exorcism as a positive experience that transforms the demonically possessed into a condition of well-being, and as a revelation of a new deity to those who witness it, the apologists attempt to use exorcism to their advantage as a focal activity in Christian mission despite social criticisms of such practices.

---

audience's opinion of Christianity. Justin's apologies tend to argue for Christianity's compatibility with Roman governance by presenting the Christian as a good citizen (Justin, *1 Apol.* 4). Tertullian also argues in favor of the name "Christian," which the Romans despise without accurately knowing either the following or its founder (Tertullian, *Apol.* 3). He further states that Christians make the best citizens who, without pay, protect the Romans from demonic affliction through exorcism (Tertullian, *Apol.* 37). Cyprian emphasizes the health benefits of exorcism where he says that Christians can adjure demons that mentally and physically disable the pagans, and that these demons confess themselves as demons upon their departures. He notes that the departure can be sudden or prolonged depending upon the faith of the sufferer or the grace of the healer (Cyprian, *Opusc.* 6.7). Wilken also points out the efforts of the apologists to refute the charge of superstition by Christianity's early critics by showing themselves god-fearers according to Greek and Roman standards (Wilken, *The Christians as the Romans Saw Them*, 66). Using Tertullian as an example, Wilken explains: "If Tertullian was to make a credible case for the truth of Christianity, he had first to show its similarity to other accepted religious and social groups within the empire" (Wilken, *The Christians as the Romans Saw Them*, 46–47). Wilken argues that Tertullian attempted this in part through judiciously avoiding Christian terminology to describe the movement (for example, *ecclesia*), and opts instead for words of associations familiar to Greco-Roman society, such as *corpus, factio Christiana, secta Dei, coitio Christianorum*, and *curia* (Wilken, *The Christians as the Romans Saw Them*, 46).

[17]As the synoptic gospels and Acts wove a theology of the kingdom of God's overthrow of the power of Satan into their exorcisms, so, too, does Barrett-Lennard see theological implications of healing (including exorcism) in later Christianity, though now with soteriological portent — "the work of God in Christ renewing the Creation." The eschatological connotations of exorcism would continue in Christian literature directed toward Christian audiences, as is evident in the writings of Irenaeus in the second century and Athanasius in the fourth (Barrett-Lennard, *Christian Healing after the New Testament*, 228). Compare also the use of exorcism by Tertullian. Tertullian, who converted to Christianity in 195, and to Montanism in ca. 212–213 (with Montanistic views reflected in his writings as early as 206), portrays exorcism differently in the texts he directs toward disputes with polytheists than he does in his writings that address intra-Christian rivalry. In writings addressed to the polytheists Tertullian argues for the proof of Christianity in the antiquity of its Scriptures and in the confession of demons during their exorcism by Christians (Tertullian, *Apol.* 46 [dated 197]), a confession that also discredits their status as gods (Tertullian, *An.* 57 [ca. 203]; *Apol.* 25). In intra-Christian debate he draws upon scriptural accounts of exorcism to provide the basis for doctrine. Thus, in *The Flesh of Christ* (ca. 207), Tertullian refers to Jesus' exorcism of devils as but one proof to justify the belief that the body is of value and worthy of healing (Tertullian, *Carn. Chr.* 4).

In keeping with the utilitarianism that underlies the traditional means for acceptance of a foreign cult into the recognized religious beliefs and practices of a state, the Christian apologists presented exorcism as pragmatically relevant to Roman society.[18] While Christianity was still in its vulnerable infancy apologists like Justin and Tertullian remained respectfully critical of Greek and Roman religious traditions by targeting its deities rather than its practitioners in the hope of improving Christianity's social standing. As Christianity began to establish itself in society, however, the tone of its critique became more confident and its language more aggressive toward the practitioners of polytheism as well as its gods, so that the respectful rhetoric that appears in the earlier apologies eventually gives way to bitter invective against all aspects of pagan religious society.[19]

---

[18]Wilken has identified "usefulness" (*utilitas*) as a defining feature of Roman religion: "Traditional Roman religion had emphasized the *utilitas* (usefulness) of religious belief for the well-being of the Roman commonwealth, and one of the outstanding theoreticians of Roman religion, Terrentius Varro (116–27 B.C.E.) had developed a theology of Roman religion based on this conception" (Wilken, *Christians as the Romans Saw Them*, 53). Elizabeth R. Gebhard discusses the traditional patterns found in the Greek and Roman legends that describe the bringing of new cults into society (Elizabeth R. Gebhard, "The Gods in Transit: Narratives of Cult Transfer," in *Antiquity and Humanity: Essays on Ancient Religion and Philosophy. Presented to Hans Dieter Betz on His 70th Birthday*, Adela Yarbro Collins and Margaret M. Mitchell, eds. [Tübingen: Mohr, 2001] 451–476). Gebhard regards the transferal and founding legends to follow a basic literary pattern of communal crisis, followed by an appeal to and revelation of divine guidance and command to found a cult, the success of which ends the crisis. As Christianity has not yet been welcomed into the Empire, some of its apologists appealed to the traditional avenues of cult transferal by emphasizing Christianity's epiphanaic aspects and its ability to solve crises. Tertullian and Arnobius are two such authors. Tertullian notes in his *Apology* that Roman law grants recognition of a deity under condition that the god has proven itself beneficial to humanity (*Apol.* 37.9; cf. 43.2). Contrary to the accusation of sacrilege and treason made against Christians for their refusal to worship Roman gods, Tertullian cites the ending of the drought in Germania by Christian prayers, an event and correlation acknowledged even by Marcus Aurelius, as an example of Christian benefaction to the Empire (Tertullian, *Apol.* 5). Arnobius cites three traditional bases for cult transferal, all of which Christianity satisfies: Christianity is effective where other gods have failed, a claim for which Arnobius refers to Asclepius' occasional inability to heal (Arnobius, *Adv. nat.* 1.49); the Sibyl and other prophetic venues have validated Christianity (Arnobius, *Adv. nat.* 1.62); despite the perception that Christianity has appeared only recently, it is an ancient religion, and recognition of such should lead to its acceptance (Arnobius, *Adv. nat.* 2.69–73). In Book 7 Arnobius reprises impending or current disasters, or recommendation by a seer, as past occasions for cult transferal, for which he cites as examples the transferal of the Asclepius cult from Epidauros to Tiber Island, and the transferal of the Great Mother cult from Phrygia (Arnobius, *Adv. nat.* 7.40, 44, 49). Compare also Lactantius, who says with respect to the inadequacy of pagan exorcism that "those insane from demons" cannot find help at temples of Zeus, Asclepius, or Apollo, yet the possessing spirits readily acknowledge the identity of Christ and flee (Lactantius, *Inst.* 4.27).

[19]Clement of Alexandria, for example, condemns the pantheon of his audience in a critique that manifestly changes the message of exorcism from an eschatological symbol of

In Lactantius' (260–330) late apologetic work, *The Divine Institutes*, the nature of Christian apologetics manifestly shifts from a genre written by the persecuted to gain respectability to a genre written from a position of privilege and devoted to destroying the credibility of its pagan opposition.[20] Despite attempts by the earlier apologists to argue Christianity's compatibility with the Roman political enterprise, it is little wonder that Christianity was viewed with suspicion by its early critics as a threat to the existing order. Compared to earlier examples of cult-transferal, Christianity's spread in the Greek and Roman world marked an aggressive expansion that aimed not at complementing existing religious practices but, by demonizing the pantheons and by displaying through exorcism God's dominion over them, sought to overpower and replace them.[21]

6.3 Magic and Early Christian Exorcism

It has been argued that the non-Christian world offered a receptive environment to the displays of power over demons performed by Christian

---

Satan's overthrow as found in the synoptic authors to the present overthrow of pagan gods (e.g. Clement, *Protr.* 4). Tatian also demonizes the Greek pantheon, with Zeus at its head (Tatian, *Oratio ad Graecos* 8–10). His apology comes as a response to a series of martyrdoms in 177 and, as Robert Grant observes, the "bitterly antagonistic" tone it assumes reflects a dramatic shift from the adulatory apologies presented just a year earlier to Marcus Aurelius by Apollinaris, Melito, and Athenagoras (Grant, *Greek Apologists of the Second Century*, 112–13).

[20]Lactantius was a student of Arnobius, who left North Africa for Gaul late in life to serve as an instructor to the Emperor Constantine's son Crispus. It was to Constantine himself that he dedicated *The Divine Institutes*. Lactantius devotes the first two of his six-book apology to pointing out the errors of polytheism. In his own earlier apology, *Against the Nations*, Arnobius offered an argument against polytheism very much from within the system. Himself a convert from polytheism and a Christian apologist from North Africa, Arnobius devotes the first six of his apology's seven books to dismantling polytheistic beliefs and practices, and he discredits the gods through the Greek and Roman myths themselves and the hypocrisies associated with those who worship them.

[21]Ramsay MacMullen, who seeks to explain why Christianity increased and eventually came to dominate Greco-Roman religious life from the first through the fourth centuries, phrases it this way: "… the unique force of Christian wonder-working that does indeed need emphasis lies in the fact that *it destroyed belief as well as creating it* — that is, if you credited it, you had then to credit the view that went with it, denying the character of god to all other divine powers whatsoever" (Ramsay MacMullen, *Christianizing the Roman Empire [A.D. 100–400]* [New Haven: Yale University Press, 1984] 108–9. MacMullen's italics). MacMullen considers Christianity to have been inherently antagonistic, and to have engaged in "a campaign of demotion" to reduce the status of gods to demons, a claim supported by their being subjugated through exorcism (MacMullen, *Christianizing the Roman Empire*, 18–19).

missionaries.[22] The apologists indeed support this view, and it finds corroboration also among the polytheists, notably in the use of the name of Christ in the *Greek Magical Papyri*.[23] But for a cultic following that sought

---

[22]Everett Ferguson says in this regard: "Greco-Roman paganism was quite demon-conscious ... A religion which offered victory over the demonic would have had a powerful appeal — especially if that religion could offer convincing evidence of its power over demons" (Ferguson, *Demonology of the Early Christian World*, 129). Ferguson's discussion of demonology in Greece spans Greek and Latin literature from epic into the first centuries of the Common Era. His comment above, however, implies the predominantly negative perception of demons that does not appear in these writings until the Common Era. MacMullen identifies belief in miracles as a principal motivation for conversion among the populus rather than among the intellectuals who were more compelled by intellectual teachings (MacMullen, *Christianizing the Roman Empire*, 62). Although Lane Fox notes that there is little indication of a formal mission effort headed by bishops in the third century (Lane Fox, *Pagans and Christians*, 282), the testimony by Irenaeus, among others, concerning exorcism in general offers support for Jesus' activity as important for setting the agenda for early Christian mission.

[23]*PGM* 3.419; 12.190–92; 13.289; 100.1–7; 123.50; 128.1–11. Acceptance of miracle working is less evident in the *belles-lettres* of the polytheists. See the Introduction for references to several of exorcism's critics among the non-Christian populace in the first centuries of the Common Era. The accounts of exorcism as a cause of conversion appear almost exclusively in the more literary and theological patristic writings. Irenaeus says that still in his own day those demoniacs who are healed through Jesus' name are motivated to join the church (Irenaeus, *Haer.* 2.32.4). Irenaeus, however, also offers hostile witness to the power of miracles to bring about conversion. Of the different Christian sects discussed by him in *Against Heresies*, some tend to be based upon doctrine while others attract converts through miracles. Irenaeus says that Marcus most resembles the antichrist because he uses miracles rather than doctrine to attract converts (Irenaeus, *Haer.* 1.13.1; cf. Mark 13:22). Compare the later pseudo-Clementine *Recognitions*, which denegrates Simon Magus' sect by saying that it is founded upon signs and prodigies (Pseudo-Clement, *Recogn.* 2.9). Tertullian refers to the importance of miracles in the founding of early churches (Tertullian, *Praescr.* 20). Origen argues that the use of Jesus' name to drive away demons proves his resurrection, and serves as a basis for attracting believers (Origen, *Cels.* 7.35). Lactantius says that Jesus conferred upon his disciples the power to work miracles as a means of founding and confirming faith (Lactantius, *Inst.* 4.21). This sentiment is also repeated in the east Syrian *Apostolic Constitutions* (ca. 380) which, with reference to Mark 16:17–18, says that miracles are worked not for the glory of the miracle worker, but to convert those disposed to believe them (*Const. ap.* 8.1). Lactantius says that some converts from paganism have become convinced of Christianity's merits after Christians have freed them from demonic possession (Lactantius, *Inst.* 5.23). These views differ from the New Testament exorcisms, which do not necessarily advocate conversion (with the possible exception of the Gerasene demoniac) or lead to possession by the Holy Spirit (compare the parable of the returning demon). Lane Fox is one who finds reason to critique the patristic evidence: "Between the Apostolic age and the fourth century, we know of no historical case where a miracle or an exorcism turned an individual, let alone a crowd, to the Christian faith" (Lane Fox, *Pagans and Christians*, 329). Although Barrett-Lennard says, "Irenaeus' testimony is that the Church practiced exorcism and did so in a highly effective manner" (Barrett-Lennard, *Christian Healing after the New Testament*, 161), he finds no evidence for exorcism at all in the private Christian

legitimacy in society as well as attention, one must also consider that the conflict created between exorcism and the existing social standards offset the advantage of its potential attraction.[24] Although the maliciousness of Christianity's demons justified to itself the practice of exorcism, such maliciousness could not be assumed from the polytheists' perspective. As seen in Chapter 4, coercive human intervention with *daimonic* powers tends to occur in magical contexts in pre-Christian Greek literary sources, so that by associating itself with power over demons Christianity associated itself with magic in the minds of its critics. In Christianity's use of exorcism it must then

---

papyrus letters prior to the fourth century, from the time such documents began to accummulate in the second half of the second century (Barrett-Lennard, *Christian Healing after the New Testament*, 137). This leads him to question whether demonic possession was considered a problem that Christians experienced at this time (Barrett-Lennard, *Christian Healing after the New Testament*, 202). Likewise, he concludes from his readings of Irenaeus and Athanasius that: "Neither writer refers to a Christian undergoing a full scale exorcism and the clear implication of their evidence is that those who did were non-Christian" (Barrett-Lennard, *Christian Healing after the New Testament*, 228–29). Irenaeus and Athanasius aside, Elizabeth Ann Leeper observes that most of the historical evidence for Christian exorcism shows it to have in fact been performed on other Christians as a post-conversion activity. She says in this regard: "... exorcism did not gain its chief importance as an impromptu evangelistic tool to attract and convert the pagan; rather, exorcism found its niche within the institutionalized church as a rite for Christians — both for the preparing and making of Christians ... and for the healing and purifying of those already Christian ... Christian teaching about demons therefore is aimed at converts from paganism, not the conversion of pagans, in order to reform their thinking about the demonic realm ..." (Leeper, *Exorcism in Early Christianity*, 182). However, it should be noted relative to Barrett-Lennard and Leeper that Tertullian's apparently spontaneous and varied references to exorcism in several of his writings suggest adjuration of demons as a familiar experience both for Christians within the church and for pagan society at large.

[24]Garrett, *The Demise of the Devil*, 20; following Anton Fridrichsen, *The Problem of Miracle in Primitive Christianity* (Minneapolis: Augsburg, 1972). Although Fritz Graf does not identify the exorcist as a specialist within the broad category of magic, he does include exorcism within the magician's repertoire, and his study is helpful in its portrayal of the suspicions the Roman Empire harbored against magic in general. Graf adopts Marcel Mauss' social view of magic and the magician as phenomena formed by social opinion, by which the accusation of magic addresses issues of social instability (Graf, *Magic in the Ancient World*, 61), and he cites as an illustration of this theory the case of Apuleius. Apuleius' marriage to an older wealthy widow much sought after by the local suitors raises the accusation against him of an outsider who disrupts the status quo through "hostile magic" (*magica maleficia*). Apuleius defends himself as an imperial citizen of urbane education and worldliness compared to the rustic ignorance and suspicions of his accusers (Graf, *Magic in the Ancient World*, 70–88). Although Roman society continued to view magic as a criminal activity subject to civil punishment especially when it sought to influence public affairs, contrary to early Greece and its agonistic use of magic to bring harm to one's adversaries, Graf sees Roman society also to have found in magic a more salutary purpose, through which it addressed a concern of becoming intimate with and knowing the Supreme God (Graf, *Magic in the Ancient World*, 232–33).

expect a struggle to gain the respect of the civil authorities who frowned upon such activities.

The exorcism that contributes toward Christian conversion appears to be that which pertains to physiological possession: illness creates a situation of openness to new options of healing, as the need for wellness leads one to hope in new cures and even new gods. Despite the fact that exorcism as a Christian missionary activity addressed physiological problems, it only occasionally appears to have been compared to the traditional healing cults.[25] Instead, Greek and Roman authors tended to classify Christian exorcism within the realm of magic, and the pagan critique of Christianity as a purveyor of magic would prove one of the most difficult for the early Christians to dispel. The shift in opinion would ultimately occur only with the supersession of Christianity over polytheism, at which point polytheistic practices would assume the defensive to the same accusation.[26]

Although the apologists use exorcism in defense of Christianity, exorcism itself becomes the subject of apology, especially in its perceived overlap with magic. Jesus' miracles afforded opponents the opportunity to label him a magician. Celsus (fl. 175–180 C.E.) advances one of the earliest associations between Jesus and the magical arts when he challenges Jesus' divinity and charges him with being a mere mortal who performed exorcisms by means of

---

[25]Justin claims that the demons raised up Asclepius as an alternative healer to Jesus (Justin, *1 Apol.* 54). Elsewhere, he defends Christianity against a prior charge of magic by countercharging that if Asclepius heals it is only an invention of the devil in imitation of Christ (Justin, *Dial.* 69). Celsus raised the comparison between the healings performed by Christ to those done by Asclepius, to which Origen responded that Christianity requires the worthiness not only of the healer, but of the healed (Origen, *Cels.* 3.24–25). Arnobius also compares the effectiveness of Christian healing to the ineffectiveness of the Asclepius cult (Arnobius, *Adv. nat.* 1.49). In the ca. late third century *Acts of Pilate*, Pilate claims that Jesus exorcizes by the power invested in him by Asclepius (*Acts Pil.* 1).

[26]Peter Brown's study of late antiquity (ca. IV–VI) technically post-dates this study, but some of his insights into sorcery of this time period are helpful for understanding the societal shift that would result in the eventual acceptance of Christian beliefs. Brown identifies two realms of power at work in late antique society: an "articulate" realm of power that is agreed upon and recognized by society at large, and the "inarticulate" realm of numinous power that lacks recognized social channels and institutions (Peter Brown, "Sorcery, Demons, and the Rise of Christianity: From Late Antiquity into the Middle Ages," in Peter Brown, *Religion and Society in the Age of Saint Augustine* [London: Faber & Faber, 1972] 124). In the first centuries of the Common Era the articulate power lay in polytheistic religious traditions supported by the empire. By the fourth century, the older system of Roman aristocratic power had become subverted, so that Christianity now influenced the recognized power sources while pagan traditions haunted society's margins. Brown portrays the sorcerer of late antiquity as the upholder and tradent of an occult wisdom grounded within old Roman religious traditions (Brown, "Sorcery, Demons, and the Rise of Christianity," 128–31).

demons and incantations.[27] The *Greek Magical Papyri* (abbreviated *PGM* from its Latin title *Papyri Graecae Magicae*), which range in date from as early as the first century of the Common Era to upwards of the sixth, offer further evidence for the basis of Christianity's association with magic.

Among the *PGM*'s conjurations, exorcisms periodically appear that parallel the characteristic indwelling demonic possession found in the New Testament. However, whereas the synoptic authors describe exorcism, the *PGM*, like the Mesopotamian formulae of Chapter 2, serve as manuals for conjuration that prescribe its performance.[28] The *PGM* provide a witness to the methods of exorcism performed in the first centuries of the Common Era that emphasized speech and invocation of divine beings to manipulate demons. The papyri arguably represent a literate, but not a literary craft, the users of which are the eclectic borrowers of signs, symbols, and words from other traditions. The exorcistic formulae that appear in the *PGM* often include Christian or Judaic features, such as the names "Jesus," "Christ," "Jahweh," or of angelic beings, in addition to their primarily polytheistic references. Yet, the practitioners who used the formulae need not have been Christians or Jews themselves, and the syncretistic and polytheistic quality of the formulae strongly suggests the contrary.[29] The papyri appear to confirm the statements one finds scattered

---

[27]E.g., Origen, *Cels.* 1.6, 38, 46, 68; 2.9, 14, 48-51; 3.5; 8.9. Jews also appear to have classified Jesus' miracles within the magical arts. Tertullian observes that exorcism was included among Jesus' repertoire of miracles that led the Jews to consider him a magician (Tertullian, *Apol.* 21). Compare Cyprian's claim that the Jews sought Jesus' execution because he was a sorcerer (Cyprian, *Opusc.* 6.13).

[28]Despite the prescriptions, the *PGM* still leaves much of the success of its incantations to the whimsy of the deities invoked (e.g., *PGM* 3.263–75).

[29]Although the *PGM* arguably draws from Christian traditions without being intended for use within the Christian cult, other collections of magical texts do appear to have been generated and employed within a Christian context. Such, for example, are the Coptic rituals edited by Marvin Meyer that concern healing generally, but also contain many specific references to exorcism of "demonic possession of the personality" (Meyer, *Ancient Christian Magic*, 130). The rituals tend to be verbal in character, whether as spoken incantations or writing on amulets. Meyer identifies these rituals as "Christian" primarily due to their date and place of composition (I–XI/XII C.E. Egypt). Although these texts are syncretistic, their borrowing reflects more a saturation of "indigenous Egyptian demonology" than reference to non-Christian deities (Meyer, *Ancient Christian Magic*, 107–8). These spells differ from the *PGM* in their exclusively negative use of *daimon*, as in other Christian writings (Meyer, *Ancient Christian Magic*, 109), and their tendency to draw its divine figures more exclusively from Jewish and Christian traditions (e.g. #88 [London Oriental Manuscript 5986] Meyer, *Ancient Christian Magic*, 187–88). Further, although in form these texts are similar to those in the *PGM*, the authors of these rituals draw the distinction between the "theurgy" that they practice and the *goeteia* of the magicians. Meyer explains: "After the third century, highbrow philosophers who practiced invocation of divine powers tried to disengage themselves from this [negative] magical tradition by rewriting the vocabulary. They called what they did theurgy, "divine work," as opposed to goeteia, howling out barbaric words"

throughout the apologetic writings that non-Christians find the name of Christ beneficial in controlling demons due not to an inherent validity of the exorcist, but to the inherent power of Jesus' name, apparently regardless of who speaks it.[30]

Aside from the insight the *PGM* gives to early exorcistic practice, it shares little in common with the purpose and meaning of exorcism as it is performed in early Christianity. Whether the *PGM* intends its formulae to be heard for effect or to be said in private, in either case their arcane quality is antithetical to the proclamatory intention of Christian exorcism as it is described by the apologists.[31] Even within the New Testament, and increasingly in the

---

(Meyer, Ancient Christian Magic, 2). That the spells use Jewish and Christian divine names in the context of broader Christian doctrine, such as explicit connections made between the invocation of Jesus' name and his history as a miracle worker, further argues for the Christian context of these Coptic spells. Compare, for example, #7 (Oxyrhynchus 1077), a fourth century parchment healing amulet with Matthew 4:23–24 written upon it that describes Jesus' pervasive healing powers (Meyer, Ancient Christian Magic, 33). Compare also #132 (London Oriental Manuscript 6796 [4], 6796), a papyrus of ca. 600 that refers to Jesus' crucifixion as the significant biographical detail rather than his healing miracles as a source of power to cast out every unclean spirit (Meyer, Ancient Christian Magic, 291).

[30]Origen critiques Aristotle's belief that names are arbitrarily bestown, and sees the name instead as a natural attribute of God that captures the essence of the deity (Origen, *Cels.* 5.45–46). Consequently, its proper pronunciation is essential to its power so that it loses its effectiveness when translated (Origen, *Cels.* 1.24–25). Compare the critique Origen raises against conjurers who manipulate evil spirits by using Hebrew names without knowledge of their divine referents (Origen, *Cels.* 1.22). Elsewhere, he says that polytheists who seek to know names and control demons are unpleasing to God (Origen, *Cels.* 8.61). In contrast, the *Clementine Homilies* says that sometimes non-Christians can effectively exorcize using the sacred name, but that these people lack personal righteousness and their cures lead neither the healed, nor the witnesses, nor the exorcists themselves to a true belief (Pseudo-Clement, *Hom.* 9.22). An anonymous *Treatise on Re-Baptism* says that one need not represent Christ and the Holy Spirit in order to exorcize, as Jesus' name is also used by those whom Jesus rejects (*Treatise on Re-Baptism* 7 [*ANF* 5.671]). From the Jewish tradition, compare *The Sword of Moses*, a magical text whose history Moses Gaster traces back to Palestinian origins in the first four centuries of the Common Era in analogy with its Greek counterparts (Moses Gaster, *Studies and Texts in Folklore, Magic, Medieval Romance, Hebrew Apocrypha and Samaritan Archaeology* [3 vols.; New York: Ktav, 1971] 1:288–337). The sword of the title likely refers to Moses' last words as recorded in Deuteronomy 33:29, and which Gaster interprets as a mystical reference "taken to denote a peculiar form of the divine Name" (Gaster, *Studies and Texts*, 1:307). This work reveals a fascination with the divine names that served as alternatives to the Tetragrammaton. Of their inherent power Gaster says: "These substitutes were considered to be no less effective for miracles, and the knowledge of these mysterious Names was no less desirable than that of the true Tetragrammaton, for they were believed to represent the exact pronunciation of the forbidden word, and thus to contain part if not the whole, of the power with which the Tetragrammaton itself was vested" (Gaster, *Studies and Texts*, 1:295).

[31]In the apologetic writings, discerning the demon's name is not used to gain power over the demon as in the *PGM*, but to expose its identity to the masses. In contrast to the

experience of the early church, the ability to perform signs, exorcism included, was insufficient in and of itself to verify the divine authority of miracle workers.[32] For early Christians the ambiguous message of miracles required a validating context based upon the miracle workers' character and the salvific content of the preaching that accompanied their wonderous acts.[33] Thus, even in its simplest form Christian exorcism constitutes a nucleus of word and deed, miracle and preaching, that encapsulates and promotes a message of Jesus' divinity and of God's subjugation of evil.

Within the New Testament itself the message of exorcism shifts from an assertion of the kingdom of God's overthrow of Satan preached by Jesus (as seen in the synoptic gospels), to Jesus himself as a source of exorcistic power for others (as seen in Acts). The patristic writings tend to convey the latter of these messages, and as a consequence early Christian literature begins to use

---

proclamatory and explanatory character of Christian exorcism, compare the abundant use of *rhesis barbarike* in the *PGM*, which Irenaeus says serves to bewilder the hearer (Irenaeus, *Haer.* 1.21.3). Justin's *Dialogue with Trypho* reveals some of the technique of Christian exorcism, in which its exorcists need only recite the name of Jesus Christ, Son of God, followed by a reverential creedal statement to effectively perform exorcisms (Justin, *Dial.* 30). Origen describes exorcistic technique as reference to the name of God, Christ, and his history (Origen, *Cels.* 3.24), and he distinguishes between Jesus' miracles and those of the conjurers by the respectable doctrine that both accompanied his deeds and denounced the practice of magic (Origen, *Cels.* 1.38). This technique shows how the mission aspect is strengthened by adding context to the name of Christ (Origen, *Cels.* 1.6). Although some of the formulae in the *Greek Magical Papyri* do suggest simple faith statements — compare "Hail, God of Abraham; hail, God of Isaac; hail, God of Jacob; Jesus Chrestos, the Holy Spirit, the Son of the Father ..." (*PGM* 4.1231–34; Coptic in Karl Preisendanz, ed., *Papyri Graecae Magicae. Die Griechischen Zauberpapyri* [2 vols., Sammlung Wissenschaftlicher Commentare; Stuttgart: Teubner, 1973–74] 1:114) — such, however, amount to a recitation of lineage and honorary titles in the interest of identifying the divine agent summoned. Any creedal potential is further diluted by an eclectic syncretism from other religious traditions.

[32]The portrayal of Simon Magus, whom Irenaeus labels as the originator of all heresies (Irenaeus, *Haer.* 1.23.2), illustrates this in early Christianity. The *Clementine Homilies* says that beneficial miracles are from God, while others, such as those done by Simon Magus, are done from wickedness (Pseudo-Clement, *Hom.* 2.33). Compare in the fifth homily, where Clement says that magicians manipulate demons (Pseudo-Clement, *Hom.* 5.5). Elsewhere the author adds that he has witnessed only mixed results of magicians (Pseudo-Clement, *Hom.* 5.4), that magic removes free-choice from the victim (Pseudo-Clement, *Hom.* 5.7), and that Simon Magus used incantations to perform his exorcisms (Pseudo-Clement, *Hom.* 2.26). This evokes the lesson that the prophet works miracles for the sake of God and goodness, while the magician does them with evil intent (Pseudo-Clement, *Hom.* 2.33; cf. *Recogn.* 3.55).

[33]The mid-fourth century *Apostolic Constitutions* sees exorcism as beneficial to the healed but, drawing support from Luke 10:20 and the Sons of Sceva episode in Acts, hesitates to assign glory or to attribute good character to the exorcists themselves based solely upon their ability to exorcize (*Const. ap.* 8.1–2).

exorcism also as an indicator of Jesus' divinity.[34] The early Christian writings add several nuances and techniques to the exorcistic practices of the New Testament of which prayer,[35] touch,[36] and the power of the cross predominate,[37] but it was the ability of others to exorcize in the name of Jesus that especially testified to his resurrection as the demons and false gods of

---

[34]Origen says that Jesus' miracles justify him as the object of worship (Origen, *Cels.* 8.9). Peter, Bishop of Alexandria (260–311), writes in a fragment on the Gospel of Matthew that Christ's miracles and signs bear witness to his divinity [*ANF* 6:283]. Methodius also interprets Jesus' miracles, exorcism included, as signs of his divinity (Methodius, *Sermo in ramos palmarum* 3 [*ANF* 6:395]). A fragment of Melito's *De incarnatione* says that miracles are a sign of Jesus' divinity and of divinity within him (recorded in Anastasius of Sinai [fl. 685], *Dux viae* 13 [*ANF* 8:760]).

[35]Tertullian mentions prayer as an exorcistic technique (Tertullian, *Or.* 29 [ca. 192], and *Idol.* 11 [pre-Montanist]). The *Selections from the Prophetic Scriptures* 15, doubtfully attributed to Clement of Alexandria, refers to Mark 9:29 as evidence of the superiority of prayer over faith for exorcism (PL 9.705; *ANF* 8:45). The *Liturgy of St. Mark* includes prayers said by the priest that drive away Satan's influence from the congregation, a spirit of weakness from the sick, and other unclean spirits (*ANF* 7:551, 555, 558). The *Liturgy of St. James* includes in prayer those troubled by unclean spirits (*ANF* 7:541). The first *Epistle to the Virgins*, credited to Clement of Rome but more likely dating to the third century Common Era (Joseph Barber Lightfoot, *The Apostolic Fathers* [2 vols.; New York: Georg Olms, 1973] 1.407–8), uses Matthew 17:20 as proof text that Christian exorcism is done through fasting and prayers, and not by grand-eloquent words (Clement, *Ep. virg.* 1.12).

[36]Touch, a major feature of healing in the New Testament, only rarely occurs in exorcisms there. Although Barrett-Lennard cites *Apostolic Tradition* 20 as the first reference to laying on of hands in Christian exorcism, and then Origen in his *Homily on Joshua* 24.1 (Barrett-Lennard, *Christian Healing after the New Testament*, 265, n. 155), Tertullian mentions touch and breath as exorcistic techniques (Tertullian, *Apol.* 23, 27; breath is also mentioned in *An.* 1 [ca. 203]). At a later date the ca. 380 *Life of Gregory Thaumaturgus* says that Gregory laid his hands upon a possessed boy to exorcize his evil spirit (Gregory of Nyssa, *Vita Gregorii Thaumaturgi* 77–78).

[37]Athanasius says that all demonic activity is put to flight by the sign of the cross (Athanasius, *C. gent.* 1.27–29). In the *Epitome of the Divine Institutes*, Lactantius says that the sign of the cross and the name of Christ cause demons to flee, and to confess their false identities as gods upon their departures (Lactantius, *Epit.* 51). Elsewhere, he reiterates that Jesus' followers exorcize by saying his name and making the sign of the cross; he adds that the cross also serves as a powerful apotropeion that protects Christians from demons (Lactantius, *Inst.* 4.27). Methodius says that the cross has the power to mitigate every evil, and symbolizes the liberty of every creature, as seen in the cross-shapes of birds in flight, or ships under sail (Methodius, *Homilia de cruce* 1 [*ANF* 6:399–400]). Gregory Thaumaturges uses the name of Christ and the sign of the cross to cause demons to flee from a pagan temple (Gregory of Nyssa, *Vita Gregorii Thaumaturgi* 34–41). The cross to drive off evil spirits is especially noteworthy for its theological implications in the writings of Athanasius, who sees proof in the exorcisms done by this means during his own day of both Jesus' resurrection (e.g, Athanasius, *C. gent.* 1.27–29; *Inc.* 47.1–21; 48.1–44; cf. 55.5–8), and divine authority (Athanasius, *Inc.* 19.1–10).

polytheism recognized his ongoing authority over them.[38] Whereas Jewish and polytheistic exorcists relied on craft, such as fumigations, incantations, and pharmacopeia, Christians claimed to control more effectively the aggressiveness of the spirit-world through the name of "Jesus Christ,"[39] which consequently served both as a validation of the Christian faith,[40] and as a means of differentiating Christianity from Judaism.[41]

---

[38]Now controlled by Christian exorcists, the supposed deities of polytheism betrayed their inferiority when exorcized in the name of the true God. MacMullen contrasts the Christian miracle, exorcism especially, with the non-Christian: "The manhandling of demons ... served a purpose quite essential to the Christian definition of monotheism: it made physically (or dramatically) visible the superiority of the Christian's patron Power over all others" (MacMullen, *Christianizing the Roman Empire*, 28). Justin (Justin, *2 Apol.* 6; *Dial.* 30, 85) and Tertullian (Tertullian, *Apol.* 21, 23–24, 46) both use the publicly displayed exorcism that is performed by Christians upon non-Christians to promote the pre-eminence of Christ and God over the demons and so-called gods that their names are able to subdue and cast out. Theophilus notes that through exorcism in the name of the true God possessing spirits confess themselves as demons (Theophilus, *Autol.* 2.8). Irenaeus says that demons recognize their superiors (Irenaeus, *Haer.* 2.6.2). Athanasius reiterates this sentiment: "For who, seeing his power over demons, or who, seeing the demons confess that he is their Lord, would still be doubtful in his mind whether he is the Son of Wisdom and Power of God." (τίς γὰρ, ἰδὼν αὐτοῦ τὴν κατὰ δαιμόνων ἐξουσίαν, ἢ τίς, ἰδὼν τοὺς δαίμονας ὁμολογοῦντας εἶναι τούτων αὐτὸν Κύριον, ἔτι τὴν διάνοιαν ἀμφίβολον ἕξει, εἰ οὗτός ἐστιν ὁ τοῦ Θεοῦ Υἱὸς καὶ ἡ σοφία καὶ ἡ δύναμις;) (Athanasius, *Inc.* 19. English translation by Robert W. Thomson, *Athanasius: Contra Gentes and De Incarnatione* [OECT; Oxford: Clarendon Press, 1971] 180–81. Greek text in PG 25:129). The demons' confession of Christ as the Son of God corroborates his divine status (Athanasius, *Inc.* 32.14–33). For Athanasius, exorcism also reveals the deception of demons at work both in false religious institutions (e.g. an oracle silenced by the sign of the cross and the name of Christ), and in such persons as the magicians and sorcerers of Egypt, Chaldea, and India. Christ's work, and the work done in his name, overthrows rather than confirms the work of these false practitioners (Athanasius, *Inc.* 46–48).

[39]Thraede, "Exorzismus," 67. Tertullian attributes the ability to exorcize to Christians alone (Tertullian, *Test.* 3), who put demons to flight by the name of Christ, and by reciting Christ's return and the impending doom of the demons. Irenaeus says that Christian exorcism is done by prayer and by calling upon the name of Jesus Christ, not by invocations and incantations (Irenaeus, *Haer.* 2.32.5). Origen also refers to the effectiveness of Jesus' name in exorcism (Origen, *Cels.* 8.58). Arnobius notes the dominical mandate to exorcize, and says that Christ permitted his followers to use his name in exorcistic command in their mission (Arnobius, *Adv. nat.* 1.50). Arnobius also argues that the current use of Jesus' name to put demons to flight and to destroy the work of the magicians proves further that Jesus was not a magician (Arnobius, *Adv. nat.* 1.46).

[40]According to Justin, exorcism illustrates the power of Jesus' name to control demons (Justin, *2 Apol.* 6); this power of Jesus' name and the acceptance of his teachings throughout the nations validates his divine status (Justin, *1 Apol.* 53).

[41]Justin compares the consistently effective use of Jesus' name in exorcism by Christians with the various powers summoned by the Jews, who sometimes effectively exorcize by the name of God, but fail when using only the names of other holy figures (Justin, *Dial.* 85).

6.4 Exorcism and Wisdom: Philostratus' *Life of Apollonius*

The *Life of Apollonius of Tyana* by Philostratus (ca. 172–ca. 249) offers a good illustration from non-Christian literature of an attempt to validate the exorcism practiced by pagan miracle workers by adapting its significance in response to criticism by the political authorities. Further, the travails of Apollonius described therein provide an analogy for the challenges faced by early Christian miracle workers.[42] In general, miracle stories establish faith in both miracle workers and the divine powers that support them. This is an aspect shared by the healing cults of Asclepius and Serapis, and one which is crucial to the Gospels' presentation of Jesus as a divine man. When we look to the healings Philostratus says were performed by Apollonius and the Indian sage Iarchas we see them also serving to generate belief, though on these occasions belief in the miracle worker as a truly wise person.[43] Several chapters from the *Life of Apollonius* show well how the concept of the wise man carried with it not only the quality of great learning and judgment, but also the ability to perform the extraordinary, exorcism included.[44] Iarchas, for

---

[42]Lactantius refers to a recent book about Apollonius of Tyana, and he compares Apollonius' miracles to those performed by Christ (Lactantius, *Inst.* 5.3). An important distinction between the two is that Apollonius appears to be considered a sorcerer (γόης) in his trial before Domitian more for reason of his reputation as a diviner than for his activities as a healer or exorcist; the charge laid against him there is that he had sacrificed an Arcadian youth that he might thereby divine the emperor's death (Philostratus, *Vit. Apoll.* 7.11).

[43]The healings performed by Iarchas and Apollonios, and for that matter by Jesus, differ from those produced by the healing cults and the medical profession in that the cults and medicine heal as their primary activity, whereas these men heal as one manifestation of their devotional lives. Temkin says: "Altogether there exists an essential difference between Asclepius and Jesus: the Greek god cured because this was his function, whereas Jesus healed in fulfillment of a divine mission" (Owsei Temkin, *Hippocrates in a World of Pagans and Christians* [Baltimore: Johns Hopkins University Press, 1991] 97). Serapis parallels Jesus more closely here in that healing is but one of his many services. Yet, even in the case of Serapis there is no indication that his many services funnel toward a single goal, such as one finds in the salvation kerygma associated with Jesus.

[44]This draws us closer to the portrayal of Jesus as teacher and miracle worker which combine to establish his status as a divine man. Although in the New Testament Jesus' teachings give him a reputation for wisdom, his healing activity is a closely related event. Mark tells how when Jesus taught in the synagogue of his hometown, he evoked the following reaction from his audience: "Where did this man get all this? What is this wisdom (τίς ἡ σοφία) that has been given to him? What deeds of power (αἱ δυνάμεις τοιαῦται) are being done by his hands?" (Mark 6:2). Compare in the *Clementine Homilies* where humanity's wisdom includes the ability to exorcize (Pseudo-Clement, *Hom.* 3.36). In the *Life of Apollonius*, the Indian sages appear to have seen themselves as more-than-human. In the conversation between Apollonius and Iarchas, Apollonius asks: "... who they [the present company of Indian sages] considered themselves to be; and the other answered 'We consider ourselves to be Gods.' Apollonius asked afresh: 'Why?' 'Because,' said the other, 'we are good men.' This reply struck Apollonius as so instinct with trained good sense, that

example, cures a demoniac boy among other healing miracles.[45] During the demonstration Philostratus identifies him as "the sage" (ὁ σοφός), and the reaction that these miracles evoke from witnesses is one of astonishment at Iarchas' "encyclopedic wisdom."[46] These healings serve not so much to show Iarchas as a great healer, as to reveal Iarchas as a truly wise person.

Demonology constitutes an important premise of the *Life of Apollonius*, as Apollonius lives in a world inhabited by spirits of various kinds. He sees the world itself as an androgenous living organism, a teaching learned from the Indian sages,[47] and in his travels to the western limits of ancient geography he interprets the ebb and flow of the ocean's tide as sub-marine spirits that come forth and recess.[48] On occasion, Apollonius actively engages this spiritual world in his exorcisms of demonic aggressors, and this wonder-working also bestows credibility upon Apollonius as a wise man. In Ephesus, Apollonius divines the onslaught of a plague, and he averts it by having the citizens stone a demon disguised as an old beggar.[49] At Corinth, he drives off a lamia, who has assumed the semblance of a beautiful woman.[50] He cures a licentious

---

he subsequently mentioned it to Domitian in his defence of himself." (... τίνας αὐτοὺς ἡγοῖντο, ὁ δέ, "θεούς," εἶπεν, ἐπερομένου δὲ αὐτοῦ, διὰ τί, "ὅτι," ἔφη, "ἀγαθοί ἐσμεν ἄνθρωποι." τοῦτο τῷ Ἀπολλωνίῳ τοσαύτης ἔδοξεν εὐπαιδευσίας εἶναι μεστόν, ὡς εἰπεῖν αὐτὸ καὶ πρὸς Δομετιανὸν ὕστερον ἐν τοῖς ὑπὲρ ἑαυτοῦ λόγοις.) (Philostratus, *Vit. Apoll.* 3.18; cf., 3.29 and 8.6 [Conybeare, LCL]). The sum of practice and wisdom as an equation toward divine status was also of consideration for the medical profession. From the Hippocratic Corpus compare the statement: "For a physician is a philosopher, is an equal to a god" (ἰητρὸς γὰρ φιλόσοφος ἰσόθεος — Hippocrates, *Decorum* 5 [post 300 B.C.E.] [Jones, LCL]). This hyperbole reflects Stoic influence in its presentation of the model of the ideal physician; W. H. S. Jones says in his introduction to the treatise that the author has made "an effort to bring the Stoic 'wise man' down to earth as a grave, self-controlled, orderly man of the world" (*Hippocrates*, 2.271 [Jones, LCL]). Though they sometimes transcend the bounds of medicine, Apollonius' own healings in the *Life of Apollonius* are not superhuman, but exceptional. There is, in fact, one instance, in his trial before the emperor Domitian, where Apollonius admits the limitations of his power to heal his friend Philiscus of Melos: "Many are the charms I would have prayed to obtain, if they could have saved his life. If, by Zeus, there are any melodies of Orpheus on behalf of the dead, I did not know them ..." (καίτοι πολλὰς ἂν ηὐξάμην ἴυγγας ὑπὲρ τῆς ἐκείου ψυχῆς γενέσθαι μοι, καί, νὴ Δί ', εἴ τινες Ὀρφέως εἰσὶν ὑπὲρ τῶν ἀποθανόντων μελῳδίαι, μηδ ' ἐκείνας ἀγνοῆσαι ...) (Philostratus, *Vit. Apoll.* 8.7.14 [Conybeare, LCL, modified]).

[45] In the same passage Iarchas also heals a lame man and a man with a paralyzed hand; he relieves a woman in childbearing, and heals the blindness of a man who is missing both of his eyes (Philostratus, *Vit. Apoll.* 3.38–39).

[46] τῆς ἐς πάντα σοφίας (Philostratus, *Vit. Apoll.* 3.40 [Conybeare, LCL]).

[47] Philostratus, *Vit. Apoll.* 3.34.

[48] Philostratus, *Vit. Apoll.* 5.2.

[49] Philostratus, *Vit. Apoll.* 4.10.

[50] Philostratus, *Vit. Apoll.* 4.25. Philostratus pronounces this the most famous of Apollonius' deeds because it took place in the heart of Greece.

youth by exorcizing from him the here-to-fore unrecognized demon of his licentiousness.[51] A common strand runs through these three events: Apollonius has the ability to perceive the demonic behind the normal facades that deceive others who are less wise. Whereas demonic possession is publicly manifest in the New Testament, this is not the case in the *Life of Apollonius*; here one needs wisdom to perceive the demons.[52]

Philostratus indicates that Apollonius' miraculous deeds brought him fame as a wise man among his supporters, but the charge of wizardry from the ranks of his rivals and opponents, a charge that Philostratus is constantly obliged to refute. By associating miraculous deeds with wisdom Philostratus attempts to reclassify Iarchas' and Apollonius' exorcisms into a category other than magic, and one that would have been received more favorably by the Roman audience for whom he writes.[53] Philostratus is quick to point out that although Apollonius consorted with sorcerers, he, like the great philosophers before him, never truly crossed into the realm of magic:

> ... some, because he had interviews with the wizards of Babylon and with the Brahmans of India, and with the nude ascetics of Egypt, put him down as a wizard, and spread the calumny that he was a sage of an illegitimate kind ... For Empedocles and Pythagoras himself and Democritus consorted with wizards and uttered many supernatural truths, yet never stooped to the black art ...[54]

---

[51]Philostratus, *Vit. Apoll.* 4.20.

[52]Compare in the pseudo-Clementine *Recognitions*, where Peter "detects" the real Simon Magus by seeing the demoniac at work behind the facade of righteousness Simon otherwise presents to the people (Pseudo-Clement, *Recogn.* 3.13). Conversely, Peter also recognizes the goodness of Faustinianus, whom Simon has maliciously made to look like Simon himself (Pseudo-Clement, *Recogn.* 10.53). By exposing Simon's hidden wickedness Peter earns a reputation as a prophet (Pseudo-Clement, *Recogn.* 3.45).

[53]Brenk notes that Philostratus' argument would likely have been unpersuasive to other Greek men of letters: "In spite of the attempt to turn Apollonius into a *sophos* or *spondaios*, the picture drawn by Philostratus would have appeared to people like Plutarch as that of pernicious, evil fraud and manipulation of folk superstition, given an aura of philosophical respectability ..." (Brenk, "In the Light of the Moon," *ANRW* 2.16.3:2138). It should be noted, however, that Plutarch lived at least two generations before Philostratus wrote, so that a change in sensibilities may have made the latter's audience more receptive to the connection between wisdom and exorcism. Compare also Lane Fox's argument against the long-standing presumption that paganism during the Antonine age onward represented an "age of anxiety" marked by a growth in superstition and irrationality. According to Lane Fox such claims are too general and find support only among a select few of the wealthy few of that period (Lane Fox, *Pagans and Christians*, 64).

[54]... οἱ δέ, ἐπειδὴ μάγοις Βαβυλωνίων καὶ Ἰνδῶν Βραχμᾶσι καὶ τοῖς ἐν Αἰγύπτῳ Γυμνοῖς συνεγένετο, μάγον ἡγοῦνται αὐτὸν καὶ διαβάλλουσιν ὡς βιαίως σοφόν, κακῶς γιγνώσκοντες· Ἐμπεδοκλῆς τε γὰρ καὶ Πυθαγόρας αὐτὸς καὶ Δημόκριτος, ὁμιλήσαντες μάγοις καὶ πολλὰ

Plato, Socrates, and Anaxagoras are also mentioned in the list. Philostratus implies that what might popularly be perceived as "magic" may involve virtues more upstanding, and that its condemnation tends to derive from the accuser's ignorance rather than from the wise man's error.

The suspicions that Philostratus confronts with regard to Apollonius' wonder-workings serve as a good analogy for how early Christians had to adapt their own presentation of exorcism to a Greco-Roman audience. As Philostratus upheld Apollonius' wonder-workings by identifying them with the fruits of true wisdom rather than the deceptions of magic, the Christian apologists likewise attempted to bolster exorcism's reputation as a legitimate practice within the authentic religion of Christianity. They did so, however, not by joining the practice of exorcism to wisdom but to ethics.

6.5 Character versus Charisma in Christian Apologetics

Exorcistic practice looks for precedent, and one of the ways the apologists dealt with the accusation of magic was by relating the Christian practice of exorcism to its ancient Scriptures. Chapter 5 sought to show that, rather than distinguishing him from other miracle workers in Israel's past, Jesus' practice of exorcism placed him in the same category as earlier prophets who possessed the spirit, power, and authority of God. In Judaism, exorcism was regarded as a *tradition noblesse* that included Moses, David, and Solomon as accredited magicians, with patriarchal ascription going back to Noah and his sons.[55] Alongside of Jesus and the disciples as the archetypal Christian exorcists, these Jewish prototypes retained their importance in Christian literature. By attributing exorcism to figures of the Old Testament Christian

---

δαιμόνια εἰπόντες, οὔπω ὑπήχθησαν τῇ τέχνῃ ... (Philostratus, *Vit. Apoll.* 1.2 [Conybeare, LCL]).

[55]In the pseudo-Clementine *Recognitions* a Jew accuses Jesus of not being a prophet but a magician, to which Philip responds by calling upon the Jewish precedent of Moses (Pseudo-Clement, *Recogn.* 1.58). The first century Common Era Pseudo-Philo attributes the practice of exorcism to David and Solomon (*Pseudo-Philo* 60.1–3 [*OTP* 2:373]). The first-to-third century *Testament of Solomon*, which presents an extended narrative of Solomon's control over the demons and forcing them to build the temple, attests to a belief in divine possession and its role in exorcism (*T. Sol.* 4.10; 26.6–7), and it describes many features of exorcistic practice, such as the determination of a demon's identity and the use of a seal to control and bind demons, that appealed to the popular imagination. *Jubilees* describes Noah's prayer to God for protection for himself and his sons from the demonic offspring of the Watchers. The spells that Noah receives in reply he records in a book and entrusts to his oldest and dearest son Shem (*Jub.* 10:3–14). The story of exorcism as an illicit practice traces back to the same mythic time period, with Ham as a magician and manipulator of demons (Pseudo-Clement, *Recogn.* 4.27), and with the antedeluvian instruction in magic given by the angels to humanity (*1 En.* 7.1–8.4).

authors historicized and added credibility to a practice otherwise anachronistic to the literary settings from which they drew. [56]

At the same time as they read exorcism back into the lives of these Old Testament figures, Christian exegetes drew forth from Scripture certain of their moral and righteous character traits to make these traits an expectation also of their own contemporary exorcists. The anonymous exorcists of the Christian apologies, however, part ways with the wisdom aspect of their Solomonic heritage. Although there is a heightened awareness in Christianity that allows the Christian to perceive the demonic nature of the pantheon that is to some extent comparable to the wisdom of Apollonius, it is not a trait that distinguishes the Christian exorcists from their fellow believers. Rather than an interest in the individual exorcists as vehicles of divine wisdom, they present them instead in an almost anti-intellectual manner as humble, non-threatening citizens, whose simple methods of exorcism both contrast with the pompous

---

[56]Early Christian exegesis followed the New Testament precedent of reading exorcism back into the prophetic language of the Old Testament. Although Justin notes similarities between Christian and polytheistic beliefs by citing analogous traditions of resurrection, virgin birth, and miraculous healings (Justin, *1 Apol.* 22), he distinguishes Christ's miracles by the fact that they fulfilled earlier prophecy (Justin, *1 Apol.* 30). They are acts analogous to the great acts of divinely inspired biblical prophets such as Moses, Elijah, and Elisha, and their message of overthrowing the forces of Satan makes them comparable to the prophetic visual displays performed by Hosea and Jeremiah. Justin directs his defense of Christianity to polytheistic audiences in his first and second apologies, and to a Jewish audience in his *Dialogue with Trypho*. It is in the latter work especially that he brings the Old Testament to bear upon exorcism. Exorcism is foretold in the Old Testament (Justin, *Dial.* 131), where such references as the "footstool" in Psalm 1:2 (Justin, *Dial.* 127; cf. Ps 110:1 ff.), and "unbinding from chains" in Isaiah 42:6–7 (Justin, *Dial.* 26) are interpreted as exorcistic allusions (cf. Justin, *1 Apol.* 40, 45). Justin applies the rebuke of the devil in Zechariah 3:1 to an activity of Jesus (Justin, *Dial.* 79, 115). Tertullian in his treatise *Against Marcion* says that casting out a dumb demon fulfills Isaiah 29:18 (Tertullian, *Marc.* 4.26). Irenaeus also says that Jesus performed his exorcisms in accordance with prophecy, and it is this prophecy that adds credibility to Jesus' miracles over against those of the heretics (Irenaeus, *Haer.* 2.32.4). For Irenaeus, the prophets anticipated the incarnation of God that liberates humanity from evil spirits. He views exorcism as an enacted prophecy that makes known the final overthrow of Satan (Irenaeus, *Haer.* 4.20.4; cf. 4.20.8, 12). Compare Peter Brown's description of exorcism in the Late Roman period as an "operetta" through which a community both acknowledges and controls the disruptive influences within it (Peter Brown, "The Rise and Function of the Holy Man in Late Antiquity," *JRS* 81 [1971] 88). In one of his treatises Cyprian says that Jesus performed exorcism and other wonders in keeping with earlier prophecy (Cyprian, *Opusc.* 6.13). In the *Epitome of the Divine Institutes* Lactantius recites Jesus' many miracles, exorcism included, and says that all were prophesied by the books of the prophets and the verses of the Sibyl (Lactantius, *Epit.* 45). Lactantius says that Jesus' miracles revealed his divine power, and that such works were the fulfillment of prophecy (Lactantius, *Inst.* 4.13). Hippolytus (170–236) relates the healing of the woman bent double in Luke 13:15–16 to the freeing from bondage in Isaiah 49:9 (Hippolytus, *Comm. Dan.* 2.18 [*ANF* 5:181]).

displays of non-Christian exorcists and divert attention away from themselves and toward the deity whom they invoke.[57] In this regard, they also differ from the glorified protagonists of the apocryphal *Acts* and early Christian hagiographies for whom exorcism serves as a sign of the true apostle or believer.

Perhaps to avoid accusations against Christian exorcists as social agitators, the apologists also downplayed their charismatic personalities. In contrast with Philostratus' portrayal of Iarchas and Apollonius, the apologists attempt to elevate the status of Christianity by locating the significance of exorcism, and of miracles in general, less in the personality of the exorcist than in the accompanying message that the exorcist brings with it. Origen (185–ca. 254) illustrates this well, and he is consistent with other apologists here in drawing upon scriptural tradition to validate Christian exorcism.[58] In *Against Celsus*,

---

[57]The Athenian apologist Aristides describes the humility of Christians in general in his address to Hadrian: "they do not proclaim in the ears of the multitude the kind deeds they do, but are careful that no one should notice them" (Aristides, *Apologia* 16, from the Syriac translation [*ANF* 10:278]). Origen says that Christian exorcists are often of plain demeanor and illiterate (Origen, *Cels.* 7.4). Arnobius counters the accusation that Jesus was a magician by distinguishing his method of miracles, exorcism included, which he performed by word, touch, and his divine nature, compared to the incantations, herbs, and divinatory methods used by the magi (Arnobius, *Adv. nat.* 1.43–45). Arnobius ranks Zoroaster among the renowned magicians, yet he challenges such legendary figures and their followers to accomplish what unlearned Christians have done by word alone (Arnobius, *Adv. nat.* 1.52). As such, Arnobius distinguishes the Christian practice from the learned, or perhaps merely pedantic practices of the magi to which the *PGM* bears witness. Eusebius notes that the apostles were of simple speech and relied on the Holy Spirit and miracles to convey the message of Christ (Eusebius, *Hist. eccl.* 3.24.3). Despite this argument for simplicity, the Christian exorcisms from this period do reveal a variety of rituals and formulae.

[58]This is reflected in the technique of exorcism, whereby Christians exorcize by reciting the name of Christ accompanied by passages from Scripture. Origen argues that the very success of Christianity testifies to the validity of Jesus' life and death as the fulfillment of earlier prophecy (Origen, *Cels.* 2.79). In keeping with the tradition of scriptural publication set by the Jews (cf. the origin of the Septuagint in the *Letter of Aristeas*), Christian Scriptures were at least made available to polytheistic audiences, even though the invitation might not have been widely accepted. At the risk of hostile interpretation by such polytheists as Celsus and Porphyry who used scripture negatively, the apologists quoted from the prophets and they referenced other parts of Scripture that validated their own belief in Christ. By this means they encouraged the critics of their faith to interpret favorably the writings by which the apologists themselves had been persuaded (e.g. Tertullian, *Apol.* 18–20; Origen, *Cels.* 5.64; Lactantius, *Inst.* 4.5; Aristides, *Apologia* 16), and even to read them for themselves (e.g. Minucius Felix, *Oct.* 33). Their apparent hope was, if not to win converts, at least to gain the respect of their critics. Irenaeus says that the Christian mission to the gentiles was more difficult than that to the Jews because it was done without the gentiles' foreknowledge of Scripture (Irenaeus, *Haer.* 4.24.2). Galen's own critique of Christianity (and Judaism) appears to have been informed by at least his partial reading of the Septuagint. Galen refers to the writings of Moses and paraphrases his style with such phrases as "God

Origen directly responds to Celsus' implication of Jesus with magic. By way of refutation Origen concedes that miracles alone cannot verify the divinity of Christ.[59] They are neutral acts, the truthfulness or deception of which depends upon the context in which they occur and the source from which they originate.[60] Origen instead emphasizes the importance of accompanying such

---

commanded," "God spoke" (Wilken, *The Christians as the Romans Saw Them*, 72). Arnobius discusses at length the misuse of Christian Scriptures by non-Christians, and their prejudice against the poor quality of its written style (Arnobius, *Adv. nat.* 1.54–59). Lactantius also laments this prejudice (Lactantius, *Inst.* 5.1; 6.21). From a later period, compare the role of Scripture in Augustine's gradual conversion from Manicheism to Christianity (e.g., *Conf.* 6.4–5, 21; 8.12).

[59]Origen, *Cels.* 2.51.

[60]In his *Commentary on the Gospel of John* Origen says that miracles were effective in their day to convert people, but now their value lies in the fulfillment of the prophecy they offer (Origen, *Comm. Jo.* 2.28), which in turn verifies their divine origin (Origen, *Comm. Jo.* 12.2). It is in *First Principles* that Origen outlines his method of exegesis based upon three levels of meaning inherent in Scripture. Listed from hierarchically least to greatest these are the corporal (literal), psychic (moral, edificatory), and spiritual (Origen, *Princ.*, Book 4). A principal for what passages require a loftier over a literal interpretation are those that are nonsensical or that contradict reason when read literally. Compare Irenaeus' suggestion that to intepret the Bible one must see a type of something else in what is otherwise morally reprehensible (Irenaeus, *Haer.* 4.31.1). Despite prohibitions against magic and his own critique of the miraculous deeds of the heretics, Origen still affirms those performed by Christians. In *Against Celsus*, Origen consistently affirms a literal interpretation of Jesus' miracles in the face of Celsus' assertion that they were the result of magical craft he had picked up while in Egypt (Origen, *Cels.* 1.38, 68). Although Origen does allegorize the healings at one point — by bringing the gospel to the people their eyes and ears are opened, and the feet of the inner man are restored to enable them to trample the serpents of the evil one (Origen, *Cels.* 2.48) — he otherwise reads exorcism and other miracles literally as historical events with analogies in his contemporary society. Jesus' name, for example, is still effective for exorcism and other powerful acts in Origen's own day (Origen, *Cels.* 1.67). Allegorical interpretation of the miracles has more relevance in Origen's commentaries, which have a different objective than does *Against Celsus* in that they intentionally seek to draw out the "spiritual" interpretation of Scripture. Even in the commentaries, however, Origen sees the literal and spiritual readings as complementary rather than conflicting interpretations, and although he does allegorize miracles in his *Commentary on the Gospel of John* — Origen interprets every healing by Jesus to refer to the healing of a disorder in the soul (Origen, *Comm. Jo.* 13.3) — Origen does not allegorize the existence of demons there. Contrast how Arnobius denies allegory to the pagans as a method of literary interpretation to dispense with the immoralities embedded in their myths (Arnobius, *Adv. nat.* Book 5). The *Clementine Homilies* attributes such a position to Appian, a friend of Simon Magus, who defends myths through allegorical interpretation (Pseudo-Clement, *Hom.* 6.2). Irenaeus suggests three criteria for determining the veracity of a miracle, exorcism included: such ought to be done through God's power, in connection with the truth, or for purposes of human well being (Irenaeus, *Haer.* 2.31.2). The pseudo-Clementine *Recognitions* makes a criterion for good miracles the benefit they bring to humanity, such as through exorcism and healing. Evil miracles are only a show which, however, when they do perchance accomplish good, reveal evil's compromised status as the demonic realm is now divided against itself (Pseudo-Clement, *Recogn.* 3.60).

works with teaching, and he identifies the source for Jesus' own miracles, exorcism included, not in the magical arts, but in the power of the Holy Spirit that Jesus received at baptism.[61] What distinguishes the miracles performed by Jesus and the disciples from those of the conjurers is the message of salvation that accompanies them.[62] In effect, those intrigued by the miracles performed by Christian missionaries were soon exposed also to the context of the Gospels, which record Jesus' power and authority through complementary words and deeds.

6.6 Exorcism as Visual Rhetoric

Christian writers adapted their gospel message to the recognized rhetoric of the day to appeal to the dominant culture, and they promoted their cause and critiqued polytheism by drawing upon the very Greek and Roman philosophers and literary figures who came out of that culture.[63] Sometimes

---

[61]Origen, *Cels.* 1.46. Origen asserts that Jesus' exorcisms demonstrate God's power at work in him (Origen, *Cels.* 2.9, 38). Among other Christian writers, Barrett-Lennard understands Irenaeus to see the ability to exorcize as a gift given by Jesus that does not signify the power of the exorcist himself (Barrett-Lennard, *Christian Healing after the New Testament*, 160).

[62]Origen, *Cels.* 2.49.

[63]Averil Cameron discusses the use of rhetoric by Christian writers to promote the spread of Christianity effectively during the second through sixth centuries: "But it is still useful and important to ask how Christians, the quintessential outsiders as they appeared to men like Nero, Pliny, Tacitus, and Suetonius, talked and wrote themselves into a position where they spoke and wrote the rhetoric of empire. For it is perfectly certain that had they not been able to do this, Constantine or no Constantine, Christianity would never have become a world religion" (Averil Cameron, *Christianity and the Rhetoric of Empire: The Development of Christian Discourse* [Sather Classical Lectures 55; Berkeley: University of California Press, 1991] 14). Robert Grant makes a premise of *Gods and the One God* that Christian doctrine was shaped by pagan thought, both in reaction to it and in using its familiar forms of expression to formulate its own distinctive doctrinal voice. Elsewhere, Grant notes that an enduring contribution made by the second century apologists to Christian thought lay in the pioneering aspect of their theological grapplings with the idiosyncracies and inconsistancies of Scripture in an effort to explain Christianity's teachings and practices to ill-informed audiences (Grant, *Greek Apologists of the Second Century*, 201–2). Robert Wilken observes that the apologists generally argued their case from reason rather than faith, and that Christianity was to great extent formed by such reasoned dialogue with its pagan critics (Wilken, *The Christians as the Romans Saw Them*, 200–1). Euhemerus (fl. early third century B.C.E.), who proposed that the gods were deified mortals, serves as one example of an earlier Greek philosopher whom the Christians utilized in their critique of polytheism. In *A Plea for the Christians* 26–28 (dated 177), Athenagoras claims that the gods of polytheism were once people whose identities had been assumed by demons. Tertullian challenges the Romans to prove that their deities are in fact gods and not merely deified humans (Tertullian, *Apol.* 10). Cyprian also traces back pagan gods to former kings (Cyprian, *Ep.* 6.1). Minucius

this is done in a scoffing manner, as when Hesiod and Homer are used to portray the foolishness and fickleness of the gods.[64] But the apologists also referred to writers whom they respected. For Lactantius, Seneca falls into this category,[65] and more importantly Cicero, whose judgment in Lactantius' opinion attained nearly the level of divine inspiration.[66] Although these earlier philosophers themselves often critiqued the polytheism that surrounded them,[67] from the Christian perspective they lacked an awareness of God and Christ to offer an alternative as viable as the apologists' own Christianity. Consequently, non-Christians also lacked the authority to exorcize since they did not have the power of Christ and the Holy Spirit with them; the name of "philosopher" is impotent in exorcism compared to that of "Christian."[68]

Apologetic literature portrays exorcism as a pedagogical tool that both educated those who witnessed it to the real identities of the exorcized demon-gods, and revealed Jesus as the divine power at work through the exorcist. Exorcism as a means of instruction in Christian mission has an analogy in rhetoric, which Averil Cameron defines as "the manner and circumstances that promote persuasion."[69] Although for the purposes of her study Cameron sets miracle-working into a separate category from rhetoric, her observations and the theory behind rhetorical criticism can be adapted to exorcism if the concept of persuasion is expanded beyond the confines of language to that of event and the meaning behind the event.[70] Accordingly, the exorcistic practice

---

Felix attributes the argument specifically to Euhemerus and other earlier persons (Minucius Felix, *Oct.* 21–22). The *Clementine Homilies* says that the gods were once tyrannical men and magicians (Pseudo-Clement, *Hom.* 5.23). In anti-heretical writings, however, Christians distanced themselves from this pagan intellectual and literary alliance, and attributed such influences to the corrupt views of the heretics. Hippolytus, for example, appears to derive the origin of thought and practice of the heresiarchs in polytheistic culture, such as in Chaldean astrology or earlier Greek philosophy, which the heretics have refashioned and attempted to pass off as their own (Hippolytus, *Haer.* 9.26). The Elchasaites, likewise, share an interest in magic with the Pythagoreans, and perform exorcisms by means of incantations, formulae, and lavations (Hippolytus, *Haer.* 9.9, 11).

[64]E.g., Justin, *1 Apol.* 25, 54; Tertullian, *Nat.* 1.10; Theophilus, *Autol.* 2.5–6, 8; Clement, *Protr.* 2, 7.

[65]E.g., Lactantius, *Inst.* 6.25.

[66]Lactantius, *Inst.* 5.23; 6.25. Lactantius' own writing skills prompted Jerome to compare his eloquence to Cicero's (Jerome, *Ep.* 58.10). Compare also where Justin finds the influence of the Holy Spirit in Plato's writings (Justin, *Cohortatio ad Graecos* 32).

[67]E.g., Tertullian, *Apol.* 46. Lactantius refers to Plato's *Timaeus*, prophecies from Hermes Trismegistus, and other ancient writers who referred to the one true God (Lactantius, *Ir.* 11).

[68]Tertullian, *Apol.* 46.

[69]Cameron, *Christianity and the Rhetoric of Empire*, 20.

[70]Cameron says of miracle-working: "Early Christianity was not purely a matter of ritual or ethical behavior, or of miracle cures done by a wonder-worker and his successors; it was always a matter of teaching, of interpretation and of definition" (Cameron, *Christianity and*

set forth in the New Testament was carried on in early Christianity as an instrument of persuasion achieved through visual proof in combination with verbal argumentation. It offered, in a sense, a visual rhetoric that drew upon scriptural imagery and typology within the Christian tradition to reveal the gospel message through sign.[71]

As Christian rhetoric incorporated the distinctive symbols, images, and typologies from its own scriptural tradition into classical literary and rhetorical forms, so, too, did the apologists attempt to identify Christian exorcism with phenomena more familiar to their polytheistic audiences while affirming its use within their own heritage. Exorcism appears to have gained its immediate and widespread popularity because it also tapped into something recognizable to Greco-Roman society. On the negative side it tapped into magic. What it attempted to tap into on the positive side, however, was the notion of divine possession long familiar to the Greeks and traceable through their own literary history. Christianity in this period defines itself to a great extent through the experience of indwelling possession. While those outside the church — whether pagan, heretical, or lapsed in faith — possessed demonic influences, those within the church possessed the Holy Spirit.[72]

---

the Rhetoric of Empire, 32). Cameron notes that Paul set as precedent for later writers "that Christianity was to be a matter of articulation and interpretation. Its subsequent history was as much about words and their interpretation as it was about belief and practice" (Cameron, *Christianity and the Rhetoric of Empire*, 11–12).

[71]Tertullian notes that earlier prophets filled with the Holy Spirit proclaimed monotheism and accompanied their message with signs (Tertullian, *Apol.* 18). Cameron notes that in certain genres, such as the *Lives* of saints, articulation fell less to argumentation than to revelation through signs and reliance on symbols. Signs and symbols offered a means of maintaining the paradoxical and mysterious aspects of the faith that otherwise defied reasoned explanation (Cameron, *Christianity and the Rhetoric of Empire*, 47).

[72]In his *Epistle to the Philippians*, Polycarp refers to heretics as the "first born of Satan" (πρωτότοκός ἐστι τοῦ σατανᾶ — Polycarp, *Phil.* 7.1), which he is also reported to have said to Marcion in person (Irenaeus, *Haer.* 3.3.4; Eusebius, *Hist. eccl.* 4.14.7). In Justin's writings persons are subject to divine or demonic influences, with the type of influence reflected in their actions (Justin, *2 Apol.* 1, 5). Thus, Justin also says that Marcion was incited by the devils to commit heresy (Justin, *1 Apol.* 58), as were the Jews to crucify Christ (Justin, *1 Apol.* 63). Irenaeus calls heretics the agents of Satan (Irenaeus, *Haer.* 3.16.1; 5.26.2). In *Antidote for the Scorpion's Sting*, Tertullian demonizes Prodicus and Valentinus in analogy with Matthew 4:10 and 16:23 (Tertullian, *Scorp.* 15). Alexander, Bishop of Alexandria (273–326), scatters language that demonizes heretics throughout his *Epistola de Ariana haeresi* (*ANF* 6:291–96). In his *Commentary on the Apocalypse of John*, Victorinus says that the arch-heretics Valentinus, Cerinthus, and Ebion are of the school of Satan (Victorinus, *Apoc. Jo.* 11.1. Compare where Irenaeus identifies "sonship" as something acquired either by birth or learning [Irenaeus, *Haer.* 4.41.2]). Later on he says that those faithful to Christ exhibit the devil bound, while those who are ensconced in vices and heresies exhibit the devil unleashed (Victorinus, *Apoc. Jo.* 20.6). Book 2 of the *Apostolic Constitutions* reveals much hostility toward heathens, Jews, and heretics, whom it labels wolves, demons, and beasts in human form (*Const. ap.* 2.21). The heretics are also called

Christianity did not seek to remove divine possession from the religious experience of the Greeks and Romans, but to disseminate that experience through baptism by offering an exchange of the polytheists' current indwelling demonic possessors with the divine Spirit of the true God. The idea of divine possession provided Christians an ethical context in which to present exorcism to their potential converts.

6.7 Possession and Ethics: The Two Ways Doctrine

It is not the act of exorcism alone, but the act in combination with the meaning of possession that becomes important in early Christianity. Exorcism came to convey a message of ethical instruction, for which it found a suitable interpretive context in the Two Ways doctrine. The Two Ways doctrine gained an increasing importance in early patristic writings and offered a pedagogical metaphor for the Christian notion of ethical possession that had precedent in both earlier Greek literature,[73] and in Jewish literature best articulated in writings from the Old Testament Pseudepigrapha.[74] The metaphor's independent history in Greek literature provided an avenue for

---

friends of Satan (*Const. ap.* 2.39), and their assemblies the synagogues of the wicked (*Const. ap.* 2.61). Book 6 refers to Simon Magus as possessed by the devil, and when Peter rebukes Simon at Rome he addresses his rebuke to the evil serpent in Simon (*Const. ap.* 6.7–8). In the same book Peter engages Simon in a competition of miracles during which Peter causes Simon's demons to depart him in mid-air so that he falls and injures himself (*Const. ap.* 6.9). Eusebius says that heretics considered themselves wiser than the Holy Spirit, but were actually possessed by demons (Eusebius, *Hist. eccl.* 5.28.18).

[73]The Two Ways doctrine has Greek literary precedent in Hesiod (*Op.* 287–92), and Xenophon (*Mem.* 2.1). M. L. West distances the metaphor from strictly ethical connotations as it appears in Hesiod, and instead sees it here to have more social and economic relevance: "κακότης and ἀρετή are not 'vice' and 'virtue' but inferior and superior standing in society, determined principly by material prosperity ..." (M. L. West, *Hesiod: Works and Days* [Oxford: Clarendon Press, 1978] 229). The metaphor finds an ethical context, however, in Xenophon, who records it as part of the sophistic teaching of Prodicus. Here Κακία and Ἀρετή personify the forces that respectively direct one toward an evil or virtuous life.

[74]The Two Ways doctrine can be discerned in Jewish literature prior to and contemporary with its appearance in Christian writings: for example, Deuteronomy 30:15–20, Psalm 1:6, Proverbs 4:10–15, *1 Enoch* 94.1–5, the third to second century B.C.E. *Pseudo–Greek Poets* (*OTP* 2:826, 828, frags. 6 and 10), 1QS 3:13–4:26, the *Sibylline Oracles* 8.399–401, and in the *Testaments of the Twelve Patriarchs* (*T. Ash.* 1.1–7; *T. Levi* 19.1–4; *T. Jud.* 20.1–5). Compare also the similar idea of two gates in the *Testament of Abraham*, one of which leads to life, the other to destruction (*T. Ab.* 11.10–12). The *Apostolic Constitutions* finds precedent for the Two Ways in Deuteronomy 30:15–20, 1 Kings 18:21, and Matthew 6:24 (*Const. ap.* 7.1).

Christians to articulate their exorcistic beliefs and practices in a context familiar to a Greco-Roman audience.[75]

The Two Ways doctrine is relevant to the study of possession and exorcism because, in the course of its employment in Christian texts, the paths of the Two Ways become less significant than the spiritual influences that guide one along them. These figures come even to be seen to inhabit the person and through their indwelling to influence one's ethical behavior. The Two Ways doctrine finds its earliest articulations in Christian writings in the *Didache* (1–6),[76] *Barnabas* (18–21),[77] and the *Doctrina Apostolorum*.[78] The

---

[75]M. Jack Suggs notes the commonplace observation of the Two Ways concept: "The metaphor of 'two paths' is such a natural rhetorical device that it should be obvious that considerably more than metaphor itself is needed to establish connections" (M. Jack Suggs, "The Christian Two Ways Tradition: Its Antiquity, Form, and Function," in *Studies in the New Testament and Early Christian Literature: Essays in Honor of Allen P. Wikgren*, David Edward Aune, ed. [NovTSup 33; Leiden: Brill, 1972] 63). Consequently, he sets forth a literary pattern for the Two Ways form as found in the earliest Christian examples: sharply dualistic introduction; lists of "virtues" and "vices"; concluding eschatological admonition (Suggs, "The Christian Two Ways Tradition," 64). By means of these criteria he distinguishes between the Old Testament form of the doctrine (Deut 30:15–20; Jer 21:8; Ps 1:1, 6; Prov 2:12–15), and the "sharply dualistic construction" that one first comes across in Qumran's *Community Rule* (1QS 3.13–4.26). Suggs sees 1QS 3.13–4.26 to function "as a kind of homiletic exhortation concerned with group identity" (Suggs, "The Christian Two Ways Tradition," 68) that would serve the same purpose for the Hellenistic Jewish Christian audience of earliest Christianity (Suggs, "The Christian Two Ways Tradition," 74).

[76]The estimated date of composition for *Didache* ranges from the second half of the first century to the mid-second century. Juan José Ayán Calvo supports an early date, and prefers to assign *Didache* to ca. 70 C.E. based upon: the teleological substratum of the eucharistic prayer; the still prevalent ministry of the apostles, prophets, and teachers; the pre-Matthaean character of the dominical sayings and instructions; the lack of allusions to heresies such as gnosticism or doceticism (Juan José Ayán Calvo, *Didaché, Doctrina Apostolorum, Epístola del Pseud-Bernabé* [Fuentes Patrísticas 3; Madrid: Editorial Ciudad Nueva, 1992]). Kurt Niederwimmer allows for a 110–120 date for the final redaction based upon what he considers a lack of compelling arguments that would dismiss such a conclusion (Kurt Niederwimmer, *The Didache: A Commentary* [Hermeneia; Minneapolis: Fortress, 1998] 52–54). Others date the *Didache* in its present form to after *Barnabas* (post 130) while allowing its source materials, such as the Two Ways, an earlier date (William R. Schoedel, "The Apostolic Fathers," in Eldon J. Epp and George W. MacRae, eds., *The New Testament and Its Modern Interpreters* [Philadelphia: Fortress, 1989] 468).

[77]The ca. 130 date for the composition of *Barnabas* is more secure than estimates for the *Didache*. *Barnabas*' anticipation of an imminent rebuilding of the Jerusalem Temple (*Barn.* 16.3–4) places it somewhere between the Temple's destruction in 70 C.E., and the hopes for its rebuilding in 130, prior to the Bar Kokhba Revolt (132–135 C.E.) (Schoedel, "The Apostolic Fathers," 468).

[78]Suggs notes that of the *Didache*, *Barnabas*, and *Doctrina*, the *Doctrina* was "most widely circulated in ancient times" (Suggs, "The Christian Two Ways Tradition," 71). The date at which the Two Ways teaching came into Latin, and whether *Doctrina* represents the first and most influential manifestation of such, remains unclear. Ayán Calvo sums up the

conclusion that the three texts draw independently from a Greek source, itself drawn from a Jewish formulation, has met with general support.[79]

---

situation in this way: "The Greek text [of the *Doctrina*] which survived on the basis of the Latin translation is, at least, earlier than the *Didache*. Nevertheless, to determine the date of the Latin translation is most difficult." (*El texto griego que sirvió de base a la traducción latina es, pues, anterior a la* Didaché. *Sin embargo, determinar la fecha de la traducción latina es más problemático.*) (Ayán Calvo, *Didaché, Doctrina Apostolorum, Epístola del Pseud-Bernabé*, 116). Berthold Altaner observes that the first solid evidence for citations from *Doctrina* by Latin authors does not appear until the third century (Berthold Altaner, "Zum Problem der lateinischen Doctrina Apostolorum," *VC* 6 [1952] 160–67). Edgar J. Goodspeed argues that *Doctrina*, *Barnabas*, and *Didache* represent independent versions of a common early second century Greek source, itself derived from a Jewish *Vorlage* (Edgar J. Goodspeed, "The Didache, Barnabas, and the Doctrina," *ATR* 27 [1945] 228–47). Goodspeed notes that *Doctrina*'s brevity relative to the other two goes counter to the early Christian tendency to expand upon literary themes, and so suggests its closer adherence to the original Greek.

[79]The "Two Ways" doctrine appears in several other early Christian writings, most of which are manifestly influenced by the *Didache*, *Barnabas*, or *Doctrina*. Thus, the fourth century *Apostolic Constitutions* retains the Two Ways doctrine in its expansion of the *Didache* (*Const. ap.* 7.1–21). The early fourth century *Apostolic Church Ordinances* (or *Ecclesiastical Canons of the Holy Apostles*), likely of Egyptian provenance, also begins with the Two Ways formula (Johannes Quasten, *Patrology* [4 vols.; Westminster, Md.: Christian Classics, 1950–1994] 2:119–20). This work attributes sins of the soul generally to demonic possession, and the emotions of wrath and desire specifically to male and female demons who, if allowed to join with the human soul (ψυχή), will bring in other demons besides (*Eccl. ap.* 7–9). Suggs considers the idea to originate in Judaism, and to have entered Christian literature even in the first century. Thus, he sees a parallel in Galatians 5:17–24, with its dualistic introduction of spirit and flesh, the double catalogue, and its eschatological threat and promise (Suggs, "The Christian Two Ways Tradition," 69). Willy Rordorf argues that the Two Ways doctrine entered into Christianity through two Jewish traditions of thought. He sees the New Testament's ethical dualism as found in Pauline and Johannine writings to have precedent in Qumran literature, and its non-dualistic ethics as found in the synoptic gospels to have precedent in the Old Testament covenant formula (*Bundesformular*). Of these, the *Didache* follows the non-dualistic heritage, while *Doctrina* and *Barnabas* follow the dualistic branch (Willy Rordorf, "An Aspect of the Judeo-Christian Ethic: The Two Ways," in *The* Didache *in Modern Research*, Jonathan A. Draper, ed. [AGJU 37; Leiden: Brill, 1996] 153). Sebastian Brock likewise argues that Christianity's interpretation of the Two Ways shows evidence of having originated out of both the traditional and sectarian Jewish perspectives of the metaphor: "Thus, whereas the *Didache* harks back more or less directly to Deut. 30.15–19, fused with Jer. 21.8 (as also witnessed in the Palestinian Targum tradition), the *Doctrina Apostolorum* and *Barnabas* do so only indirectly, by way of the intrusion of the non-biblical moral opposition of light and dark, also to be found in 1QS" (Sebastian Brock, "The Two Ways and the Palestinian Targum," in *A Tribute to Geza Vermes: Essays on Jewish and Christian Literature and History*, Philip R. Davies and Richard T. White, eds. [JSOTSup 100; Sheffield: Sheffield Academic Press, 1990] 143).

The *Didache* describes two ways, of life and death.[80] Although a divine presence accompanies one along the way of life,[81] the *Didache* offers little suggestion that demons play a direct role in contrary human actions. Instead, the way of death represents more the absence of God than the presence of a demonic guide.[82] The *Didache* places the Two Ways instruction within the context of a pedagogical process, specifically as catechesis prior to baptism. Through its juxtaposition of demonic with divine possession, the Two Ways doctrine offers a theological basis for exorcism before baptism, a ritual that itself places the initiates in a point of time that necessitates their renunciation of evil in favor of a commitment to God.[83] Exorcism before baptism is, in fact,

---

[80]"There are two ways, one of life and one of death" (ὁδοὶ δύο εἰσί, μία τῆς ζωῆς καὶ μία τοῦ θανάτου — *Did.* 1.1. English translation in *The Apostolic Fathers*, translated by Kirsopp Lake [2 vols. LCL; New York: MacMillan, 1924–25]).

[81]"... for where the Lord's nature is spoken of, there is he present" (ὅθεν γὰρ ἡ κυριότης λαλεῖται, ἐκεῖ κύριός ἐστιν — *Did.* 4.2 [Lake, LCL]).

[82]Although the advice to flee from "every evil one and everyone like him" (παντὸς πονηροῦ καὶ ἀπὸ παντὸς ὁμοίου αὐτοῦ — *Did.* 3.1) may refer to demons, it is just as conceivable that humans are intended here (similarly for *Did.* 6.1). Compare other ambiguous passages, such as the *Didache*'s "free us from (the) evil (one)" (ῥῦσαι ἡμᾶς ἀπὸ τοῦ πονηροῦ — *Did.* 8.2) in its version of the Lord's Prayer, which suggests the satanic agent in Matthew's version of the same (ἀλλὰ ῥῦσαι ἡμᾶς ἀπὸ τοῦ πονηροῦ — Matt 6:13); the Eucharistic prayer that asks God to "release [the church] from every evil" (τοῦ ῥύσασθαι αὐτὴν ἀπὸ παντὸς πονηροῦ — *Did.* 10.5); and "the deceiver of the world" (ὁ κοσμοπλανὴς), who will appear as a son of God but will lead people astray in the concluding apocalypse (*Did.* 16.4).

[83]Origen also sees exorcism as a pre-baptismal ritual, more relevant to the period of catechesis. This leads him to distinguish between Christianity and polytheism in the value Christianity bestows upon the worthiness of the healed in addition to the character of the healer. Thus, whereas the mystery cults invite even the wicked to be healed, Christianity only admits the purified (Origen, *Cels.* 3.25). Willy Rordorf notes that "the rite of renunciation of Satan the *abrenuntiatio* during the baptismal cermony implies the existence of a prior ethical instruction," such as the Two Ways satisfies: "... there was, without doubt, an uninterrupted tradition of prebaptismal ethical instruction in the Christian church of the first two centuries, a tradition which has its roots in Judaism, which has its *Sitz im Leben* in the context of the initiation of Gentile converts, and which led to the institution of the Christian catechumenate at the end of the second century. The *duae viae* has its place in this tradition" (Rordorf, "An Aspect of the Judeo-Christian Ethic," 158–59). Although Rordorf acknowledges that this renunciation is missing in the *Didache*, and remains otherwise unattested until the end of the second century, he considers it: "... unthinkable that one could have created, at the end of the second century, a rite of renunciation of Satan, of his angels and his works, a rite which expresses a very marked eschatological dualism. This rite must be connected to a Jewish and Jewish Christian dualistic conception, to which was attached in its turn ... certain forms of the *duae viae*. But the right [*sic*] of renunciation of Satan implies the existence of a prior ethical catechesis" (Rordorf, "An Aspect of the Judeo-Christian Ethic," 158).

evident in orthodox tradition as early as the third century in the writings of Cyprian.[84]

Like the *Didache, Barnabas* describes the two ways in terms of light and darkness.[85] *Barnabas*, however, assigns angels of light and of darkness to each of the two ways, respectively, so that the doctrine takes on spiritual embodiments.[86] *Barnabas* 16 portrays demons dwelling in one before belief in God, and the indwelling of God after one comes to faith. Consequently, rather than initiation, *Barnabas'* doctrine appears in a context of secondary instruction for those already baptized,[87] and it evokes the complementary

---

[84]Cyprian, *Ep.* 75.15–16. Based in part upon the gospel's dominical commands to exorcize and baptize (Matt 10:8; 28:19; Mark 16:17), the Seventh Council of Carthage (258) viewed exorcism as a preliminary step toward the re-baptism of heretics (PL 3.1089–1116; *ANF* 5.565–72). Dölger considers the practice consequently to have been in place at least by the first half of the third century (Dölger, *Exorzismus im altchristlichen Taufritual*, 17). Although Tertullian mentions exorcism on numerous occasions, including prior to baptism in *De corona militis* 3.4 (written 211), Dölger notes that it is noticably absent from his *De baptismo* (ca. 200–206), a treatise otherwise devoted to the subject (Dölger, *Exorzismus im altchristlichen Taufritual*, 14–17. For references to exorcism elsewhere in Tertullian's writings, see *Praescr.* 41 [ca. 200] and *Idol.* 11 [ca. 211]). Exorcism also appears before baptism in the *Apostolic Tradition*, the final redaction of which, however, may date to the early fourth century (see Chapter 1, note 32). The earliest evidence for the existence of baptismal exorcism in the eastern church appears in the early third century East Syrian *Acts of Thomas*, where exorcism takes place before the baptismal "sealing" (σφραγίς) (*Acts Thom.* 157. Cited in Dölger, *Exorzismus im altchristlichen Taufritual*, 12).

[85]"There are two ways of instruction and authority, that of light and that of darkness" (ὁδοὶ δύο εἰσὶν διδαχῆς καὶ ἐξουσίας, ἥ τε τοῦ φωτὸς καὶ ἡ τοῦ σκότους — *Barn.* 18.1). *Barnabas* also calls the way of darkness "the black way" (τοῦ μέλανος ὁδός — *Barn.* 20.1). Cf. the exhortation "that the Black One may have no opportunity of entry" (ἵνα μὴ σχῇ παρείσδυσιν ὁ μέλας — *Barn.* 4.9 [Lake, LCL]).

[86]"For over the one are set light-bringing angels of God, but over the other angels of Satan. And one is Lord from eternity to eternity, and the other is the ruler of the present time of iniquity." (ἐφ' ἧς μὲν γάρ εἰσιν τεταγμένοι φωταγωγοὶ ἄγγελοι τοῦ θεοῦ, ἐφ ' ἧς δὲ ἄγγελοι τοῦ σατανᾶ. καὶ ὁ μέν ἐστιν κύριος ἀπὸ αἰώνων καὶ εἰς τοὺς αἰῶνας, ὁ δὲ ἄρχων καιροῦ τοῦ νῦν τῆς ἀνομίας — *Barn.* 18.1–2 [Lake, LCL]). Compare also the "innerworking one" (αὐτοῦ τοῦ ἐνεργοῦντος) who has authority while the days are evil (*Barn.* 2.1), and "the evil one" (ὁ πονηρός) who threatens "deceitful entry" (παρείσδυσιν πλάνης) into the believer (*Barn.* 2.10). He is also called "the evil ruler" (ὁ πονηρὸς ἄρχων — *Barn.* 4.13). In contrast, the author himself claims to have attained his own understanding by accompanying the Lord in the way of righteousness (*Barn.* 1.4).

[87]Jonathan Draper argues that *Barnabas* has turned the earlier catachetical context for the Two Ways as found in the *Didache* into post-baptismal instruction intended only for a select few. The author's introduction to the doctrine as "another knowledge and teaching" (ἑτέραν γνῶσιν καὶ διδαχήν — *Barn.* 18.1) reveals it as a higher gnosis beyond, if not superfluous to, catechetical instruction (Jonathan A. Draper, "Barnabas and the Riddle of the Didache Revisited," *JSNT* 58 [1995] 89–113, 110). In an excursus on "Barnabas, the Two Ways and Polemic," James Carlton Paget responds to Draper's interpretation, and suggests

metaphor of the body as a temple of God to describe their possession of the Holy Spirit.[88] In this regard, *Barnabas* foreshadows later orthodox arguments against the Gnostic belief of simultaneously indwelling good and evil spirits.

Like *Barnabas*, the *Doctrina* also assigns spiritual overseers to the Two Ways. The *Doctrina* begins:

> In the world there are two ways:
> of life and of death,
> of light and of darkness.
> Two angels were appointed over these:
> one of equity,
> the other of inequity.[89]

The *Doctrina* then sets forth the characteristics of each way. The way of life consists both of prohibitions against wrongful behavior and exhortations to do good, as typified by the commandments to love God and neighbor. The way of death constitutes the juxtaposing vices.

More so than the *Didache*, *Barnabas*, or the *Doctrina*, the *Testaments of the Twelve Patriarchs*, a pseudepigraphic work perhaps from the end of the second century of the Common Era, exemplifies well the emphasis upon the

---

that the inclusion of the Two Ways at the end of *Barnabas* could rather "reinforce his strong commitment to the ethical dimension of Christianity" set forth throughout the previous chapters of the epistle (James Carleton Paget, *The Epistle of Barnabas: Outlook and Background* [WUNT 2.64; Tübingen: Mohr ((Siebeck)), 1995] 49–51). Reider Hvalvik sees the Two Ways in *Barnabas* to promote its cause as a letter of Christian self-definition, written for the Christian community in an effort to distinguish itself from Judaism: "The contrast between the two peoples and the Two Ways is in fact a governing idea throughout the letter — and serves to promote the right choice between Judaism and Christianity. That is the purpose of *Barnabas*" (Reider Hvalvik, *The Struggle for Scripture and Covenant* [WUNT 2.82; Tübingen: Mohr ((Siebeck)), 1996] 204). Hvalvik considers the "semantic field" of the Two Ways doctrine, explicitly stated in *Barnabas* 18–20, with vocabulary such as "way and walking," "life and death," "salvation and destruction/death," "righteousness and sin, evil, and going astray" to occur in relation to one another throughout the epistle (Hvalvik, *Struggle for Scripture and Covenant*, 64). Accordingly, whereas from the Jewish perspective the way of darkness constituted paganism, from the perspective of *Barnabas* it constitutes Judaism (Hvalvik, *Struggle for Scripture and Covenant*, 143).

[88] *Barn.* 16.7–10.

[89]   *Viae duae sunt in saeculo,*
    vitae et mortis,
    lucis et tenebrarum.
    In his constituti sunt angeli duo,
    unus aequitatis,
    alter iniquitatis. (*De Doctrina Apostolorum* 1.1–7).
Goodspeed includes the Latin *Doctrina*, and English translations of *Didache* and *Barnabas* in his synopsis of the Two Ways (Goodspeed, "The Didache, Barnabas, and the Doctrina," 238–47).

spirits over against the ways.[90] Although Two Ways language does appear here,[91] the document shows greater interest in the idea of two spiritual influences at work upon the individual. This emphasis on possession as an inner struggle relates demonic influence to a context not so much concerned with physical afflictions, but with ethical decision making. The *Testament of Judah* expresses well this twofold understanding of the human situation:

two spirits await an opportunity with humanity: the spirit of truth and the spirit of error. In between is the conscience of the mind which inclines as it will.[92]

---

[90]H. W. Hollander and M. de Jonge's extensive study of the internal and external evidence associated with the *Testaments of the Twelve Patriarchs* has led them to conclude that the extant work "functioned meaningfully in Christian circles at the end of the second century A.D." (H. W. Hollander and M. de Jonge, *The Testaments of the Twelve Patriarchs: A Commentary* [SVTP 8; Leiden: Brill, 1985] 83). Although this does not preclude the possibility of a Jewish *Vorlage* — and parallel ethical concepts may indeed be found in earlier Jewish and hellenistic writings — Hollander and de Jonge argue that by this date such parallels could have as easily been drawn from prior Christian writings. De Jonge observes of the entwined Jewish-Christian(-Greek) heritage of the *Testaments*' ethical instruction: "The Testaments give, first and foremost, ethical instruction — influenced by the Psalms and the Wisdom books of the LXX; the Cynic-Stoic philosophical tradition and early Christian sources offer many parallels. In the field of ethics there has been a considerable measure of continuity between Hellenistic Judaism and certain circles in early Christianity. Many utterances in the Testaments are Jewish as well as Christian, and at the same time acceptable to Hellenistic fellow-citizens of Jews and Christians" (Marinus de Jonge, "The So-Called Pseudepigrapha of the Old Testament and Early Christianity," in *The New Testament and Hellenistic Judaism*, Peder Borgen and Søren Giversen, eds. [Aarhus: Aarhus University Press, 1995] 70; see also, M. de Jonge, "The Transmission of the *Testaments of the Twelve Patriarchs* by Christians," *VC* 47 [1993] 19–22). With reference to parallels between the *Testaments* and New Testament literature, see M. de Jonge, "Light on Paul from the *Testaments of the Twelve Patriarchs*," in *The Social World of the First Christians: Essays in Honor of Wayne A. Meeks*, L. Michael White and O. Larry Yarbrough, eds. [Minneapolis: Fortress, 1995] 100–15).

[91]The *Testament of Asher* 1.3–9 refers to "two ways" (δύο ὁδοί) of good and of evil that God has given to humanity, of which Beliar controls the way of evil.

[92]δύο πνεύματα σχολάζουσι τῷ ἀνθρώπῳ τὸ τῆς ἀληθείας καὶ τὸ τῆς πλάνης· καὶ μέσον ἐστὶ τὸ τῆς συνέσεως τοῦ νοός, οὗ ἐὰν θέλη κλῖναι (*T. Jud.* 20.1–2; trans. Kee [*OTP*]; Greek text in M. de Jonge, *The Testaments of the Twelve Patriarchs: A Critical Edition of the Greek Text* [PVTG; Leiden: Brill, 1978]). To this we can compare the "soul" (ψυχή) as the place of residence and control for both the Lord and Beliar in the *Testament of Dan* (*T. Dan* 4.7). In contrast, Suggs cites the *Testament of Asher* as a case where human intentions are in conflict within the individual, rather than spiritual powers: "The genre has been ethicized and relatively demythologized" (Suggs, "The Christian Two Ways Tradition," 68). Yet, it is precisely through ethics and the Two Ways ethical metaphor that Christianity maintains its mythological heritage by providing a venue for spiritual beings to interact with human beings.

As a malady takes on a demonic persona in the cases of physical possession, the *Testaments* shows how the passions can also become demonized to affect moral judgment.[93]

The apologists also employ the Two Ways doctrine in their arguments, and they do so in such a way that its ethical concerns interact with the apologists' interest in exorcism. For Justin, exorcism implies a judgment against the demons, that is, those angels and angelic offspring who work against God's creation in an abuse of their freedom of choice.[94] It is in the intimation of the eternal punishment due the demons that we find Justin's *raison d'etre* for exorcism: as exorcism is the judgment against and the fate imagined for the demon that rebels against the divine will, so, too, does the same divine

---

[93]We see this where the *Testaments of the Twelve Patriarchs* mentions seven spirits of error or deceit — the spirits of promiscuity, insatiability, strife, flattery/trickery, arrogance, lying, and injustice — that commingle in the human body with seven other spirits — the spirits of life, sight, hearing, smell, speech, taste, and procreation — necessary for sustaining human life (*T. Reu.* 2.1–3.7). Of the first three deceitful spirits the author writes: First, the spirit of promiscuity resides in the nature and the senses. A second spirit of insatiability, in the stomach; a third spirit of strife, in the liver and the gall ..." (πρῶτον τὸ τῆς πορνείας ἐν τῇ φύσει καὶ ταῖς αἰσθήσεσιν ἔγκειται· δεύτερον πνεῦμα ἀπληστίας ἐν τῇ γαστρί· τρίτον πνεῦμα μάχης ἐν τῷ ἥπατι καὶ τῇ χολῇ ...) (*T. Reu.* 3.3–4; trans. Kee). To these seven, the spirit of sleep acts as an accomplice that causes error and delusion. In the *Testament of Judah*, desire, heated passion, debauchery, and sordid greed are four evil spirits that reside in wine, and invade the person who drinks too much (*T. Jud.* 16.1–4). The spirit of deceit enters into the "mind" (νοῦς) in cases of drunkenness (*T. Jud.* 14.8). The spirit of error is associated with Beliar in the *Testament of Judah* 25.3. Spirits are the cause of sin in the *Testament of Dan* 5.6. In the *Testament of Joseph* a spirit is associated with lust (*T. Jos.* 7.1–8). In the *Testament of Issachar* spirits of "deceit" (πλάνη) corrupt the "mind" (νοῦς) (*T. Iss.* 4.4). In the *Testament of Zebulon* people are susceptible to spirits of deceit because they are "flesh" (σάρξ) (*T. Zeb.* 9.7). In the *Testament of Naphtali* those who do not do what is good "the devil will inhabit him as his own instrument" (ὁ διάβολος οἰκειοῦται αὐτὸν ὡς ἴδιον σκεῦος) (*T. Naph.* 8.6; trans. Kee). The testaments also include language suggestive of divine possession, as where the *Testament of Benjamin* says that the Lord "dwells in [the good person]" (ἐν αὐτῷ κατοικεῖ) (*T. Benj.* 6.4).

[94]Justin, *2 Apol.* 5. For reason of their decision to choose evil, Justin makes the Jews and polytheists guilty of the same abuse of free will as the demons (Justin, *Dial.* 140–41). Tertullian also exhibits an interest in the role of human decision making in a dualistic cosmos. In *The Soul*, likely a pre-Montanist work, he speculates that the human soul exists independently of the Holy Spirit or Satan but that either of these two can come to influence it (Tertullian, *An.* 11, 16). In Tertullian's view sin is not natural to humanity, but has been instigated by the serpent (Tertullian, *An.* 21), and it is the devil that continues to encourage human sinfulness. Compare in his *Apology* where Tertullian envisions the demons as swift, winged spirits that manipulate deception through prophetic half-truths, and who afflict humanity out of hatred and jealousy (Tertullian, *Apol.* 27).

rejection await the unrepentant evil person.[95] By placing exorcism within a moral framework Justin uses exorcism to illustrate the fate of evil humanity, of those who willingly choose evil over good and vice over virtue. Justin relates his notion of free will in Greek literary terms by referring to Heracles' encounter with Virtue and Vice at the divided road, a *topos* that first enters Greek literature in Xenophon's retelling of Prodicus' parable.[96]

Lactantius also uses exorcism as a means of indoctrinating his audience both to a new cosmogony and to the dualistic hierarchies sprung from Near Eastern precedent. The essential dualism of Lactantius' belief is captured in a recurrent theme in *The Divine Institutes* that "There is no virtue if an adversary is wanting."[97] In Lactantius' view, the devil punishes evil persons, but strengthens the patience and endurance of those who are righteous. Lactantius' juxtaposition of virtue and vice leads him to present the Two Ways doctrine in Book 6, where he compares the Christian teaching to its non-Christian counterpart. Lactantius finds the principal difference to lie in Christianity's assigning to God and the devil the role of guides along the paths of good and evil, respectively, while the pagan version assigns a guide only along the way of good. From this we see how prominent, even essential, the concept of evil becomes to understanding the *modus operandi* for Christian exorcism according to Lactantius, for whom error involves an intentional misleading.[98] For Lactantius, Christianity needs a demonic adversary in opposition to the salvation given by God.

6.8 Heresy and the Further Articulation of Spiritual Possession

To some extent, the utility of miracle-working in Christian mission, exorcism included, was sabotaged by its abuses or misuses within the Christian communities themselves. Consequently, exorcism and the character of the exorcist are also recurrent issues in heresiological writings. Although orthodox writers acknowledged that heretics did perform exorcisms, they attributed

---

[95] Justin, *2 Apol.* 8. Justin draws upon Matthew's references to the casting out from the Kingdom of God into the outer darkness to apply both to the demons and those unworthy of salvation (Justin, *Dial.* 76; cf. Matt 8:11–12).

[96] Justin, *2 Apol.* 11.

[97] *virtus nulla sit, si adversius desit* (Lactantius, *Inst.* 3.29; 6.15; *ANF* 7.99, 180; PL 6.443, 689). In Book 7 Lactantius states a similar essential juxtaposition by which wisdom cannot exist without evil, so that each gives the other its value (Lactantius, *Inst.* 7.5). Yet, he considers this situation as temporary. Lactantius sees his own moment in time to fall within the thousand year period when the devil is let loose and the righteous are persecuted; a time that will be followed by God's judgment and the vindication of the righteous (Lactantius, *Epit.* 72). Lactantius' eschatology envisions an immortal existence free from evil and wisdom alike, since at that time all will be ignorant of evil (Lactantius, *Inst.* 7.5).

[98] Lactantius, *Inst.* 6.3–7.

their authority for doing so to demonic forces rather than to the power of God.[99] The intra-Christian debate that heresiology involved has bearing upon Christian mission relative to the proper representation of Christ's name before non-Christians: by their illegitimate miracles and false teachings, the heretics slandered the Church and tarnished the reputations of true believers.[100]

Heresiology also provides a context for debating the subtleties of demonic and divine states of possession that lead to a further articulation of humanity's relationship to good and evil spiritual forces. The Pauline metaphor of the human body as the temple of God that earlier helped to articulate this relationship in the New Testament also appears in a variety of contexts in early patristic literature. It appears occasionally in apologetic writings, where it is used primarily to establish a basis of common belief between Christians and non-Christians as to the nature of the human being and the possibility of divine possession.[101] It finds more frequent reference,

---

[99]Justin links the prophet's ability both to foretell future events and to work miracles with the same inner-working of the Holy Spirit. When false prophets attempt the same they do so through demons of error (Justin, *Dial.* 7). Tertullian says that exorcism is even performed by female heretics, apparently in disparaging trivialization of heretical practices compared to those he favors (Tertullian, *Praescr.* 41). Early Christian writings point especially toward Simon Magus as an archetypal practitioner of magical deception in the name of Christ, and whose followers are also said to have included exorcism in their magical repertoire (e.g. Justin, *1 Apol.* 26, 56; Irenaeus, *Haer.* 1.23.4). Irenaeus charges that miracle workers such as Simon perform their wonders through demons and Satan in order to deceive and to swindle their victims from their financial resources; if Simon and others do exorcize it is only because they have first sent the demons into the victims of demonic possession (Irenaeus, *Haer.* 2.31.2). This charge against heretics (and pagans) is inconsistent with Irenaeus' interpretation elsewhere in *Against Heresies*, where he appears to consider physical illness or disability a consequence of humanity's disobedient nature (Irenaeus, *Haer.* 5.15.2; cf. 5.12.6). Thus, the paralytic of Matthew 9:6 suffers as a result of his own sin (Irenaeus, *Haer.* 5.17.2). Certain maladies may even be due to God, who makes this an opportunity to heal publicly, such as the case with the man born blind (Irenaeus, *Haer.* 5.15.2; cf. John 9:1–41). By this unfortunate argument Irenaeus puts Christian miracle workers into the similar position he earlier sought to place the heretical magicians: they cast out demons or rid maladies that they have first implanted in their victims.

[100]Hippolytus, *Haer.* 7.20.

[101]For example, Tatian argues that the Christians follow Greek philosophical views that the human being consists of soul and flesh, but he adds that those whom God favors, namely the Christians, also permits them to serve as temples that house God's spirit (Tatian, *Oratio ad Graecos* 15). Origen responds to Celsus' claim that Christians build no temples to their God by belittling the polytheistic practice and comparing their temples to prisons in which the demons are confined and where their lusts are satisfied by sacrifices (Origen, *Cels.* 7.35; cf. Arnobius, *Adv. nat.* 6.3–7). He later upholds it as a Christian belief both as a metaphor of divinity joining with the individual believer, who is consequently required to lead a virtuous life, and as an image of corporate divine possession (Origen, *Cels.* 8.19–20). Although Tertullian sees the body to constrain the soul, he contrasts the Greek belief that sees the soul fully imprisoned by it (Plato, *Phaedo* 62.6) with Paul's view of it as a temple (Tertullian,

however, in heresiologies and other writings that promote orthodoxy and orthopraxy. In these contexts the metaphor only infrequently represents the corporate church.[102] Instead, it is more commonly used to identify the individual believer and to argue for the need to lead a pure life that maintains the sanctity of the Holy Spirit's residence.[103] In this respect the exhortation also comes to advocate asceticism and mortification of the flesh, and often it does so by claiming the Pauline usages of the temple metaphor as the archetypal basis for such guidance.[104]

The ethics of early patristic writers tend to emphasize free will at work in a dualistic cosmos, so that states of both sinfulness or sanctification lie within human potential. Clement of Alexandria articulates this well in the course of his conflict with Gnosticism concerning the freedom of the human will. Although Clement upholds the independence of the will either to strive toward God or regress toward the demons, he also sees this independence as

---

An. 53). Compare also where Justin Martyr claims to find common ground with Judaism in the belief that bodies serve as "residences" (οἰκοί) for the spirit of God, and that Adam was created for this reason (Justin, *Dial.* 40).

[102]Lactantius, for example, sees the temple of God manifest in the catholic Church rather than in heretical gatherings (Lactantius, *Inst.* 4.30). Although he upholds the body-as-temple image elsewhere (e.g. Lactantius, *De mortibus persecutorum* 15 [*ANF* 7:306]; cf. *Inst.* 2.13, where he calls the body a "temporary residence" [*domicilio temporali*]), he also adopts Seneca's teaching that the human heart serves as a more appropriate metaphor of the divine residence and the place where humanity and divinity merge rather than to think of the body as a temple. As such, Lactantius emphasizes the activities that take place within the sanctuary — namely in the "gift" (*donum*) and "sacrifice" (*sacrificium*), which for the Christian translate into innocence, and praise and hymnody — instead of the maintenance of the temple itself (Lactantius, *Inst.* 6.25; cf. *Ir.* 23).

[103]Cyprian, for example, uses the metaphor frequently in the writings he addresses to fellow believers. In his *Epistles* he uses it as an encouragement to adorn the body-temple with precious virtues (Cyprian, *Ep.* 1.15; cf. *Opusc.* 10.14), and to preserve its sanctity by avoiding sinful activity (Cyprian, *Ep.* 51.27). Adherence to the faith also retains the Holy Spirit's presence within, and when faith fails the Holy Spirit departs and the devil returns (Cyprian, *Ep.* 75.15–16; cf. *Const. ap.* 6.27).

[104]In Book 5 of *Against Heresies*, Irenaeus expands upon his understanding of the corporal merger of the Holy Spirit with the human being. Drawing upon Pauline precedents (e.g., 1 Cor 3:16; 2 Cor 12:7–9; Eph 5:30), Irenaeus argues against docetic and Ebionite views that would deny the possibility for divinity to participate in human flesh, and claims the temple of God metaphor as an appropriate representation of how this participation can be envisioned (Irenaeus, *Haer.* 5.2.1–9.4). Irenaeus argues for the exclusivity of divine or demonic occupancy of the person (Irenaeus, *Haer.* 5.12.1), so that in order to maintain the Holy Spirit within requires one to maintain the body-temple's purity (Irenaeus, *Haer.* 5.9.4). This leads to a consequent argument for the mortification of the flesh, which Irenaeus also justifies through Paul (Col 3:5; Irenaeus, *Haer.* 5.12.3). For other early patristic uses of the temple of God metaphor to justify asceticism, see Tertullian, *The Apparel of Women* 2.1; *Apostolic Constitutions* 4.14; Pseudo-Clement, *Epistles to the Virgins* 1.12, and *Recognitions* 4.17.

susceptible to spiritual influences that incline a person toward one or the other goal.[105] Clement considers Christians to have God constantly with them, and he consequently rejects the possibility of Satan dwelling within the human being once the body has become the residence of the Holy Spirit. Instead, sinfulness in Clement's view is due to one's lack of self-discipline and obedience rather than to one's nature, and he cites *Barnabas* as proof that sins, not demons, occupy the human body-temple of God.[106] Clement's position comes in response to Valentinus (fl. 138–158) and Basilides (fl. 120–145), who taught that evil spirits occupy the soul as passions.[107] Whereas Valentinus considered good and evil spirits to coexist within the person, Clement argues that one comes to possess either a demon or the Holy Spirit through one's own actions. Clement contends that those who sin become like demoniacs, but do so of their own choosing, not because of a pre-existing demonic spiritual presence within them. To say otherwise is to say that they are guiltless of their sins, a conclusion to which he sees the Valentinian doctrine to lead.[108]

A similar notion of free will appears in the writings of Clement's contemporary Irenaeus (ca. 140–ca. 202), Bishop of Lyon, and fellow spokesperson for "orthodox" Christianity. Irenaeus' work *Against Heresies* provides him a forum not only for dismantling the beliefs of the heretics, but for stating his own as he has learned them from his predecessors. For Irenaeus

---

[105]Clement, *Strom.* 1.17 (*ANF* 2:319); 4.26 (*ANF* 2:440); 6.12 (*ANF* 2:502); 7.11 (*ANF* 2:541). This view also appears in the *Testaments of the Twelve Patriarchs*, which portrays the moral character as being influenced by and acquiescing to, on the one hand, spirits of Beliar-Satan and, on the other, those of God (*T. Jud.* 20.1–5). Compare where the spirit of deceit and envy is driven away when one turns to the Lord (*T. Sim.* 3.1–6).

[106]Clement, *Strom.* 2.20 (*ANF* 2:372). Clement also refers to the body as the temple of God in *Exhortation to the Greeks* 11. In *Stromata* Book 4 Clement argues that sin is an activity not an existence (Clement, *Strom.* 4.13 [*ANF* 2:426]).

[107]Clement, *Strom.* Book 2. Though in the course of this conflict Clement attempts to reclaim "gnostic" as an appellation for the Christian, since in his opinion the heretics do not have true knowledge (Clement, *Strom.* 2.20 [*ANF* 2:370]), elsewhere he claims virtue as the objective of pedagogy rather than the acquisition of intelligence (Clement, *Paed.* 1.1–2). As a physician is a healer of bodies, the pedagogue is a healer of souls, who heals the soul of its disease of sins and passions (Clement, *Paed.* 1.1–2).

[108]Clement, *Strom.* 6.12 (*ANF* 2:502). Compare also Archelaus who, in his polemic against Manichaeism, attributes evil not to the devil, but to the freedom granted to the will (Archelaus, *Acta disputationis cum Manete* 15 [*ANF* 6:189]). Ioan Couliano locates the first appearance of dualistic possession in *Pistis Sophia* 111–115, where the breath of the Holy Spirit and a spark of the Pleroma (the "Fullness," as the sum of all hypostases) exist in the human body along with an evil spirit (Ioan P. Couliano, *The Tree of Gnosis: Gnostic Mythology from Early Christianity to Modern Nihilism* [San Francisco: HarperCollins, 1992] 102). For the exchange of spiritual dependencies, compare the Messalians, first mentioned around 370, who believed that evil abides in the human as a demon and only after three years of prayer is expelled and replaced by the Holy Spirit (Couliano, *The Tree of Gnosis*, 34).

there is one Creator and one creation within which evil exists as the product of choice and free will.[109] In Book 5 Irenaeus denies that divine and demonic states of possession can co-exist within the body. He argues instead for exclusive states of divine or demonic possession, with the former condition true of the Christian and the latter of the heretic.[110]

Origen, a student of Clement and his successor at the catechetical school in Alexandria, also expresses his views on the freedom of the will in *First Principles*. Origen divides demonic possession into those who suffer complete domination by evil forces, as in the New Testament stories of exorcism, and those who succumb to evil influences that lead to sin, as in the case of Judas.[111] Rather than demons as the cause of sin, Origen maintains humanity's

---

[109]Irenaeus says that evil, whether done by the devil, angels, or humanity is done from free will (Irenaeus, *Haer.* 4.41.1), and that the same destiny of fire and darkness awaits them all (Irenaeus, *Haer.* 4.40.1–2).

[110]In the first half of Book 5 of *Against Heresies*, Irenaeus argues against the Ebionite view that divinity cannot merge with humanity. Instead, it is possible for the Holy Spirit to take up residence in the Christian, whose purified body serves as a temple of God (Irenaeus, *Haer.* 5.6.1–2). In contrast with the Christians, Irenaeus considers Gnostics to be filled with a satanic spirit for reason of their apostasy from the Creator (Irenaeus, *Haer.* 5.26.2). The Montanist controversy also serves as a good case in point. In the 170's the Asian bishops excommunicated Montanus and his followers, whose prophetic spirit they interpreted to be of demonic rather than divine origin. Asterius Urbanus (ca. 232) distinguished the "spurious ecstasy" (ἐν παρεκστάσει) of the leaders of this movement from the Old Testament and New Testament prophetic traditions (Asterius Urbanus, *Fr. Mont.* 9 [PG 10:153–56; *ANF* 7:337]). When Montanus appealed his case to the western episcopacies, Irenaeus led the successful effort at Rome to uphold the earlier ruling. Once excommunicated, the Montanists were thereafter subject to exorcism for their demonic possession (Lane Fox, *Pagans and Christians*, 407–8; cf. Eusebius, *Hist. eccl.* 5.16.6–19.4). Exorcism may be implied when Montanus is "rebuked" (ἐπετίμων) by those who first hear his prophecy and consider him possessed by demons (Asterius Urbanus, *Fr. Mont.* 2 [PG 10:147–50; *ANF* 7:335]).

[111]Origen, *Princ.* 3.3.4. These divisions anticipate the corporal and ethical types of demonic possession identified by Dölger. Origen also says that one's state of demonic or divine possession can occur as early as the womb, and he refers to John the Baptist as one divinely so possessed, and to others who are born into a state of demonic possession (Origen, *Princ.* 3.3.5). Compare Augustine's later distinction between two types of "unclean spirit" that suggests a continuing belief in demonic possession as a physiological affliction as well as an ethical one: the invasive spirit subject to exorcism, and the impure soul defiled by sin (Augustine, *Beat.* 18; trans. Mary T. Clark, *Augustine of Hippo: Selected Writings* [New York: Paulist Press, 1984] 184). Compare also Augustine's rebuttal to the philosophical claim that true goodness is found in the human being: "What shall I say of those who are afflicted by attacks of demons? In what hidden or submerged places do their intellects lurk, when the evil spirit is using their souls and bodies according to its own will?" (*Quid dicam de his, qui daemonum patiuntur incursus? Ubi habent absconditam vel obrutam intellegentiam suam, quando secundum suam voluntatem et anima eorum et corpore malignus utitur spiritus?*) (Augustine, *Civ.* 19.4. English translation in Augustine, *The City of God against the Pagans*, translated by William Chase Greene et al. [7 vols. LCL; Cambridge: Harvard University Press, 1960]). Here, Augustine uses demonic possession as

free will as the seat of responsibility for whether one follows the divine calling or succumbs to temptation.[112] It is not surprising, then, to find an ethical concern in the text, and a reference to *Barnabas'* Two Ways teaching with its angels of light and darkness as guides.[113] The importance that these early patristic authors bestow upon the freedom of the will lends import to the decision and commitment necessary for one to convert to Christianity, and adds further incentive for the inclusion of exorcism in the third century baptismal ceremony.

6.9 Exorcism and Initiation

The exorcisms described in the New Testament dealt with physiological rather than ethical concerns. Writings from the later Old Testament Pseudepigrapha also associate exorcism with physiological possession. The driving out of demonic influences that involves inner human conflict rather than physical or emotional disturbances is less an exorcistic act that requires a mediator between the victim of possession and the divine relief-bringing power, than a means of personal spiritual purification. In the *Testaments of the Twelve Patriarchs* seeking the Lord and loving others causes the evil spirit to depart,[114] and a divestiture of envy and hardness of heart leads to domination over the evil spirits.[115] There also the Anointed One shall bind Beliar, and "grant to his children the authority to trample on wicked spirits."[116] Issachar

---

part of his contemporary parlance to create an example for non-Christians. In his biography of Augustine, Peter Brown compares the belief in demons in Augustine's day to our own sense of fear at "the presence of myriads of dangerous bacteria. The 'name of Christ' was applied to the Christian like a vaccination" (Peter Brown, *Augustine of Hippo: A Biography* [Berkeley: University of California Press, 1967] 41).

[112]Origen, *Princ.* 3.2.4. Although *First Principles* is only partly preserved, and that mainly through Latin translation, it is interesting that exorcism, apart from those performed by Jesus, makes no appearance in the extant text. Where references to Jesus' exorcisms do occur, Origen finds in them evidence of the unseen adversaries against whom humanity struggles (Origen, *Princ.* 3.2.1–2). This offers insight into his sense of humanity's place in the dualistic cosmos of good and evil hierarchies that he sets forth in Book 1. In the good hierarchy God, Jesus Christ, and the Holy Spirit, are good by nature. Otherwise, the angels and demons that populate the good and evil orders respectively are good or evil by choice, and it is only through their conscious efforts that they abide in the one or the other realm. Humanity constitutes a third order of rational creatures who, with the encouragement of the angels, makes moral progress toward the good, yet whose intermediary status makes it subject also to the temptations of demons.

[113]Origen, *Princ.* 3.2.4.

[114]*T. Sim.* 3.1–4.9.

[115]*T. Sim.* 6.1–7.

[116]δώσει ἐξουσίαν τοῖς τέκνοις αὐτοῦ τοῦ πατεῖν ἐπὶ τὰ πονηρὰ πνεύματα (*T. Lev.* 18.12; trans. Kee). Cf. *T. Zeb.* 9.8.

advises his children that, should they live a life of piety as he has, "every spirit of Beliar will flee from you, and no act of human evil will have power over you."[117] Further, in a passage similar to Jesus' parable of the returning demon, *Psalms of Solomon* says:

> ... sin after sin does not visit the house of the righteous.
> The righteous constantly searches his house,
>   to remove his unintentional sins.
> He atones for (sins of) ignorance by fasting and humbling his soul,
>   and the Lord will cleanse every devout person and his house.[118]

Here, a constant personal vigil keeps one's body inwardly pure. Nevertheless, it is the ethical aspect that came to dominate the responsibilities of the exorcist-as-office-holder in the church, especially in the areas of catechesis and baptism.

Exorcism appears to have developed its ethical concern correlative to the association of baptism with the invocation of the Holy Spirit.[119] As an

---

[117]πᾶν πνεῦμα τοῦ Βελιὰρ φεύξεται ἀφ ' ὑμῶν, καὶ πᾶσα πρᾶξις πονηρῶν ἀνθρώπων οὐ κυριεύσει ὑμῶν (*T. Iss.* 7.7; trans. Kee. Cf. *T. Benj.* 5.2).

[118]... ἐν οἴκῳ δικαίου ἁμαρτία ἐφ ' ἁμαρτίαν· ἐπισκέπτεται διὰ παντὸς τὸν οἶκον αὐτοῦ ὁ δίκαιος τοῦ ἐξᾶραι ἀδικίαν ἐν παραπτώματι αὐτοῦ. ἐξιλάσατο περὶ ἀγνοίας ἐν νηστείᾳ καὶ ταπεινώσει ψυχῆς αὐτοῦ καὶ ὁ κύριος καθαρίζει πᾶν ἄνδρα ὅσιον καὶ τὸν οἶκον αὐτοῦ (*Pss. Sol.* 3.6–8; trans. R. B. Wright, "Psalms of Solomon," *OTP* 2). The psalms date to the first century C.E. (R. B. Wright, "Psalms of Solomon," *OTP* 2:640–41).

[119]Baptism underwent significant embellishment in early Christianity to become an initiation rite and the hinge between the exorcism of demonic possessors and the invocation of the Holy Spirit. There are two conflicting views of exorcism's relationship to baptism. On the one hand, Dölger posits exorcism as a later addition to the baptismal ceremony, and suggests that exorcism of corporal possession faded from the Christian landscape until the point of its virtual replacement by its ethical counterpart that became consolidated in the baptismal ceremony; a consolidation made possible by early Christianity's association of sin with Satan (Dölger, *Exorzismus im altchristlichen Taufritual*, 25–38, 127). On the other hand, Otto Böcher considers Christian baptism essentially to have been an exorcistic ritual of purification, despite the early theologians' best efforts to evoke from it a higher sense: "[Baptism] is simply an exorcistic sacrament of the old church; the fear of demons ... is stronger than the awareness of the new freedom sent by God. The second hand interpretations of baptism, especially by Paul, are re-transformed into rites, and the protest of the New Testament against an understanding of baptism as a material lustration (1 Peter 3:21) went unheeded." (*Sie [die Taufe] wird zum exorzistischen Sakrament der alten Kirche schlechthin; die Dämonenfurcht ... ist stärker als das Bewusstsein der gottgeschenkten neuen Freiheit. Die vor allem von Paulus gebrauchten Bilder für die Taufe werden in Riten zurückverwandelt, und der Protest des Neuen Testaments gegen ein Verständnis der Taufe als einer dinglichen Lustration [1 Petr 3,21] verhallt ungehört.*) (Böcher, *Christus Exorcista*, 318–19). Adela Yarbro Collins' own study of the origins of Christian baptism appears to offer a compromise between these differing opinions by seeing sinfulness as an original cause for the baptism administered by John, which Dölger sees later to have been

initiation rite, baptism appears originally to have implied a sense of renunciation and commitment.[120] As exclusion from and membership in the Christian community came to be identified with demonic and divine states of spiritual possession, exorcism and invocation became the rituals for renunciation and commitment respectively: exorcism as the renunciation of

---

personified by Satan. According to Yarbro Collins, John's own baptism, which served as precedent and model for Christian baptism, was steeped in prophetic symbolism that reinterpreted the sense of defilement in ethical terms as sinfulness from which one needed cleansing in anticipation of a coming judgment by God, "the day of the Lord" (Adela Yarbro Collins, "The Origin of Christian Baptism," in Maxwell E. Johnson, ed., *Living Water, Sealing Spirit: Readings on Christian Initiation* [Collegeville, Minn.: Liturgical Press, 1995] 47).

[120]The scriptural portrayals of baptism at the Jordan provide the basis for viewing baptism either as a catharsis (consistent with John's message of remission of sins), or for the bestowal of charisma (the descent of the spirit upon Jesus). Acts' use of the phrase "into the name of Christ" (Acts 2:38) or "into the name of the Lord Jesus" (Acts 19:5) suggests baptism as an initiation ceremony to be more a ritual of commitment to a life in Christ than an invocation of the Holy Spirit per se. Although Acts uses the phrase "baptised with the Holy Spirit" on several occasions (Acts 1:5; 11:16; 19:1–7), in Acts 2:38 Peter's command to "be baptized" (βαπτισθήτω: aorist imperative) followed by the future tense of the verb "to receive" (λήμψεσθε) indicates that baptism anticipates the reception of the Holy Spirit, but does not itself accomplish it. Acts further distinguishes between baptism and invocation of the Holy Spirit, where Philip baptizes the Samaritan believers, but Peter and John bestow upon them the Holy Spirit by a separate action of laying on of hands (Acts 8:14–17). The distinction between what baptism accomplishes and what is accomplished by the imposition of hands is critical here for denying that Simon Magus ever possessed the Holy Spirit despite his baptism by Philip (Acts 8:13). Compare also the case of the heretic Novatian (Novatus), who, during a severe illness, received baptism but not the Holy Spirit, and was, in fact, considered a demoniac by those who opposed him (Eusebius, *Hist. eccl.* 6.43.13–15). Laying on of hands is the means by which the Holy Spirit is conveyed not only at reception into the church (Irenaeus, *Haer.* 4.38.2; Tertullian, *Res.* 8 and *Bapt.* 8; Origen, *Princ.* 1.3.2; anonymous, *Treatise on Re-baptism* 3 [*ANF* 5:668]; *Const. ap.* 2.32, 41), but also at the bestowal of ordination to each of the clerical ranks as described in the *Apostolic Tradition.* Compare Cyprian's story of a woman who received a demon while at the bath and died as a result. By contrasting this event to her having received the Holy Spirit at her baptism, Cyprian highlights the exchange of spiritual dependencies and suggests baptism as the ritual that bestows the Holy Spirit (Cyprian, *Opusc.* 3.24). Elsewhere, Cyprian interprets baptism as an exorcistic washing away of a demonic presence (Cyprian, *Ep.* 75.15–16). The invocation of the Holy Spirit comes about through the separate stages of prayer, imposition of hands, and sealing (Cyprian, *Ep.* 72.6, 9; 73.7). 1 Corinthians 12:13 offers the most tantalizing evidence for baptism as an invocation ceremony in the New Testament, where Paul, perhaps in allusion to the waters of baptism, describes those who are baptized as "drinking in" (ἐποτίσθημεν) the one spirit. Hermann Gunkel cites 1 Corinthians 12:13 (cf. 6:11) as evidence for Paul's belief that the Holy Spirit was conveyed through baptism. Gunkel also notes, however, that Galatians 3:2 offers a different interpretation, whereby the spirit is conveyed through "hearing with faith" (Hermann Gunkel, *The Influence of the Holy Spirit: The Popular View of the Apostolic Age and the Teaching of the Apostle Paul: A Biblical-Theological Study* [Philadelphia: Fortress, 1979] 91).

former things that prepares for the invocation of the Holy Spirit as a partial fulfillment of the promises of a life in Christ.[121]

This shift in ritual context from healing to initiation also underscores the exorcist's transformation from a charismatic personality, in the sense of one invested with authority directly from God, to a representative of authority bestowed by the church.[122] This clericalization of the exorcist, however,

---

[121]Exorcism's role in baptism goes beyond our stated interests to the extent that it concerns catechumens who have already committed themselves to the church rather than its potential converts. In her work on baptismal exorcism, Leeper has observed that the incorporation of exorcism into the process of Christian catechesis arose from the perceived need to purify the catechumens from their prior devotions to the deities of pagan cults (Leeper, *Exorcism in Early Christianity*, 271–73). Several early patristic writers attest to exorcism as part of the convert's re-orientation from a life of idolatry to a life in Christianity, which reveals the tensions between their own beliefs and pagan culture. In *Miscellanies* 2.13 Clement speaks of repentance from a polytheistic lifestyle, as well as a repentance of the soul for one to make way for faith (Clement, *Strom.* 2.13 [*ANF* 2.360–61]). On the *Public Shows*, attributed to Cyprian, associates the devil and demons with public entertainments (Cyprian, *De spectaculis* 4). The author would prefer Christians to read Scripture instead, which humbles the devil before Christ (Cyprian, *De spectaculis* 10). In the pseudo-Clementine *Recognitions* Peter tells Clement that he will not dine with pagans until they have had the unclean spirits of polytheism removed through baptism (Pseudo-Clement, *Recogn.* 2.71–72). Elsewhere, the text identifies idolatry as the inroad of demonic influence upon the individual, so that by avoiding idolatry one not only avoids this influence, but also receives the ability to drive it away from others (Pseudo–Clement, *Recogn.* 4.14). Compare Book 8 of the *Apostolic Constitutions*, where magicians, amulet makers, and users of magical verses must prove that they have abandoned these practices before their baptism into the church (*Const. ap.* 8.32).

[122]In his work on early ordination rites, Paul Bradshaw notes a pattern evident from the end of the first century that shifts divine authority from one's charismatic disposition toward a given office, to the bestowal of charisma through ordination (Paul Bradshaw, *Liturgical Presidency in the Early Church* [Grove Liturgical Study; Bramcote, Notts.: Grove Books, 1983] 9–13). What has been observed for ordained offices in general, others have pursued of the office of exorcist in detail. The earliest evidence for exorcism as an office in western Christianity comes from a letter sent to Cyprian by the confessors (Cyprian, *Ep.* 16 [dated 250]), and Cornelius' letter to Fabius (dated 251) as recorded in Eusebius, *Hist. eccl.* 6.43.11 (Thraede, "Exorzismus," *RAC* 7:74–75). Thraede concludes that the western church led the push toward exorcism's status as an office, while in the east the practice continued on as a free charisma until the beginning of the fourth century (Thraede, "Exorzismus," *RAC* 7:72–75). According to Thraede, the impetus for this transformation locates within the intra-mural debates in Christianity's developing sense of orthodoxy rather than as an adaptation to the sensibilities of pagan sceptics. Thraede argues that as Christian doctrine developed in apposition to heresy, so, too, did exorcism's regulation come about through its perceived misuse in heretical circles. According to Thraede, orthodox Christianity attempted to distinguish its own exorcistic practice from that of the heretics by making it a regulated office based upon liturgy, Scripture, and dogma rather than "folk superstition" (*Volkaberglauben*) and gnosis (Thraede, "Exorzismus," *RAC* 7:113). Leeper also understands exorcism to have undergone a process of "institution building," through which exorcism increasingly concedes its original basis as a charisma to an office authorized by the church. She cites the bishop's

appears to play a complementary role in the history of Christian exorcism rather than an exclusionary one. By performing exorcism in the baptismal ceremony, Christians now apply the practice of exorcism to the ethical context of Christian initiation, and consequently to an area of theological speculation that had otherwise not been exposed to it in the New Testament.[123] Although the role of the exorcist can be seen to have become

---

role in the *Apostolic Tradition* as evidence that the "charismatic gift of discernment of spirits mentioned earlier [e.g. 1 Cor 12:10] has not only been institutionalized; it has been subsumed by the highest ecclesiastical office" (Leeper, *Exorcism in Early Christianity*, 304). Exorcism as seen in the *Apostolic Tradition* came to imbue the initiate with respect for the authority of the bishop and, hence, a respect for ecclesiastical authority, as it was the bishop who performed the climactic exorcism and gave final approval for entry into the Christian community (Leeper, *Exorcism in Early Christianity*, 273). As a consequence, this "routinization of charisma" (Leeper, *Exorcism in Early Christianity*, 293), that is, the transfer of charisma from the individual to an office, marks a significant change in exorcistic practice as the church became the mediated source of the exorcist's divine power.

[123]The influences that led to exorcism's attachment to baptism, and the consequent shift in the perception of demonic possession from a physiological problem to an ethical one, have been seen as an abberation from mainstream Christian theology and practice, with origins instead in Gnostic theology. According to Thraede, it is in the gnostic attempt to disentangle humanity's divine nature from its demonic nature, a dual-nature first advanced by Valentinus (fl. 138–158), that constitutes the theological underpinnings of the baptismal exorcism (Thraede, "Exorzismus," *RAC* 7:79–84). Leeper follows Thraede's argument, and has attempted to identify Valentinus as "the conduit between Alexandria and Rome," whose own teachings on the importance of pre-baptismal exorcism contributed to the "longstanding tradition" which Hippolytus describes for the Roman church some sixty years later in the *Apostolic Tradition* (Leeper, *Exorcism in Early Christianity*, 248; this assumes the traditional date of composition in 214). Leeper bolsters her assertion by identifying commonalities between the *Apostolic Tradition* and the *Excerpts* preserved of Theodotus, a student of Valentinus' at Alexandria. (For relevant quotations from the *Excerpts*, see above, Chapter 1, note 31). A redating of the *Apostolic Tradition* to the early fourth century (see above, Chapter 1, note 32) need not derail her central argument for a Valentinian source of the orthodox rite. Leeper admits that her interpretation rests on tenuous evidence (Elizabeth A. Leeper, "From Alexandria to Rome: The Valentinian Connection to the Incorporation of Exorcism as a Prebaptismal Rite," *VC* 44 [1990] 20), yet, it is a constructive hypothesis, and one that gains plausibility with the recent efforts to reclassify Valentinus within the realm of orthodoxy. Valentinus appears to have received the label of arch-heretic only after or near the end of a life of devoted service to the orthodox church that had until then recognized him as a distinguished teacher first in Alexandria and then in Rome. Christoph Markschies, for example, argues that Valentinus was not a Gnostic, but a Platonizing biblical exegete whose ideas were later connected into a mythological Valentinianism by Ptolemaius (Christoph Markschies, *Valentinus Gnosticus? Untersuchungen zur valentinianischen Gnosis mit einem Kommentar zu den Fragmenten Valentins* [WUNT 65; Tübingen: Mohr, 1992]). For a general study of the relationship between orthodoxy and heresy, compare Walter Bauer's thesis that heresy in many regions was the original manifestation of Christianity rather than a development out of orthodoxy (Walter Bauer, *Orthodoxy and Heresy in Earliest Christianity* [Philadelphia: Fortress, 1971] xi). Even in the New Testament writings Christianity appears to advance ahead of its own named apostles: for example, the anonymous exorcist who casts

increasingly institutionalized in ecclesiological writings such as the *Apostolic Tradition*, evidence for the continuation of charismatic exorcism does occur in other types of literature, so that instead of a narrowing of contexts and applications for practicing exorcism its use in baptism represents an addition to the exorcist's repertoire.

6.10 The Continuation of Charismatic Exorcism: Pseudepigraphy and Hagiography

Exorcism proceeds into the first centuries of Christian development under a dominical mandate for the disciples to employ it in their mission of spreading the message of Christ throughout the world.[124] The closest parallels to the New Testament stories of exorcism may be found in those patristic writings that share the biographical and narrative interests of the gospels and Acts, and that highlight similar disciple-like figures. For the most part, references to charismatic exorcism continue in the fictive realms of the later Old Testament Pseudepigrapha,[125] the New Testament apocryphal *Acts*,[126] and the hagiographical *Lives* that concerned inspirational church leaders.[127] These writings were likely written by the faithful for the faithful, as they offer a familiar literature with predictable themes and scenarios earlier established by

---

out demons in Jesus' name apart from his following (Mark 9:38–40//Luke 9:49–50); Philip and the Ethiopian eunuch (Acts 8:26–40); Peter and Cornelius (Acts 10:1–48); Paul writing to a church already established at Rome (Romans 1:13). From later Christian writings compare Peter's follow-up to Simon Magus' earlier arrival in Rome (Pseudo-Clement, *Recogn.* 3.63).

[124]Mark 16:15–18. Compare from the *Epitome of the Divine Institutes*, where Lactantius says that Jesus breathed the Holy Spirit upon his disciples to enable them to work miracles in their mission (Lactantius, *Epit.* 47).

[125]Exorcism tends to appear in the apocalyptic and testamentary writings from this collection that are attributed to the Common Era and, whether or not of Christian origin, have undergone Christian redaction in their received forms. Passing references to exorcism appear in the *Apocalypse of Elijah* (I–IV C.E.), which notes that fasting can drive out demons (*Apoc. El.* [C] 1.21) and that exorcism will be an activity of the antichrist (*Apoc. El.* [C] 3.10). The *Testament of Jacob* (ca. II–III) says that the ability to exorcize is achieved through leading a religious life (*T. Jac.* 7.17). The *Testament of Adam* (II–V) refers to Jesus' exorcisms (*T. Adam* 3.1), and it may also refer to the use of oil in exorcism (*T. Adam* 2.10).

[126]Exorcism appears prominently in the second and third century apocryphal *Acts* (e.g. *Acts Andr.* [*NTAp.* 2:123–28, 135–39]; *Acts Paul* 10 [*NTAp.* 2:259]; *Acts John* 41, 57; *Acts Pet.* 11; *Acts Thom.* 43–46, 75–81), and the later fifth century *Acts of Pilate* (*Acts Pil.* 1.1; 6.1; 8.1; 14.1; 4[20].1). *NTAp.* refers to Wilhelm Schneemelcher, ed., *New Testament Apocrypha* (rev. ed., 2 vols.; Louisville: Westminster/John Knox Press, 1992).

[127]For example, see below for references to exorcism in Athanasius' *Life of Antony* and Gregory of Nyssa's *Life of Gregory Thaumaturgus*.

Scripture that both reinforced existing beliefs and appealed to Christian devotion and spirituality.[128]

Whereas the authors of the apocryphal *Acts* expanded upon the portrayals of the disciples in the New Testament, those of the hagiographical biographies tended to incorporate the analogous activities of Jesus and the disciples into the lives of their own revered contemporaries or the recently departed.[129] Both the apocryphal *Acts* and the *Lives* offer their stories of exorcism in similar literary forms as one finds for them in the synoptic tradition.[130] They

---

[128]Averil Cameron notes that the apocryphal *Acts* of the second and third centuries, and their successors, the fourth through sixth century *Lives* of saints, offer paradigms for action (Cameron, *Christianity and the Rhetoric of Empire*, 89). Of the *Acts* she says, "The apocryphal *Acts* cannot be marginalized; they too were integrally related to the general culture of the second and third centuries. But more specifically, they provided for Christians a set of texts in which the Christian self was expounded, first in narrative terms and then in terms of asceticism; the writing of Christian texts would shape Christian lives" (Cameron, *Christianity and the Rhetoric of Empire*, 116). Of the lives of saints Cameron says, "Sacred lives functioned as ideological and literary exemplars" intended to inspire their readers to such like actions as the piety and asceticism of their heroes (Cameron, *Christianity and the Rhetoric of Empire*, 145). Ramsay MacMullen also sees Scripture and the apocryphal writings to have been written chiefly for the Christian community (MacMullen, *Christianizing the Roman Empire*, 20–21). The *Lives* were a genuinely popular literature that both appealed to all classes of society, and also afforded the theologians who authored them an opportunity to disseminate their Christian ideals to a far broader audience than would have otherwise read their theological writings (e.g. Athanasius's *Life of Antony*; Gregory of Nyssa's *Life of Gregory Thaumaturgus*, Jerome's lives of Paul the First Hermit, Hilarion, and Malchus). Cameron notes the popularity of the *Life of Antony*, which was promoted by Jerome, and was read in the highest Roman circles after its translation into Latin only ten years after its original composition in Greek (Cameron, *Christianity and the Rhetoric of Empire*, 113).

[129]To some extent the importance of the dominical example can be discerned from the similarity of exorcistic methods between early Christian exorcists and the portrayals of Jesus and the disciples in the synoptic authors. S. Vernon McCasland observes that although the gospels portray Jesus as the one who commanded the disciples to include exorcism in their missionary work, it is the disciples themselves, in their use of the name of Jesus to perform exorcisms, who serve as the paradigm for the practice in early Christianity (McCasland, *By the Finger of God*, 111). McCasland refers to Justin (*2 Apol.* 6; *Dial.* 76, 85), Tertullian (*Apol.* 23), Irenaeus (*Haer.* 2.32.4), Origen (*Cels.* 1.6, 68; 2.33; 5.2; 7.4), Lactantius (*Inst.* 2.16; 5.22), and Augustine (*Civ.* 22.8) as early Christian writers who portray exorcism similarly to New Testament practice (McCasland, *By the Finger of God*, 55–56). In contrast, Thraede sees apologists like Irenaeus and Justin to portray exorcism after the model of Hellenistic-Jewish aretalogies (Thraede, "Exorzismus," 71). Although arguments for both scriptural and hellenistic paradigms can be made due to the lack of any clear prescription for exorcism in the New Testament, the hellenistic parallels tend to appear in post-New Testament times, and are themselves likely to have been influenced by a familiarity with Jewish and Christian writings and practices.

[130]The previous chapter mentioned Rudolf Bultmann's six typical features of the New Testament exorcism story: 1) encounter with the demoniac; 2) description of the affliction; 3)

also tend to follow the New Testament exorcism stories by highlighting the exorcists and their message rather than those who are freed from demonic possession. As such, exorcisms are performed not for their own sake, but to legitimize the exorcists as envoys of Christ in whom the Holy Spirit dwells and to illustrate or punctuate their preaching.[131]

---

demon recognizes the exorcist and offers resistance; 4) exorcism; 5) expulsion of the demon accompanied by a sign of its departure; 6) impression left upon the spectators. Several passages from the apocryphal *Acts* and early Christian hagiographies contain these primary elements in their own exorcism stories. The *Life of Antony*, for example, contains many exorcism stories that reveal similarities of presentation with those in the New Testament, and there is a summary of Antony's exorcism compared to Christ's mandate in *Life of Antony* 83–84. Compare, for example, Antony's rebuke of an evil spirit of a youth in the name of Jesus Christ (Athanasius, *Vit. Ant.* 63), which Barrett-Lennard calls "a classic case of exorcism," replete with New Testament terminology (Barrett-Lennard, *Christian Healing after the New Testament*, 244). Compare also Antony's exorcisms in Chapter 48 (Martinian's daughter), Chapter 64 (a young man), Chapter 71 (a young girl), and Chapter 80 (several demoniacs). These exorcism stories tend to place Antony in public settings where his exorcisms are done through calling upon the name of Christ, prayer, and making the sign of the cross. The miracle stories associated with Gregory Thaumaturgus (ca. 213–270), a student of Origen's at Caesarea, and later Bishop of Neo-Caesarea in Pontus, also illustrate the influence of the New Testament. Although Gregory's own writings reveal little of the miracles later attributed to him, his biographer, Gregory of Nyssa (ca. 335–394), sprinkles miracles that include exorcisms throughout his own tribute. The miracle stories as they appear here generally follow the essentials of presentation seen in the synoptic writings, and they also contribute to the preaching, discerning, directing, and teaching of Gregory's public ministry (e.g. Gregory of Nyssa, *Vita Gregorii Thaumaturgi* 47). Other examples of exorcism stories in early Christian writings that follow New Testament paradigms include the *Acts of Andrew* [*NTAp.* 2:135–36], Cyprian's account of a woman possessed of a prophetic demon (Cyprian, *Ep.* 74.10), Lactantius' reference to a Christian who exorcizes a priest of Apollo that results in his inability to divine (Lactantius, *Inst.* 4.27; cf. the exorcism of the slave girl in Acts 16:16–18), and passages in the *Recognitions* (Pseudo-Clement, *Recogn.* 4.7; 9.38).

[131]In the *Life of Antony*, Antony's exorcisms differ from those in the New Testament in their application to ethical possession. Antony heals not by playing the part of Jesus, but through prayer and speaking Jesus' name. It is not the Christian who performs wonders, but Christ through the Christian. Barrett-Lennard finds in *Life of Antony* 56 the epitome of the author's "theology of healing" (if not Antony's as well), where the ability to heal and healing itself derive from God: those cured praise God, not the healer; those not cured live in consolation of the words of healing and learn patience (Barrett-Lennard, *Christian Healing after the New Testament*, 185). To this qualification note also *Life of Antony*'s agreement with the critique of exorcism offered in Matthew 7:22 and Luke 10:20 (Athanasius, *Vit. Ant.* 38). Although Antony attains a reputation for exorcism and other wonders, the biographer emphasizes that what is truly important is not Antony's wonders, but his virtue, and by extension the virtue of the Christian. Compare also the pseudo-Clementine *Recognitions*, which illustrates how Peter's ability to exorcize proves his faith (Pseudo-Clement, *Recogn.* 5.2), and validates his teaching (Pseudo-Clement, *Recogn.* 10.70–71).

What these texts lack with respect to historical credibility they make up for in their contribution to our understanding of popular theological perceptions. In spite of any formal influence, the underlying eschatology of the synoptic exorcisms that both anticipated the overthrow of Satan and was reinterpreted in early Christianity during times of persecution recedes to the background in Christian hagiography. Instead, passions are the spiritual powers against which humanity struggles,[132] which the later hagiographical writings portray as chronic foes to be engaged repeatedly in battle. In hagiography the idea of demonic possession becomes a matter of personal struggle with evil: as external reifications of inward temptations, the demons test the resolve of the pious and thereby strengthen that resolve.[133]

The struggle between the human will and the will of the demon seen in the earlier heresiologies anticipates the engagements between the early eremitic ascetics led by Antony and their temptations by hostile spirits.[134] In the *Life*

---

[132]Early indications of the demonization of the passions appear in the writings of Cyprian, who equates such human emotions as jealousy and envy with the inner workings of the adversary (Cyprian, *Opusc.* 10.1). The association of sin with Satan, and the metaphor of Christ as the physician who heals one from sin is found throughout Clement of Alexandria's *Paedagogus*, in which he also calls passions a disease of the soul (Clement, *Paed.* 1.2). Origen also finds intemperance, negligence, or sloth to afford the opportunity for demonic intrusion (Origen, *Princ.* 3.3.5). Compare also Lactantius, who personifies the three corrupting affections of anger, desire, and lust, as Furies (Lactantius, *Inst.* 6.19). The pseudo-Clementine *Recognitions* teaches that doing good and living in moderation keep evil away and permit God to dwell within. Otherwise, demons find inroads through excess and evil actions, which enable them to enter a body where they remain to corrupt the soul (Pseudo-Clement, *Recogn.* 4.15–18). Compare also Gregory Thaumaturgus, who at one point in his extant writings compares envy to a wicked spirit, and so internalizes spiritual possession as an ethical concern (Gregory Thaumaturgus, *Metaphrasis in Ecclesiasten Salomonis* 4). Compare also the passage quoted above in Chapter 5, note 213, from the life of Pityrion (ca. 400) that equates demonic possession with the passions (Pityrion 15.2–3; *Hist. mon.* 110).

[133]The theology behind such perceptions of demonic possession appears early on, where Tertullian asserts God's sovereignty by saying that demons possess only with God's permission and that such possession strengthens the endurance of holy men (Tertullian, *Fug.* 2 [dated ca. 208]). Tertullian makes much of the distinction between one's being handed over to Satan for the punishment of unpardonable sins (e.g. Hymenaeus and Alexander in 1 Tim 1:20), and Paul's own affliction by an angel of Satan as a means for edification: "Hold my grace sufficient; for virtue is perfected in infirmity" (*Satis habe gratiam meam; virtus enim in infirmitate perficitur* — 2 Cor 12:9; referred to in Tertullian's *Pud.* 13 [dated as early as 208]; PL 2:1058). At a later date Lactantius argues that persecution benefits the persecuted because it has the potential to prove the loyalty of Christians to God and to strengthen them in their faith (Lactantius, *Inst.* 5.23). Compare the pseudo-Clementine *Recognitions*, which says that demonic possession and other maladies are caused by demons that serve through their maliciousness to strengthen the righteous (Pseudo-Clement, *Recogn.* 9.8).

[134]Compare also the *Narrative of Zosimus on the Life of the Blessed*, a work that in its original form perhaps dates to 250, which says that Zosimus' cave was a place of healing for sick pilgrims, but of trial for himself. The devil and 1,360 demons abuse Zosimus for forty

of Antony, written ca. 356–362 and attributed to Athanasius,[135] the biographer records Antony as the object of hatred by the devil and demons because of his virtue. Compared to the public settings of the exorcism stories in the New Testament and those before pagan audiences in the apologies, Antony's temptations tend to take place in isolation. His victories over the demons serve as examples for the Christian ascetic and spiritualist rather than for public display.

This early form of Christian asceticism transforms the earlier battles against civil persecution, as seen earlier with Cyprian, into personal confrontations with the demonic hierarchy. As a consequence, asceticism's role in exorcism acquires an increasing importance in early Christianity,[136] and it is an aspect of the lives of the saints for which Christian writers found precedent in Paul's writings.[137] What is interesting in the patristic use of Paul, however, is that it

---

days, but he chases them off through prayer (*Narrative of Zosimus on the Life of the Blessed* 18–20 [*ANF* 10:223–24]). In general, Tatian's *Address to the Greeks* provides an excellent resource for early Christian demonology with respect to the nature of the demons and their interaction with the material world. The *Address* anticipates the use of asceticism to battle demons that would become a prominent feature in the lore about the early desert ascetics (Tatian, *Oratio ad Graecos* 15). Tatian, himself the founder of the Encratites ("Self-controlled") believed that matter, though created good, could be perverted into a conduit of demonic influence (Tatian, *Oratio ad Graecos* 17–18), and that repudiation of matter diminished this influence (Tatian, *Oratio ad Graecos* 16). Tatian's outlook sees a confrontation between those who devote their attention to the knowledge of God and the demons who consequently assail them (Tatian, *Oratio ad Graecos* 12).

[135]Barrett-Lennard considers the *Life of Antony* as "essentially the work of Athanasias" since the attribution was never seriously challenged in antiquity (Barrett-Lennard, *Christian Healing after the New Testament*, 351).

[136]Otto Böcher identifies the renunciation of clothing, hygene, food and drink, sex, sleep, sight, and speech as passive treatments for both the apotropaic warding off (*dämonen-abhaltend*) and exorcistic driving out (*dämonen-vertreibend*) of demons (Böcher, *Dämonenfurcht und Dämonenabwehr*, 239). Tertullian says that fasting contributes toward a demon's egress and the Holy Spirit's ingress (Tertullian, *Jejun.* 8). Tertullian also notes that sexual deprivation from one's wife gives a man greater confidence when adjuring demons (Tertullian, *Exh. cast.* 10). Asceticism in exorcism also appears in one of the *Clementine Homilies* which reasons that the demon's motivation for possessing a body is to delight in the senses otherwise deprived to their own spiritual existence. To deprive the senses of their pleasure, and even to bring to them discomfort, compels the demons to depart (Pseudo-Clement, *Hom.* 9.10). From the pseudo-Clementine *Epistles to the Virgins* mortification of the flesh accomplishes the will of God and maintains the presence of the Holy Spirit within one. Those who mortify the flesh become a temple of God, and with God's help such people are able to exorcize the sick (Pseudo-Clement, *Ep. virg.* 1.9–12).

[137]Paul appears as a paradigmatic figure for asceticism in *Life of Antony* 21, 51 (e.g., Eph 6:12), and Clement of Alexandria, *Miscellanies* 2.20. Irenaeus refers to Paul (Col 3:5) as an authority for exchanging carnal desires for the Holy Spirit through the mortification of the flesh (Irenaeus, *Haer.* 5.12.3). Origen enlists Paul as a spokesman for asceticism when he interprets "flesh" (σάρξ) as the corporal body, and cites Galatians 5:17 as proof text that

is not Paul as the exorcist of Acts who serves as paradigm. If this were the case, we should as readily expect to see also any number of the other disciples said to perform exorcisms in the New Testament. Instead, it is Paul as known through his own letters, or the letters attributed to him, to whom the patristic writers refer, and who more directly appealed to the contemplative and reflective character of personal devotion inherent in the act of asceticism.

Charismatic exorcism will come to have a more historically grounded basis after the fourth century in the healings associated with the Christian cult of the saints.[138] In his study of the third-to-fourth century rise of this cult, Peter Brown discusses the *potentia* of the saints, that is, the divine power channeled through the *praesentia*, or the "physical presence of the holy."[139] Brown says that "possession and exorcism in the great basilicas of Catholic Gaul was held to be the one irrefutable sign of the *praesentia* within them of the saints,"[140] and for which cure by exorcism became for the Christian Church "the paradigm of the exercise of the *potentia* of the saints."[141] Although Brown speaks of Gaul at the end of the sixth century, the evidence he discusses supports the conclusion that the *praesentia* of those who had died maintained a form of charismatic exorcism within Christianity.[142]

---

flesh works against the spirit (Origen, *Princ.* 3.2.3). For Cyprian, Paul is a model not so much for asceticism as for the virtue of patient suffering during the days of persecution endured by the Christians of Carthage. Cyprian draws upon the example of Paul, as one who gains strength through suffering (2 Cor 12:7–9), as a way of associating the execution of martyrs with the crucifixion of Jesus (Cyprian, *Opusc.* 7.13). Paul also figures prominently in Methodius, who considers him to be a paradigm for sexual continence (Methodius, *Symp.* [e.g. Discourse 3.1–14 — "Thaleia"]).

[138]Thraede considers the exorcisms attributed to monks and saints, and rooted in the life of the monastery, to continue to portray exorcism as a charisma, still distinct from its role as an office in the church (Thraede, "Exorzismus," *RAC* 7:104).

[139]Peter Brown, *The Cult of the Saints: Its Rise and Function in Latin Christianity* (The Haskell Lectures on History of Religions, New Series 2; Chicago: University of Chicago Press, 1981) 88.

[140]Brown, *The Cult of the Saints*, 106.

[141]Brown, *The Cult of the Saints*, 107.

[142]Compare also in Peter, Bishop of Alexandria's (ca. 260–311), *Genuine Acts of Peter*, where Peter's burial site is a place of miracles, exorcism included (*ANF* 6:268), and in the *Acts of Thomas* where dust from Thomas' sepulchre heals a demoniac boy (*Acts Thom.* 170). For Hebrew Biblical precedent, compare Elisha's grave and corpse as a source of revitalization (2 Kgs 13:20–21). Such miraculous powers show God to honor holy people after their death. Frend also notes that miraculous cures by dead or living Christian saints were a significant cause of conversion in the mid-fourth century (Frend, *The Rise of Christianity*, 565).

6.11 Conclusion

The practice of exorcism presented difficulties for the very expansion of Christianity into the Greco-Roman world that it was intended to facilitate. Christian exorcism necessitated a dualistic cosmological view that was foreign to the Greeks and Romans of the early Common Era, a foreignness they more readily identified with the socially marginal activity of magic than with their own conventional cults. Even so, the early patristic writers showed an active interest in upholding possession and exorcism as defining features of their faith, and they used exorcism as a pedagogical tool that exposed the demonic nature of the cults and revealed the inherent cosmic dualism that otherwise went unrecognized by the polytheists. The apologists addressed the wariness toward exorcism on the part of the civil authorities by downplaying the eschatological aspects of exorcism that could be viewed as a threat to the existing political powers, and instead they appealed to the traditional criteria by which the Greeks and Romans had earlier accepted new cults into their societies. In this context they appealed to exorcism's utilitarian benefits to the Empire, especially with respect to the healthfulness it brought to its citizenry even where the traditional means of healing had failed.

Christian writers also related exorcism to the good character of its exorcists, and they distanced the practice as a whole from magic by placing it instead within a moral framework founded upon Scripture and the gospel message that accompanied it. In their appeal to the non-Christian populace, early patristic writers also presented exorcism as a kind of visual rhetoric that related their practice of exorcism and its underlying theology and demonology to concepts already familiar to their critics and potential converts. By tying exorcism to ethics these authors were able to connect exorcism and its attendant belief in demonic possession also to the concept of divine possession long familiar to the Greeks and readily traceable through their literature. To this end, Christian writers found an exemplary illustration in the Two Ways metaphor, which offered a common point of reference between the Greek and Christian intellectual heritages.

Within the context of intra-Christian debate the heresiologists further articulated the meaning of demonic and divine states of possession. By and large, they upheld the independence of the human will to pursue good or evil, while at the same time they acknowledged its susceptibility to demonic and divine spiritual influences. This belief came to be expressed also in the Christian initiation ceremony, with its attendant renunciation of evil achieved in part through the exorcism of the catechumen and baptizand, and the subsequent commitment to a life in Christ accomplished through the invocation of the Holy Spirit through the imposition of hands. Although the role of exorcism in the baptismal ceremony attests to an institutionalization of the exorcist as an ordained church official, charismatic exorcism continued within the Christian literary landscape both as a staple of the pseudepigraphic and hagiographic stories of holy persons, and in the exorcisms that came to attend the late antique cult of the saints. These latter contexts suggest that, rather than its abandonment to the esoteric rite of initiation, the charismatic exorcism of physiological ailments continued on even as its applications expanded into ethical and institutional contexts not previously evident for it in the New Testament.

Chapter 7

Conclusion

The preceeding discussion of demonic possession and exorcism has asked how Christianity maintained its exorcistic tradition in those areas of mission where it conflicted with social convention. An answer to this question has in part been found in the relationship between demonic possession and the divine indwelling spirit. Although monographs have dealt with demonic and divine possession as separate phenomena, the contribution of this work lies in showing how they came to be viewed correlatively with respect to exorcism. The correlation becomes evident from a consideration of both the internal and external stimuli for the development of exorcism and the role of the exorcist within Christianity. The internal stimulus arose as Christians reflected upon their exorcistic heritage for purposes of catechetical instruction and liturgical practice. The external stimulus arose from Christianity's encounter with Greek and Roman sensibilities and its effort to find acceptance within their geographic realms.

I have argued that exorcism retained its relevance within Christianity through three principal means: cultural adaptation, authoritative tradition, and innovative theological interpretations applied to that tradition. In regard to cultural adaptation, I have traced the origins of Christianity's view of possession out of the Near Eastern environment. The reason behind looking to the Near East for the origins of demonic possession and the practice of exorcism in the New Testament lies in the fact that its cultures had well established traditions of technical practice with regard to the treatment of illness due to demonic affliction. Chapter 2 showed Mesopotamian conjurers to provide a precedent for the New Testament exorcists in their attribution of maladies to hostile spiritual forces, especially in their mediating role between healing deities whom they solicited to ease the sufferings of human beings. Although the ancient Mesopotamian societies lacked a well-defined belief in hostile spiritual aggressors capable of indwelling the bodies of those whom they afflicted, precedent for indwelling possession does appear in Zoroastrianism, whose dualistic cosmology identified human beings with the good or evil spiritual forces to whom they offered their allegiances.

Despite an overt resistance to Near Eastern conjuration in the Hebrew Bible, Chapter 3 described how analogous practices found acceptance in

Judaism when practiced under the aegis of Yahweh. The influence of these Near Eastern cultures upon Jewish demonology in general becomes increasingly apparent during the post-exilic period, and it is in the inter-testamental writings that Judaism first begins to articulate a belief in indwelling demonic possession and to develop a corresponding practice of exorcism. The influence of Near Eastern beliefs and practices upon the post-exilic Jews allowed for the unapologetic acceptance of exorcism evident in the writings of the Synoptic authors.

Whereas the New Testament authors inherited their demonology from a hellenistic Jewish environment in which exorcists circulated without apparent cultural stigma, their status changed in a Greco-Roman environment that met them with suspicion and even hostility. The Greeks and Romans in the central Mediterranean were relatively uninformed about the demonologies of earlier Near Eastern cultures at the turn of the era, and such activities as exorcism were identified more with the magical practices that lurked on the fringes of their societies than with those practices associated with the publicly sanctioned cults. Chapter 4 argued that, although the elements for demonic possession and exorcism are nearly all in place within Greek society, they are not yet connected in a way that would require the services of an exorcist. Exorcism appears to presuppose a belief in evil as a self-willed entity, a belief that earlier Greek literature either lacks or leaves undeveloped. Although spiritual possession appears frequently and explicitly in early Greek writings, especially with respect to oracles, ailments, and madness, malevolent occasions of such, even when due to the presence of *daimonic* figures, tend to be motivated by divine retribution in response to an offense taken at some human action. The general tendency in early Greece toward seeing *daimones* as divine agents resulted in treating them with propitiation and appeasement, a view that contrasts with the contempt paid the hostile demons in the New Testament. It was the Jewish and early Christian views of evil entities capable of being subjected by a superior divine power that helped to generate a need for the exorcist in Greco-Roman society during the Common Era.

Exorcism continued as a concern of the early church in part because of its importance for the portrayals of Jesus in the gospels. Jesus' own exorcistic activity and his command to his disciples to do likewise established exorcism at the earliest stages of Christian tradition, a tradition with which the church would eventually have to come to terms in its missionary appeal to Greek and Roman audiences. Chapter 5 argued that, while the Synoptic Gospels and Acts served as literary exemplars for the practice of exorcism in early Christianity, the Pauline writings served as an interpretive basis for what it meant to be possessed. The New Testament writings, especially the Pauline letters, used the language of indwelling possession to identify humanity's relationship with divine and demonic spiritual forces. Whereas demonic possession represented an impure state, the exorcism of which restored one to a pure yet profane condition, divine possession represented an elevation from a profane condition to one of sanctification for which the human body as a temple of God served as metaphor. Demonic possession and exorcism consequently served Christianity's missionary objectives by making known the possibility for the divine possession that identified membership within the community of believers, a possibility that Christians sought to disseminate to their converts through baptism.

Demonic possession continued to frequent Christian literature during the first centuries of Christianity's expansion under the dual impetuses of a dominical mandate and an influx of Near Eastern beliefs and practices upon the Roman Empire. The direction of influence, however, was not one-sided, and exorcism itself underwent metamorphoses that adapted it to Greek and Roman sensibilities. Although the mandate for exorcism in Christian mission does appear in New Testament writings, the lack of a prescription for its performance allowed for innovations to its practice. This is apparent not only in the variety of rituals and formulae employed in exorcism, but also in the theological interpretations it received. Chapter 6 argued that the correlation of demonic possession with the concept of a divine indwelling spirit became a means by which Christians were able to relate their otherwise unfamiliar practice of exorcism to an ambivalent, even hostile Greco-Roman culture.

The correlation of divine and demonic possession gained prominence in early Christianity when Christianity began to articulate possession in ethical terms. Christianity found a suitable metaphor for the expression of this correlation in the Two Ways doctrine, an instruction which itself had antecedents in the Greek literary heritage as well as in Christianity's own sacred writings. As it developed within Christianity, the two ways of the doctrine became of less interest than the angelic or demonic guides who encouraged one along them, and it was their influence that encouraged an association of spiritual possession with moral behavior. This adaptation led to an expansion of exorcism's use: by correlating demonic and divine states of possession, early Christianity now applied exorcism not simply to demons that manifested themselves through physiological maladies, as was the case in the synoptic writings, but to the evil motivations within humanity.

The association between ethics and exorcism has long been observed by others, but the interest in such observations has been upon the development of exorcism with respect to later Christian baptismal practices. In baptism, however, exorcism appears in an esoteric Christian context as an act of initiation into the community of believers for those who have already been exposed to and accepted its traditions. The present approach has explored to a greater extent than in previous works the ways in which an ethical contextualization of exorcism was motivated by Christianity's engagement with the non-Christian world. Interpreting exorcism through an ethical lens helped to diffuse the associations of foreignness it held among non-Christians.

Attaching a familiar interpretation to its exorcistic practice enabled Christianity to employ exorcism more effectively as a means of persuading a Greco-Roman audience to Christian values and beliefs. Christianity attempted to use its exorcistic heritage to persuasive advantage by emphasizing the exemplary character of Christian exorcists, by identifying the demonic nature of the gods that revealed themselves as subservient to the name of Christ through exorcism, and by the beneficial results that successful exorcisms brought to society at large. All such means, however, benefited from Christianity's own reinterpretation of its exorcistic heritage, a reinterpretation that affected its use and significance not only within Christianity as an esoteric rite of initiation, but also in its use as an outward indicator of Christianity's intentions toward non-Christian culture.

BIBLIOGRAPHY OF WORKS CITED

Abusch, Tzvi. *Babylonian Witchcraft Literature: Case Studies*. Atlanta: Scholars Press, 1987.

————. "The Demonic Image of the Witch in Standard Babylonian Literature: The Reworking of Popular Conceptions by Learned Exorcists." Pages 27–58 in *Religion, Science, and Magic: In Concert and Conflict*. Edited by Jacob Neusner. New York: Oxford University Press, 1989.

————. "Maqlû." Pages 346–51 in vol. 7 of *Reallexikon der Assyriologie*. Edited by Erich Ebeling et al. Berlin: de Gruyter, 1928–.

Achtemeier, Paul J. "Toward the Isolation of Pre-Markan Miracle Catenae." *Journal of Biblical Literature* 89 (1970): 265–91.

Aeschylus. Translated by Herbert Weir Smyth. 2 vols. Loeb Classical Library. Cambridge: Harvard University Press, 1938–1946.

Aeschines. *The Speeches of Aeschines*. Translated by Charles Darwin Adams. Loeb Classical Library. Cambridge: Harvard University Press, 1958.

Alderink, Larry J. "Stoicheia στοιχεῖα τοῦ κόσμου." Pages 815–18 in *Dictionary of Deities and Demons in the Bible*. Edited by Karel van der Toorn, Bob Becking, and Pieter W. van der Horst. 2d ed. Leiden: Brill, 1999.

Alexander, William Menzies. *Demonic Possession in the New Testament: Its Historical, Medical and Theological Aspects*. Grand Rapids, Mich.: Baker Book House, 1980.

Altaner, Berthold. "Zum Problem der lateinischen Doctrina Apostolorum." *Vigiliae christianae* 6 (1952): 160–67.

The Ante-Nicene Fathers. Edited by Alexander Roberts and James Donaldson. 1885–1887. 10 vols. Repr. Peabody, Mass.: Hendrickson, 1994.

The Apostolic Fathers. Translated by Kirsopp Lake. 2 vols. Loeb Classical Library. New York: MacMillan, 1924–25.

Appian. *Roman History*. Translated by Horace White. 4 vols. Loeb Classical Library. New York: MacMillan, 1912–1913.

Arnold, Clinton E. "Returning to the Domain of the Powers: *Stoicheia* as Evil Spirits in Galatians 4:3,9." *Novum Testamentum* 38 (1996): 55–76.

The Assyrian Dictionary of the Oriental Institute of the University of Chicago. Edited by Ignace J. Gelb et al. Chicago: Oriental Institute of Chicago, 1956–.

Augustine. *The City of God against the Pagans.* Translated by William Chase Greene et al. 7 vols. Loeb Classical Library. Cambridge: Harvard University Press, 1960.

Aune, David E. *Prophecy in Early Christianity and the Ancient Mediterranean World.* Grand Rapids, Mich.: Eerdmans, 1983.

―――. "Revelation." Pages 1187–1202 in *HarperCollins Bible Dictionary.* Edited by Paul J. Achtemeier et al. 2d ed. San Francisco: HarperSanFrancisco, 1996.

―――, ed. *Studies in the New Testament and Early Christian Literature: Essays in Honor of Allen P. Wikgren.* Novum Testamentum Supplements 33. Leiden: Brill, 1972.

Ayán Calvo, Juan José. *Didaché, Doctrina Apostolorum, Epístola del Pseud-Bernabé.* Fuentes Patrísticas 3. Madrid: Editorial Ciudad Nueva, 1992.

Barrett-Lennard, R. J. S. *Christian Healing after the New Testament: Some Approaches to Illness in the Second, Third, and Fourth Centuries.* Lanham: University Press of America, 1994.

Bauer, Walter. *Orthodoxy and Heresy in Earliest Christianity.* Philadelphia: Fortress, 1971.

Bauernfeind, Otto. *Die Worte der Dämonen im Markusevangelium.* Beiträge zur Wissenschaft vom Alten und Neuen Testament 44. Stuttgart: Kohlhammer, 1927.

Beckman, Gary. "Medizin. B. Bei den Hethitern." Pages 629–31 in vol. 7 of *Reallexikon der Assyriologie.* Edited by Erich Ebeling et al. Berlin: de Gruyter, 1928–.

Benveniste, Emile. *The Persian Religion according to the Chief Greek Texts.* Ratanbai Lecture Series 1. Paris: Librairie Orientaliste Paul Geuthner, 1929.

Betz, Hans Dieter. "The Concept of the 'Inner Human Being' (ὁ ἔσω ἄνθρωπος) in the Anthropology of Paul." *New Testament Studies* 46 (2000): 315–41.

―――. "Corinthians, Second Epistle to the." Pages 1148–54 in vol. 1 of *The Anchor Bible Dictionary*. Edited by D. N. Freedman. 6 vols. New York: Doubleday, 1992.

―――. *Galatians: A Commentary on Paul's Letter to the Churches in Galatia*. Hermeneia 62. Philadelphia: Fortress, 1979.

―――. *The Greek Magical Papyri in Translation: Including the Demotic Spells.* 2d ed. Chicago: University of Chicago Press, 1992.

―――. "Jewish Magic in the Greek Magical Papyri (*PGM* VII.260–71)." Pages 45–63 in *Envisioning Magic: A Princeton Seminar and Symposium*. Edited by Peter Schäfer and Hans G. Kippenberg. Leiden: Brill, 1997. Repr. pages 187–205 in *Antike und Christentum. Gesammelte Aufsätze IV*. Tübingen: Mohr (Siebeck), 1998.

―――. "Legion λεγιών." Pages 507–8 in *Dictionary of Deities and Demons in the Bible*. Edited by Karel van der Toorn, Bob Becking, and Pieter W. van der Horst. 2d ed. Leiden: Brill, 1999.

Böcher, Otto. *Christus Exorcista: Dämonismus und Taufe im Neuen Testament*. Beiträge zur Wissenschaft vom Alten und Neuen Testament 16; Stuttgart: Kohlhammer, 1972.

―――. *Dämonenfurcht und Dämonenabwehr. Ein Beitrag zur Vorgeschichte der christlichen Taufe*. Beiträge zur Wissenschaft vom Alten und Neuen Testament 90. Stuttgart: Kohlhammer, 1970.

―――. *Das Neue Testament und die dämonischen Mächte*. Stuttgarter Bibelstudien 58. Stuttgart: KBW, 1972.

Borgen, Peder, and Søren Giversen, eds. *The New Testament and Hellenistic Judaism*. Aarhus: Aarhus University Press, 1995.

Bormann, Lukas, ed. *Religious Propaganda and Missionary Competition in the New Testament World: Essays Honoring Dieter Georgi*. Leiden: Brill, 1994.

Bourguignon, Erika. *Possession*. Chandler and Sharp Series in Cross Cultural Themes. San Francisco: Chandler & Sharp, 1976.

Bourguignon, Erika, ed. *Religion, Altered States of Consciousness, and Social Change*. Columbus: Ohio State University Press, 1973.

Boyce, Mary. *A History of Zoroastrianism*. 3 vols. Leiden: Brill, 1975–1991.

———. *Textual Sources for the Study of Zoroastrianism*. Textual Sources for the Study of Religion. Totowa, N.J.: Barnes & Noble Books, 1984.

———. *Zoroastrianism: Its Antiquity and Constant Vigour*. Columbia Lectures on Iranian Studies 7. Costa Mesa, Calif.: Mazda Publishers, 1992.

Bradshaw, Paul F. *Liturgical Presidency in the Early Church*. Grove Liturgical Study 36. Bramcote, Notts.: Grove Books, 1983.

———. "Redating the *Apostolic Tradition*: Some Preliminary Steps." Pages 3–17 in *Rule of Prayer, Rule of Faith: Essays in Honor of Aidan Kavanagh, O.S.B.* Edited by Nathan Mitchell and John F. Baldwin. Collegeville, Minn.: Liturgical Press, 1996.

———. *The Search for the Origins of Christian Worship: Sources and Methods for the Study of Early Liturgy*. London: SPCK, 1992.

Braumann, Georg. *Vorpaulinische christliche Taufverkündigung bei Paulus*. Beiträge zur Wissenschaft vom Alten und Neuen Testament 82. Stuttgart: Kohlhammer, 1962.

Bréhier, Louis. *La sculpture et les arts mineurs byzantins*. Histoire de l'art byzantin. Paris: Éditions d'art et d'histoire, 1936.

Bremmer, Jan N. "Scapegoat Rituals in Ancient Greece." *Harvard Studies in Classical Philology* 87 (1983): 299–320.

Brenk, Frederick E. "In the Light of the Moon: Demonology in the Early Imperial Period." *Aufstieg und Niedergang der römischen Welt: Geschichte und Kultur Roms im Spiegel der neueren Forschung* 2.16.3.2068–145. Edited by W. Haase. New York: de Gruyter, 1986.

Brock, Sebastian. "The Two Ways and the Palestinian Targum." Pages 139–52 in *A Tribute to Geza Vermes: Essays on Jewish and Christian Literature and History*. Edited by Philip R. Davies and Richard T. White. Journal for the Study of the Old Testament: Supplement Series 100. Sheffield: Sheffield Academic Press, 1990.

Brown, Francis et al. *A Hebrew and English Lexicon of the Old Testament.* Oxford: Clarendon Press, 1951.

Brown, Peter Robert Lamont. *Augustine of Hippo: A Biography.* Berkeley: University of California Press, 1967.

—————. *The Cult of the Saints: Its Rise and Function in Latin Christianity.* The Haskell Lectures on History of Religions. New Series 2. Chicago: University of Chicago Press, 1981.

—————. *Religion and Society in the Age of Saint Augustine.* London: Faber & Faber, 1972.

—————. "The Rise and Function of the Holy Man in Late Antiquity." *Journal of Roman Studies* 81 (1971): 80–101.

—————. "Sorcery, Demons and the Rise of Christianity: From Late Antiquity into the Middle Ages." Pages 119–46 in *Religion and Society in the Age of Saint Augustine.* London: Faber & Faber, 1972.

Büchsel, Friedrich. "διάκρισις." Volume 3 pages 949–50 in *Theological Dictionary of the New Testament.* Edited by G. Kittel and G. Friedrich. 10 vols. Grand Rapids, Mich.: Eerdmans, 1964–1976.

Buck, Carl Darling. *The Greek Dialects: Grammar, Selected Inscriptions, Glossary.* Chicago: University of Chicago Press, 1955.

Bultmann, Rudolf. *The History of the Synoptic Tradition.* 2d rev. ed. New York: Harper & Row, 1968.

Burkert, Walter. "Apokalyptik im frühen Griechentum: Impulse und Transformationen." Pages 235–54 in *Apocalypticism in the Mediterranean World and the Near East.* Edited by David Hellholm. 2d ed. Tübingen: Mohr, 1989.

—————. *Greek Religion.* Cambridge: Harvard University Press, 1985.

—————. *The Orientalizing Revolution: Near Eastern Influence on Greek Culture in the Early Archaic Age.* Cambridge: Harvard University Press, 1992.

—————. "Towards Plato and Paul: The 'Inner Human Being.'" Pages 59–82 in *Ancient and Modern Perspectives on the Bible and Culture: Essays in Honor of Hans Dieter Betz.* Edited by Adela Yarbro Collins. Atlanta: Scholars Press, 1998.

Cameron, Averil. *Christianity and the Rhetoric of Empire: The Development of Christian Discourse*. Sather Classical Lectures 55. Berkeley: University of California Press, 1991.

Cathcart, Kevin J., and Michael Maher, eds. *Targumic and Cognate Studies: Essays in Honour of Martin McNamara*. Journal for the Study of the Old Testament: Supplement Series 230. Sheffield: Sheffield University Press, 1996.

Cecchelli, Carlo et al., eds., *The Rabbula Gospels*. Monumenta occidentis 1. Olten: Urs Graf-Verlag, 1959.

Charlesworth, James H. "Pseudepigrapha, OT." Pages 537–40 in vol. 5 of *The Anchor Bible Dictionary*. Edited by D. N. Freedman. 6 vols. New York: Doubleday, 1992.

————, ed. *The Old Testament Pseudepigrapha*. 2 vols. New York: Doubleday, 1985.

Christensen, Arthur. *Essai sur la démonologie iranienne*. Historisk-filologiske Meddelelser 27:1. Copenhagen: Ejnar Munksgaard, 1941.

Clark, Mary T. *Augustine of Hippo: Selected Writings*. New York: Paulist Press, 1984.

Clifford, Richard J. "Isaiah, Book of (Second Isaiah)." Pages 490–501 in vol. 3 of *The Anchor Bible Dictionary*. Edited by D. N. Freedman. 6 vols. New York: Doubleday, 1992.

Cogan, Mordechai, and Hayim Tadmor. *2 Kings*. Anchor Bible 11. New York: Doubleday, 1988.

Collins, Adela Yarbro, ed. *Ancient and Modern Perspectives on the Bible and Culture: Essays in Honor of Hans Dieter Betz*. Atlanta: Scholars Press, 1998.

————. "Apocalypses and Apocalypticism (Early Christian)." Pages 288–92 in vol. 1 of *The Anchor Bible Dictionary*. Edited by D. N. Freedman. 6 vols. New York: Doubleday, 1992.

————. "Finding Meaning in the Death of Jesus." *Journal of Religion* 78 (1998): 175–96.

Collins, Adela Yarbro. "The History-of-Religions Approach to Apocalypticism and the 'Angel of the Waters' (Apoc 16:4–7)." *Catholic Biblical Quarterly* 39 (1977): 367–81.

———. "The Origin of Christian Baptism." Pages 35–57 in *Living Water, Sealing Spirit: Readings on Christian Initiation*. Edited by Maxwell E. Johnson. Collegeville, Minn.: Liturgical Press, 1995.

———. "Pergamon in Early Christian Literature." Pages 163–84 in *Pergamon, Citadel of the Gods: Archaeological Record, Literary Description, and Religious Development*. Edited by Helmut Koester. Harvard Theological Studies 46. Harrisburg, Pa.: Trinity Press International, 1998.

Collins, Adela Yarbro, and Margaret M. Mitchell, eds. *Antiquity and Humanity: Essays on Ancient Religion and Philosophy. Presented to Hans Dieter Betz on His 70th Birthday*. Tübingen: Mohr (Siebeck), 2001.

Collins, John J. *Daniel: A Commentary on the Book of Daniel*. Hermeneia 27. Minneapolis: Fortress, 1993.

———, ed. *The Origins of Apocalypticism in Judaism and Christianity*. Vol. 1 of *The Encyclopedia of Apocalypticism*. New York: Continuum, 1998.

———. "The Mythology of Holy War in Daniel and the Qumran War Scroll: A Point of Transition in Jewish Apocalyptic." *Vetus Testamentum* 25 (1975): 596–612.

———. "Prayer of Nabonidus: 4Q242. 4Q Prayer of Nabonidus ar." Pages 83–93 in *Qumran Cave 4, 17: Parabiblical Texts, Part 3*. Edited by George Brooke et al. Discoveries in the Judean Desert 22. Oxford: Clarendon Press, 1996.

Conzelmann, Hans. *1 Corinthians: A Commentary on the First Epistle to the Corinthians*. Hermeneia. Philadelphia: Fortress, 1975.

Couliano, Ioan P. *The Tree of Gnosis: Gnostic Mythology from Early Christianity to Modern Nihilism*. San Francisco: HarperCollins, 1992.

Crossan, John Dominic. *The Historical Jesus: The Life of a Mediterranean Jewish Peasant*. San Francisco: HarperSanFrancisco, 1991.

Davies, Philip R., and Richard T. White, eds. *A Tribute to Geza Vermes: Essays on Jewish and Christian Literature and History*. Journal for the Study of the Old Testament: Supplement Series 100. Sheffield: Sheffield Academic Press, 1990.

Davies, Stevan L. *Jesus the Healer: Possession, Trance, and the Origins of Christianity*. New York: Continuum, 1995.

Demosthenes. Translated by C. A. Vince et al. 7 vols. Loeb Classical Library. Cambridge: Harvard University Press, 1964–1989.

Dictionary of Deities and Demons in the Bible. Edited by Karel van der Toorn, Bob Becking, and Pieter W. van der Horst. 2d ed. Leiden: Brill, 1999.

Diels, Hermann. *Die Fragmente der Vorsokratiker: Griechisch und Deutsch*. 3 vols. Zurich: Weidmann, 1974–75.

Dion, Paul E. "Medical Personnel in the Ancient Near East. *asû* and *āšipu* in Aramaic Garb." *ARAM* 1 (1989): 206–16.

Dix, Gregory. *The Treatise on the Apostolic Tradition of St. Hippolytus of Rome, Bishop and Martyr*. 2d rev. ed. reissued with additional corrections by Henry Chadwick. London: Alban Press, 1992.

Dodds, E. R. *The Greeks and the Irrational*. Berkeley: University of California Press, 1964.

Dölger, Franz Joseph. *Der Exorzismus im altchristlichen Taufritual: Eine religionsgeschichtliche Studie*. Studien zur Geschichte und Kultur des Altertums 3:1–2. Paderborn: Ferdinand Schöningh, 1909.

Draper, Jonathan A. "Barnabas and the Riddle of the Didache Revisited." *Journal for the Study of the New Testament* 58 (1995): 89–113.

———, ed. *The* Didache *in Modern Research*. Arbeiten zur Geschichte des antiken Judentums und Urchristentums 37. Leiden: Brill, 1996.

Duling, Dennis C. "Solomon, Exorcism, and the Son of David." *Harvard Theological Review* 68 (1975): 235–52.

Dupont-Sommer, André. "Exorcismes et guérisons dans les écrits de Qoumrân." Pages 246–61 in *Congress Volume: Oxford 1959*. Edited by G. W. Anderson. Vetus Testamentum Supplements 7. Leiden: Brill, 1960.

Eddy, Samuel K. *The King Is Dead: Studies in the Near Eastern Resistance to Hellenism 334–31 B.C.* Lincoln, Nebr.: University of Nebraska Press, 1961.

Edelstein, Emma J., and Ludwig Edelstein. *Asclepius: A Collection and Interpretation of the Testimonies.* New York: Arno Press, 1975.

Edelstein, Ludwig. *Hippocrates The Oath: Or the Hippocratic Oath.* Baltimore: Ares Publishers, 1943.

Eitrem, Samson. *Some Notes on the Demonology in the New Testament.* Symbolae osloenses Fasc. Supplet. 20. 2d ed. Oslo: Universitetsforlaget, 1966.

Euripides. Translated by Arthur S. Way. 4 vols. Loeb Classical Library. New York: MacMillan, 1912.

Euripides. Translated by David Kovacs. 4 vols. Loeb Classical Library. Cambridge: Harvard University Press, 1994–1999.

Eusebius. *The Ecclesiastical History.* Translated by Kirsopp Lake and J. E. L. Oulton. 2 vols. Loeb Classical Library. Cambridge: Harvard University Press, 1964–1965.

Everling, Otto. *Die paulinische Angelologie und Dämonologie: Ein biblisch-theologischer Versuch.* Gottingen: Vandenhoeck & Ruprecht, 1888.

Faraone, Christopher A. "The Agonistic Context of Early Greek Binding Spells." Pages 3–32 in *Magika Hiera: Ancient Greek Magic and Religion.* Edited by Christopher A. Faraone and Dirk Obbink. New York: Oxford University Press, 1991.

Faraone, Christopher A., and Dirk Obbink, eds. *Magika Hiera: Ancient Greek Magic and Religion.* New York: Oxford University Press, 1991.

Ferguson, Everett. *Demonology of the Early Christian World.* Symposium Series 12. New York: Edwin Mellen, 1984.

Festugière, André–Jean, ed. *Historia monachorum in Aegypto.* Brussels: Société des Bollandistes, 1971.

Fiensy, David A. *Prayers Alleged to Be Jewish: An Examination of the Constitutiones Apostolorum.* Brown Judaic Studies 65. Chico, Calif.: Scholars Press, 1985.

Foerster, Werner. "δαίμων et al." Volume 2 pages 1–20 in *Theological Dictionary of the New Testament*. Edited by G. Kittel and G. Friedrich. 10 vols. Grand Rapids, Mich.: Eerdmans, 1964–1976.

———. "πύθων." Volume 6 pages 917–20 in *Theological Dictionary of the New Testament*. Edited by G. Kittel and G. Friedrich. 10 vols. Grand Rapids, Mich.: Eerdmans, 1964–1976.

———. "σατανᾶς." Volume 7 page 151-63 in *Theological Dictionary of the New Testament*. Edited by G. Kittel and G. Friedrich. 10 vols. Grand Rapids, Mich.: Eerdmans, 1964–1976.

Frankfurter, David. "Narrating Power: The Theory of Magical *Historiola* in Ritual Spells." Pages 457–76 in *Ancient Magic and Ritual Power*. Edited by Marvin Meyer and Paul Mirecki. Religions in the Graeco-Roman World 129. New York: Brill, 1995.

Frend, W. H. C. *The Rise of Christianity*. Philadelphia: Fortress, 1984.

Fridrichsen, Anton. *The Problem of Miracle in Primitive Christianity*. Minneapolis: Augsburg, 1972.

Gager, John G. *Curse Tablets and Binding Spells from the Ancient World*. Oxford: Oxford University Press, 1992.

García Martínez, Florentino. *The Dead Sea Scrolls Translated. The Qumran Texts in English*. Translated by Wilfred G. E. Watson. 2d ed. Leiden: Brill, 1996.

García Martínez, Florentino, and Eibert J. C. Tigchelaar, eds. *The Dead Sea Scrolls Study Edition*. 2 vols. Leiden: Brill, 1997–1998.

Garland, Robert. *Introducing New Gods: The Politics of Athenian Religion*. Ithaca, New York: Cornell University Press, 1992.

Garrett, Susan R. *The Demise of the Devil: Magic and the Demonic in Luke's Writings*. Minneapolis: Fortress, 1989.

Garrucci, Raffaele. *Storia della arte cristiana nei primi otto secoli della chiesa*. 6 vols. Prato: G. Guasti, 1872–1881.

Gaster, Moses, ed. *Studies and Texts in Folklore, Magic, Medieval Romance, Hebrew Apocrypha, and Samaritan Archaeology*. 3 vols. New York: Ktav, 1971.

Gebhard, Elizabeth R. "The Gods in Transit: Narratives of Cult Transfer." Pages 451–76 in *Antiquity and Humanity: Essays on Ancient Religion and Philosophy. Presented to Hans Dieter Betz on His 70th Birthday.* Edited by Adela Yarbro Collins and Margaret M. Mitchell. Tübingen: Mohr (Siebeck), 2001.

Geller, Markham J. *Forerunners to Udug-hul: Sumerian Exorcistic Incantations.* Freiburger Altorientalische Studien 12. Stuttgart: Steiner Verlag Wiesbaden, 1985.

Georgi, Dieter. *The Opponents of Paul in Second Corinthians.* Philadelphia: Fortress, 1986.

Goodspeed, Edgar J. "The Didache, Barnabas, and the Doctrina." *Australasian Theological Review* 27 (1945): 228–47.

Gould, Ezra P. *A Critical and Exegetical Commentary on the Gospel According to St. Mark.* International Critical Commentary. Edinburgh: T&T Clark, 1955.

Graf, Fritz. "Alastor." Pages 434–35 in vol. 1 of *Der neue Pauly: Enzyklopädie der Antike.* Edited by H. Cancik and H. Schneider. Stuttgart: Metzler, 1996–.

———. *Magic in the Ancient World.* Revealing Antiquity 10. Cambridge: Harvard University Press, 1997.

Grant, Robert McQueen. *Gods and the One God.* Philadelphia: Westminster Press, 1986.

———. *Greek Apologists of the Second Century.* Philadelphia: Westminster Press, 1988.

———. *Miracle and Natural Law in Graeco-Roman and Early Christian Thought.* Amsterdam: North Holland, 1952.

Gray, John. *1 and 2 Kings: A Commentary.* Philadelphia: Westminster Press, 1970.

Grayson, A. Kirk. "Mesopotamia, History of (Assyria)." Pages 732–55 in vol. 4 of *The Anchor Bible Dictionary.* Edited by D. N. Freedman. 6 vols. New York: Doubleday, 1992.

A Greek-English Lexicon of the New Testament and Other Early Christian Literature, revised and edited by Frederick William Danker (3d ed.; Chicago: University of Chicago Press, 2000).

Greenspoon, Leonard J. "Versions, Ancient (Greek)." Pages 793–94 in vol. 6 of *The Anchor Bible Dictionary*. Edited by D. N. Freedman. 6 vols. New York: Doubleday, 1992.

Guelich, Robert. *Mark 1–8:26*. Word Biblical Commentary 34A. Dallas, Tex.: Word Books, 1989.

Gunkel, Hermann. *The Influence of the Holy Spirit: The Popular View of the Apostolic Age and the Teaching of the Apostle Paul: A Biblical-Theological Study*. Philadelphia: Fortress, 1979.

Güterbock, Hans G., and Thorkild Jacobsen, eds. *Studies in Honor of Benno Landsberger on His Seventy-Fifth Birthday April 21, 1965*. Assyriological Studies 16. Chicago: University of Chicago Press, 1965.

Hartman, Sven S. "Datierung der jungavestischen Apokalyptik." Pages 61–75 in *Apocalypticism in the Mediterranean World and the Near East*. Edited by David Hellholm. 2d ed. Tübingen: Mohr, 1989.

Haussleiter, Johannes. "Deus internus." Pages 795–842 in vol. 3 of *Reallexikon für Antike und Christentum*. Edited by T. Kluser et al. Stuttgart: Hersmann, 1950–.

Hayes, Christine. "Intermarriage and Impurity in Ancient Jewish Sources." *Harvard Theological Review* 92 (1999): 3–36.

Hellholm, David, ed. *Apocalypticism in the Mediterranean World and the Near East: Proceedings of the International Colloquium on Apocalypticism, Uppsala, August 12–17, 1979*. 2d ed. Tübingen: Mohr, 1989.

Hendel, Ronald S. "Vampire עלוקה." Page 887 in *Dictionary of Deities and Demons in the Bible*. Edited by Karel van der Toorn, Bob Becking, and Pieter W. van der Horst. 2d ed. Leiden: Brill, 1999.

Henten, J. W. van. "Python Πυθών." Pages 669–71 in *Dictionary of Deities and Demons in the Bible*. Edited by Karel van der Toorn, Bob Becking, and Pieter W. van der Horst. 2d ed. Leiden: Brill, 1999.

Herodotus. *The History*. Translated by David Grene. Chicago: University of Chicago Press, 1987.

Herrero, Pablo. *La Thérapeutique mésopotamienne*. Mémoire 48. Paris: Éditions Recherche sur les civilisations, 1984.

Hesiod, The Homeric Hymns and Homerica. Translated by Hugh G. Evelyn-White. Loeb Classical Library. Cambridge: Harvard University Press, 1959.

Hillgarth, J. N., ed. *Christianity and Paganism, 350–750: The Conversion of Western Europe*. Philadelphia: University of Pennsylvania Press, 1986.

Hippocrates. *Ouevres complétes*. Edited by Émile Littré. 10 vols. Paris: J.-B. Bailliére, 1839–1861.

Hippocrates. Translated by W. H. S. Jones et al. 8 vols. Loeb Classical Library. Cambridge: Harvard University Press, 1972–1995.

Hippolytus. *La Tradition Apostolique*. 2d ed. Sources chrétiennes 11. Paris: Cerf, 1984.

Hodgson, Robert, Jr. "Holiness (NT)." Pages 249–54 in vol. 3 of *The Anchor Bible Dictionary*. Edited by D. N. Freedman. 6 vols. New York: Doubleday, 1992.

Hollander, Harm W., and Marinus de Jonge. *The Testaments of the Twelve Patriarchs: A Commentary*. Studia in Veteris Testamenti pseudepigraphica 8. Leiden: Brill, 1985.

Honoré, Tony. *Ulpian*. Oxford: Clarendon Press, 1982.

Horsley, Richard A. *Jesus and the Spiral of Violence: Popular Jewish Resistance in Roman Palestine*. San Francisco: Harper & Row, 1987.

Hübner, Hans. "Unclean and Clean (NT)." Translated by Ronald B. Thomas, Jr. Pages 741–45 in vol. 6 of *The Anchor Bible Dictionary*. Edited by D. N. Freedman. 6 vols. New York: Doubleday, 1992.

Hughes, Dennis D. *Human Sacrifice in Ancient Greece*. London: Routledge, 1991.

Hultgård, Anders. "Persian Apocalypticism." Pages 39–83 in *The Origins of Apocalypticism in Judaism and Christianity*. Vol. 1 of *The Encyclopedia of Apocalypticism*. Edited by John J. Collins. 3 vols. New York: Continuum, 1998.

Hutter, Manfred. "Asmodeus Ἀσμοδαῖος." Pages 106–108 in *Dictionary of Deities and Demons in the Bible*. Edited by Karel van der Toorn, Bob Becking, and Pieter W. van der Horst. 2d ed. Leiden: Brill, 1999.

————. "Lilith לילית." Pages 520–21 in *Dictionary of Deities and Demons in the Bible*. Edited by Karel van der Toorn, Bob Becking, and Pieter W. van der Horst. 2d ed. Leiden: Brill, 1999.

Hvalvik, Reider. *The Struggle for Scripture and Covenant*. Wissenschaftliche Untersuchungen zum Neuen Testament 2.82. Tübingen: Mohr (Siebeck), 1996.

Inscriptiones Graecae. 2d ed. Berlin: de Gruyter, 1929.

Insler, Stanley. *The Gāthās of Zarathustra*. Acta Iranica 8. Leiden: Brill, 1975.

Jacoby, Felix. *Die Fragmente der griechischen Historiker*. Vols. Berlin: Weidmann, 1923–; Leiden: Brill, 1940–.

Jameson, Michael H., David R. Jordan, and Roy Kotansky, *A Lex Sacra from Selinous*. Greek, Roman, and Byzantine Monographs 11. Durham, N.C.: Duke University Press, 1993.

Janowski, Bernd. "Azazel עזאזל." Pages 128–31 in *Dictionary of Deities and Demons in the Bible*. Edited by Karel van der Toorn, Bob Becking, and Pieter W. van der Horst. 2d ed. Leiden: Brill, 1999.

Jewett, Robert. *Paul's Anthropological Terms: A Study of Their Use in Conflict Settings*. Arbeiten zur Geschichte des antiken Judentums und Urchristentums 10. Leiden: Brill, 1971.

Johnson, Maxwell E., ed. *Living Water, Sealing Spirit: Readings on Christian Initiation*. Collegeville, Minn.: Liturgical Press, 1995.

Jonge, Marinus de. "Light on Paul from the *Testaments of the Twelve Patriarchs*." Pages 100–15 in *The Social World of the First Christians: Essays in Honor of Wayne A. Meeks*. Edited by L. Michael White and O. Larry Yarbrough. Minneapolis: Fortress, 1995.

————. "The So-Called Pseudepigrapha of the Old Testament and Early Christianity." Pages 59–71 in *The New Testament and Hellenistic Judaism*. Edited by Peder Borgen and Søren Giversen. Aarhus: Aarhus University Press, 1995.

Jonge, Marinus de. *The Testaments of the Twelve Patriarchs: A Critical Edition of the Greek Text*. Pseudepigrapha Veteris Testamenti Graece 1.2. Leiden: Brill, 1978.

————. "The Transmission of the *Testaments of the Twelve Patriarchs* by Christians." *Vigiliae christianae* 47 (1993): 1–28.

Jordan, David Randolph. *Contributions to the Study of Greek Defixiones*. Ph.D. diss., Brown University, 1982.

Josephus. Translated by H. St. J. Thackeray et al. 9 vols. LCL. Cambridge: Harvard University Press, 1926–1965.

Kee, Howard Clark. *Medicine, Miracle and Magic in New Testament Times*. Society for New Testament Studies Monograph Series 55. Cambridge: Cambridge University Press, 1986.

Kelhoffer, James A. *Miracle and Mission: The Authentication of Missionaries and Their Message in the Longer Ending of Mark*. Wissenschaftliche Untersuchungen zum Neuen Testament 2.112. Tübingen: Mohr (Siebeck), 2000.

Kellens, Jean, and Eric Pirart. *Les Textes Vieil-Avestiques*. 3 vols. Weisbaden: Ludwig Reichert Verlag, 1988.

Kingsley, Peter. "The Greek Origin of the Sixth-Century Dating of Zoroaster." *Bulletin of the School of Oriental and African Studies* 53 (1990): 245–65.

Kloppenborg, John S. *Q Parallels: Synopsis, Critical Notes, and Concordance*. Sonoma, Calif.: Polebridge Press, 1988.

Koester, Helmut, ed. *Pergamon, Citadel of the Gods: Archaeological Record, Literary Description, and Religious Development*. Harvard Theological Studies 46. Harrisburg, Pa.: Trinity Press International, 1998.

Koster, W. J. W., ed. *Scholia in Aristophanem*. Groningen: Bouma's Boekhuis, 1978.

Lambert, W. G. *Babylonian Wisdom Literature*. Oxford: Clarendon Press, 1960.

Lane Fox, Robin. *Pagans and Christians*. New York: Knopf, 1987.

Langton, Edward. *Essentials of Demonology: A Study of Jewish and Christian Doctrine, Its Origins and Development*. London: Epworth Press, 1949.

Lanpher, James E. *The Miraculous in Mark: Its Eschatological Background and Christological Function.* Ph.D. diss., University of Notre Dame, 1994.

Lee, J. A. L. *A Lexical Study of the Septuagint Version of the Pentateuch.* Pages 129–44 in Society of Biblical Literature Septuagint and Cognate Studies 14. Chico, Calif.: Scholars Press, 1983.

Leeper, Elizabeth Ann. *Exorcism in Early Christianity.* Ph.D. diss., Duke University, 1991.

———. "From Alexandria to Rome: The Valentinian Connection to the Incorporation of Exorcism as a Prebaptismal Rite." *Vigiliae christianae* 44 (1990): 6–24.

Leidinger, Georg. *Miniaturen aus Handschriften der Kgl. Hof- und Staatsbibliothek in München. Heft 1: Das sogenannte Evangeliarium Kaiser Ottos III.* Munich: Riehn & Tietze, 1912.

Lienhard, Joseph T. "On 'Discernment of Spirits' in the Early Church." *Theological Studies* 41 (1980): 505–29.

Lieu, Samuel N. C. *Manichaeism in the Later Roman Empire and Medieval China.* 2d rev. ed. Wissenschaftliche Untersuchungen zum Neuen Testament 63. Tübingen: Mohr, 1992.

Lightfoot, Joseph Barber. *The Apostolic Fathers.* 2 vols. New York: Georg Olms, 1973.

———. *Saint Paul's Epistle to the Galatians.* 10th ed. Grand Rapids, Mich.: Zondervan, 1971.

Lois sacrées des cités grecques. Supplement. Edited by Franciszek Sokolowski. Ecole français d'Athènes. Travaux et mémoires; fasc. 11. Paris: E. de Boccard, 1962.

Louw, J. P. *Semantics of New Testament Greek.* Philadelphia: Fortress, 1982.

Lucian. Translated by A. M. Harmon et al. 8 vols. Loeb Classical Library. Cambridge: Harvard University Press, 1959–1967.

Lührmann, Dieter. "Neutestamentliche Wundergeschichten und Antike Medizin." Pages 195–204 in *Religious Propaganda and Missionary Competition in the New Testament World: Essays Honoring Dieter Georgi.* Edited by Lukas Bormann. Leiden: Brill, 1994.

Lysias. Translated by W. R. M. Lamb. Loeb Classical Library. Cambridge: Harvard University Press, 1960.

MacMullen, Ramsay. *Christianizing the Roman Empire (A.D. 100–400)*. New Haven: Yale University Press, 1984.

Malandra, William W. *An Introduction to Ancient Iranian Religion: Readings from the Avesta and Achaemenid Inscriptions*. Minneapolis: University of Minnesota Press, 1983.

Marcovich, Miroslav, ed. *Iustini Martyris Apologiae pro Christianis*. Patristische Texte und Studien 38. Berlin: de Gruyter, 1994.

Marcus Aurelius Antoninus. *The Communings with Himself*. Translated by C. R. Haines. Loeb Classical Library. Cambridge: Harvard University Press, 1961.

Marcus, Ralph. "Jewish and Greek Elements in the Septuagint." Pages 227–45 in *Louis Ginzberg: Jubilee Volume on the Occasion of His Seventieth Birthday*. Edited by Saul Lieberman et al. New York: American Academy for Jewish Research, 1945.

Markschies, Christoph. *Valentinus Gnosticus? Untersuchungen zur valentinianischen Gnosis mit einem Kommentar zu den Fragmenten Valentins*. Wissenschaftliche Untersuchungen zum Neuen Testament 65. Tübingen: Mohr, 1992.

Martin, Ralph P. *Carmen Christi: Philippians ii.5–11 in Recent Interpretation and in the Setting of Early Christian Worship*. Society for New Testament Studies Monograph Series 4. Cambridge: Cambridge University Press, 1967.

Marx, Werner G. "Luke, the Physician, Re-examined." *Expository Times* 91 (1980): 168–72.

McCasland, Selby Vernon. *By the Finger of God: Demon Possession and Exorcism in the Light of Modern Views of Mental Illness*. New York: MacMillan, 1951.

Metzger, Bruce M. *A Textual Commentary on the Greek New Testament*. Stuttgart: United Bible Societies, 1975.

Meyer, Marvin, and Richard Smith, eds. *Ancient Christian Magic: Coptic Texts of Ritual Power*. San Francisco: HarperSanFrancisco, 1994.

Meyer, Marvin, and Paul Mirecki, eds. *Ancient Magic and Ritual Power*. Religions in the Greco-Roman World 129. New York: Brill, 1995.

Michel, Otto. "ναός." Volume 4 pages 880–90 in *Theological Dictionary of the New Testament*. Edited by G. Kittel and G. Friedrich. 10 vols. Grand Rapids, Mich.: Eerdmans, 1964–1976.

Milik, J. T. "'Prière de Nabonide' et autres écrits d'un cycle de Daniel." *Revue biblique* 63 (1956): 407–11.

Minor Attic Orators. Translated by K. J. Maidment and J. O. Burtt. 2 vols. Loeb Classical Library. Cambridge: Harvard University Press, 1953–1954.

Mitchell, Margaret M. *Paul and the Rhetoric of Reconciliation: An Exegetical Investigation of the Language and Composition of 1 Corinthians*. 1st American ed. Louisville, Ky.: Westminster/John Knox, 1991.

Mitchell, Nathan, and John F. Baldwin, eds. *Rule of Prayer, Rule of Faith: Essays in Honor of Aidan Kavanagh, O.S.B.* Collegeville, Minn.: Liturgical Press, 1996.

Mommsen, Theodore, and Paul Krueger, eds. *The Digest of Justinian*. Translated and edited by Alan Watson. 4 vols. Philadelphia: University of Pennsylvania Press, 1985.

Müller, Karl, ed. *Fragmenta historicorum graecorum*. 5 vols. Paris: Didot, 1851–1885.

Muraoka, Takamitsu, ed. *Melbourne Symposium on Septuagint Lexicography*. Society of Biblical Literature Septuagint and Cognate Studies 28. Atlanta: Scholars Press, 1990.

Myers, Ched. *Binding the Strong Man: A Political Reading of Mark's Story of Jesus*. Maryknoll, N.Y.: Orbis Books, 1988.

Neusner, Jacob, ed. *Religion, Science, and Magic: In Concert and Conflict*. New York: Oxford University Press, 1989.

Nickelsburg, George W. E. "Enoch, First Book of." Pages 508–16 in vol. 2 of *The Anchor Bible Dictionary*. Edited by D. N. Freedman. 6 vols. New York: Doubleday, 1992.

Niederwimmer, Kurt. *The Didache: A Commentary*. Hermeneia. Minneapolis: Fortress, 1998.

Nilsson, Martin P. *Geschichte der Griechischen Religion. Zw. B.: Die Hellenistische und Römische Zeit*. Munich: C. H. Beck'sche, 1961.

Oppenheim, A. Leo. *Ancient Mesopotamia: Portrait of a Dead Civilization*. Revised and edited by Erica Reiner. Chicago: University of Chicago Press, 1977.

————. "Man and Nature in Mesopotamian Civilization." Pages 634–66 in *Dictionary of Scientific Biography* 15 Supplement 1. New York: Scribners, 1978.

Origen. *Origenis Hexaplorum quae supersunt sive Veterum interpretum graecorum in totum Vetus Testamentum fragmenta*. Edited by Friedrich Field. 2 vols. Oxford: Clarendon Press, 1875.

Oxford English Dictionary. 2d ed. 20 vols. Oxford: Clarendon Press, 1989.

Pagels, Elaine H. *The Origin of Satan*. New York: Random House, 1995.

Paget, James Carleton. *The Epistle of Barnabas: Outlook and Background*. Wissenschaftliche Untersuchungen zum Neuen Testament 2.64. Tübingen: Mohr (Siebeck), 1995.

Parker, Robert. *Miasma: Pollution and Purification in Early Greek Religion*. Oxford: Clarendon Press, 1983.

Parpola, Simo. *Letters from Assyrian and Babylonian Scholars*. State Archives of Assyria 10. Helsinki: Helsinki University Press, 1993.

————. *Letters from Assyrian Scholars to the Kings Esarhaddon and Assurbanipal. Part 2: Commentary and Appendices*. Alter Orient und Altes Testament 5:2. Neukirchen-Vluyn: Butzon & Bercker, 1983.

Patrologiae cursus completus. Series graeca. Edited by J.-P. Migne. 162 vols. Paris: Migne, 1857–1886.

Patrologiae cursus completus. Series latina. Edited by J.-P. Migne. 217 vols. Paris: Migne, 1844–1864.

Pearson, Alfred Chilton. *The Fragments of Sophocles*. 3 vols. Cambridge: Cambridge University Press, 1917.

Penny, Douglas L., and Michael O. Wise. "By the Power of Beelzebub: An Aramaic Incantation Formula from Qumran [4Q560]." *Journal of Biblical Literature* 113 (1994): 627–50.

Philostratus. *The Life of Apollonius of Tyana*. Translated by F. C. Conybeare. 2 vols. Loeb Classical Library. Cambridge: Harvard University Press, 1960.

Pietersma, Albert, ed. *The Apocryphon of Jannes and Jambres the Magicians: P. Chester Beatty XVI (with New Additions of Papyrus* vindobonensis *Greek inv. 29456 + 29828* verso *and British Library Cotton Tiberius B. v f. 87)*. Religions in the Graeco-Roman World 119. Leiden: Brill, 1994.

Pilch, John J. *Healing in the New Testament: Insights from Medical and Mediterranean Anthropology*. Minneapolis: Fortress, 2000.

Plato. Translated by R. G. Bury et al. 12 vols. Loeb Classical Library. Cambridge: Harvard University Press, 1917–1929.

Plummer, Alfred. *A Critical and Exegetical Commentary on the Second Epistle of St Paul to the Corinthians*. International Critical Commentary. Edinburgh: T&T Clark, 1956.

Preisendanz, Karl, ed. *Papyri Graecae Magicae: Die Griechischen Zauberpapyri*. 2 vols. Sammlung Wissenschaftlicher Commentare. Stuttgart: Teubner, 1973–74.

Preisker, Herbert. "λεγιών." Volume 4 pages 68–69 in *Theological Dictionary of the New Testament*. Edited by G. Kittel and G. Friedrich. 10 vols. Grand Rapids, Mich.: Eerdmans, 1964–1976.

Puech, Émile. "La prière de Nabonide (4Q242)." Pages 208–27 in *Targumic and Cognate Studies: Essays in Honour of Martin McNamara*. Edited by R. J. Cathcart and M. Maher. Sheffield: Sheffield University Press, 1996.

Pulleyn, Simon. "The Power of Names in Classical Greek Religion." *Classical Quarterly* 44 (1994): 17–25.

Quasten, Johannes. *Patrology*. 3 vols. Westminster, Md.: Christian Classics, 1992.

Reiner, Erica. "First Millennium Babylonian Literature." Pages 293–321 in vol. 3.2 of *Cambridge Ancient History*. Edited by I. E. S. Edwards, G. J. Cadd, and N. G. L. Hammond. 3d ed. Cambridge: Cambridge University Press, 1970–.

———. "Fortune Telling in Mesopotamia." *Journal of Near Eastern Studies* 19 (1960): 23–35.

Reiner, Erica. *Šurpu: A Collection of Sumerian and Akkadian Incantations.* Archiv für Orientforschung 11. Graz: Ernst Weidner, 1958.

Religionsgeschichtliche Versuche und Vorarbeiten. Giessen: J. Ricker, 1903–.

Ritter, Edith K. "Magical-Expert (= *ašipu*) and Physician (= asû)." Pages 299–321 in *Studies in Honor of Benno Landsberger on His Seventy-Fifth Birthday April 21, 1965.* Edited by Hans G. Güterbock and Thorkild Jacobsen. Assyriological Studies 16. Chicago: University of Chicago Press, 1965.

Rordorf, Willy. "An Aspect of the Judeo-Christian Ethic: The Two Ways." Pages 148–64 in *The* Didache *in Modern Research.* Edited by Jonathan A. Draper. Arbeiten zur Geschichte des antiken Judentums und Urchristentums 37. Leiden: Brill, 1996.

Rose, H. J. "Possession." Page 869 in *The Oxford Classical Dictionary.* Edited by N. G. L. Hammond and H. H. Scullard. 2d ed. Oxford: Clarendon Press, 1970.

Rose, H. J., and B. C. Dietrich. "Erinyes." Pages 406–7 in *The Oxford Classical Dictionary.* Edited by Simon Hornblower and Antony Spawforth. 3d ed. Oxford: Oxford University Press, 1996.

Rouse, W. H. D. *Greek Votive Offerings.* Cambridge: Cambridge University Press, 1902.

Roux, Georges. *Ancient Iraq.* 3d ed. London: Penguin Books, 1992.

Ruge, W. "Pharmakos." Columns 1841–42 in vol. 38 of *Paulys Realencyclopädie der classischen Altertumswissenschaft.* Edited by G. Wissowa. 49 vols. Munich: Druckenmüller, 1980.

Russell, Jeffrey Burton. *The Devil: Perceptions of Evil from Antiquity to Primitive Christianity.* Ithaca, N.Y.: Cornell University Press, 1977.

Saggs, H. W. F. *Civilization before Greece and Rome.* New Haven: Yale University Press, 1989.

Sagnard, Francois, ed. *Extraits de Théodote.* 2d ed. Sources chrétiennes 23. Paris: Cerf, 1970.

Sanders, E. P. *Paul.* Past Masters. Oxford: Oxford University Press, 1991.

Schäfer, Peter, and Hans G. Kippenberg, eds. *Envisioning Magic: A Princeton Seminar and Symposium.* Leiden: Brill, 1997.

Schlier, Heinrich. *Principalities and Powers in the New Testament.* Quaestiones disputatae 3. New York: Herder & Herder, 1961.

Schneemelcher, Wilhelm, ed. *New Testament Apocrypha.* 2 vols. Rev. ed. Louisville: Westminster/John Knox, 1991–92.

Schürer, Emil. *The History of the Jewish People in the Age of Jesus Christ (175 B.C.–A.D. 135).* Revised and edited by Geza Vermes and Fergus Millar. 3 vols. Edinburgh: T&T Clark, 1986.

Schweizer, Eduard. "Slaves of the Elements and Worshippers of Angels: Gal 4:3, 9 and Col 2:8, 18, 20." *Journal of Biblical Literature* 107 (1988): 455–68.

Seeberg, Alfred. *Der Katechismus der Urchristenheit.* Leipzig: Deichert, 1903.

Selwyn, Edward Gordon. *The First Epistle of St. Peter.* London: MacMillan, 1946.

Seneca. *Ad Lucilium, Epistulae, Morales.* Translated by Richard M. Grummere. 3 vols. Loeb Classical Library. New York: Putnam, 1925.

Smith, Jonathan Z. "Towards Interpreting Demonic Powers in Hellenistic and Roman Antiquity." *Aufstieg und Niedergang der römischen Welt: Geschichte und Kultur Roms im Spiegel der neueren Forschung* 2.16.1:425–39. Edited by Wolfgang Haase. New York: de Gruyter, 1978.

Smith, Morton. *Jesus the Magician.* San Francisco: Harper & Row, 1978.

Smith, Wesley D. "So-called Possession in Pre-Christian Greece." *Transactions of the American Philological Association* 96 (1965): 403–26.

Smyth, Herbert Weir. *Greek Grammar.* Cambridge: Harvard University Press, 1984.

Sophocles. Translated by Hugh Lloyd-Jones. 3 vols. Loeb Classical Library. Cambridge: Harvard University Press, 1994–1996.

Stendahl, Krister. "The Apostle Paul and the Introspective Consciousness of the West." Pages 78–96 in *Paul among Jews and Gentiles.* Philadelphia: Fortress, 1976.

Stol, Marten. "Diagnosis and Therapy in Babylonian Medicine." *Jaarbericht van het Vooraziatisch-Egyptisch Gezelschap (Genootschap) Ex oriente lux* 32 (1991–92): 42–65.

Stol, Marten. *Epilepsy in Babylonia.* Cuneiform Monographs 2. Groningen: Styx, 1993.

Stowers, Stanley. *A Rereading of Romans: Justice, Jews, and Gentiles.* New Haven: Yale University Press, 1994.

Stukey, Harold J. "The Cyrenean *hikesioi.*" *Classical Philology* 32 (1937): 32–43.

Suggs, M. Jack. "The Christian Two Ways Tradition: Its Antiquity, Form, and Function." Pages 60–74 in *Studies in the New Testament and Early Christian Literature: Essays in Honor of Allen P. Wikgren.* Edited by David Edward Aune. Novum Testamentum Supplements 33. Leiden: Brill, 1972.

Supplementum epigraphicum Graecum. Amsterdam. A. W. Sijthoff, 1923–.

Tambornino, Julius. *De antiquorum daemonismo.* Religionsgeschichtliche Versuche und Vorarbeiten 7.3. Giessen: Töpelmann, 1909.

Temkin, Owsei. *The Falling Sickness: A History of Epilepsy from the Greeks to the Beginning of Modern Neurology.* 2d rev. ed. Baltimore: Johns Hopkins University Press, 1994.

———. *Hippocrates in a World of Pagans and Christians.* Baltimore: Johns Hopkins University Press, 1991.

Tertullian. *Apology.* Translated by T. R. Gover. Loeb Classical Library. Cambridge: Harvard University Press, 1966.

———. *De Corona.* Érasme; Paris: Presses Universitaires de France, 1966.

Theissen, Gerd. *The Miracle Stories of the Early Christian Tradition.* Translated by Francis McDonah. Philadelphia: Fortress, 1983.

Theological Dictionary of the New Testament. Edited by G. Kittel and G. Friedrich. 10 vols. Grand Rapids, Mich.: Eerdmans, 1964–1976.

Thomson, Robert W. *Athanasius: Contra Gentes and De Incarnatione.* Oxford Early Christian Texts. Edited by H. Chadwick. Oxford: Clarendon Press, 1970–.

Thraede, Klaus. "Exorzismus." Pages 44–117 in vol. 7 of *Reallexikon für Antike und Christentum.* Edited by T. Kluser et al. Stuttgart: Hersmann, 1950–.

Tov, Emanuel. "Greek Words and Hebrew Meanings." Pages 83–126 in *Melbourne Symposium on Septuagint Lexicography*. Edited by Takamitsu Muraoka. Society of Biblical Literature Septuagint and Cognate Studies 28. Atlanta: Scholars Press, 1990.

————. *Textual Criticism of the Hebrew Bible*. Minneapolis: Fortress, 1992.

Twelftree, Graham H. *Jesus the Exorcist: A Contribution to the Study of the Historical Jesus*. Wissenschaftliche Untersuchungen zum Neuen Testament 2.54. Tübingen: Mohr, 1993.

VanderKam, James C. "Jubilees, Book of." Pages 1030–32 in vol. 3 of *The Anchor Bible Dictionary*. Edited by D. N. Freedman. 6 vols. New York: Doubleday, 1992.

Vermes, Geza. *The Complete Dead Sea Scrolls in English*. New York: Allen Lane/Penguin Press, 1997.

Versnel, H. S. "possession, religious." Page 1233 in *The Oxford Classical Dictionary*. Edited by Simon Hornblower and Antony Spawforth. 3d ed. Oxford: Oxford University Press, 1996.

Vielhauer, Philipp. "Oikodome. Das Bild vom Bau in der christlichen Literatur vom Neuen Testament bis Clement Alexandrinus." Pages 1–168 in vol. 2 of *Oikodome: Aufsätze zum Neuen Testament*. Theologische Bücherei 65. Munich: Chr. Kaiser, 1979.

Vliet, Jacques van der. "Satan's Fall in Coptic Magic." Pages 401–18 in *Ancient Magic and Ritual Power*. Edited by Marvin Meyer and Paul Mirecki. Religions in the Graeco-Roman World 129. New York: Brill, 1995.

Weisman, Ze'ev. "The Personal Spirit as Imparting Authority." *Zeitschrift für die alttestamentliche Wissenschaft* 93 (1981): 225–34.

West, M. L. *Hesiod: Works and Days*. Oxford: Clarendon Press, 1978.

White, L. Michael, and O. Larry Yarbrough, eds. *The Social World of the First Christians: Essays in Honor of Wayne A. Meeks*. Minneapolis: Fortress, 1995.

Widengren, Geo. "Leitende Ideen und Quellen der iranischen Apokalyptik." Pages 77–162 in *Apocalypticism in the Mediterranean World and the Near East*. Edited by David Hellholm. 2d ed. Tübingen: Mohr, 1989.

Wilken, Robert L. *The Christians as the Romans Saw Them*. New Haven: Yale University Press, 1984.

Winkler, Gabriele. "The Original Meaning and Implications of the Prebaptismal Anointing." *Worship* 52 (1978): 24–45.

Winston, David. "Solomon, Wisdom of." Pages 120–27 in vol. 6 of *The Anchor Bible Dictionary*. Edited by D. N. Freedman. 6 vols. New York: Doubleday, 1992.

Zaehner, R. C. *Zurvan: A Zoroastrian Dilemma*. Oxford: Clarendon Press, 1955.

The Zend-Avesta. Part 1: The Vendîdâd. Translated by James Darmesteter. American ed. Sacred Books of the East 3. New York: Christian Literature Company, 1898.

Reference Index

Contents: 1. Hebrew Bible; 2. New Testament; 3. Apocrypha and Pseudepigrapha; 4. Josephus; 5. Philo; 6. Dead Sea Scrolls; 7. Rabbinic and Other Jewish Literature; 8. Apostolic Literature and Christian Apocrypha; 9. Patristic and Medieval Literature; 10. Greek and Roman Literature; 11. Persian Literature; 12. Semitic Texts and Inscriptions.

7. Rabbinic and Other Jewish Literature

8. Apostolic Literature and Christian Apocrypha

9. Patristic and Medieval Literature

Author Index

Subject Index

Aaron 48–49, 56
Acts, apocryphal 191, 214–17
Ahura Mazda 32, 35–38, 40–41, 118
Alastor (see Avenging spirits)
Angelology 49–50, 54, 60, 82, 121,
    144–46
Angra Mainyu 35–37, 39–44, 118
Animals, demonic possession of 61, 79
Anthropology (Platonic) 83–84
Antony (Saint) 216–18
Aphrodite 79
Apocalypticism 37 n 79, 44 n 108,
    44–46, 128–31, 172–75
Apollo 80, 98, 111–12, 150
Apollonius of Tyana 8, 186–89, 191
Apologetics, exorcism in 9–10, 173–77,
    180–82, 194–95, 203–5
Apuleius 179 n 24
Arab (exorcist in Lucian) 8–9
Ares 78, 98
Artemis, Temple of 150
Asalluḫi (see Marduk)
Asceticism 63 n 69, 206, 218–19
Asclepius, cult of 3–6, 107–9, 180 n 25,
    186
Āšipu (conjurer) 19–32, 48, 53 n 37, 59,
    72
Āšipūtu (conjuration) 20–25, 31, 64
Asmodeus (Aeshma) 40, 45 n 111, 49 n
    8, 50, 54–55
Asû (doctor) 19, 23, 30–31
Athanasius 10 n 30
Avenging spirits 114
- *alastor* 85–87, 89–90, 110
- *hikesios* 111–13

Bacchic frenzy 78–80, 92, 98–99, 104
Baptism 12–15, 161–62, 196, 199–200,
    210–12
Bārû (diviner) 19, 29–31
Bārûtu (divination) 29–30
Basilides 207

Beelzeboul (Beelzebub) 69, 121
- Controversy 140–43
Belial (Beliar) 49 n 7, 65–66, 69, 159,
    209
Bondage 102, 104, 114–15, 133, 140–42

Cambyses 100–1, 103
Cassandra 80, 86 n 55, 92 n 92, 98
Catharsis (see Rituals, purificatory)
Celsus 173–74, 180–81, 191–93
Christian self-definition 185, 201 n 87
Cicero 194
Cleomenes 100–4
Cornelius (Bishop of Rome) 2, 12
Cosmomachy 125 n 52, 128–31, 135,
    172, 183, 217
Cults
- authority of 4–6, 28, 48–49, 153
- competition between 48–49, 57, 59,
    149–53, 173–77, 180, 185
- cooperation with medicine 30–31, 41 n
    99
- of saints 219
- transferal of 169–77
Curse tablets (see *Defixiones*)

Daimon
- evil 80, 82, 84, 121, 169
- good (ἀγαθὸς δαίμων) 82, 93–95
- morally ambiguous 15, 55, 80–85, 169
Daniel 48–49, 52, 57, 59, 152
David 53, 68, 139 n 127, 189
Defixiones 9, 114–16
Demoniac, literary presentation of 40,
    124–27, 153–55
Demonic possession (see Possession,
    demonic)
Demonization
- of opponents 39, 43, 87–90, 154
- of pantheons 15, 150, 169–77, 190,
    193–94

Wissenschaftliche Untersuchungen zum Neuen Testament

Alphabetical Index of the First and Second Series

Burnett, Richard: Karl Barth's Theological Exegesis. 2001. *Volume II/145.*

Byrskog, Samuel: Story as History – History as Story. 2000. *Volume 123.*

Cancik, Hubert (Ed.): Markus-Philologie. 1984. *Volume 33.*

Capes, David B.: Old Testament Yaweh Texts in Paul's Christology. 1992. *Volume II/47.*

Caragounis, Chrys C.: The Son of Man. 1986. *Volume 38.*

– see *Fridrichsen, Anton.*

Carleton Paget, James: The Epistle of Barnabas. 1994. *Volume II/64.*

Carson, D.A., O'Brien, Peter T. and *Mark Seifrid* (Ed.): Justification and Variegated Nomism: A Fresh Appraisal of Paul and Second Temple Judaism. Volume 1: The Complexities of Second Temple Judaism. *Volume II/140.*

Ciampa, Roy E.: The Presence and Function of Scripture in Galatians 1 and 2. 1998. *Volume II/102.*

Classen, Carl Joachim: Rhetorical Criticsm of the New Testament. 2000. *Volume 128.*

Crump, David: Jesus the Intercessor. 1992. *Volume II/49.*

Dahl, Nils Alstrup: Studies in Ephesians. 2000. *Volume 131.*

Deines, Roland: Jüdische Steingefäße und pharisäische Frömmigkeit. 1993. *Volume II/52.*

– Die Pharisäer. 1997. *Volume 101.*

Dettwiler, Andreas and *Jean Zumstein (Ed.):* Kreuzestheologie im Neuen Testament. 2002. *Volume 151.*

Dietzfelbinger, Christian: Der Abschied des Kommenden. 1997. *Volume 95.*

Dobbeler, Axel von: Glaube als Teilhabe. 1987. *Volume II/22.*

Du Toit, David S.: Theios Anthropos. 1997. *Volume II/91*

Dunn , James D.G. (Ed.): Jews and Christians. 1992. *Volume 66.*

– Paul and the Mosaic Law. 1996. *Volume 89.*

Dunn, James D.G., Hans Klein, Ulrich Luz and *Vasile Mihoc* (Ed.): Auslegung der Bibel in orthodoxer und westlicher Perspektive. 2000. *Volume 130.*

Ebertz, Michael N.: Das Charisma des Gekreuzigten. 1987. *Volume 45.*

Eckstein, Hans-Joachim: Der Begriff Syneidesis bei Paulus. 1983. *Volume II/10.*

– Verheißung und Gesetz. 1996. *Volume 86.*

Ego, Beate: Im Himmel wie auf Erden. 1989. *Volume II/34*

Ego, Beate and *Lange, Armin* with *Pilhofer, Peter (Ed.):* Gemeinde ohne Tempel – Community without Temple. 1999. *Volume 118.*

Eisen, Ute E.: see *Paulsen, Henning.*

Ellis, E. Earle: Prophecy and Hermeneutic in Early Christianity. 1978. *Volume 18.*

– The Old Testament in Early Christianity. 1991. *Volume 54.*

Endo, Masanobu: Creation and Christology. 2002. *Volume 149.*

Ennulat, Andreas: Die 'Minor Agreements'. 1994. *Volume II/62.*

Ensor, Peter W.: Jesus and His 'Works'. 1996. *Volume II/85.*

Eskola, Timo: Messiah and the Throne. 2001. *Volume II/142.*

– Theodicy and Predestination in Pauline Soteriology. 1998. *Volume II/100.*

Fatehi, Mehrdad: The Spirit's Relation to the Risen Lord in Paul. 2000. *Volume II/128.*

Feldmeier, Reinhard: Die Krisis des Gottessohnes. 1987. *Volume II/21.*

– Die Christen als Fremde. 1992. *Volume 64.*

Feldmeier, Reinhard and *Ulrich Heckel* (Ed.): Die Heiden. 1994. *Volume 70.*

Fletcher-Louis, Crispin H.T.: Luke-Acts: Angels, Christology and Soteriology. 1997. *Volume II/94.*

Förster, Niclas: Marcus Magus. 1999. *Volume 114.*

Forbes, Christopher Brian: Prophecy and Inspired Speech in Early Christianity and its Hellenistic Environment. 1995. *Volume II/75.*

Fornberg, Tord: see *Fridrichsen, Anton.*

Fossum, Jarl E.: The Name of God and the Angel of the Lord. 1985. *Volume 36.*

Frenschkowski, Marco: Offenbarung und Epiphanie. Volume 1 1995. *Volume II/79* – Volume 2 1997. *Volume II/80.*

Frey, Jörg: Eugen Drewermann und die biblische Exegese. 1995. *Volume II/71.*

– Die johanneische Eschatologie. Volume I. 1997. *Volume 96.* – Volume II. 1998. *Volume 110.*

– Volume III. 2000. *Volume 117.*

Freyne, Sean: Galilee and Gospel. 2000. *Volume 125.*

Fridrichsen, Anton: Exegetical Writings. Edited by C.C. Caragounis and T. Fornberg. 1994. *Volume 76.*

Garlington, Don B.: 'The Obedience of Faith'. 1991. *Volume II/38.*

– Faith, Obedience, and Perseverance. 1994. *Volume 79.*

Garnet, Paul: Salvation and Atonement in the Qumran Scrolls. 1977. *Volume II/3.*

Gese, Michael: Das Vermächtnis des Apostels. 1997. *Volume II/99.*

Gräbe, Petrus J.: The Power of God in Paul's Letters. 2000. *Volume II/123.*

Gräßer, Erich: Der Alte Bund im Neuen. 1985.
Volume 35.
– Forschungen zur Apostelgeschichte. 2001.
Volume 137.
Green, Joel B.: The Death of Jesus. 1988.
Volume II/33.
Gundry Volf, Judith M.: Paul and Perseverance.
1990. *Volume II/37.*
Hafemann, Scott J.: Suffering and the Spirit.
1986. *Volume II/19.*
– Paul, Moses, and the History of Israel. 1995.
Volume 81.
Hahn, Johannes (Ed.): Zerstörungen des
Jerusalemer Tempels. 2002. *Volume 147.*
Hannah, Darrel D.: Michael and Christ. 1999.
Volume II/109.
Hamid-Khani, Saeed: Relevation and Con-
cealment of Christ. 2000. *Volume II/120.*
Hartman, Lars: Text-Centered New Testament
Studies. Ed. von D. Hellholm. 1997.
Volume 102.
Hartog, Paul: Polycarp and the New Testament.
2001. *Volume II/134.*
Heckel, Theo K.: Der Innere Mensch. 1993.
Volume II/53.
– Vom Evangelium des Markus zum viergestal-
tigen Evangelium. 1999. *Volume 120.*
Heckel, Ulrich: Kraft in Schwachheit. 1993.
Volume II/56.
– Der Segen im Neuen Testament. 2002.
Volume 150.
– see *Feldmeier, Reinhard.*
– see *Hengel, Martin.*
Heiligenthal, Roman: Werke als Zeichen. 1983.
Volume II/9.
Hellholm, D.: see *Hartman, Lars.*
Hemer, Colin J.: The Book of Acts in the Setting
of Hellenistic History. 1989. *Volume 49.*
Hengel, Martin: Judentum und Hellenismus.
1969, ³1988. *Volume 10.*
– Die johanneische Frage. 1993. *Volume 67.*
– Judaica et Hellenistica.
Kleine Schriften I. 1996. *Volume 90.*
– Judaica, Hellenistica et Christiana.
Kleine Schriften II. 1999. *Volume 109.*
– Paulus und Jakobus.
Kleine Schriften III. 2002. *Volume 141.*
Hengel, Martin and *Ulrich Heckel* (Ed.): Paulus
und das antike Judentum. 1991. *Volume 58.*
Hengel, Martin and *Hermut Löhr* (Ed.):
Schriftauslegung im antiken Judentum und
im Urchristentum. 1994. *Volume 73.*
Hengel, Martin and *Anna Maria Schwemer:*
Paulus zwischen Damaskus und Antiochien.
1998. *Volume 108.*
– Der messianische Anspruch Jesu und die
Anfänge der Christologie. 2001. *Volume 138.*

Hengel, Martin and *Anna Maria Schwemer*
(Ed.): Königsherrschaft Gottes und himm-
lischer Kult. 1991. *Volume 55.*
– Die Septuaginta. 1994. *Volume 72.*
Hengel, Martin; Siegfried Mittmann and *Anna
Maria Schwemer* (Ed.): La Cité de Dieu /
Die Stadt Gottes. 2000. *Volume 129.*
Herrenbrück, Fritz: Jesus und die Zöllner. 1990.
Volume II/41.
Herzer, Jens: Paulus oder Petrus? 1998.
Volume 103.
Hoegen-Rohls, Christina: Der nachösterliche
Johannes. 1996. *Volume II/84.*
Hofius, Otfried: Katapausis. 1970. *Volume 11.*
– Der Vorhang vor dem Thron Gottes. 1972.
Volume 14.
– Der Christushymnus Philipper 2,6-11. 1976,
²1991. *Volume 17.*
– Paulusstudien. 1989, ²1994. *Volume 51.*
– Neutestamentliche Studien. 2000. *Volume 132.*
– Paulusstudien II. 2002. *Volume 143.*
Hofius, Otfried and *Hans-Christian Kammler:*
Johannesstudien. 1996. *Volume 88.*
Holtz, Traugott: Geschichte und Theologie des
Urchristentums. 1991. *Volume 57.*
Hommel, Hildebrecht: Sebasmata. Volume 1 1983.
Volume 31 – Volume 2 1984. *Volume 32.*
Hvalvik, Reidar: The Struggle for Scripture and
Covenant. 1996. *Volume II/82.*
Joubert, Stephan: Paul as Benefactor. 2000.
Volume II/124.
Jungbauer, Harry: „Ehre Vater und Mutter".
2002. *Volume II/146.*
Kähler, Christoph: Jesu Gleichnisse als Poesie
und Therapie. 1995. *Volume 78.*
Kamlah, Ehrhard: Die Form der katalogischen
Paränese im Neuen Testament. 1964. *Volume 7.*
Kammler, Hans-Christian: Christologie und
Eschatologie. 2000. *Volume 126.*
– see *Hofius, Otfried.*
Kelhoffer, James A.: Miracle and Mission. 1999.
Volume II/112.
Kieffer, René and *Jan Bergman (Ed.):* La Main de
Dieu / Die Hand Gottes. 1997. *Volume 94.*
Kim, Seyoon: The Origin of Paul's Gospel.
1981, ²1984. *Volume II/4.*
– "The 'Son of Man'" as the Son of God.
1983. *Volume 30.*
Klein, Hans: see *Dunn, James D.G..*
Kleinknecht, Karl Th.: Der leidende Gerechtfer-
tigte. 1984, ²1988. *Volume II/13.*
Klinghardt, Matthias: Gesetz und Volk Gottes.
1988. *Volume II/32.*
Köhler, Wolf-Dietrich: Rezeption des Matthäus-
evangeliums in der Zeit vor Irenäus. 1987.
Volume II/24.

Korn, Manfred: Die Geschichte Jesu in veränderter Zeit. 1993. *Volume II/51.*

Koskenniemi, Erkki: Apollonios von Tyana in der neutestamentlichen Exegese. 1994. *Volume II/61.*

Kraus, Thomas J.: Sprache, Stil und historischer Ort des zweiten Petrusbriefes. 2001. *Volume II/136.*

Kraus, Wolfgang: Das Volk Gottes. 1996. *Volume 85.*

– see *Walter, Nikolaus.*

Kreplin, Matthias: Das Selbstverständnis Jesu. 2001. *Volume II/141.*

Kuhn, Karl G.: Achtzehngebet und Vaterunser und der Reim. 1950. *Volume 1.*

Kvalbein, Hans: see *Ådna, Jostein.*

Laansma, Jon: I Will Give You Rest. 1997. *Volume II/98.*

Labahn, Michael: Offenbarung in Zeichen und Wort. 2000. *Volume II/117.*

Lange, Armin: see *Ego, Beate.*

Lampe, Peter: Die stadtrömischen Christen in den ersten beiden Jahrhunderten. 1987, [2]1989. *Volume II/18.*

Landmesser, Christof: Wahrheit als Grundbegriff neutestamentlicher Wissenschaft. 1999. *Volume 113.*

– Jüngerberufung und Zuwendung zu Gott. 2000. *Volume 133.*

Lau, Andrew: Manifest in Flesh. 1996. *Volume II/86.*

Lee, Pilchan: The New Jerusalem in the Book of Relevation. 2000. *Volume II/129.*

Lichtenberger, Hermann: see *Avemarie, Friedrich.*

Lieu, Samuel N.C.: Manichaeism in the Later Roman Empire and Medieval China. [2]1992. *Volume 63.*

Loader, William R.G.: Jesus' Attitude Towards the Law. 1997. *Volume II/97.*

Löhr, Gebhard: Verherrlichung Gottes durch Philosophie. 1997. *Volume 97.*

Löhr, Hermut: see *Hengel, Martin.*

Löhr, Winrich Alfried: Basilides und seine Schule. 1995. *Volume 83.*

Luomanen, Petri: Entering the Kingdom of Heaven. 1998. *Volume II/101.*

Luz, Ulrich: see *Dunn, James D.G..*

Maier, Gerhard: Mensch und freier Wille. 1971. *Volume 12.*

– Die Johannesoffenbarung und die Kirche. 1981. *Volume 25.*

Markschies, Christoph: Valentinus Gnosticus? 1992. *Volume 65.*

Marshall, Peter: Enmity in Corinth: Social Conventions in Paul's Relations with the Corinthians. 1987. *Volume II/23.*

Mayer, Annemarie: Sprache der Einheit im Epheserbrief und in der Ökumene. 2002. *Volume II/150.*

McDonough, Sean M.: YHWH at Patmos: Rev. 1:4 in its Hellenistic and Early Jewish Setting. 1999. *Volume II/107.*

McGlynn, Moyna: Divine Judgement and Divine Benevolence in the Book of Wisdom. 2001. *Volume II/139.*

Meade, David G.: Pseudonymity and Canon. 1986. *Volume 39.*

Meadors, Edward P.: Jesus the Messianic Herald of Salvation. 1995. *Volume II/72.*

Meißner, Stefan: Die Heimholung des Ketzers. 1996. *Volume II/87.*

Mell, Ulrich: Die „anderen" Winzer. 1994. *Volume 77.*

Mengel, Berthold: Studien zum Philipperbrief. 1982. *Volume II/8.*

Merkel, Helmut: Die Widersprüche zwischen den Evangelien. 1971. *Volume 13.*

Merklein, Helmut: Studien zu Jesus und Paulus. Volume 1 1987. *Volume 43.* – Volume 2 1998. *Volume 105.*

Metzler, Karin: Der griechische Begriff des Verzeihens. 1991. *Volume II/44.*

Metzner, Rainer: Die Rezeption des Matthäusevangeliums im 1. Petrusbrief. 1995. *Volume II/74.*

– Das Verständnis der Sünde im Johannesevangelium. 2000. *Volume 122.*

Mihoc, Vasile: see *Dunn, James D.G..*

Mittmann, Siegfried: see *Hengel, Martin.*

Mittmann-Richert, Ulrike: Magnifikat und Benediktus. *1996. Volume II/90.*

Mußner, Franz: Jesus von Nazareth im Umfeld Israels und der Urkirche. Ed. von M. Theobald. 1998. *Volume 111.*

Niebuhr, Karl-Wilhelm: Gesetz und Paränese. 1987. *Volume II/28.*

– Heidenapostel aus Israel. 1992. *Volume 62.*

Nielsen, Anders E.: "Until it is Fullfilled". 2000. *Volume II/126.*

Nissen, Andreas: Gott und der Nächste im antiken Judentum. 1974. *Volume 15.*

Noack, Christian: Gottesbewußtsein. 2000. *Volume II/116.*

Noormann, Rolf: Irenäus als Paulusinterpret. 1994. *Volume II/66.*

Obermann, Andreas: Die christologische Erfüllung der Schrift im Johannesevangelium. 1996. *Volume II/83.*

Okure, Teresa: The Johannine Approach to Mission. 1988. *Volume II/31.*

Oropeza, B. J.: Paul and Apostasy. 2000. *Volume II/115.*

Ostmeyer, Karl-Heinrich: Taufe und Typos. 2000. *Volume II/118.*

Paulsen, Henning: Studien zur Literatur und Geschichte des frühen Christentums. Ed. von Ute E. Eisen. 1997. *Volume 99.*

Pao, David W.: Acts and the Isaianic New Exodus. 2000. *Volume II/130.*

Park, Eung Chun: The Mission Discourse in Matthew's Interpretation. 1995. *Volume II/81.*

Park, Joseph S.: Conceptions of Afterlife in Jewish Insriptions. 2000. *Volume II/121.*

Pate, C. Marvin: The Reverse of the Curse. 2000. *Volume II/114.*

Philonenko, Marc (Ed.): Le Trône de Dieu. 1993. *Volume 69.*

Pilhofer, Peter: Presbyteron Kreitton. 1990. *Volume II/39.*

– Philippi. Volume 1 1995. *Volume 87.* – Volume 2 2000. *Volume 119.*

– Die frühen Christen und ihre Welt. 2002. *Volume 145.*

– see *Ego, Beate.*

Pöhlmann, Wolfgang: Der Verlorene Sohn und das Haus. 1993. *Volume 68.*

Pokorný, Petr and *Josef B. Souček:* Bibelauslegung als Theologie. 1997. *Volume 100.*

Pokorný, Petr (Hrsg.): Philosophical Hermeneutics and Biblical Exegesis. 2002. *Volume 153.*

Porter, Stanley E.: The Paul of Acts. 1999. *Volume 115.*

Prieur, Alexander: Die Verkündigung der Gottesherrschaft. 1996. *Volume II/89.*

Probst, Hermann: Paulus und der Brief. 1991. *Volume II/45.*

Räisänen, Heikki: Paul and the Law. 1983, ²1987. *Volume 29.*

Rehkopf, Friedrich: Die lukanische Sonderquelle. 1959. *Volume 5.*

Rein, Matthias: Die Heilung des Blindgeborenen (Joh 9). 1995. *Volume II/73.*

Reinmuth, Eckart: Pseudo-Philo und Lukas. 1994. *Volume 74.*

Reiser, Marius: Syntax und Stil des Markusevangeliums. 1984. *Volume II/11.*

Richards, E. Randolph: The Secretary in the Letters of Paul. 1991. *Volume II/42.*

Riesner, Rainer: Jesus als Lehrer. 1981, ³1988. *Volume II/7.*

– Die Frühzeit des Apostels Paulus. 1994. *Volume 71.*

Rissi, Mathias: Die Theologie des Hebräerbriefs. 1987. *Volume 41.*

Röhser, Günter: Metaphorik und Personifikation der Sünde. 1987. *Volume II/25.*

Rose, Christian: Die Wolke der Zeugen. 1994. *Volume II/60.*

Rüegger, Hans-Ulrich: Verstehen, was Markus erzählt. 2002. *Volume II/155.*

Rüger, Hans Peter: Die Weisheitsschrift aus der Kairoer Geniza. 1991. *Volume 53.*

Sänger, Dieter: Antikes Judentum und die Mysterien. 1980. *Volume II/5.*

– Die Verkündigung des Gekreuzigten und Israel. 1994. *Volume 75.*

– see *Burchard, Christoph*

Salzmann, Jorg Christian: Lehren und Ermahnen. 1994. *Volume II/59.*

Sandnes, Karl Olav: Paul – One of the Prophets? 1991. *Volume II/43.*

Sato, Migaku: Q und Prophetie. 1988. *Volume II/29.*

Schaper, Joachim: Eschatology in the Greek Psalter. 1995. *Volume II/76.*

Schimanowski, Gottfried: Die himmlische Liturgie in der Apokalypse des Johannes. 2002. *Volume II/154.*

– Weisheit und Messias. 1985. *Volume II/17.*

Schlichting, Günter: Ein jüdisches Leben Jesu. 1982. *Volume 24.*

Schnabel, Eckhard J.: Law and Wisdom from Ben Sira to Paul. 1985. *Volume II/16.*

Schutter, William L.: Hermeneutic and Composition in I Peter. 1989. *Volume II/30.*

Schwartz, Daniel R.: Studies in the Jewish Background of Christianity. 1992. *Volume 60.*

Schwemer, Anna Maria: see *Hengel, Martin*

Scott, James M.: Adoption as Sons of God. 1992. *Volume II/48.*

– Paul and the Nations. 1995. *Volume 84.*

Shum, Shiu-Lun: Paul's Use of Isaiah in Romans. 2002. *Volume II/156.*

Siegert, Folker: Drei hellenistisch-jüdische Predigten. Teil I 1980. *Volume 20* – Teil II 1992. *Volume 61.*

– Nag-Hammadi-Register. 1982. *Volume 26.*

– Argumentation bei Paulus. 1985. *Volume 34.*

– Philon von Alexandrien. 1988. *Volume 46.*

Simon, Marcel: Le christianisme antique et son contexte religieux I/II. 1981. *Volume 23.*

Snodgrass, Klyne: The Parable of the Wicked Tenants. 1983. *Volume 27.*

Söding, Thomas: Das Wort vom Kreuz. 1997. *Volume 93.*

– see *Thüsing, Wilhelm.*

Sommer, Urs: Die Passionsgeschichte des Markusevangeliums. 1993. *Volume II/58.*

Souček, Josef B.: see *Pokorný, Petr.*

Spangenberg, Volker: Herrlichkeit des Neuen Bundes. 1993. *Volume II/55.*

Spanje, T.E. van: Inconsistency in Paul? 1999. *Volume II/110.*

Speyer, Wolfgang: Frühes Christentum im antiken Strahlungsfeld. Volume I: 1989. *Volume 50.*
– Volume II: 1999. *Volume 116.*
Stadelmann, Helge: Ben Sira als Schriftgelehrter. 1980. *Volume II/6.*
Stenschke, Christoph W.: Luke's Portrait of Gentiles Prior to Their Coming to Faith. *Volume II/108.*
Stettler, Christian: Der Kolosserhymnus. 2000. *Volume II/131.*
Stettler, Hanna: Die Christologie der Pastoralbriefe. 1998. *Volume II/105.*
Strobel, August: Die Stunde der Wahrheit. 1980. *Volume 21.*
Stroumsa, Guy G.: Barbarian Philosophy. 1999. *Volume 112.*
Stuckenbruck, Loren T.: Angel Veneration and Christology. 1995. *Volume II/70.*
Stuhlmacher, Peter (Ed.): Das Evangelium und die Evangelien. 1983. *Volume 28.*
– Biblische Theologie und Evangelium. 2002. *Volume 146.*
Sung, Chong-Hyon: Vergebung der Sünden. 1993. *Volume II/57.*
Tajra, Harry W.: The Trial of St. Paul. 1989. *Volume II/35.*
– The Martyrdom of St.Paul. 1994. *Volume II/67.*
Theißen, Gerd: Studien zur Soziologie des Urchristentums. 1979, ³1989. *Volume 19.*
Theobald, Michael: Studien zum Römerbrief. 2001. *Volume 136.*
Theobald, Michael: see *Mußner, Franz.*
Thornton, Claus-Jürgen: Der Zeuge des Zeugen. 1991. *Volume 56.*
Thüsing, Wilhelm: Studien zur neutestamentlichen Theologie. Ed. von Thomas Söding. 1995. *Volume 82.*
Thurén, Lauri: Derhethorizing Paul. 2000. *Volume 124.*
Treloar, Geoffrey R.: Lightfoot the Historian. 1998. *Volume II/103.*
Tsuji, Manabu: Glaube zwischen Vollkommenheit und Verweltlichung. 1997. *Volume II/93.*
Twelftree, Graham H.: Jesus the Exorcist. 1993. *Volume II/54.*

Urban, Christina: Das Menschenbild nach dem Johannesevangelium. 2001. *Volume II/137.*
Visotzky, Burton L.: Fathers of the World. 1995. *Volume 80.*
Vollenweider, Samuel: Horizonte neutestamentlicher Christologie. 2002. *Volume 144.*
Vos, Johan S.: Die Kunst der Argumentation bei Paulus. 2002. *Volume 149.*
Wagener, Ulrike: Die Ordnung des „Hauses Gottes". 1994. *Volume II/65.*
Walter, Nikolaus: Praeparatio Evangelica. Ed. von Wolfgang Kraus und Florian Wilk. 1997. *Volume 98.*
Wander, Bernd: Gottesfürchtige und Sympathisanten. 1998. *Volume 104.*
Watts, Rikki: Isaiah's New Exodus and Mark. 1997. *Volume II/88.*
Wedderburn, A.J.M.: Baptism and Resurrection. 1987. *Volume 44.*
Wegner, Uwe: Der Hauptmann von Kafarnaum. 1985. *Volume II/14.*
Welck, Christian: Erzählte ‚Zeichen'. 1994. *Volume II/69.*
Wiarda, Timothy: Peter in the Gospels . 2000. *Volume II/127.*
Wilk, Florian: see *Walter, Nikolaus.*
Williams, Catrin H.: I am He. 2000. *Volume II/113.*
Wilson, Walter T.: Love without Pretense. 1991. *Volume II/46.*
Wisdom, Jeffrey: Blessing for the Nations and the Curse of the Law. 2001. *Volume II/133.*
Wucherpfennig, Ansgar: Heracleon Philologus. 2002. *Volume 142.*
Yeung, Maureen: Faith in Jesus and Paul. 2002. *Volume II/147.*
Zimmermann, Alfred E.: Die urchristlichen Lehrer. 1984, ²1988. *Volume II/12.*
Zimmermann, Johannes: Messianische Texte aus Qumran. 1998. *Volume II/104.*
Zimmermann, Ruben: Geschlechtermetaphorik und Geschlechterverhältnis. 2000. *Volume II/122.*
Zumstein, Jean: see *Dettwiler, Andreas*

For a complete catalogue please write to the publisher
Mohr Siebeck • P.O. Box 2030 • D–72010 Tübingen/Germany
Up-to-date information on the internet at www.mohr.de